LIVES IN COMMON

MENACHEM KLEIN

Lives in Common

Arabs and Jews in Jerusalem, Jaffa, and Hebron

Translated by
Haim Watzman

HURST & COMPANY, LONDON

First published in the United Kingdom in 2014 by
C. Hurst & Co. (Publishers) Ltd.,
41 Great Russell Street, London, WC1B 3PL
This paperback edition first published in 2026 by
C. Hurst & Co. (Publishers) Ltd.,
New Wing, Somerset House, Strand, London, WC2R 1LA
© Menachem Klein, 2026
All rights reserved.
Printed in the United Kingdom

The right of Menachem Klein to be identified as the author
of this publication is asserted by him in accordance with the
Copyright, Designs and Patents Act, 1988.

A Cataloguing-in-Publication data record for this book
is available from the British Library.

ISBN: 9781805266037

EU GPSR Authorised Representative
Easy Access System Europe Oü, 16879218
Address: Mustamäe tee 50, 10621, Tallinn, Estonia
Contact Details: gpsr.requests@easproject.com, +358 40 500 3575

www.hurstpublishers.com

This book is printed using paper from registered sustainable
and managed sources.

CONTENTS

About this Book   vii
Prologue to the Paperback Edition   xiii

PART I
CONNECTED TO PLACE

Introduction: Jerusalem, Jaffa Gate/Bab al-Khalil   3
The Gate of Forked Ways   3

1. Arab Jews   19
   Neither Oxymoron nor Aspersion   19
   The Locals   22

2. Mixed Cities   65
   A Holy Site Chooses a City—A City Chooses a Holy Site   87
   Coexistence Disturbed by Confrontation   94

3. Life On the Verge of the Future   111
   A Large Problem in a Small Place   111
   Conflict as Routine   121

PART II
CONNECTED BY FORCE

4. Expanding the Boundaries of the Possible   139
   A New Land   139
   An Ambiguous V   157

5. Like Owners   171
   Transferring the Deed   171
   Houses from Within, People from Without   188

CONTENTS

6. Occupation, Assimilation, Opposition	213
Jerusalem: A Bustling and Noisy Place	213
Jaffa: Abandoned and Attractive	246
Hebron and Jerusalem: The Force of History	258
Epilogue	285
Notes	291
Bibliography	307
Index	327

ABOUT THIS BOOK

Historians should not adopt the past, but rather investigate the relationship between past and future.

– Alon Confino[1]

Modern history has connected and disconnected Jaffa, Hebron, and Jerusalem, showing them to have much in common but also much that separates them. Jerusalem and Hebron, two mountain cities and the two holiest cities in Palestine, have been contrasted with Jaffa, the worldly coastal city. Each of these cities is home to a Palestinian community with its own character and status, and each of them is also home to a Jewish community of a different sort. The conflict between Israeli Jews and Palestinian Arabs is different in each of these cities, only about 40 miles distant from each other, yet it is also much alike. In the same way, the Jews and Arabs in each of these cities have evolved relationships that, while similar in some ways, are different in others.

All three cities have a long history. Jerusalem and Hebron were founded about 5,000 years ago. Jaffa is younger—only about 3,800 years old. Many books have been written about each of these cities but no work has been devoted to comparing them. However, it is important to make such a comparison because each of them has become a focus of modern Israeli or Palestinian national identity (or of both). The confrontation between these two peoples has played out in each of these cities, dividing them and setting into motion a series of demographic, urban, and political changes. But—and this is one of the book's original insights—urban life has also created types of common

ABOUT THIS BOOK

identity and coexistence. Only at a few points in time did the conflict become total. The following chapters reveal this by focusing on daily life. It is a new approach in the history of the Israeli–Palestinian conflict. Whereas the existing historical literature stresses national institutions and leaderships, this book views the cities from the bottom up, concentrating on the day-to-day interactions between Jews and Arabs. The national struggle broke out within this context, impairing the previous web of relations and reorganizing daily life.

The triangle formed by Jaffa, Jerusalem, and Hebron lies in the geographical, political, religious, and historical center of the Land of Israel, as the Jews call it, or Palestine, as the Arabs call it. Another triangle, formed by Haifa, Acre, and Nazareth, lies to the north. Jews and Arabs who lived in that triangle fashioned a system of relationships that differed from that of the central triangle. It was less fervent religiously and nationally, and exhibited more cooperation between ethnic groups.[2] But the northern triangle lies in the country's geographical and historical periphery. None of the three cities that formed it had ever been a capital, nor were any of them holy to Muslims or Jews. Jews and Muslims together constitute an overwhelming majority of the country's inhabitants, and for more than a century have contested who the country belongs to. The focal point of this contest is the Jaffa–Jerusalem–Hebron triangle. Furthermore, up until 1948 Jaffa was a much more important city than Arab Haifa or Nazareth.

By telling the stories of these three cities, the book casts new light on the larger story of the Jewish–Palestinian conflict. It reveals aspects of the conflict that have been missed by previous studies which examined the subject from the top down and whose starting point was Zionism or Palestinian nationalism and the conflict between them. Unlike the approach generally taken by historians of the Jewish national movement or its Palestinian rival, this book's starting point is not an event that was constitutive of Zionism or Palestinian nationalism—say, for example, the inception of Jewish immigration motivated by national sentiments or the Palestinian riots of 1920. This book's story instead begins at an earlier point in time, toward the end of the nineteenth century, when a local Palestinian identity began to form, an identity in which Jews and Arabs were partners. It did not arrive from the outside, like Arab nationalism and Zionism, but grew out of the daily lives of the country's inhabitants during a rapidly modernizing and Westernizing period, in which the authority of the Ottoman regime was

ABOUT THIS BOOK

growing weaker. The voice of this identity has not yet been heard. The growing scholarship on Arab Jews in the Middle East—Jews who identified culturally and nationally as Arabs—skips over the cities of Palestine because, unlike in other cities of the region, in Palestine's cities such an identity was not formulated by writers, intellectuals, and ideologues, but by the fabric of everyday life. I term this local identity an Arab–Jewish one because that is the term that historians give to a similar sort of joint identity that developed in Baghdad and Cairo during the 1930s and 1940s. In other words, when Jewish and Arab nationalism reached Palestine, it did not encounter people who lacked identities, but rather a local community where everyday life created connections among its members and between them and the place in which they lived. ("Place" is used here in the broadest sense of the word, beyond the location in which a person was born or lived.) Following the collapse of the Ottoman Empire during World War I, each of the rival national movements sought to take over this local identity and to define the local population as either Zionist or Palestinian.

At its inception, the conflict was a disturbance in this local identity. In the mid-1930s, and even more so after World War II, the conflict expanded and became routine. The Zionist–Palestinian conflict of 1948 finally defeated the local identity that had previously flourished, in different ways, in Jaffa, Jerusalem, and Hebron. It is for this reason that Part I of the book is called "Connected to Place." The second part, entitled "Connected by Force," describes the development of relations on the streets of Jaffa, Jerusalem, and Hebron after 1948. To offer a broad generalization, the two national movements at this time were preoccupied not only with nation-building but also with expunging or taking over the previous identity. The Israeli victory in 1948 was redoubled in the war of 1967, fixing Israeli power as a shaper of identity. In this second part of the book I describe how force shapes the streets of Jaffa, Jerusalem, and Hebron—not only their present form, but also their takes on the past—that is, how they depict the period prior to 1948. I devote special attention to some emotionally and politically charged encounters. One category of these involves refugees bearing searing memories showing up at the doors of their former homes and asking to visit, where they encounter the current residents of these houses who are members of the opposing nation. This sort of meeting between the victor and the defeated is also a confrontation between the past and the present. As this part of the book shows, such

ABOUT THIS BOOK

encounters have not followed a rigid pattern. Only in some cases did the people facing each other in the doorway act in accordance with national ideology. This fact offers cause for optimism, suggesting that it might be possible, in the future, to reach an accommodation on the refugee issue.

A comparison of the period prior to 1948 with the period that followed leads to the conclusion that Jewish–Arab identity no longer exists in its original form. Anyone who advocates such an identity today needs to grant it new meaning. If Israel were to accept the Arab League's peace initiative, Prince Turki al-Faisal of Saudi Arabia has said, "We will start thinking of Israelis as Arab Jews rather than simply as Israelis." He does not and cannot propose turning the clock back and doing away with nation-states as prime shapers of identity. A contemporary Jewish–Arab identity, he maintains, means close ties between Israel and the Arab countries:

> One can imagine the integration of Israel into the Arab geographical entity. One can imagine not just economic, political and diplomatic relations between Arabs and Israelis but also issues of education, scientific research, combating mutual threats to the inhabitants of this vast geographic area.[3]

This indicates a possibility for reframing the old Jewish–Arab identity in a way that would make it appropriate for the present. But, as the final chapter of this book shows, strong forces seek to sabotage this possibility by deepening the fissure between Jews and Arabs and seeking exclusive ownership of the land.

A book of scholarship is not an encyclopedia, and *Lives in Common* does not include everything that took place during the period that the book covers. The book is not intended to serve as a comprehensive history of Jaffa, Jerusalem, and Hebron, nor does it aim to provide an exhaustive account of the Jews and Arabs who have lived in these cities. Many others have written such books. But no one has yet written of the Jewish–Arab interface in its various guises over the last 150 years, and it is this interface which is the subject of this book. I broaden my account of matters that have not received appropriate scholarly attention thus far, and in places where I have discovered sources that cast new light on what has already been written. The book is a mosaic formed of myriad tesserae, as can be seen by a glance at its footnotes and bibliography, and contains the names of many people and streets. So as not to impose too heavily on the reader and not to disturb the flow of the prose, I have minimized biographical informa-

ABOUT THIS BOOK

tion and I do not include maps. In the age of the Internet, both are just a click away for readers who seek further detail.

The book takes its readers on a tour of the streets of Jaffa, Jerusalem, and Hebron. It frequently jumps from one city to another, offering points of view, life experiences, and the voices of the cities' inhabitants. The book intentionally avoids generalizations, as daily life and contacts between Jews and Arabs in these mixed cities do not fit into any rigid mold but instead take on different and sometimes opposing forms. The chapters are composed of small scraps of the fabric of life, with all their contrasts and different paths. Only in retrospect can one see where they eventually arrived. A historian who seeks to describe life as it was then, when the future had not been determined and was only a possibility, must also portray those parts of the flow of life that were eventually blocked. As Carlo Ginzburg has argued, it must be depicted as we look from the present back on the past.[4] From the here and now the book sends its gaze back to the middle of the nineteenth century, from which it then makes its way to our time. This movement from the past to the present and back means that the book's chapters do not proceed in a simple chronology, nor is there a hard-and-fast division into periods. The past flashes forward into chapters that address the present and vice-versa. The book must be read in its entirety to grasp the full picture.

This book was written over a period of several years. The idea for it took form and I began to collect material in 2008. In addition to the European University Institute and Leiden University, which hosted me during the writing of the book, I also received cooperation and a great deal of assistance from the staff of the National Library of Israel on the Hebrew University campus; my wife, Rivka Klein, at the Hebrew University Law Library; Iris Sardis of the Israel Defense Forces Archive; the staff of the Jerusalem Municipal Archive; the Israel State Archive; the HaShomer HaTza'ir Archive, Yad Ya'ari, at Givat Haviva; the St Antony's College Archive at Oxford University; the British Museum; and the United States National Archives in Maryland. Prof. Elhanan Reiner, Na'ama Tzifroni, Attorney Gilead Sher, Rafi Levi, Meron Benvenisti, Attorney Michael Ben-Ya'ir, General [ret.] Shlomo Gazit, Eli Amir, Gershom Gorenberg, Prof. Yair Wallach, Prof. Yoram Peri, Professor Salim Tamari, Professor Joel Migdal, Dr. Abigail Jacobson, the author Diana Pinto, and Avrum Burg were generous with their time and shared with me their notes, memories, and documents in their possession. The book has been translated and edited by Haim Watzman, whose professional and skillful contribution can be felt in every word. I am deeply indebted to all of them. I, of course, am solely responsible for the book's contents.

The book's principal sources were the writings of Israeli Jews. This community has published far more diaries and memoirs than the Palestinian community, and Israel's archives are open to scholars. There are not yet any official Palestinian archives. The Israeli Jews won the wars and did well. Unlike the Palestinians, only a few became refugees and most of their documents were not lost. The Jewish–Israeli side has the material resources and psychological wherewithal to look back, and it has been better at fostering its historical memory than the Palestinians. Israeli archives thus provided a wealth of material, including photographs that I used as historical sources. I found more material on Jerusalem than on Jaffa, and more on Jaffa than on Hebron. The reason for this is the fact that Jerusalem had a Jewish majority by the end of the nineteenth century, while Jaffa's population, until 1948, included many more Jews than Hebron's. Israeli Jerusalem is stronger and larger than Arab Jerusalem, just as Tel Aviv gazes out over Jaffa as a strong victor. The number of Israeli settlers in Hebron and adjacent Kiryat Arba is much smaller than the number of Palestinians in that city, and the Israeli settlers live distant from any large Jewish city.

This book is not based solely on archival documents, diaries, and other papers. I also deliberately introduced into it my personal experience as an inhabitant of Jerusalem and an Israeli citizen. I lived through some of the events that I portray and have formed opinions about them, as well as about the personalities and movements that appear in the book. In this I drew encouragement from Tony Judt, a historian who described his later books in this way: "Their value rests on essentially impressionistic effect: the success with which I have related and interwoven the private and the public, the reasoned and the intuitive, the recalled and the felt."[5] I hope that the texts listed in my biography have helped me in the endeavor of writing good history and in better understanding the era that I describe. As another historian, Eric Hobsbawm, has written, "Historical understanding is what I am for, not agreement, approval or sympathy."[6]

PROLOGUE TO THE PAPERBACK EDITION

At first glance, there was nothing special about this particular group photograph[1] of teenage Jerusalem boys lined up in three rows. Beside them stands a man wearing a coat. Some boys have a vacant or indifferent look, while others stretch their torsos to appear upright and well-built. Similar photos were taken in schools at the end of the school year, at weddings, and when distinguished guests arrived in the city. All the boys are dressed uniformly in white shirts and dark pants. A mustache adorns the faces of two of those in the bottom row, making them look slightly older than the other boys. The young man in the middle of the bottom row holds up a sign and has a football next to him.

"The Jerusalem Yeshiva Youth Association," the sign announces. In the lower right corner, the photographer added in his own handwriting, "Gymnastics [= sports] group," and the Hebrew calendar year, which is 1913/4 in the common era. About ten years earlier, sports classes were introduced into the curricula of European schools in Jerusalem, and since then, football matches have been held between Jerusalem and Beirut school teams. Sport was a major component in shaping young adults as English gentlemen, and some of this reached Ottoman Jerusalem. On the eve of World War I, Western norms were adopted and institutionalized not only in European schools but also in *yeshivas* (Jewish religious schools) in Jerusalem. These norms existed alongside the traditional patterns, as evidenced by the Ottoman fez that everyone in the photographs wore.

These modern norms created a new local patriotic identity at the end of the nineteenth century. In the contemporary era, religious affiliation has lost its exclusive status, and the barrier to separation from other religions has been lowered. The connection to a place beyond one's residence or birthplace, the larger space, and its diverse inhabitants forged an identity. Geographically, this refers to central Palestine, in the area between Jerusalem, Jaffa, Hebron, Beersheba, and Gaza. Jerusalem was at the heart of this region because of its religious significance.

This book challenges the commonly held view that a Palestinian identity developed only after the British occupation boundaries (1917) and establishment of the Mandate government (1922), namely, with the establishment of borders and an administration that both unified the region. But it was not a foreign administration that created a local identity; it preceded the British. When their colonialism gave it an administrative form, it developed from an identity to a national movement. Palestinian-Arab resistance to foreign rule and Zionism were expressed shortly afterward.

Local patriotism connected Jews, Muslims, and Christians, as well as people from different social classes. Alongside political affiliation and membership in a religious collective, local patriotism existed in the main cities and gradually influenced peripheral towns and the surrounding villages. Contrary to the Zionist myth and the apologetic argument used by British imperialism, none of them introduced Western norms of life to the center of Palestine. They accelerated the process of change, which began before their arrival.

Recent studies refer to these local patriotic Jews as Arab Jews, but they can also be called Palestinian Jews. The title Palestine was an identity marker. It is no coincidence that the newspaper *Al-Munadi*, published in Jerusalem from 1912–13, presented itself as one that specifically addressed "Palestinian affairs."[2] It is widely assumed that the French-Tunisian author Albert Memmi[3] was the first to use the term Arab Jew in 1975 as an alternative identity signifier. Later, post-Zionist Jews endorsed it in their cultural-political campaign against mainstream Zionist-Israeli ideology.[4] Nevertheless, it was the Polish Jew Abraham Shmuel Hirschberg (1858–1943), visiting Jerusalem in 1910, who invented the term. After mingling with these city-dwellers, Hirschberg wrote that Sephardi Jews in Jerusalem "are characteristic of the people among whom they settle. They are Arab Jews—having good manners exteriorly but uncivilized internally."[5] According to him, Jews and Arabs share the same character and manner, not just language. Due to the impact of their Sephardi compatriots, Hirschberg adds that Jerusalem's Ashkenazi men and women form a hybrid Ashkenazi-Sephardi-Arab-Jew personality.[6]

Until the 1948 war, the mixed Jerusalem elite of Jews, Muslims, and local and foreign Christians formed a cosmopolitan community. "Dr Helena Kagan emerged as one of the leaders speaking for mutual respect and tolerance. As she had treated Jewish and Arab patients since her arrival in Palestine, her home had become a social meeting for the leading women of all communities. In the autumn of 1921, she introduced Zakiyya Kazim, the wife of the former mayor of Jerusalem, who became one of the leaders of the Palestinian Arab nationalist movement, to the Jewish women in her circle. The common language "in the afternoon... was not English, Arabic, or Hebrew; instead, the women spoke French."[7] Philologist Eliezer Ben-Yehuda and his wife Hemda "hosted an eclectic group of linguistics and archeologists—Christian, Muslims, and Jews, speaking French, German, English, Hebrew, and Arabic—on Friday nights. Dr Ticho, the ophthalmologist... and his wife, Anna, an artist, conducted their parties in German with a cosmopolitan guest list."[8]

Jerusalem's elite women were also publicly active. After World War I they established the Social Service Association to take care of girls that, under the privations of war, had turned to prostitution. In 1921, Annie Landau founded the Jerusalem Ladies' Club, in which Jewish, Arab, and English women worked together to improve the city's welfare. The escalating national conflict in the years 1945–8 split its membership along lines of national identity, and they stopped meeting.[9] As this volume shows, the working classes expressed their joint Jewish–Arab identity in the public sphere too. In the early 1930s, it was powerfully expressed by Jewish survivors of the 1929 Hebron massacre. "It was amazing how many of the Jews—even in Hebron—were saved by Arabs. And more extraordinary—how already the Hebron Jews are talking of returning to their homes right in the ghetto there," wrote Helen Bentwich.[10]

The Zionist establishment was alienated from—if not directly hostile to—such joint local identity. Zionism was founded in Europe, and as the Balfour Declaration of 1917 stated, it enjoyed the backing of imperial Britain. The young Palestinian national movement sought Jewish partners. "To our Jewish fellow natives of the homeland, to those who were cheated by Zionism," wrote Jamal al-Husseini to his compatriot Jews, on behalf of the Arab Executive Committee in the local newspaper *al-Sabbah*. His appeal was published in *Haaretz* on 26 February 1922, in Hebrew. "To those who understand the goals and damage of Zionism—to them we extend our hands today and call: Come to us! We are your friends! You share the same rights and duties in our mother Palestine as we do... because you and we are the sons of the same homeland whether the Zionist like it or not."[11]

However, only a few were ready to cooperate. In 1921, two local intellectuals, Haim Ben Kiki and Yosef Haim Castel, opposed the Balfour Declaration and Zionist leadership collaboration with Britain. Ben Kiki saw the declaration as a clear expression of Western colonialisms. Castel suggested rewriting the Balfour Declaration to recognize the national rights of the Palestinian majority alongside the Jewish ones. Palestine, he argued, is also the homeland of local Arabs.[12] In November 1929, following riots that August, David Avissar, the chairperson of the Association of the Pioneers of the East, criticized the Zionist leadership for ignoring the Arabs. Instead, he suggested, "a single, joint homeland for Jews and Arabs should be established in Palestine... both peoples would enjoy national self-determination through the egalitarian allocation of governmental powers and the autonomy of each people to nurture its own life".[13] In December 1927, Eliyahu Sasson, a Syrian-born Jew who joined the Arab nationalist movement, argued: "the Palestinian country will not gain its freedom and independence unless all forces—Jews, Christians and Muslims—unite to free it from foreign powers."[14] In other words, he opposed the Zionist political strategy of relying exclusively on Britain. Later Sasson and his contemporaries transformed from fierce critics of Zionist political strategy to a political operator serving the Zionist–Ashkenazi establishment and its pro-British policy. He accepted Zionist hegemony both in policymaking and in determining social status hierarchy. Thus, during the British Mandatory years, the role of Zionist Arab Jews changed from loyal opposition to subordinated operators in the service of the national movement.

Beyond the political echelon, Jewish-Arab common life continued in the public domain, with ups and downs determined by the national conflict. The 1948 war destroyed it forever. "Many Jewish residents at the time of the British Mandate came looking for their pre-1948 acquaintance" in the Old City of Jerusalem where John Tleel lived. "Old friends met again after nineteen years of separation. My father's friends and patients and some of my university classmates came to see us. All were very polite and offered to be of any help... The enthusiasm was great, but the bonds, with the passage of time and the circumstances, never regained their old strength and even died out."[15] Tleel's post-1967 war encounter with Jews led him to conclude that "there is a difference between the Jews we knew during the British Mandate and the ones we have known after the 1967 occupation. With the first ones the attachment remains a nostalgic one, with the second ones the relationship is rather business-like and intellectual."[16]

The second half of *Lives in Common* sets out the deterioration of Jewish–Arab relations since 1967. Indeed, both the Zionist movement and then the Palestinian national movement worked to split the joint identity that had existed on the ground. Each national movement claimed exclusive attachment to the land. However, neither prior to 1948 war nor after 1967 was escalation unavoidably deterministic. *Lives in Common* demonstrates that, along the historical avenue and junctions, several roads that might have led to less violent and disastrous results were not taken.

My book ends around 2010 without of course referring to the genocide and atrocities of the war in Gaza. However, its origins are to be found in the settler–indigenous clashes in Hebron as described in the final chapter. Watching the horrific crimes committed on an unprecedented scale in Gaza, I wonder how we can sustain any hope. "Hope remains," argues Alon Confino, a historian of Nazi Germany and of the 1948 war, "even if constrained, as long as we keep the human capacity to see the world through the eyes of others, telling a story, be it as a writer or historian, enables us to look outward and provide a way of seeing the world, of being in it, of offering the possibility of freeing our imagination."[17] It is time we freed our political imagination from the exclusive claim of belonging to this land and examine the possibility of restoring, albeit in a different manner, what is missing from our recollection of the past.

PART I

CONNECTED TO PLACE

INTRODUCTION

JERUSALEM, JAFFA GATE/BAB AL-KHALIL

> The Mediterranean speaks with many voices.
> – Fernand Braudel[1]

The Gate of Forked Ways

I am about to enter the Old City via the Alrov–Mamilla Mall. A pedestrian avenue of cafés and tastefully designed brand stores silences the buzz of the street and channels me toward the Jaffa Gate. Attractive window displays—Nike, Gap, Nautica, and H. Stern Jewelers—are implanted in chiseled, clean Jerusalem stone. Innocuous muzak sounds in my ears as I pass by modern sculptures with a crowd that includes Israeli teenagers seeking the latest fashions, Haredi families on an outing, and hijab-clad window-shopping mothers from East Jerusalem. Nothing here evokes nearby Jaffa Road. Once West Jerusalem's modern downtown thoroughfare, Jaffa Road is now an ugly, down-at-the-heel street that the municipality is trying to revive. Until the mid-twentieth century, it was the artery that linked Jerusalem to Tel Aviv and Jaffa, the major cities of the coastal plain. Jaffa Road's long decline began in 1948. The roofless Alrov–Mamilla Mall, which opened in 2007, was built to mask the old road's sorry appearance. The architecture seeks to create the impression that it is not a mall, but is instead an authentic Jerusalem street that links the modern Western part of the city to its historical core.

The word "Alrov" in the mall's title refers to the company that built the complex, which also includes a luxurious hotel and exclusive apartments, of which the shopping area is a part. The second half of the mall's name, Mamilla, is there as a sop, a kind of apology, a flash from the past. The complex stands on the site of old Mamilla (the name comes from the Arabic *ma'man Allah*, God's refuge), a neighborhood built at the end of the nineteenth century. It was inhabited by both Jews and Arabs until the 1948 war abruptly separated its inhabitants. Mamilla now belongs to the past, Alrov to the twenty-first century.

It presents itself today as though private initiative and modernization have overcome this sad heritage. Or is this just the impression that this modern mall wants to impress upon me? Have we returned to a common Jewish–Arab experience that will stitch up the rip in that fabric?

I consider the fact that, beginning at the end of the nineteenth century, Jews from the city's new neighborhoods mixed with the Old City's Arabs in the open area outside the gate. Travelers from Jaffa and Hebron encountered foreign tourists mingling with natives. It was a time when distances were shrinking and the pace of life was accelerating. Then the Great War and national conflict between Jew and Arab made the city's life more turbulent. Jaffa Gate and its environs became a meeting place not only for people but also for ideas and lifestyles. Knowledge of distant events arrived, as did ideas from other lands, all of which became part of the local conversation.

That the Arabs call the Jaffa Gate Bab al-Khalil—the Hebron Gate— is no coincidence. The Jerusalem–Hebron route was traveled by pilgrims visiting the two cities' holy sites. But it also brought fine grapes, eggs, and chickens to Jerusalem from Hebron. Jerusalem paid Hebron for this with newspapers and books, which prompted the discussion of new questions in Hebron, questions of the sort argued in the homes of Jerusalem's intellectuals and in the city's cafés. In 1919 a small English-style club, consisting of several rooms, opened in Hebron. Its members could go there to read books and newspapers, to play games, to listen to music, and to eat.[2] And horse-drawn carriages brought residents of West Jerusalem to the Jaffa Gate, where they shopped at the *suk* (the bazaar or market) and perhaps continued on foot to pray at the holy sites. Jewish and Arab coachmen drove tourists and pilgrims, in German-made carriages, from the gate to waiting boats in Jaffa's port.

Jaffa Gate ceased to be a central meeting point when the conflict between the Jews and Palestinians escalated in the second half of the

INTRODUCTION

1940s. The war severed the gate from its hinterland. For all intents and purposes, its names in Arabic, Hebrew, and English lost their original reference points. Old Jerusalem was cut off from the Palestinian coastal plain, of which Jaffa was the center. Jaffa also lost its connection to Hebron Road. Jaffa Road was left in a slightly better position than the gate, retaining something of the status it had gained in the first half of the century—that of the New City's main street—up until the 1980s. It remained at the center of the downtown area, serving as provincial Jerusalem's artery to the more sophisticated center of the country. But until 1967 it was blocked on its eastern end by an ugly wall of steel and concrete that marked the cease-fire line between Israel and Jordan. A small crack in the wall enabled Jerusalem's inhabitants, on either side, to view the enemy city. But there was not a great deal that could be seen through it. In 1954 the Hebrew poet Natan Alterman peered and declared categorically: "From here to Shanghai is Asia; from here to Hayarkon Street in Tel Aviv is the state of Israel."[3] Jordanian Jerusalem would become visible to Jewish Jerusalem only in June 1967, and then not for long. Within a few years, Israeli development would leave nothing of it. Israel's European (as the new country defined itself) alienation from Asia was replaced by a sense of ownership and desire to expand into the new territory. After June 1967, what Alterman had termed "Asia" became Jewish and Israeli.

Hebron Road suffered a worse fate than Jaffa Road. The 1948 war cut Jaffa Gate off from the former street, most of which lay on the Israeli side of the cease-fire line. The road could no longer be used to travel from the gate to the city of Hebron. The section from Jaffa Gate to Abu Tor became a no-man's land entered by no one. The section from Abu Tor to the end of Talpiot lay in Jewish Jerusalem, cut off in the south by the cease-fire line. Today, Hebron Road is an anodyne urban street, a gray stretch of asphalt, no less drab for running past sites of historical and religious significance. One of these is the Valley of Hinnom, mentioned in the Bible as a place of death and slaughter, where fathers sacrificed their sons to the pagan god Moloch. Further south is the Hill of Evil Counsel where, according to Christian tradition, the Jewish council of elders resolved to hand Jesus over to the Romans to be crucified. According to Jewish tradition it is the place from which Abraham first viewed Mount Moriah, which God designated as the place where Abraham was to sacrifice his son Isaac; there he left his servants and continued on foot to the mountain with his son.

A mile or so further south is the Mar Elias Monastery, where Christians believe the Prophet Elijah stopped to rest while in flight from Queen Jezebel. And not far south of that lies the tomb of Rachel the Matriarch. Each of these sites exists in its own right, without connection to the road that links them. After the 1967 war, Israel reestablished the link between Jaffa Gate and Jaffa Road, but not the Hebron Road with Bab al-Khalil. Hebron Road and Bab al-Khalil are separated by a section of road with a different name—Jerusalem Brigade (Hativat Yerushalayim) Street, named after the Israeli army unit that failed in its attempt to break through to the Old City's Jewish Quarter in 1948, and which fought against the Jordanians in southern Jerusalem in 1967. Hebron Road does not begin until the edge of Abu Tor.

Abu Tor itself was founded by a Swiss banker, Johannes Frutiger, and his Jewish partners Shalom Konstrum and Joseph Navon. They aspired to establish a mixed Christian–Jewish neighborhood. Their original intention failed—Christians were not attracted by the idea and it ultimately became a Jewish area.[4] Over the years an Arab Abu Tor took root on the slope to the east.

Jerusalem Brigade Street does not stand alone. In commemoration of the Israeli victory in June, the Jerusalem municipality decided in September to replace the Arabic names of the major roads in East Jerusalem with the names of Israeli army units that had fought in the city that year. It was as if the city government was saying that the Israeli army had to retake the Arab city each day. The municipality also granted the general staff of the Israel Defense Forces (IDF) the right to determine which units would be memorialized in asphalt and on signs mounted on stone walls. The square that had been Allenby Square since the Mandate period was renamed IDF (TZaHa"L) Square, and the main street that descended from there to the Old City wall was named Paratrooper (Tzanhanim) Road, in honor of the Paratrooper Brigade, which took the glory for the "liberation of Jerusalem." Just a few years later, the municipality further resolved to rename other East Jerusalem streets after medieval Arab geographers, cultural figures, scientists, and historians. Henceforth there were streets honoring the philosopher Avicenna, the traveler Ibn Batuta, and the historian Ibn Khaldun. In January 1975, the street in the Sheikh Jarrah neighborhood where the home of former Jerusalem mayor Raghib Nashashibi stood was named for him. But other Palestinian mayors were not so honored.[5]

INTRODUCTION

The role of a link between Jerusalem and Hebron, which the Jaffa Gate had previously served, was now taken over by the Damascus Gate. The small cab stand that had operated there during the Mandate period[6] was turned into a central bus and cab station whose vehicles linked Arab Jerusalem with the Palestinian interior. Public transportation that ran on the East Jerusalem–Hebron route left from the Damascus Gate, passing Jaffa Gate as if it had never been called Bab al-Khalil. Damascus Gate—which is called Bab al-'Amud in Arabic—served only the Palestinian population. Jews who wanted to reach the Israeli settlements that had sprung up in the Hebron area used a separate transportation system, buses that left from the Central Bus Station on the western end of Jaffa Road. Today, Palestinian minibuses and Jewish buses drive side by side on the Hebron road until they reach the roadblock at the southern end of the city, where they are channeled on to two separate routes.

Jerusalemites from a varied spectrum of the city's population saunter alongside me at Mamilla Mall. Jews and Arabs alike are tempted to imagine, for this brief moment, that they are in some other country, or on one of Tel Aviv's fashionable shopping streets. Both tourists and Israeli inhabitants bracket their visit to the Old City with a pleasant walk through the mall. It creates for them, simultaneously, two illusions—first, of being in a modern Western city, and second, of being in the real Jerusalem. Israeli Jews and Palestinian Arabs pass one another but do not mingle. The cafés, entry to which requires being checked by a security guard, are filled with Jews. Arabs keep walking—few stop for coffee. But most of the kitchen workers, hidden from the patrons, are Arabs.

In the two or three years since my initial visit to the mall, this situation has changed only slightly. Now, in 2013, Arabs take advantage of end-of-season sales at the Jewish-owned brand-name clothing stores. Arab women sit down to have quiet conversations in Jewish restaurants. This is something they are able to do here but not in the traditional coffee houses on the Arab side of the city, just to the east of Jaffa Gate.

The *suk* within the gate has been in operation since the Middle Ages. It is roofed, clamorous, and congested, not to mention colorful, aromatic, and sometimes putrid. As the accounts of nineteenth-century travelers make clear, the latter was also the case in previous times, when the city's air was said to be full of fetid vapors.[7] When the

Swedish author Selma Lagerlöf called Jerusalem a city that kills people, she was not referring to martyrdom in holy wars. Every visitor took a grave risk of infection from contaminated water and other filth, a risk that cast a pall over Jerusalem's physical beauty. Leather tanning shops were located within the walls and emitted a stench that could not be evaded. On top of this was the smell of rotting flesh from the offal left along the side of the streets. The moat at the foot of David's citadel, right next to the Jaffa Gate, stank from the dung of horses, donkeys, sheep, and goats. Men and animals walked the streets side by side, and the sweat of both hung in the summer air. The only respite was in the public bathhouses. Or, instead, one could divert one's gaze (and nose) from the physical city to a purer and cleaner place, the heavenly Jerusalem.

The *suk* is paved with gray-black stone, smoothed from the caresses of centuries of rain and the soles that have trodden upon it, and looks quite different from the mall to the west, with its chiseled limestone. Unlike the Mamilla Mall, the marketplace is not linear, alienating, or domineering. It does not lead a walker toward a fixed destination. Instead, it offers the freedom to meander off on its branching byways. The *suk* is alluring, vibrant, and expansive, sending out fingers into narrow alleys. Before coming to a sudden end at Haram al-Sharif (which Westerners call the Temple Mount), it takes a sharp right turn into the Jewish Quarter. But for the most part it turns left, toward the Damascus Gate and East Jerusalem's business center on Salah al-Din Street. Shoppers who enter the stores adjacent to the Jaffa Gate can buy items from an eclectic selection—a Jewish ritual object, such as a shofar, *talit* (prayer shawl), or kiddush cups; a black-and-white-checked *khefiyyah* (Arab headdress); a colorful silk scarf made in the Far East; an Armenian ceramic bowl or tile, made in Arab Jerusalem; a pair of simple pilgrim sandals, like those worn by Christian clergymen in the city; a *nargilah* (water pipe); a backgammon set; and t-shirts bearing the symbols and names of IDF units. Arab–Jewish interaction is limited to commerce and tourism, underscoring the Arab merchants' economic dependence on buyers coming in from the western side of the city.

The colorful merchandise in the stores reflects how today's tourists differ from their predecessors, and how different their perception of Jerusalem is from that of travelers more than a century ago. At the end of the nineteenth century Jerusalem was visited largely by pilgrims, most of them poor, from Russia, Eastern Europe, and the eastern

Mediterranean. For wealthier tourists from the West, Jerusalem was a stop on their grand tour of the exotic orient. With enthusiasm and awe they came to see the places in which the stories of the Old and New Testaments "really happened." Together, at this time, they numbered more than 20,000 a year. In the years just before World War I approximately 10,000 Russian pilgrims arrived each year.[8] The Russians purchased Christian religious souvenirs, including paintings by local artists that depicted biblical scenes. The Bible, both Hebrew and Christian, was the most-used guidebook for visitors at that time.

During the first half of the twentieth century the flow of wealthier tourists increased, supplemented by members of the middle class. They combined religious pilgrimage with vacations and shopping. The *suk* offered them emblematic goods of the East, such as oriental rugs and damask fabric. Then, from 1949 to 1967, when the Old City came under Jordanian rule, wealthy tourists from the Arabian Peninsula became the majority. They were interested in the same goods, and became the main source of livelihood for the *suk*'s storekeepers and artisans.

The *suk*'s appearance was again changed following the Israeli conquest in 1967. Under Jordanian rule, no more than a handful of souvenir stores had been allowed to operate. The Israelis loosened up. In the new regime, Arab tourists no longer came. Their place was taken, at first, by ravenous Israelis who found in the *suk*—the name of which they Hebraicized to *shuk*—goods that had long been unavailable or overpriced in Israel. They bought everything they could lay their hands on, and in large quantities—fountain pens from China, camels carved out of olive wood, and rural Arab ceramics. Large clay jugs became fashionable living-room ornaments, providing an oriental accent that told guests that their hosts were native-born Israelis rather than immigrants.

In the 1970s American tourists of all faiths visited the *shuk* in ever-growing numbers. To appeal to them, the merchants began stocking what they claimed were Bedouin or Palestinian wares, even though most of the items had actually been manufactured in the Far East. In the 1980s the tourists were mostly American Jews, and the *shuk* began to offer Jewish ritual objects and Jewish and Israeli souvenirs, including t-shirts emblazoned with the names and insignia of IDF units or with militaristic slogans that most certainly did not express the sentiments of the Palestinian shopkeepers. But for American Jewish tourists, with their unbounded enthusiasm for Israel, they represented the authentic Jerusalem as a blend of the Bible, oriental exoticism, Judaism, and Israeli army-inspired patriotism.[9] The result was a complex and interesting relationship between the merchants and their customers. Palestinian storekeepers offered American Jewish tourists a Jerusalem that matched their expectations. The buyers disregarded the actual here-and-now Jerusalem and the Palestinian identity of the people they bought from. By providing the tourist with a dose of illusion, the seller locked his patrons into an imaginary space. For his part, he made a profit that enabled him to live in the real world.

The *shuk* changes its character the deeper one penetrates it. It turns from a place that encloses tourists in an illusion of authenticity to one that provides for the needs of the city's inhabitants. Tourists are less evident; most of the patrons are Palestinians doing their daily or weekly shopping. This part of the *shuk* is full of meat, cloth, real and artificial leather goods, jewelry, kitchenware, spices, and produce. Tiny restaurants that cater to laborers offer hummus and kebabs, along with pita rounds from the bakery down the street, which also displays trays of baklava dripping with sugar syrup. The names of the streets preserve the memory of the ancient marketplace: Suk Han al-Zeit (Oil Market), Suk al-Lahamin (Butchers' Market), Suk al-'Atarin (Perfume Market), Suk al-Khawajat (Silversmiths' Market), Suk al-Katanin (Cotton Merchants' Market). The ruckus of daily life is cut short by the Via Dolorosa, where shoppers are likely to encounter groups of pilgrims singing hymns at the Stations of the Cross. The shoppers cross the road, dividing the pilgrims into isolated islands. It is the physical manifestation of the intersection of the sacred and profane Jerusalems.

During the Jerusalem Film Festival movies are screened in the mall, but not in the *shuk*. At the mall, on summertime Thursday evenings, middle-aged Israelis relive their youths by participating in folk dances. A svelte model dressed in tight Levis watches them from a large poster in a nearby store. In the Old City coffee is not served in comfortable chairs but in tiny niches. These coffee stands supply nearby shops with their wares by sending out delivery boys, who snake deftly through the crowd with copper trays bearing small cups of bitter brew and tumblers of syrupy tea, together with glasses of cold water. The flow and clamor of life give the Arab *shuk* a feeling of being truly alive, unlike the mall to the west of Jaffa Gate, which intentionally frames its visitors inside the consumer culture of a prosperous society.

INTRODUCTION

In Mamilla, the stores are ranged like sentries on either side of the central promenade. On 11 December 1917, on the spot where the mall now stands, a British honor guard stood in formation with bayoneted rifles, ammunition belts, and steel helmets. The soldiers were drilling in preparation for the ceremony that would mark the advent of British rule. Two days previously, at the western end of Jaffa Road, a band of exhausted Turkish soldiers had surrendered to a small British patrol. Ottoman Turkish rule, which had lasted for 400 years, suddenly came to an end without any of the blood and heroism that had typified previous battles for the Holy City. Although the British would govern the territory for a mere thirty-one years, this was a formative period. General Allenby's entry into Jerusalem left as much of a mark on Palestine as Napoleon did on Egypt following his invasion in 1798.

The empire did not intend to take charge of Jerusalem in an offhanded fashion, even if that was the way it acquired the city in practice. The honor guard was commanded by a tall officer whose roars can almost be heard from Eric Matson's photograph. During the practice drills the Turkish flag, red crescent and star on white background, still flew on either side of Jaffa Gate's broad opening through the city wall. The clock over the gate showed that it was 7.30 when the commander of the 60th Division, General Edmund Allenby, reviewed the guard and strode through the gate in his dress uniform, followed by other senior officers. The city's notables received him at the entrance to David's Citadel, next to the gate. Crowds on either side of the road, on the gate's roof, and on nearby balconies, cheered. Jews were among them. Did anyone reflect on the historical irony that the Christian British Empire was taking control of the city from the Muslim Ottomans on Hanukah, the Jewish holiday that commemorates the ancient Jewish conquest of Jerusalem and the liberation of the Holy Temple? The Turkish flags had been removed before Allenby went through the gate, but one remained on a house right next to it as a reminder. The British general walked straight past it before mounting his horse in order to ride at the head of his staff. Four days later, on the west side of the gate where the mall now stands, a small ceremony was held at which Allenby was promoted to field marshal.[10]

The British, like many of the conquerors before and after them, did not like what they saw in their new possession. Nine days after entering the city, its temporary military governor, General William Borton, told his replacement Ronald Storrs that "the only tolerable places in

Jerusalem [are] bath and bed."[11] Storrs, however, preferred not to stay in bath or in bed. He worked hard to make the real Jerusalem look like the one he imagined.

Uniforms are still a presence at the Jaffa Gate—not the uniforms of tourist police but those of soldiers making a display of force. On one side of the plaza inside the gate stands a fortified police station, situated in the Kishla, an Ottoman prison and army base built in the mid-nineteenth century. The Ottoman soldiers were replaced by British ones, who were in turn replaced by Jordanians, who were then replaced by Israelis. The contingent stationed at the Gate keeps order in the Old City on foot and on horseback, assisted by video cameras deployed on the walls and roofs. Israeli soldiers patrol the Jaffa Gate plaza as if it were a dangerous and violent place. Fitted out with flak jackets, they are armed with rifles and pistols, and equipped with walkie-talkies. Everyday life happens around them. Tourists, rabbis, nuns, and priests cross the square in colorful array. In their traditional dress, headdresses, and haircuts, the clergymen look as if they had arrived here from some previous century. They bear a message from older times, refusing to allow Jerusalem to live its life in the here and now.

Shortly after the Israeli annexation of Jordanian Jerusalem in September 1967, the Jerusalem municipality's Culture and Names Committee changed the name of the plaza inside the gate from Caliph 'Omar ibn al-Khatab Square, named after the Muslim conqueror of Jerusalem, to Citadel Square. The committee's chairman, Ben-Zion Luria, declared that 'Omar promised that "no Jew would be allowed to live in Jerusalem." Furthermore, he said, the hallmark Islamic laws discriminating against the Jews were named after 'Omar. In contrast, the citadel is David's Citadel. The decision was lambasted by Mayor Teddy Kollek and the poet Haim Guri, and three months later the Jordanian name was restored.[12]

Today the plaza is full of people from East Jerusalem going about their daily business. The sound of donkeys braying and the smell of their droppings have been replaced by the growl of diesel-engine taxicabs and the stench from their exhausts. Several cab drivers stand in the same place that was, until the 1930s, the preserve of beggars, many of them deformed, who harangued the passersby, asking for handouts. No Israelis sell street food here. Arabs with green wooden wagons ply falafel balls and rings of sesame-covered bread, offered with a small cone of newspaper filled with powdered *za'atar*—Middle Eastern hyssop—classic Palestinian Arab food. These small, narrow, three-wheeled wagons have been present in the plaza since the nineteenth century, if not before, arriving here after their drivers had trundled them through the Old City alleys. They replaced the donkeys that used to haul merchandise to and from the *suk*. The fact that the municipality demands that each peddler displays a license serves as another sign of modernity. This licensing system enforces tough standards that govern the build of the wagons and where they may be placed. Unlicensed hawkers receive heavy fines.[13]

The municipal museum is situated across the street from the police station, in David's Citadel. Like the Kishla, it exudes power and authority. While the police exert these qualities physically, the museum does so in the realms of history and consciousness. The two institutions complement each other. In the past, physical control of the citadel was vital in order to conquer Jerusalem. Today, the regime requires historical justification, as the domination of consciousness supplements physical domination. The Jews were the losers throughout most of history; now their state writes the city's history as a victor.

David's Citadel went through a number of fascinating incarnations before its current Jewish–Israeli one. Its name derives from a biblical reading by fourth-century Byzantine monks who identified the spot as being the place where David composed the psalms. The monks seem to have made the connection via a passage in Josephus Flavius's *The Wars of the Jews*. Josephus described a stronghold in the upper part of the walled city that had three towers. He called the fortress, which was built by Herod the Great, the Citadel of King David.[14] Josephus gave the name, and the Byzantine monks imbued the name with meaning. In the centuries that followed, the Christian tradition was supplemented by Muslim tradition. The latter sees the spot as the prayer niche of the Prophet Da'ud (the Arabic form of David). Muslims believe that 'Omar ibn al-Khatab prayed there upon conquering Jerusalem in 638. They thus called the gate next to the Citadel *Bab Da'ud*—David's Gate—or *Bab Mahrab Da'ud*—David's Prayer Niche Gate. The two traditions went through further incarnations, in which each side sought to reinforce its version, during the Muslim–Crusader wars of the twelfth century. The Mamluks, who defeated the Crusaders and ruled Palestine from the thirteenth to the sixteenth century, built their own citadel over the old Crusader one. In the sixteenth century, the next conqueror, Ottoman Sultan Suleiman the Great, replaced it with an even more impressive citadel, the one that stands there today, as part of his project of fortifying Jerusalem and building a city wall. A turret, which the Jews later named David's Tower, was built a century later. It was the minaret of a mosque built inside the citadel.[15]

The identification of the citadel and the minaret as a Jewish holy place linked to King David dates to 1837. In that year, Yehosef Schwartz, a Jerusalem scholar and writer, drew the Citadel, following the lead of British scholars, his friends, who examined religious traditions searching for places mentioned in the Bible in the real landscape of Palestine. Schwartz's painting was part of a series depicting Jewish holy places which also included views of the Western Wall, Rachel's Tomb, Absalom's Tomb, and the Cave of the Patriarchs. Schwartz's pictures were made into prints, first in Germany and then by the press that Israel Beck established in Jerusalem in 1841. Schwartz sent the prints to Jews overseas where they quickly became part of popular European Jewish culture, hung on synagogue walls and used to illustrate books. They were the basis for the way Diaspora Jews imagined Jerusalem. The advent of the Zionist movement and the founding of the Bezalel Art Academy in Jerusalem in 1906 further strengthened the site's identification with King David. Bezalel's faculty and students aimed to create a national Jewish art inspired by the Bible, and David's Citadel was perfect for their purposes. Depictions of it appeared on Jewish sacred objects, souvenirs, and in popular art disseminated around the world, turning it into a kind of icon representing the Land of Israel. Bezalel artists went beyond the regular dissemination of works of art depicting the land in Jewish-biblical guise. Using as a model a famous photograph from 1897, showing Herzl standing on a balcony in Basel during the First Zionist Congress, they produced a painting showing Herzl looking out over David's Citadel. By depicting Herzl gazing out at an ostensibly biblical site, they linked Zionism to King David, who had conquered Jerusalem and made it his capital. The picture was made into a tapestry, and in 1940 it was used for a stamp issued by the Keren Kayemet (Jewish National Fund), all of these reinforcing the link between David's Citadel and the Jewish national movement. In the 1920s the British Mandate administration issued a series of postage stamps and banknotes that showed the Citadel alongside Rachel's Tomb and the Dome of the Rock. It provided official sanction to this popular symbol of the Jewish connection to Jerusalem, even if the intent of the British had been, it would seem,

INTRODUCTION

to use the impressive fortress as an emblem of the city as a whole. At the time the city of Jerusalem did not have an official seal, so David's Citadel became its unofficial crest. In mid-1943 the British officials who ran the city launched a process to create an official seal; one of the proposals was that it would include a drawing of the Citadel. But the 1948 war cut this process short.[16]

As the status of David's Citadel as a Jewish holy site grew stronger, al-Haram al-Sharif's standing as a Muslim symbol gained as well. Its prominence grew as a result of the national–religious contention with the Jews over the Western Wall and Temple Mount. Muslim attention was diverted from the area of Jaffa Gate, where David's Citadel lay, to al-Haram al-Sharif. There were ancient Muslim traditions that identified the place where David had prayed as being somewhere on al-Haram al-Sharif, but that tradition had been abandoned when, in the conflict with Christianity, the claim to the Citadel became a primary Muslim concern. Now, with the Jews returning to Palestine and demanding changes in the regulations regarding Jewish prayer at the Western Wall while trumpeting their historical connection to the Temple Mount, the Muslims moved to shore up their claim to that site. In the process, they left the Zionist narrative on David's Citadel uncontested.

The British in the meantime divested David's Citadel of its religious significance. They renovated the site and used it for performances and cultural activities. An art exhibition sponsored by the Pro-Jerusalem Society, led by Ronald Storrs, the governor of Jerusalem, opened there in April 1921. In the same year drafts of urban renewal plans were also displayed there, as well as an exhibit of Palestinian arts and crafts. Between 1922 and 1927 Bezalel artists, as well as the painter Reuven Rubin, mounted exhibits there. In 1935 the gallery was redone as a museum with a collection of local Arab and Jewish arts, crafts, and folklore which displayed the material culture of the various communities that lived in Palestine—clothing, jewelry, and ceramics. The site's multicultural character was reflected under British rule by the names given to the nearby streets. The road that ran by the Citadel was called David Street in English, Tariq Mahrab Da'ud (David's Prayer Niche Road) in Arabic, and Rehov David HaMelekh (King David Street) in Hebrew. The square next to the Citadel, just inside Jaffa Gate, was called Citadel Square in English, Midan al-Qal'ah (with the same meaning) in Arabic, and Kikar Migdal David (David's Citadel Square) in Hebrew.[17]

Despite its high standing in the Zionist consciousness, David's Citadel suddenly disappeared from Israeli awareness in the period from 1949 to 1967. It was not a focus of Zionist longing, nor did it figure in dreams of national liberation. It stood on the neglected seam between Israel and Jordan, manned by Jordanian troops. When a seal was finally designed for the Jerusalem municipality, the Citadel was not featured in it. The committee that oversaw the process decided from the start that the seal would not include "the forms of ancient buildings, Jewish or otherwise, that are referred to by traditional names that have no justification."[18] With the exception of a single stamp, the structure made no appearance in the post, nor was it engraved on the medals produced by the Israeli mint. Nor was it used by the Hashemite regime that ruled Jordan, which preferred the Dome of the Rock and al-Aqsa Mosque as symbols.

The Israeli victory in 1967 restored to the Citadel and its tower some of their former importance. In 1968 Israel issued a medal imprinted with their images, and Keren Kayemet a stamp with a picture of the site. This signification of the Citadel was followed by actions. The Israeli government renovated the site and opened it once again as a museum. In 1983 the Jerusalem municipality made it into its municipal museum, with a permanent exhibit that opened in 1989. A program outline for the museum in 1985 states that it should stress Jerusalem's centrality to the three monotheistic religions, while at the same time emphasizing "the exclusive role which Jerusalem played and continues to play in the life of the Jewish nation."[19]

The homepage of the museum's website states that it presents the history of Jerusalem as the Jewish capital and stresses its importance to Jews, Christians, and Muslims.[20] When the historian Meron Benvenisti visited the museum in the mid-1990s, he found that the Canaanite period, which lasted for nearly 2,000 years, was presented only in passing, in comparison with the space devoted to the Israelite period, which lasted only 600 years. He also noted that the term "Arab" did not appear at all. Instead of speaking of the Arab-Muslim conquest, the exhibit referred to it only as Muslim. The exhibit had nothing to say about how the city had been run during this period or about its important people. But the Jewish nation was mentioned in every period. The exhibit stressed the presence of a Jewish community in Jerusalem in all of these eras, depicting its way of life and the hopes of Diaspora Jews to return to the city. The Arab-Muslim period in the

INTRODUCTION

city's history lasted from the seventh through the twentieth centuries, interrupted only by a brief 88-year hiatus of Crusader rule. The museum divided this entire epoch into small periods labeled with the names of the different ruling dynasties. This manipulation of history created the impression that all were very different regimes, each of which ruled the city for less time than the Jews. The Zionist struggle against the British was presented dramatically, including the 1946 bombing of the King David Hotel, which can be seen from the Citadel, on the other side of the Hinnom Valley. The Zionist struggle against the Palestinian national movement was not mentioned at all. Israel's War of Independence was depicted as a war against British imperialism and the Arab Legion, Jordan's army. The Palestinians were presented as a disorganized mass that rioted and opposed the UN partition resolution blindly and illogically. The Palestinian national struggle after 1967 was cast, in the museum catalogue that Benvenisti saw, as a municipal problem.[21]

When I viewed the museum's website in 2010, in order to see the museum's permanent exhibit as displayed online, it was clear that very little had changed in the period since Benvenisti's visit. The section devoted to the Canaanite period said nothing about the city's institutions or the regime of the Jebusites, whom the Palestinians claim as their ancestors. The section on the Muslim period includes the Umayyad and Abbasid Caliphates, without mentioning that both were not only Muslim but also Arab.[22] These rulers are presented as distinct from the post-Crusader dynasties of the Ayyubids, the Mamluks, and the Ottomans, even though all of these were Muslims. History is thus enlisted to underline the double importance of Jerusalem to the Jews—as both its holiest city and as the center of its nationhood. According to the exhibit, Jerusalem is important as a national symbol only to Israel. The Jews are the only nation to have lived in Jerusalem in the past and to have returned to it in the present—another proof that the city belongs to them and only to them. The same message is conveyed to visiting groups of Jews by Israeli Jewish tour guides. Palestinians who come to the museum hear a different script and are taken on a shorter route to see the Citadel structure and the archaeological site in its courtyard, but not the museum. The central message of the Arabic tour is that the Citadel is a military installation rather than a focus of identity. Nor is Jerusalem's importance to the three monotheistic religions a theme of the Arab tour.[23]

The museum stresses that Jewish history reached its climax with the creation of the State of Israel in 1948 and the unification of Jerusalem in 1967. The depiction of the past as a circle, closing with the arrival at a historical destination at which the Jewish people had always aimed, brings to mind the point made by the historian Tony Judt:

> The final decades of the [twentieth] century had seen an escalating public fascination with the past as a detached artifact, encapsulating not recent memories but *lost* memories: history not so much as a source of enlightenment about the present but rather as an illustration of how very different things had once been. History on television—whether narrated or performed; history in theme parks; history in museums; all emphasized not what bound people to the past but everything that separated them from it. The present was depicted not as heir to history but as its orphan: cut off from the way things were and the world we have lost.[24]

1

ARAB JEWS

Beneath the official harmony of the past lie the vaster regions of sediment traces and variable topography of discarded memories and forgotten lives.[1]

Neither Oxymoron nor Aspersion

Before nationalism brutally separated the two words "Arab" and "Jew" and required the inhabitants of Palestine to count themselves as one or the other, there were people who thought of themselves as Arab Jews, just as today there are American Jews. Arab–Jewish identity was a fact of life, something encountered daily by the country's natives. Ideologues did not codify it in a clear-cut way in articles and books, poets did not write of it, and no conferences and fundraising drives were held to promote it or bring it about. Members of some social strata simply lived it. It contained incongruent and sometimes contradictory elements—life never conforms to a single model but rather flows in different directions. That is why the evidence below is disparate and sometimes contradictory. The process of creating the "Arab Jew" identity was not a smooth one. It was full of spurs and bumps, exceptions and oppositions. Despite its internal disharmony, it is a discernible whole when viewed from the outside. It emerged from the juxtaposition of several factors. The flagging Ottoman Empire was trying to restore some of the vigor it had lost through reforms and modernization projects. Ways of life and patterns of thinking were changing.

Palestine opened up and a growing stream of Westerners arrived, thanks to advances in transportation that made it possible to travel farther in less time. Old identities weakened and were replaced by more complex and multidimensional ones. Local identity, the sense of belonging to the place where one lived and the surrounding society, grew stronger as the Ottoman regime declined, culminating in the Young Turk rebellion of 1908. At the same time, new trans-local identities arrived in Palestine—Arab and Jewish nationalism.

Arab–Jewish identity differed from the Jewish–Muslim coexistence of the previous period in a number of ways. First, it grew in parallel with the attenuation of traditional identities. Arab–Jewish identity was not an element of Jewish–Muslim coexistence in Islam's Golden Age. Second, Arab–Jewish identity in Palestine was very much a local identity, much more so than the religious and ethnic identities that connect their adherents to distant places and other lifestyles, such as those encompassed by the categories of Jew and Muslim. It meant more than coexistence and residing one beside the other. Lifestyles, language, and culture created a common identity that centered on a sense of belonging to a place and to the people who live there. Intellectuals expressed this in articles they published in the local press. *Falastin* and *al-Quds* were not just the names of newspapers—they defined terms of local identity.[2] Later, Arab–Jewish identity, shunted into the margins by the two rival identities of Arab and Jew, declined and disappeared. It became something abstract, a concept looked on from a distance in time and place, and sometimes from a mental and emotional distance as well. The Arab–Jewish life experience became a subject for memoirs, an object of longing, and a goal for artificial attempts of re-creation, in particular by people who lived on the margins of society, who suffered from a feeling that their previous identity was now illegitimate due to the deadly Arab–Jewish conflict. Until now, historical research has barely touched on Arab–Jewish identity. Its incarnation in Palestine/the Land of Israel, the place where the fate of Arab–Jewish identity throughout the Middle East was decided, has been studied even less.

Arab–Jewish identity did not develop only in Jerusalem, Jaffa, and Hebron. It was a fact of life throughout the Arab world. By the end of the nineteenth century it was a self-conscious identity in the major cities of the East, such as Cairo, Beirut, and Baghdad. In these urban centers Jews took part in the Arab cultural renaissance and in local national movements. Up until the mid-1930s it evolved without reference to the Zionist–Palestinian conflict. The first repercussions of that struggle were felt at the time of the Arab revolt of 1936–9 in Palestine, which dealt a devastating blow to Arab–Jewish identity, one that would reverberate throughout the Arab world in the mid-1940s.[3] However, beyond its local nature, Palestine's Arab–Jewish identity had two unique aspects that were not present elsewhere in the East. First, in Jerusalem, one of its focal points, Jews were a majority by the end of the nineteenth century. Likewise, a Jewish city, Tel Aviv, sprang up alongside Arab Jaffa. Second, Jerusalem had a large population of Ashkenazim—Jews of European origin—many of whom adopted an Arab–Jewish identity.

At the end of the nineteenth century, Palestine was not a single administrative or political entity, as it would become under the British Mandate. But the inhabitants of its central cities developed new types of ties and affiliations among themselves, and between them and the land in which they lived, a land that meant more than simply the place where they had been born or where they resided. Arab–Jewish identity and local patriotism emerged alongside a sense of belonging to the Ottoman Empire. The Arab natives distinguished between Arab Jews and Ashkenazi Zionists. Whereas Arabs viewed the former as natives of a somewhat inferior status, the latter were seen as European invaders who had to be repelled. "We knew they were different from 'our Jews,' I mean Arab Jews. We thought of them as foreigners from Europe rather than Jews as such," wrote Ghada Karmi, a Palestinian physician and writer who grew up in West Jerusalem.[4] In the words of Ya'akov Yehoshua, the father of Israeli novelist A.B. Yehoshua, "The residential courtyards of the Jews and Muslims were common. We were like one family, we were all friends." "Our mothers poured out their hearts to Muslim women and they poured out their hearts to our mothers. The Muslim women accustomed themselves to speaking the Ladino language. They frequently used that language's proverbs and idioms." The Ashkenazim, he claimed, lived in their own exclusive courtyards that they did not share with Muslims. "Muslim women descended to us from the roofs to while away the evening talking to our mothers," he recalled. "Our children played with their children and when other children in the neighborhood hurt us our Muslim friends who lived in our courtyard came to defend us. We were their allies."[5] Aryeh Sasson, who grew up in the Old City's Muslim Quarter, recalled that his Arab neighbors "scolded Arab children if they bullied a Jewish child and a girl or woman had no need to be afraid of walking down a street or alley because it was known that any passing Arab would defend the honor of Jewish women."[6]

There is something both nostalgic and authentic about the recollections of the last two of these writers, both of whom were members of the old Sephardi Yishuv (Jewish community) in Jerusalem. Nationalism suddenly intruded on their lives and those of their Muslim neighbors and imposed its hatreds and wars on them. The construction of the national "I" involved the rejection of prior identities, including that of being Arab Jews. The entire spectrum of Arab–Jewish identity dissipated from 1929 onward. Zionism on the one side and Palestinian nationalism on the other drew boundaries of animosity against the Other. Native Arab Jews were relegated to inferiority in the Central and East European Zionist establishment. The Zionists invented and promoted their own ideal of the native-born, Hebrew-speaking Jew—the *Tzabar* or Sabra. Sabra culture was created by the children of immigrants who viewed themselves as natives. They adopted dances, melodies, and dress from Palestinian Arab and Arab–Jewish folk culture. They also borrowed words and phrases from Arabic and emulated Arab standards of masculinity. Like the Bedouin, they trekked from one end of the country to the other as a way of knowing it in the most concrete way. Maps were relabeled, with Arab place names replaced by Hebrew ones.[7] The intention behind these new designations was not only to relabel the immigrants as natives but also to place them ahead of the natives who had been there before them—or, at the very least, to establish a new order in which the immigrants, who viewed themselves as authentic natives, would enjoy a superior position to the land's original inhabitants. The initial Sabra generations persuaded themselves that they were indeed natives, but they did not convince the Palestinian Arabs, the country's original inhabitants. Zionism had to do so by force.

The Locals

Up until the mid-nineteenth century, Jerusalem was a small city that locked its identity and lifestyle within its city walls. In 1840 it had only 13,000 inhabitants.[8] Jaffa Road was the axis along which Jerusalem warily opened itself up to the West. To no small extent this opening was forced on the city as a result of the Ottoman Empire's defeats at the hands of European powers, whereupon the victors compelled the

Ottomans to grant special legal status to Europeans in its territories. Furthermore, the debilitated empire adopted a set of Western-inspired administrative and technological reforms with the intent of using the West's own means to fight against it. Jerusalem was one of the first Ottoman provincial cities in which a municipal administration was set up. It was founded in 1867 on the model of a municipality that had run one of Constantinople's neighborhoods for eight years. It brought about the integration of the local elite into the imperial administration and helped turn Jerusalem into a political center.[9]

Jaffa Road first appeared in the 1860s as a dirt road leading from the Old City to *Nuva Yerushama*, New Jerusalem. This New Jerusalem was a compound built by the Russian government in 1859–69 that included a consulate, a hospital, and a lodge for religious pilgrims. The name signaled the same sort of pretention that the Zionists shared. According to the classic Zionist narrative, New Jerusalem to the west of the walled city resulted from a Jewish and Israeli initiative against the backward Arab East. In both the Russian and Zionist stories, the innovation is tied up with the fact that its founders were not Arabs. But history says otherwise.

In anticipation of the visit of Emperor Franz Joseph of Austria in 1869, Jaffa Road was widened and graded so that horse-drawn carriages could travel on it. But carriages could not enter the Old City until the gate was replaced by a broad archway thirty years later, in 1898. An American tourist who arrived from Europe was, quite appropriately, the first person to drive a motorcar through Jaffa Gate.[10] A market where African girls could be purchased operated in the Old City until 1889, despite the fact that the sultan had outlawed the slave trade throughout his realm in 1846. In about 1880, Haim Aharon Valero bought an Ethiopian girl who was around ten years old. When the central government enforced the emancipation of slaves in Jerusalem, the girl chose to stay with Valero's family and converted to Judaism.[11] A few hundred descendants of these slaves still live in the Old City, in what is called the Black or Slave Compound.

Even before the modern age made its way into the Old City, its Arab and Jewish residents were going outside the walls to greet it. The nineteenth century's strength was petering out and Jerusalem's inhabitants left the walls to receive the twentieth, which looked promising and fresh. A new Jewish Jerusalem had its inception with the construction of the Nahalat Shiv'ah quarter, across from the Russian Compound, in

1869. Nahalat Shiv'ah was followed by a series of other neighborhoods built along Jaffa Road—Even Yisrael (1874); Beit Ya'akov (1877); Mahaneh Yehuda (1887), next to which stood the Alliance Israélite Universelle school (1882) and Sephardi Orphanage (1908); Sha'arei Yerushalayim, Ohel Shlomo (1891) and Ezrat Yisrael (1892), and the Feingold houses next to Nahalat Shiv'ah (1898). An old-age home was built at the western end of Jaffa Road (1901). The Jewish exodus from within the walls at this time was a group action, involving ad hoc organizing of families to settle in the new quarters. It was only under British rule in the 1920s and 1930s that Jewish families began to build individual homes in these new areas.

Jews were not the only ones to leave the Old City, and not all Jews segregated themselves from the Arabs into their own spaces. In the 1890s Arabs and Jews began building neighborhoods and buildings that together created a new downtown stretching west from Jaffa Gate along nearby streets, in the direction of the Russian Compound and the *ma'man Allah* (Mamilla) cemetery. This new urban area included a central station from which carriages set out for Jaffa and Hebron, a customs office, a modern commercial center, post offices, banks, hotels, workshops, stores, travel agencies, restaurants, and cafés. Photographs taken in the 1880s show that the signs over these establishments in the Jaffa Gate area were largely written in European languages, with almost no Arabic lettering.[12] Some of the stores physically abutted the Old City wall, a phenomenon that would later exasperate Ronald Storrs, who served as British governor of Jerusalem from 1917 to 1926. At the beginning of the 1920s he ordered the demolition of these establishments so as to expose the wall over its entire length. He also pulled down the clock tower that the Turks had built on the northern side of Jaffa Gate in 1907, vying in height with David's Tower to the south.[13] The clock symbolized progress and innovation, its prominence conveying the message that Jerusalem kept pace with time. The Turks constructed a similar tower in Jaffa's central square, next to its administrative center there, which remains a landmark to this day. But Storrs did not identify Ottoman Turkish Jerusalem with modernization. It was the British Empire, he maintained, that was the embodiment of progress, replacing the rule of the "sick man on the Bosphorus." For Storrs, Jerusalem in his day was its past:

> The city is indeed quick with every time and kind of tragic memory, and has perhaps passed the age of its productivity, though surely not of its interest and

attraction ... something past yet unalloyed and throbbing, that seems to confound ancient and modern, and to undate recorded history.[14]

He wanted to preserve Jerusalem's charm by baring its wall. Storrs was the first man in modern Jerusalem to understand that stone could make history a salient presence in the city, and he did all he could to amplify this effect. He issued an edict which required every new building subsequently built in Jerusalem to be faced in stone. It is no coincidence that the three monotheistic faiths are all represented in Jerusalem by stones: the foundation stone over which the Dome of the Rock is built, the Western Wall, and the Holy Sepulcher. Yet all this stone gives Jerusalem the image of being a hard and cruel city, a place of religious wars and fanatics, in which the present buckles under the heavy burden of the past.

One Saturday in 1896, David Yellin, a Jewish educator, went out for a walk and counted the number of Jewish stores in the Old City. He found that twenty of the seventy-five stores along the street leading from Jaffa Gate down into the *shuk* belonged to Jews. Most of these were produce and food stands. On Batrak (Patriarchate) Street he found that forty out of sixty shops belonged to Sephardi Jews who dealt in fabric. In the area of Damascus Gate he counted fifty Jewish stores out of 300, most of them selling leather goods and owned by Sephardi Jews.[15] These retailers bought their merchandise in Jaffa from Arab wholesalers. In the 1920s and 1930s the horse-drawn carriages that traveled between the two cities were replaced by taxis. Those who could not afford the taxis traveled on Arab trucks that had been equipped with benches in the back.[16] The businesses in the Jaffa Gate area were owned by Jews, German Templers, Greeks, Armenians, and Arabs. Hadoar Café, next to Barclay's Bank, was owned by a Jew from Russia. Al-Mukhtar Café, which opened in 1918 on the inside of the gate, was a favorite of the Greek Orthodox community. Four years later, the Bristol Gardens Café became the meeting place for the British. It was a modern establishment, at the back of Jaffa Road, and boasted a garden in which patrons could relax under shade trees and listen to the burble of water in a fountain and the music of a live orchestra. Western music helped the British feel at home in the city.[17] From the end of the nineteenth century onward, more people from more countries came to Jaffa and Jerusalem, and the cities' inhabitants changed their traditional lifestyles. It was not only that human and cultural diversity increased. Political and military events followed each other in rapid succession and at a pace that the region had never experienced before. People gathered in cafés to talk politics, discuss cultural issues, and to exchange opinions and information. At a café one could read the latest news in *al-Quds*, founded in 1908, or *Falastin*, founded in 1911, as well as meet professional colleagues and members of one's community. (Hebrew newspapers had preceded them—*Hazvi* [1884], *Hahavatzelet* [1863], and *Hashkafa* [1896], but they do not seem to have been read in these establishments.) Those who had trouble reading might prefer one of the traditional cafés where a literate patron would read the newspaper out loud for the benefit of others. When the reader fell silent, the local storyteller (*hakawati*) would begin, weaving current events into his tales.[18] In between, one could play backgammon and smoke. Later the gramophone and radio would find their way into traditional cafés. On special occasions, there might be live music. Rashid Khalidi described the changes in Jerusalem at the end of the nineteenth century as being just short of a revolution insofar as they turned the city into an intellectual, cultural, and educational center, not just a religious one. By 1931, Jerusalem was the largest city in Palestine.[19]

The city's most important and finest hotels stood just inside the Jaffa Gate. The Grand New Hotel (today the Imperial) and Amdursky's (today the Petra) stood next to the Austrian post office. The plaza was not just the city's center of tourism—it was also part of a business district that began there and extended along Jaffa Road to the west. Arab moneychangers had booths there, alongside the Jewish Valero family bank. At the end of the nineteenth century, other Jewish establishments could also be found there. Yitzhak Shirion opened a shop that supplied paper to printers. It later became a kitchen supply and small furniture store. Down in the *shuk* one could buy sweets at Havilio's or handbags and briefcases from Ben-Naim. Fresh fish could be purchased from the Jewish fishmonger Aroches. He received his wares, laid in beds of cracked ice, from the Port Said–Jaffa–Jerusalem train. "Among all the [Arab] stores ... also lay the fancy wholesale outlet of R. Berl Baiover, a Habad Hasid, who supplied flour and pulses to many of the city's inhabitants," Judge Gad Frumkin wrote in his memoirs. "I almost skipped over Maimon, a Sephardi Jew who owned an establishment for blocking tarbushes ... Up David Street were [the establishments of a mixture of] Jews, Arabs, and Christians, selling cloth and fabric and other goods ... Valero's bank was among them."[20] This bank "had close commercial relations with overseas, and served as agents of the

House of Rothschild and of other banks in England."[21] Situated at the outer side of the gate were the photo shops of Sevidas the Greek and Krikorian the Armenian. Berman's bakery next door emitted mouth-watering aromas. Jerusalem's new westward development was the impetus for the opening of a new gate in the city wall, the New Gate, in 1889–90.[22]

The train line from Jaffa to Jerusalem and the steamships that sailed between Europe and Jaffa brought in increasing numbers of tourists, further changing Palestine. The transformation accelerated when the new century began and motor vehicles replaced horse-drawn carriages. More people became mobile and it took less time to get from one place to another, which encouraged the inhabitants to focus on the country rather than the village, town, or city as the focal point of their identities. The inhabitants of Jaffa and Jerusalem were exposed more than they had ever been in the past to Western ideas and ways of life. The area around Jaffa Gate was cosmopolitan, at least in terms of that place and time. Local and foreign nationals mixed, walking the streets alongside tourists and pilgrims. A babel of languages were spoken. Storekeepers, café patrons, and tourists made Jerusalem as a whole and Jaffa Gate in particular a place where the modern world wore away at the traditional life that, hitherto, Jerusalem had so zealously fostered. From 1900 to 1911 the Loretz and Zarsifi cafés next to Jaffa Gate screened silent films. The popularity of such entertainment prompted the opening of the Zion cinema in 1912. During the first decade of the twentieth century, physical education was introduced into the curricula of the city schools run by organizations based overseas. The city's inhabitants would walk over to the soccer field outside Damascus Gate to watch games between teenagers from Jerusalem and Beirut.[23]

The way people dressed also changed. In a photograph taken in 1896 at the Jewish Lemel elementary school for boys, some of the pupils are wearing sailor hats, others caps or Ashkenazi-type homburgs. But most of them stand erect with Turkish tarbushes on their heads.[24] The soccer team of the Anglican St George's school for boys (founded in 1899) posed for the camera, some of its members bareheaded, others with tarbushes, and others, apparently as a compromise between tarbush and nothing, with cloth caps. Teachers and students at al-Dusturiyah (founded in 1908) went even further. In a photograph taken a year after the school had opened, most of the boys are not wearing hats, although a few wear tarbushes. All wear Western-style blazers, but only some a tie. Some of the teachers sport tarbushes, but one has a modern European summer hat.[25] Similar variety can be seen in a photograph, taken in 1910, of craftsmen working at the Bezalel Academy of Art. Some are clad in Western suits, complete with bowties and hats. Others wear caps, tarbushes, or no hats at all. Only a few appear in the traditional *galabiya*.[26] Boys' clothes were not the only ones in flux. Girls were also dressing differently. A photograph from 1892 of a school for Jewish girls run by Christian missionaries in Jerusalem shows about a third of the girls bareheaded, while most have kerchiefs over their hair. In a photograph taken at the same school four years later, none of the girls have their heads covered.[27]

Jerusalem was thus, at this time, not a cloistered holy city but rather a multilingual, multicultural place. Its men and women wore a wide variety of clothing and spoke a gamut of languages. At the beginning of the 1960s, the Jerusalem Municipal Archive asked thirty-eight Jews about their lives at the turn of the century. In this group, fourteen knew five languages, with two who used only two languages. The most common languages cited, other than Hebrew, were Arabic, English, Yiddish, Ladino, German, and French. Some spoke Russian, Turkish, or Italian. Movement between Jerusalem and Europe went both ways. Jerusalem's inhabitants not only met tourists on the streets of their cities, but were at times themselves tourists. Most of the people interviewed by the archive made overseas trips at that time, whether for their studies or for business, a vacation, or a family visit. Others went for medical treatment, or to flee mandatory service in the Turkish army.[28]

In 1896 the municipal offices moved into a new building at the intersection of Mamilla and Jaffa Roads, so that the Ottoman regime could display its power in the new urban center. (In 1932 the municipality moved again, into a new building on Allenby Square.) Parades were held on Jaffa Road to mark the visits of heads of states; criminals sentenced to death were hung publicly on the road, in front of the municipal building. Its central location attracted foreign consulates, such as those of Austria, Italy, France, and Germany, who followed Russia. The downtown area spread from either side of the main road. To the north it reached to Prophets Street, where, in addition to the consulates, there were hospitals, missionary societies, and Christian religious centers. Interspersed among them were fine homes, Jewish schools, and the B'nai B'rith library, the first Jewish lending library to operate in the city. At the lower end of Prophets Street, near the

Damascus Gate, lay the city's old commercial center, where Arab farmers sold their produce.[29]

During this same period, Palestinian families built summer homes in Wadi Joz, a valley to the northeast, to which they escaped from the crowded and suffocating Old City. This area would later attract the middle classes that densely populate it today. But at the beginning of the nineteenth century, Wadi Joz had been the dwelling of the pariahs, the lowest rung on the social ladder, the Romany or Gypsies. Despite being Muslims, these people were shunned. The majority viewed them as primitive and forced them to live as a closed-off community, helping them to preserve their Domari language. In the twentieth century the Romany moved into cramped apartments vacated by poorer residents of the Muslim Quarter, and into the Ras al-'Amud neighborhood. Around 1,000 of them now reside in Arab Jerusalem.[30]

Well-off and elite Palestinians exited the Old City at the end of the nineteenth century and founded neighborhoods outside the walls—Sheikh Jarrah and Musrara to the north, and Baq'a and Qatamon to the south. In this first stage of the Palestinians exodus from the walled city, extended families built a residential compound and moved into them as a group. Most Jews, in contrast, were immigrants who did not have these kinds of large extended families who had lived in the city for centuries. Others did not have money to build and lived off philanthropy. In the 1920s and 1930s another Arab neighborhood, Talbiyeh, came into being. By this time, Palestinians constructed homes for their nuclear families, not compounds for entire clans.

At the end of the nineteenth century the road connecting Jerusalem with Nablus was repaved and provided a spine along which Jerusalem expanded to the north, just as it was developing westward along Jaffa Road. The new Wadi Joz and Sheikh Jarah neighborhoods enhanced the status of Damascus Gate, making it the major entryway into the Old City from the north. Unlike Jaffa Gate, the area inside this gate was not modernized. The marketplace pressed up against it. Ever more inhabitants moved out of the Old City in the 1920s; from an area of scattered houses, Sheikh Jarah turned into a real neighborhood. A house owned there by the Hussayni family was rented out to a devout Christian sect from the United States and Sweden that established the American Colony. At the beginning of the century a young man named Shmuel Meir Mashaiof resolved to learn English. He presented himself at the American Colony, where he found "Americans who came to settle in Palestine out of belief in the Bible, who it was known were not missionaries ... These people taught willingly and did not preach Christianity." But his family did not share his positive opinion of the American Colony's inhabitants. Maschoieff belonged to the Habad Hasidic community, the members of which continued to wear traditional clothing and grew long sidelocks. Even the fact that two of his fellow students, David Yellin and Yosef Meyuhas, were religious Jews did not change his parents' mind. "My studies there did not last long because in the meantime someone told my family that I was learning English from gentiles and they compelled me to stop." But his parents permitted him to learn English from a Jewish teacher.[31]

Today the American Colony compound operates as a cosmopolitan hotel with a whiff of the Orient. Its magical courtyard and dimly lit bar have, since the Intifada of 1987, hosted unofficial talks between Israelis and Palestinians and between each of them and well-meaning mediators from around the world who seek to help the two sides to end the lengthy discord between them. Foreign correspondents prowl nearby—they like to stay at the American Colony, viewing it as Jerusalem at its best. No doubt some of the people in the corridors are spies and double agents—the American Colony provides all the necessary ambience for espionage.

Jews lived in these new northern neighborhoods as well. One of them was Judah Leib Magnes, the president of the Hebrew University, who lived for a time on Ibn Batuta Street, near Herod's Gate, which lies just east of Damascus Gate. He rented his home from the Khalidis, one of the leading Jerusalem clans. But when a Jewish driver who came to pick Magnes up was shot dead during the Arab Revolt, Magnes and his family moved to the Jewish neighborhood of Rehavia.[32] Not far away lived a Jewish doctor, Aryeh Boehm, the philosopher Hugo Bergman, and Yaakav Tahon, a leading Zionist. Henrietta Szold, a member of the Zionist Executive and a founder of Hadassah, also lived in the area, in an apartment she rented from Mohammad Salah Hussayni. Among her neighbors were Dr Israel Klieger of Hadassah Hospital and the Jewish Agency's treasurer, Siegfried van Vriesland. Edwin Samuel, son of British High Commissioner Herbert Samuel, also lived in the neighborhood, in a home he rented from a member of another prominent Jerusalem Arab family that led the opposition to the leadership of the Hussayni family—Hasan Sadqi al-Dajani. Edwin Samuel's children went to a Jewish preschool that operated nearby. But when tensions between the two communities grew worse, the Samuels moved to Qatamon.

The prominent Arab clans that contended for leadership of the Jerusalem Arab community all had homes in Sheikh Jarah—the Hussaynis, Nashashibis, Dajanis, Jarallahs, and al-'Afifis. Their Jewish neighbors in this area north of Damascus Gate, near the American Colony, included the Levis and Simhas, who lived in the Sa'd WaSa'id compound, next to the Arab Nusseibehs. In 1876 the boards of the Sephardi and Ashkenazi communities purchased the Simon the Just cave and surrounding property, where they built the Jewish Shimon HaTzadiq neighborhood. Thirteen families lived there in 1916, along with another ninety-three Jewish families who lived on the other side of the road in the Nahalat Shimon neighborhood.[33] In an autobiographical story, Yonah Cohen, the son of Hakham Gershon, the rabbi of the Shimon HaTzadiq Jewish community, wrote that even "the Arab shepherds knew the Jews well and knew every Jewish precept and custom." Hakham Gershon ran a *heder*, a traditional one-room Jewish school for boys. When parents from Sheikh Jarrah sought to enroll their sons, the rabbi expressed his surprise, objecting that a Jewish education was not appropriate for Arab boys. The parents replied: "It's not a problem, rabbi, the boy will learn good behavior from you ... when he gets older he'll go to our school."[34] Between Shimon HaTzadiq and Damascus Gate stood the Nisan Beq house (built in 1877) and the Eshel Avraham compound (1893), where Jews from Russian Georgia lived. All these Jewish homes were abandoned during the 1948 war.

In 1967, Cohen went to visit his boyhood neighborhood and found an Arab family cowering in the cave. His story (in which he is represented by a character named Yonatan) relates: "Yonatan's command [of Arabic] and his good manners surprised the frightened Arab. A moment later they shook hands. He asked in an anxious voice: Will they take us out of here? Yonatan responded candidly: Undoubtedly. This cave is the tomb of a righteous man, Simon the Just. The Arab accepted the justice of the claim and mumbled: It is. But will they give us some other place?" Yonah-Yonatan's response was unambiguous: "The state of Israel does not throw families out into the street."[35] Yonah Cohen did not demand that the Palestinians living in his family's former home leave; he only demanded that the holy site not be used as a dwelling. He was certain, then, that the Israeli government would find the evacuated family alternative housing. At the end of the 1990s, Jewish settlers evicted Arab families living in former Jewish homes in the neighborhood. The settlers received title to the houses from the Jewish organizations that had originally built them, after their claim to the houses was affirmed by an Israeli court, for all intents and purposes enforcing a "Jewish right of return." None of the evacuated families was offered alternative housing. Two of them, the al-Kurd and Rawi families, now live in tents next to the homes they were forced to leave.[36]

Michael Ben-Yair, formerly Israel's attorney general, lived in a house in Nahalat Shimon prior to 1948, after which he and his family became refugees. He and one of his sisters went to visit the childhood home in 2011 in order to lend their support to the Palestinian tenants who were threatened with evacuation by the settlers. Soon after the end of the 1967 war, he, his parents, and his sisters went to see their former home. He recalled that the rest of the family was very emotional, but that he was not. He was a young child when his family had fled, and he had no memories of the house. The families who then lived in the house were afraid that the Ben-Yairs had come to claim their property and evacuate the squatters. But the Ben-Yairs reassured them by telling them that they would not go to court as they had received compensation for the house they had lost—a house in West Jerusalem where a Palestinian family had once lived.[37]

Until the 1880s, the majority of Jerusalem's Jews were Sephardim. They lost their majority with the arrival of Ashkenazi immigrants under the patronage of the European powers, whose nationals benefited from special rights in Palestine. A 1905 Ottoman census shows that Jerusalem was a mosaic of communities. Jews made up more than half the population, but were subdivided into Ashkenazi, Sephardi, Moroccan, Yemenite, Kurdish, Georgian, and Aleppo communities. The Muslims consisted of Jerusalem natives, blacks, Romany, and Mughrabis. The Christian community included Armenians, Armenian Catholics, Armenian Orthodox, Greeks, Catholics, Protestants, Maronites, Russian Orthodox, and Chaldeans-Syrians. The economic standing of these different communities can be divined from data on who was entitled to vote in municipal elections. Suffrage was not universal—it was limited to male Ottoman subjects who owned property or paid high levels of taxes. In 1898, voters numbered 700 out of 7,000 Muslims; 300 out of some 13,000 Christians; and 178 Jews (ninety-two Sephardim and eighty-six Ashkenazim) out of 35,000.[38]

Even if the population figures err at the high end, they offer a snapshot of the relative status of the various communities.

In 1874 Jerusalem's administrative status was upgraded when it became an independent *sanjaq* of the Ottoman government, with its governor appointed directly by the sultan's court. This conferred on Jerusalem a special standing when compared to other parts of Palestine, and Jerusalem's leaders accordingly had a direct channel of communication with the central government. In 1891, Jerusalem notables petitioned the government to prevent Zionist immigration and to forbid the sale of land to the Jews. They viewed this immigration as a cultural and physical invasion by European aliens. The leaders of the Hussayni family, who lobbied the court to place restrictions on the Zionists, also sold them land. Jerusalem's mayor, Taher al-Hussayni, approved the sale of land to the Zionists and engaged in such transactions himself. In 1891 Rabah al-Hussayni sold the Qaloniyah lands west of Jerusalem to the Zionists, where the latter built the farming village Motza. He also helped Jewish land buyers get around the Ottoman land law's stipulation that land which had not been farmed for three years automatically became state property, thereby preventing it from being sold. Ibrahim Sa'id al-Hussayni worked for Baron Edmond de Rothschild's land company (JCA); he later resigned and signed protests against the Zionists. Salim al-Hussayni made a fortune in real estate ventures with the Jewish community and partnered in a hotel with Yitzhak Rokach, an Ashkenazi resident of Jerusalem who received from the Ottoman government the concession to levy a carriage (transit or travel) tax on the Jaffa–Jerusalem road.[39] In 1884, Rokach sent his son Shimon to Jaffa to direct his operation there. Two years after arriving in Jaffa, Shimon Rokach was the head of the Jewish community and the founder of Agudat Bnei Tzion, an organization that provided assistance to the Jewish immigrants who landed there. The organization founded a guest house for immigrants, a Jewish hospital, and the Sha'ar Tzion library. Unlike his father, Shimon had no interest in partnering with Jaffa's Arabs—he wanted to keep his distance from them, becoming one of the initiators of the construction of Neve Tzedek, the Jewish neighborhood outside Jaffa's walls that became the nucleus of Tel Aviv. Shimon's son, Israel, was elected mayor of the new city. "Jaffa played no role in world history, nor in Israeli history, and one cannot find there any relic of ancient culture from any period at all," Mayor Rokach said.[40] Unlike his grandfather, Israel Rokach was in a position of power, one which he used to erase the Palestinians from local history.

The intense rivalry within Jerusalem's Arab elite meant that the Jews could hold the balance of power if they voted together. Jewish leaders offered their support to the Hussaynis but demanded a quid pro quo. One of their demands was that the narrow and crowded alley that ran along the Western Wall, the holiest site where Jews prayed, be widened. The Hussaynis owned the houses on the other side of the alley and if these were sold to Jews the alley could be broadened. Mustafa al-Hussayni thus decided in 1887, out of electoral considerations, to sell some of those properties to Nisim Bechar and Baron Edmond de Rothschild. But the deal was never completed, in part because Jerusalem's rabbis feared a harsh Muslim reaction. Ten years later, the city's Hussayni governor nearly signed a deal to sell Rothschild the alley itself, which was owned by the Waqf, the Muslim religious trust, but other Arab families prevented the sale.[41] In 1914, David Yellin, representing the Association to Maintain Historical Sites in the Land of Israel, wrote to the US ambassador to the sultan's court, Henry Morgenthau Jr, asking him to press the Ottoman government to enable the Association to buy the Western Wall. Yellin did not have the money to do so—he estimated that the price would be at least 1 million French francs, including a 10 percent bribe for the relevant municipal officials—but he presumed he could obtain it from Jewish millionaires as soon as the Ottomans agreed to the sale in principle.[42] Yellin's initiative never got off the ground. The Zionist leadership would later make yet another attempt to buy the site, with the help of the British administration, as will be recounted below.

Political considerations led to cooperation in obtaining immigration permits for Jews. Menasheh Hai Elyashar recalled in his memoirs:

As a public official who was acquainted with broad swathes of Jerusalem's Arabs, I had friendly ties for many years with two senior officials in the Mandate government, both of them Arabs. They were Tewfiq Efendi al-Hussayni and Jajati Efendi Nashashibi ... The two were sworn enemies because of the historic competition and rivalry between the Hussayni and Nashashibi families. It was all about key positions in the government and municipality. Both these families were involved among the Palestinian Arabs, and when I understood the extent of the huge animosity between them I thought of exploiting it for the purpose of Jewish immigration from Italy.

Elyashar took advantage of a provision in the Ottoman immigration law according to which "only a person who has capital in the amount of 1,000 [British] pounds may apply for a certificate, that is an immigration permit to Palestine. "That was an obstacle we could overcome." He meant by bribery. Elyashar was a well-off man and his Arab partners knew that.

Each time I benefited from the assistance of one of the two Arabs, the second would put on a show of anger and each of them told me this, each at different times: "You prefer him to me." What it meant, by implication, was the purchase of land, tax exemptions, even hush money. Al-Hussayni helped in his way. Nashashibi went even farther. He set up a "system" with me in order to defraud the British Mandate authorities. This is how we did it: when I requested to bring over a Jew who did not have the necessary "capital," I would put his name on the door of my house as if he were a member of my family and a business partner, and Nashashibi would send over an "inspector." He would show up at my house and see that the name of the Jew in question was on my door. That fact served as Nashashibi's confirmation that this Italian Jew who wanted to immigrate to Palestine was not poor.[43]

There were those among the Hussaynis who realized where Zionism would lead. In 1914, Jamil al-Hussayni declared that Zionism should be fought because its success would mean that the Palestinians would lose their land. But that was not the common wisdom. From the point of view of Palestinian sellers, they were doing land deals with Jewish purchasers whom they viewed as capitalists of foreign nationality. At the end of the nineteenth and the beginning of the twentieth century, the Zionist movement was still in its infancy, whereas the Arabs had more of a cultural consciousness than a national movement. Furthermore, neither the Arab nor the Jewish national movement had its base in Palestine. The leaders of the Palestinian public warned that Zionism threatened the character of their country, but they did not see it as a concrete threat. They did not perceive European Jews as genuine locals, nor as people who could become such under the sponsorship of a foreign power. The Palestinian Arabs had not yet developed a model of Arab nationalism that viewed Zionism as a menace and they were not determined to fight it. They trusted the Ottoman establishment and their representatives who had become part of that establishment to prevent the influx of foreign nationals, even though the Ottomans were too weak to withstand the European powers. The Palestinians did not suspect that the end of the 400-year-old empire was approaching, or imagine that the region would be conquered by a Western power and sponsor of Zionism. Unsurprisingly, then, Jerusalem's mayor, Salim al-Hussayni, elected with the help of Jewish votes, claimed that Zionism represented no real danger "because it is not a political movement but a settlement one, and I am certain that no intelligent and rational Zionist would consider the establishment of a Jewish government in Palestine."[44] Many years would go by before the Palestinians would give credence to a statement made by Najib 'Azuri, a Maronite Christian from Lebanon who served in the Ottoman administration in Jerusalem and was one of the heralds of Arab nationalism. In 1905 he declared that "these two movements are doomed to constant struggle, until one overwhelms the other. The fate of the entire world depends on the outcome of this struggle between these two nations, which represent two opposing principles."[45]

The unit of local identity, beyond the family and clan, was the neighborhood, or more correctly, the residential compound surrounding a common yard.[46] While the Jews were in the majority in Jerusalem by the end of the nineteenth century, most of the housing was owned by Arabs. Jews lived among Arabs, and more Jews rented homes and apartments from Arabs than vice-versa. One example of the latter was the al-Hatibs, who lived in Meah She'arim, the only Arab family in this devoutly Jewish neighborhood.[47] Several Christian families lived in Mahaneh Yisrael, not far from Mamilla. The rental contract for the compounds, or courtyards, as they were called, was registered in the Muslim Shar'iah court before a *qadi* and written in Arabic. In many other cases, however, such a deal was concluded in the Sephardi religious court, with the contract being written in Hebrew.[48] A family's religion did not dictate where its members lived. At the end of the Ottoman period none of the city's quarters was homogeneous. Yehoshua Yellin's family moved into a house in the Bab al-Hutah section of the Muslim Quarter in the mid-nineteenth century. In the 1860s and 1870s Jews lived all along al-Wad Street in the Muslim Quarter, up to its northeastern end. The Valero family owned homes in the Muslim and Christian Quarters. At the end of the nineteenth century Ashkenazi Jews rented a house from them in the Muslim Quarter, near Herod's Gate. In 1908 Haim Aharon Valero leased land near to the Muslim Ruzat al-Ma'araf school, and donated the rent money to the school. According to Ya'akov Elazar, a Jewish native of the Old City, Jews lived in about 70 percent of the homes in the Armenian Quarter and 30 percent of those in the Muslim Quarter.[49]

David Aflalao was born in the Old City and, before he left it in the wake of the disturbances of 1929, his social ties were entirely within the walls. His friends were his Jewish and Arab neighbors in the courtyard where he lived. He never went for a walk outside the walls, and knew the new city only from his work there as a wagon driver.⁵⁰ Arabs brought charcoal, chickens, vegetables, and eggs to Jewish homes. Some delivered goatskin bags of water to homes that did not have wells in their yards. Before the founding of Tenuva in 1926, the Jewish cooperative to supply milk produced on Jewish farms to the cities, Arab farmers would bring their goats into courtyards and milk them straight into cans under the watchful eyes of their customers.⁵¹

Neighbors shared celebrations and tragedies, in consideration of each other's religious sensibilities. Ya'akov Elazar related:

> Muslim women respected Jewish religious customs. Their Jewish neighbors would ask them not to draw water from the communal well in the courtyard on the Sabbath, so as not to dirty the yard that the Jewish women had worked so hard to clean the day before. The Muslim women acceded to the request of their Jewish neighbors and drew the water they needed for their households before the Sabbath began."⁵²

Muslim women were not religiously obligated to observe the Jewish Sabbath. But they wanted to show that they appreciated the work that the Jewish women had done and their desire to observe the Sabbath in spotless surroundings.

The Sephardi Jews who lived in the Old City "dressed much like the Arabs. The men wore a long coarse linen caftan tied at the waist with a broad red belt to which they attached their watch and purse, and thongs on their feet," related Hannah Lunz-Boltin. "The Ashkenazim wore round black hats under which a white *yarmulke* with a homemade braid ... while the Sephardim donned tarbushes ... the women [wore] substantial broad dresses, over which was a large kerchief with rolled edges ... on their heads [they wore] a thin, colorful kerchief embroidered with flowers ... the Ashkenazi women added ... a thicker kerchief fastened under the chin like a sort of tie. On their feet, the women wore wooden clogs with high heels."⁵³ The Yemenites who lived in Silwan, a village just south of the city walls, were employed as construction workers and wore traditional Yemenite garb. Only when the English arrived did they adopt European dress when they left their homes to visit the new city or to shop in the Old City *shuk*. They and other Sephardi Jews ate their meals sitting cross-legged around a low table, and spent the evening hours sitting on mattresses spread out on the floor.⁵⁴

"We heard Arabic and spoke it utterly freely with our neighbors," Eliahu Eliyashar wrote.[55] Most of the owners of the homes in which Jews lived in the Old City were Muslims; relations were far more cordial than usual between landlord and tenant. "Each Sephardi family maintained close and friendly relations with Muslim families," Yehoshua wrote.[56] Muslims demonstrated more than just friendship toward their Jewish neighbors when they, too, recited Jewish devotions. "In time both learned to speak Ladino. Especially the women. And those who became friends with their Jewish neighbors also learned a few Hebrew sentences, especially from prayers," Elazar wrote in his memoirs, adding that the Arabs would often make a point of reciting the appropriate Jewish blessing when they were served a cup of water or a piece of cake. "They were well-versed in the Jewish holidays and took part in their neighbors' celebrations," he added, noting that they acquired this knowledge because "they also had the reason of enjoying the company of Jewish girls and women."[57] Elazar argued that the life of Jews in the Old City was part of the Zionist story, but this, like his cynicism about Arab motives in joining in Jewish festivities, did not keep him from acknowledging that Jews and Arabs lived integrated lives in Jerusalem.

Islam's doctrine that Jews were of inferior status did not prejudice daily life nor create an inflexible barrier between the members of the two faiths. "If, during the Ottoman regime, Jews were treated as inferior it was because that was the standing of the Jewish community in the eyes of the ruling authorities," Gad Frumkin wrote. "But personal relations between Muslims and Jews were good and even friendly."[58] The central government indeed operated in accordance with this official position, imposing extra taxes on the Jews and denying them legal equality. But this was not evident in everyday affairs.

It is important to note that these testimonies about close relations between Jews and Muslims come from the minority that would have felt the sting of official inequality had it been pervasive. They come, for the most part, from Ottoman subjects and not from Jews, like most Ashkenazim who, as subjects of foreign powers, enjoyed more rights and benefited from the protection of European consuls. Muslim–Jewish relations were hardly ideal. Religious distinctions came to the fore in tense times. But these were brief interruptions against a background of close relations in everyday life.

"[Meir] Hefetz's wife remembers the Muslim infant Shihab whom she raised for nine months with her own son after the death of his mother. When he grew up he did not forget them and he was like a member of the family," Yehoshua related, quoting the woman: "'He ate of my bread and drank my milk. I not only gave him my breast but I also cared for him like a mother cares for her child. I washed him and diapered him. His father came each day to see how his son Shihab was growing and developing.'" Hefetz himself related: "'I remember Dib Nimer, a Muslim who was circumcised on the eighth day by Hakham Elazar Mizrahi because several of his brothers had died before him and his father decided that being circumcised on the eighth day by a Jewish *mohel* [ritual circumciser] would mark him for long life. When he grew up he was given the additional name of Ben Zion, a name he used among us, the Jews.'"[59]

Yosef Meyuhas came from a Sephardi family that moved from the Old City to Silwan in 1874, when he was five years old. In later life he recalled that for ten years "I was a constant guest in the homes of the fellahs [peasants]" in Silwan. "In the evening, when I returned from the *heder*, or during vacations and holidays, I would always visit Mohammad and Fatma, as well as 'Ali and Khadijah, my favorite neighbors. They fed me of their bread, I drank of their water, and sometimes when they honored me with their conversations and stories as 'dessert,' until late at night, I would also sleep in their homes, and in this manner all their manners, values, way of life, speech, and the stories I loved, served as my childhood education."[60] In his nostalgia, Meyuhas overlooked the abject poverty of Silwan's Jews. The poorest of the Yemenite immigrants of 1882–1914 lived in houses purchased for them by the Sephardi Community Board in 1905, into which they moved from the caves they had previously squatted in.[61] Meyuhas wrote just prior to the Arab–Jewish clashes of the Arab Revolt that began in 1936. He was disturbed by the growing alienation between the two communities. Meyuhas was a teacher of Hebrew, Arabic, and French at the Evelina de Rothschild school for girls and wrote books in which he sought to endear Arab culture to Jews. The life of the *fellahs*, he wrote enthusiastically, was "a living explication of our living book, the Book of Books."[62] Meyuhas viewed the *fellahs* as the original Arabs, as opposed to the desert nomads and the merchants of the cities. The *fellahs*, he wrote, were "the descendants of the Canaanites [who are] considered the most ancient inhabitants of Palestine." They "fully preserved all the ancient customs and mores that [the Jews] have forgotten" because of their exile. He nevertheless stressed that "all the

Arabs' ways of life," not just those of the *fellahs*, "are important to us as Jews because they are very close to the life of our nation and to the spirit of the biblical period." Arab folktales preserve the spirit of the ancient Israelites. The common land of the Jews of the Bible and the Canaanites, who were in fact ancient Arabs, created a shared consciousness that was much stronger than the distinctions between the two peoples. Meyuhas knew that this was not sufficient to convince his Jewish readers. He had to give them utilitarian reasons. "By reacquainting ourselves with these customs and mores, we will be able to understand more precisely problematic or even entirely incomprehensible verses in our Book of Books." In other words, he advocated close Jewish–Arab relations as a way of gaining a better understanding of the Bible. But he had another practical argument based in the present, in the return of the Jews to Zion. Through Arab folktales, "we realize to what extent the Arabs are close to us Jews in spirit as well. The benefits that will accrue to us from such an acquaintance, at a time when we are renewing our life in our land, which is really a small island in a broad sea of Arabs surrounding us on all sides, hardly need be stated."[63] Meyuhas's point of departure here is a fundamental one—the Arabs and Jews are close in spirit because they live in the same land. But he pulled this basic claim in a functional direction. The awareness that Jews are close to the Arabs was, he claimed, vital to the success of the Zionist project. He wrote that he had no need to expand on the importance of this point. Were he writing today he most likely would have done so. Jews moved into Meyuhas's home in 1991 under the sponsorship of the Elad Organization, which has as one of its goals the establishment of an Israeli settlement in Silwan. Ever since, the house has been a source of friction between the settlers and the residents of the Palestinian neighborhood.

Arab–Jewish identity developed primarily among Jews from the East. While many Ashkenazim did speak Arabic, they did so less regularly than did Sephardi Jews. "The Arabic spoken by Ashkenazim was incorrect and a subject of jest" by Sephardim, Ya'akov Yehoshua asserted with no little arrogance.[64] Ashkenazi Jews lived for the most part on charity from the Diaspora. "When Ashkenazi Jews arrived in Palestine, they brought with them customs and clothing and did not change their way of life in this country," Yeshayahu Pres wrote. "They speak Yiddish and preserve in this country the accent of the Jewish street in their countries of origin. They differ from their Sephardi brethren not only in language and external appearance, but also in their views, and the two are as distant as east and west."⁶⁵ East and West? Not really. Even according to Pres himself:

Proper neighborly relations were generally maintained between Jews and Muslim Arabs. ... [A]nd one example is the ten-year-old son of Salim Efendi al-Hussayni, mayor of Jerusalem, who fell ill with typhus. When my grandmother, who had helped bring the boy to the light of day, visited the mayor's home to ask how he was doing, the concerned father asked her to go to the Western Wall with a quorum of Jews to pray for the sick boy's health. She did as he requested and the night after the prayers at the Western Wall the boy's condition took a turn and he slowly returned to full strength. Rejoicing at his son's recovery, the mayor invited the prayer quorum to his home for a feast prepared for them by a kosher restaurant on the Jews' street. Over time these neighborly relations changed. When he grew up and inherited his father's position as the elder of the Hussayni family after World War I and the Balfour Declaration, the boy, named Musa Kazem, for whom the innocent Jews had prayed at their sacred wall, would be one of the great nemeses of Israel.⁶⁶

Ashkenazi Jews also had daily contact with Arabs. Amin, who in the 1870s sold the charcoal that the Lunz family used for heating and cooking, spoke fluent and piquant Yiddish with them in a Lithuanian accent. Ashkenazi Jews who lived in the relatively spacious apartments in the Batei Mahaseh compound in the Jewish Quarter, which was under Jewish ownership, nevertheless spoke Arabic. Ashkenazi women learned from their Sephardi neighbors not only to speak Ladino but also to cook Oriental dishes.⁶⁷

The interplay of their lives led to the absorption of Arabic words, expressions, and proverbs into colloquial Palestinian Yiddish. Arabs adopted and adapted the term that Jews used to designate a person who rented an apartment from an Arab, *ba'al hahzakah*, coining the word *hazqir*.⁶⁸ Arabic made far greater inroads into the local Yiddish dialect than did Turkish or Ladino. The linguist Mordecai Kosover catalogued 454 Arab words that made their way into Yiddish, as opposed to only thirty-five Ladino words. Among these were *masari* (money), *basta* (stand in the *shuk*), *zift* (bad mood), *harkah* (movement), *sponja* (washing the floor), *kifta* (meatball), *mezeh* (salads and condiments served as a first course), *muhram* (moving to a new home, from the name of the Muslim month in which people customarily moved house), and *joba* (a coat with pockets that Ashkenazi tailors made for Arab clients). These Arab incursions into local Yiddish demonstrated a web of ties between the two communities that went far beyond trade. These words evidence norms of conversation and mutual respect, refer to moods, foods, administrative institutions, and types of buildings and dress. A teach-yourself-Arabic book for Yiddish speakers was published in Jaffa, apparently in 1912, and another one appeared in Tel Aviv in 1936. The first of these promised to teach its buyer the local language in just four weeks.[69] Of course, words moved in the opposite direction as well, from Jewish languages into spoken Arabic. Among these were the Ladino *donsi* (a type of sweet) and *dobles* (for free) and the Yiddish *shlekhteh* (shrewish woman), *lekkah* (honey cake), and *meshugineh* (madman).[70]

In 1887 the philanthropist Moshe Montefiore awarded a sum of money to enable Jewish religious schools for boys to hire Arabic-language teachers. The head of the Etz Hayyim Yeshiva, Rabbi Moshe Nehemiah Kahanov, found a suitable candidate, and received the support of Jerusalem's two chief rabbis, the Ashkenazi Shmuel Salant and the Sephardi Ya'akov Shaul Elyashar. But the followers of the zealous Rabbi Diskin opposed the initiative and were able to put an end to it.[71] At around that time, a senior figure in the Jerusalem Ashkenazi community entered his neighborhood synagogue wearing a tarbush instead of the traditional fur hat or *streimel* and scandalized the worshipers. It might have been Yosef Rosenthal, the "*mukhtar haprushim*," whom Gad Frumkin relates as being "dressed in Sephardi clothes." Whoever it was, the Ashkenazim saw this as a violation of propriety, a symbol of adopting a non-Jewish lifestyle. Rabbi Salant, the highest religious authority in the city, offered muted support for the violator, noting that Jaffa's Jews customarily wore the tarbush and thus that it could not be condemned. Perhaps he had in mind Meir Hamburger, an Orthodox Ashkenazi Jew who lived in that city from 1887 to 1914 and who regularly wore such a hat.[72] Whatever the case, what passed in Jaffa was considered indecent, illegitimate, and unauthentic by Jerusalem's Ashkenazim.

Yosef Rivlin, a scion of one of the Ashkenazi families that founded the Nahalat Shiv'ah neighborhood, recalled:

I would sometimes descend the steps of Batraq [Patriarchate] Street—David Street in the time of the British Mandate—and get pleasure from the Arab stores with their fruit and vegetables arranged with great taste in baskets and piles; enjoy the sight of the vendors in their special Eastern dress. The storekeeper would sit serenely, sometimes with a nargileh in his mouth, without going after the buyer. Even when the buyer comes up to him he does not rush up to him, he rises tranquilly, responds placidly, weighs with equanimity, accepts payment indifferently, and returns to his serenity.

Rivlin learned Arabic as a boy at the turn of the century. When he grew up he became one of Israel's foremost experts on Arabic and Islam, translating the Qur'an into Hebrew and publishing his recollections of his childhood during the months just before and just after the 1967 war. He portrayed the Sephardim as utterly different from the Arabs. "I would veer to the left when I came to the wide [part of] Batraq Street, to the haberdasheries and toy stores, a polished street compared to all the others, 'shining' with its clothing and fabrics. The proprietors were for the most part Sephardi Jews, alert and sprightly, the exact opposite of the serenity of the Arabs of the narrow [part of] Batraq, the fruit and vegetable market."[73]

Like Rivlin, Gad Frumkin came from the Ashkenazi elite. His father, Israel Dov Frumkin, edited and published *Havatzelet*, a Hebrew-language newspaper. Gad grew up in the Old City's Muslim Quarter. He had Arab neighbors, but not in his courtyard. The Frumkins lived in a large house of their own, in the basement of which Israel Dov printed his newspaper.

Muslims and Christians lived on both sides of the street, and only one house on the left was in the possession of [a Jew,] the wife of R. Eli Yaffe, a teacher or student of Torah ... All the houses on either side belonged to Arabs and were largely occupied by the heads of the myriad branches of the Hussayni family, but many of the homes were 'held' by Jews [rented to Jews who sublet apartments or rooms to other Jews], so it was mixed habitation.

As a boy, Gad Frumkin was a silent witness to his father's close relations with his Hussayni neighbors. "Frequently, when I descended Gemilut Hesed Alley, before turning onto Hashalshelet Street, 'Ali Efendi Qutub, one of the most important Arabs in the city and a good friend of my father's, a literary man who even knew some Hebrew, would stop me next to his doorway" and start a conversation. "I was acquainted with this Arab notable from his visits to my father's house. Sometimes I would listen to the conversation between them, in Arabic of course, on politics and relations between the province of Jerusalem and the Ottoman capital."[74]

The more integrated life was, the better the personal relations. The intimacy described by Ya'akov Yehoshua, Yosef Meyuhas, and Ya'akov Elazar, who lived in the same compound as Arabs, is not evident in Gad Frumkin's account. Also noteworthy is the fact that the latter did not have friendships with the Arab children who lived close by of the type his father had with adults. "Relations between Jewish and Arab children were not normal and the only contact between them was getting hit by one of the stones that they used to throw at each other. Women also knew that once twilight fell they should not walk alone along Han al-Zayt Street and the Maʻaqhelah Alley if they did not want to run into ogling neighbor boys." This went beyond the usual sort of boyhood rivalries. The difference between father and son, and to a certain extent between men and women, had to do with the differing intensity of their contact with Palestinian Arabs. Frumkin the elder had closer relations with Arabs than his son or wife, who spent more time in their Jewish family compound or at school. "I lived in an Arab environment from childhood," Frumkin testified. "In terms of place, in particular, since the Arab and Jewish courtyards were adjacent, and the children would encounter and clash with each other, like two separate worlds that shared nothing in terms of mindset or culture. That was the rule of that world. In my father's house it was a bit different because Arab intellectuals frequently visited him." As was customary between Arabs and Jews, on the night after the last day of the Pesach holiday, "father's Arab friends would send him gifts of *hametz* [leavened food forbidden on the Jewish holiday]—pita bread, butter, honey—in exchange for the gifts of *matzot* he would send them during the holiday. The Arabs' servants would stand in the alley, holding their trays, waiting for the stars to come out so as not to bring *hametz* into the house before Pesach was over."[75]

Years later, in 1927, when religious and national tension over Jerusalem's holy places intensified, Frumkin's brother-in-law, Rabbi Yeshayahu Rafaelowitz, paid him a visit. He hoped that "perhaps I could obtain a permit [for him] to visit the Makhpelah Cave [the Tomb of the Patriarchs in Hebron, which the Muslims call the Ibrahimi Mosque]." Jews were not allowed to get any closer than the seventh step to the shrine, except when Jewish artisans were needed to carry out maintenance work at the Muslim-controlled site. "I telephoned the mufti of Jerusalem, Hajj Amin al-Hussayni," to whose family his neighbors belonged. As the head of the Supreme Muslim Council, the mufti made such decisions. "A few minutes later the mufti's secretary arrived with a letter to the sheikh of the mosque." To the astonishment of the head of Hebron's Jewish community, Frumkin and his brother-in-law were given the privilege of visiting the tomb—and of being given a detailed guided tour by the sheikh. A year earlier the mufti had given an unusual wedding present to the son of Yehiel Amdursky, the owner of a hotel next to the Jaffa Gate—a permit for his entire family to visit the tomb. They were forbidden, however, to speak Hebrew while inside. Jews with beards and sidelocks were not allowed in, lest they rouse the ire of Muslim worshipers.[76]

This common but multifaceted network of relations between Jews and Arabs appears not only in the memoirs of Jews, but in the memoirs of Arabs of that generation as well. Wasif Jawhariyyeh's family was friendly with the Elyashar, Navon, Antebi, and Mani families. The Arabs describe the oriental Jews as natives (*awlad al-balad*) and as Arab Jews (*yahud awlad 'arab*). Jewish–Muslim business partnerships were standard, and not just in land deals with the Zionists. Members of the two communities also worked together in charitable and public welfare organizations. The Red Crescent was founded in 1916 in Jerusalem, and members of the Antebi, Mani, and Elyashar families were involved, as well as the Hussayni and Khalidi families. Jawhariyyeh led a band that included Jewish musicians. It played at the café he ran next to the Russian Compound, as well as at parties held in private homes. The group played at the homes that men from the Hussayni and Nashashibi families bought in the city's suburbs in order to tryst with their Jewish lovers. Liquor and hashish were served at these parties, with members of both faiths partaking. Jewish musicians were often invited to play Andalusian music at Arab weddings, when the families wanted to wax nostalgic over the lost province of Iberia, the culture of which was preserved by the descendants of the Jews who had been expelled from Spain.[77]

There was no mental boundary separating Muslim and Jew. The walls of language and culture were low ones, and Jews and Arabs who entered the physical or linguistic zone of the Other felt no sense of being alien. Ya'akov Yehoshua's grandmother taught Ladino to the girls of the Ja'uni family.[78] Muslims from other neighborhoods patronized the cafés run by David Elbaz and Ben-Zion Dabash on the Jews' street. The al-Bashurah and al-Muna cafés on al-Wad Street attracted young Jewish customers because they were more modern than those of the Jews. Music played there from gramophones and, on Ramadan nights, a puppet theater presented the popular show *Karagoz waHajawat*, performed throughout the Arab world during the holy month. Young Jews also liked the cafés near the Jaffa Gate, where they could hear Egyptian bands. To compete with the popularity of the Arab cafés, Jewish establishments began offering recorded music and dominos. Arabs frequently visited their Jewish neighbors. As gentiles not bound by the strictures of the Sabbath, they would light candles for their Jewish neighbors on Friday nights. Jews invited their Arab neighbors in to share their *hamin*, the traditional stew eaten on Sabbath afternoons.[79]

The extent of the intimacy and lack of barriers between the two communities was most obvious in the bathhouses constructed during the Mamluk period in the center of the Old City marketplace. According to Ya'akov Yehoshua, Jewish and Arab men went to the baths in the early afternoon and spent hours there, first bathing and then lounging on sofas and armchairs, "sipping steaming coffee, drinking cold lemonade, and eating fruit and baked goods." Still half-naked, "we would chat about subjects, ranging from prattle about social life to commercial business dealings." Most of the Ashkenazim preferred the bathhouses adjoining their synagogues in the Jewish Quarter. But those establishments "were not known for their cleanliness and did not have the serene atmosphere of the Arab bathhouses." Women went to the baths in the afternoons and evenings, and the Arab bathhouses were also used by Jewish women for the ritual immersion required of them after their monthly periods and at other times. Yehoshua noted that "the proprietors of the Arab bathhouses carefully observed the rules of purifying immersion ... a Jewish woman expert in the laws of immersion was stationed in each bathhouse" to oversee the performance of this requirement.[80]

Both Jews and Muslims believed that rabbis could work wonders, and that demons and spirits residing around or in their common courtyards could hurt them. It was in this context that the members of both faiths, of all ages, shared their fears and their ways of coping with them. When Arab youths wanted to persuade their Arab–Jewish neighbors of their sincerity, Yehoshua wrote, they did so "by swearing in the name of Moses and the holiness of the Ten Commandments, and we were convinced."[81] When Muslims returned from their pilgrimages to Mecca, their Jewish neighbors congratulated them and the Muslims shared with them dates from the holy city. The members of both religions had similar or even identical customs, which tightened the bonds between them. Muslims bought meat from Jews, and similar burial and mourning rituals made it easier for them to console one another in times of tragedy. There was also intimacy at the inception of life.

Jewish and Muslim women nursed each other's babies and watched over each other's children.[82]

Sexual relations and marriage between Jews and Arabs, both Muslim and Christian, were not unheard of, but they were considered illegitimate. The son of Um Jabara of Baq'a married a Jewish woman from Poland, as did Taher, Fuad, and Darwish al-Khalidi and 'Abdallah Dajani al-Daoudi.[83] The headmaster of the Muslim orphanage, Jamil Wahaba, married an Ashkenazi Jew and taught Ya'akov Yehoshua Arabic before Yehoshua began to study with the imam of Lifta, Sheikh Salah al-Liftawi.[84] In 1930, the famous beauty Leah Tannenbaum married a Christian, Mikhail (Nasib Bey) Abkarius, the most well-known criminal lawyer of the Mandate period. In 1934 Abkarius built the Villa Leah in Rehavia for his wife, which still stands at the head of Ben-Maimon Street. In 1935 the house was rented to Haile Selassie, the Ethiopian emperor who had gone into exile after the conquest of his country by Italy. Abkarius later fell into financial difficulties, and the couple divorced in 1945. After the 1948 war, Villa Leah passed into the hands of the custodian of abandoned properties and was made available to Moshe Dayan, the commander of the Jerusalem region in the 1950s. Later occupants included Yosef Burg, a long-standing member of Israel's cabinet.[85] The number of marriages between Jewish women and Palestinian men of high social status increased during the 1930s, when many European Jewish women came to Palestine. But Jewish men rarely married Palestinian women. The marriage of a man from the Luria family of Tel Aviv to a Muslim woman from Jaffa was exceptional. When the national conflict intensified in the 1940s, the number of intermarriages plunged and many mixed families separated. In those cases in which Jewish women stayed with their Palestinian husbands, they had to conceal their Jewish origins.[86]

Jerusalem Mayor Raghib Nashashibi's second wife was a Jewish woman named Palumba of Rhodes, while another member of the Nashashibi family in 1940 married Esther Weiner, niece of the writer Shmuel Yosef Agnon. The Agnon family did not welcome the wedding and severed its relations with Esther. No one then imagined that more than fifty years later two women from the Nashashibi and Agnon families would meet. After the Oslo agreements were signed, Dafna Golan-Agnon and Rene Nashashibi worked together to organize meetings of Israeli and Palestinian women to promote peaceful relations. In 1996 they together visited wounded Palestinians in Hadassah hospital in

Jerusalem.[87] At the beginning of the 1940s a Jerusalem dentist, Dr Issa Dajani, married Chava Rechtman of Rehovot. Other members of the Dajani families of Jerusalem and Jaffa married Jewish women. So did two other men from Jaffa, from the Badas and Shanti families. The latter moved to Tel Aviv with his Jewish wife, as did Mohammad al-Siksik whose move was prompted by the Arab Revolt of 1936–9—Siksik sold land to the Jews and feared for his life. His two sons, Ibrahim and Isma'il, attended the Herzliya Hebrew Gymnasium, where they went by the names of Avraham and Shmuel. Ibrahim received a diploma after passing all his Hebrew examinations, including one in Talmud. Another Arab student at the same high school was Salim Abu-Ghosh. Fearing the Jews, Mohammad al-Siksik and his two sons fled to Jaffa at the beginning of the 1948 war, but Iraqi volunteers who had come to defend the city captured and beat them. After Jewish forces took the Arab city, soldiers from Israeli military intelligence imprisoned and beat them. They were eventually released due to the intervention of the minister of minorities, Bechor Shitrit, only to find that all of their family's considerable property had been confiscated by the state on the grounds that they were absentees. Ibrahim and Isma'il also married Jewish women. The former emigrated to Canada with his family. The latter married Rivka Gradstein and settled in Tel Aviv. Their son is the well-known opera conductor Daniel Oren, who lives as an Orthodox Jew.[88]

Religious holidays were not private family events conducted at home, but were celebrated in the streets and neighborhoods, with the participation of members of other faiths. As a boy, Wasif Jawhariyyeh took part in the jovial Purim celebrations held in his Jewish neighborhood, dressing up in a costume just as they did. For him, Purim was not a holiday celebrating a miracle but simply a reason for a party to lighten the winter gloom. With the arrival of spring, the young people of all religions would go out for a picnic on the lawn at the edge of al-Haram al-Sharif.[89] The Jawhariyyeh family also took part, along with other Muslim and Christian families, in the pilgrimage to the tomb of Simon the Just in Sheikh Jarrah on Lag BeOmer. In his diary, Jawhariyyeh describes it as a springtime family picnic. The pilgrimage in 1892 was attended by everyone in the nearby neighborhoods, Jews and Muslims of all classes, including black slaves. During the Mandate period, according to another memoir, "masses of Arabs" celebrated "the pilgrimage, just like the Jews, with food and sweets."[90] Another festival of Simon the Just was held in the fall, on the traditional date of his death. The custom then was to pray for his intercession in bringing rain during the coming winter.[91] A similar role was played by Nebi Samuel, a site outside Jerusalem identified as the tomb of the Prophet Samuel. Jews and Muslims from the Jerusalem region and villages to its north were already celebrating a pilgrimage festival there in the twelfth century. The belief that the prophet could assure the arrival of the rains was held by all the region's inhabitants. At the beginning of the rainy season, and later as well if the year was a dry one, Jews and Muslims would go to the tomb and pray side by side for the prophet's intercession. Jews also visited the tomb on the 28th of their month of Iyar, the traditional day of the Prophet Samuel's death. The Ottoman authorities allowed them to spend the entire night and day praying there, despite Muslim protests and demands to do away with the Jewish custom.[92] When Israel conquered the site in the month of Iyar 1967, religious Jews saw this as a sign from heaven, an invitation to return to the tomb, reestablish it as a Jewish site, and push the Muslim presence to its margins. In 1995 Israel converted a large area around the tomb, one that included Palestinian homes, into a national park, imposing considerable restrictions on the daily lives of the residents. The separation fence built by Israel during the 2000s circles around Nebi Samuel, placing it on the Israeli side of the structure even though the site was never formally annexed by Israel. This Muslim holy site was thus cut off from its surroundings and local Palestinians do not have free access to it.

The leaders and many members of Jerusalem's Jewish community took part in receiving the processions of pilgrims who arrived from Hebron and Nablus to take part in the traditional festivities held at Nebi Musa near Jericho. According to Ya'akov Yehoshua, Jews displayed a combination of indulgence, arrogance, and understanding for the Muslim tradition that this was the site of Moses's burial. According to the Torah, Moses never crossed the Jordan and his burial site is unknown. The Jews nevertheless found a place for the Muslim tradition in their own lives, and to a large extent identified with it, making it part of their common experience with their Muslim neighbors. Jerusalem's Jews felt a special tie to the pilgrims from Hebron. "We imagined," Yehoshua wrote, "that the inhabitants of Hebron and its surrounding villages, who, according to legend, were the descendants of the Jews who had remained in the Holy Land after the destruction of the Second Temple, were making their pilgrimage to the Temple in Jerusalem."

The pilgrims walked from the al-Aqsa plaza to the governor's residence, from which they took the Prophet Moses's standard and palanquin. These two were placed before the standard and palanquin of Abraham. They represented the pilgrims from Hebron and were kept for them in Jerusalem. Jews feared walking by the Tomb of the Holy Sepulcher in the Easter season, dreading they would be attacked, but at the Nebi Musa festival "a warm and happy atmosphere prevailed among us. We knew that they were honoring the memory of a prophet and man of God whom we also accepted."[93] A similar ceremony was held when the celebrants returned to Jerusalem. Even in 1919, when the pilgrimage had already turned into an anti-Zionist and anti-British nationalist demonstration, Hakham Bashi Rabbi Nissim Danon and other leading Jews took part in the reception held for the returning pilgrims. But then, and in the years that followed, Jewish feelings were mixed. They "remembered the old times," Ezra Menachem related, when "youths and old men reported in the early morning to the gate in the wall to receive the celebrants with cheers. Their procession, displaying many flags, passed through the Jewish alleys to the sound of drums and cymbals. The Jews cheered as they came and sprinkled rose water on them." But after 1919 the Jews, apprehensive, kept their stores half-closed and quickly shut them when the procession turned violent and anti-Jewish. "Just a few days went by," he wrote, after spirits had been fired and violence broke out, "and life got back on track. Jews and Arabs again met with each other and both apologized for the spilt blood."[94]

Hebron's Jews also turned out to welcome the Muslims returning from Nebi Musa. Led by their leading citizens—those whose families claimed descent from the Prophet Muhammad—Hebron's inhabitants met the pilgrims and strode with them along Hebron's streets, singing and dancing. "As the *birq* [the banners of Abraham, Isaac, and Jacob, kept in the Tomb of the Patriarchs and taken out for this event] crossed the city's streets, all the inhabitants, Arabs and Jews, stood along the way. The procession entered the Makhpelah Cave where a special service was held, and the celebrants dispersed," Menasheh Mani of Hebron wrote. "When the pilgrims returned home, an atmosphere of festivity spread through the city, in the Jewish compound and outside it, and the Jews would then go out to walk along the main road to Jerusalem, and along the roads, on the hills, clusters of families ate and drank."[95]

In contrast with the close relations evident in common neighborhoods and ways of life, schools were highly segregated. Still, it was not infrequent to find Jewish children being taught by Arab teachers or attending Arab schools, and vice-versa. Muslim boys also attended Jewish schools, among them the first agricultural school in Palestine, the prestigious Mikveh Israel, founded in 1870. 'Omar al-Salah and Sa'id al-Hussayni (Jerusalem's mayor from 1905 to 1908) attended the Alliance Israélite school. Julia Buhbut attended the Tabitha missionary school at the edge of Jaffa's 'Ajami quarter.[96] Othman al-Khalidi's two sons were enrolled in the Jewish Lemel school during the first decade of the twentieth century.

When the children entered fourth grade, when they began to study Mishnah, the principal exempted them [the Arab pupils] from that class. The next day Othman Efendi appeared at the school to lodge a complaint about this discrimination. He demanded that his sons take part in all classes, without exception. Starting in sixth grade, the two boys also spent four hours a week learning Talmud. They graduated with good marks."[97]

Jewish children from the established Sephardi families of Mani, Moial, and Amzaleg attended the modern Arab school, al-Madrasah al-Dusturiyyah, founded in 1909 by Khalil Sakakini. Sakakini named his school after the constitution promulgated in 1908 by the Young Turks, whom he very much admired.[98] The student body of the St George school for boys and college for girls, noted Shulamit Laskov, was attended by "no few boys and girls of our nation, and no few of them were from pious homes."[99]

Sakakini was a committed anti-Zionist who was active in the Arab, and later the Palestinian, national movements. But this did not stop him from giving private lessons to Jewish and Zionist pupils. One of his students was Binyamin Ivri, a Zionist who purchased land for Jewish settlement. Sakakini tutored Ivri in 1914, and wrote in his memoir about the debates over Zionism that he and Ivri had during the lessons. But Sakakini's anti-Zionist stance did not elide into anti-Jewish sentiment. In 1917, during World War I, Sakakini was arrested and imprisoned in Damascus on charges of giving shelter to Alter Levin, an American Jew. The United States, as an enemy power, and all its citizens were presumed by the Ottomans to be spies. Levin, who wrote under the pseudonym Assaf Halevy, viewed himself as a man of both the East and West. In his office hung two portrait photographs taken in Jerusalem in 1929 by the photographer Khalil Riad. One showed Levin clad in a Western suit and the second dressed as a sheikh of the desert. Levin was a man of powerful contradictions. He thought of himself as oriental but represented Western concerns and insurance companies, and viewed the Arabs as primitive.

Sakakini had other Jewish friends as well—Ya'akov Yehoshua; Judah Leib Magnes, president of the Hebrew University; and Avinoam Yellin, a colleague of his in the Mandate administration's education department. Among the students at the Kulliyyat al-Nahda school that he founded in 1938 on the boundary between Arab Baq'a and Jewish Talpiot were Yehuda Piamenta and Gideon Weigert. The latter, who had come all the way from Haifa, wanted to live in the home of an Arab family, close to the school, so that he could improve his Arabic and make up the gap in his knowledge at the high level that the school demanded. Sakakini sent him to the neighborhood *mukhtar* (chief), who arranged for him to live with a widow from the Tarazi family who apparently needed extra income. While he was living there he and a girl from the family who helped him with his studies fell in love. But the couple was separated when the *mukhtar* made it clear to the young Jewish man that he would not accept a romance between a Jewish boy and a Muslim girl. Weigert was the school's first Jewish graduate and, after completing his studies, he became a member of the group that used to gather around Sakakini at Café Piccadilly on Mamilla Street each evening to smoke and talk about the issues of the day. Weigert maintained his friendships with his Arab schoolmates, sleeping over at their houses on weekends and going out on hikes with them. The ties held fast even during the violent years of the Arab Revolt, and when the Jewish–Palestinian conflict escalated after World War II.[100]

This is not to say that everything was ideal. Relations between young Jews and their Christian and Muslim fellows sometimes grew strained. Shulamit Laskov lived in Baq'a in the early 1920s, in an apartment that the Karikorians, an Armenian family, rented to her parents and to English tenants. She played with the Karikorian children, and when she ate at their home she would occasionally participate in Christian prayers with them. But when they fought, her erstwhile friends would sneer "Jewess!" at her.[101] It seems probable that when Jews and Arabs lived as neighbors there were more serious incidents as well, like those described by Gad Frumkin. Yehoshua and Elyashar, who published their memoirs in the late 1970s and early 1980s, mentioned that Arab boys sometimes bullied them, but did not offer any details. The dark shadow cast by the conflict at the time they wrote could well have muddied the nostalgia of these two scions of the old elite for their Sephardi identity and squelched their desire to hark back to another more peaceful and harmonious age. Elyashar was elected to the first two Knessets and served as president of the Sephardi community in Jerusalem; Yehoshua's family had come to Palestine in the sixteenth century, after the Spanish Exile. Yet, even if Jewish–Muslim relations were more acrimonious than they describe, it does not obviate the wealth of evidence for a local Arab–Jewish identity. Members of the two nations conducted their web of daily interactions on a different plane from that laid out by official theology. On the doctrinal level, Islam accepted the Jews, but in a position of inferiority, institutionalized in a set of regulations.

The relative sizes of the two populations were not the cause of Arab–Jewish identity. It developed in Jerusalem, a city with a Jewish majority, but also in Hebron, where the Jews were a tiny and shrinking minority. Jerusalem's population in 1880 was 30,000, of whom 18,000 were Jews; by 1914 the population had grown to 70,000, including 45,000 Jews. In 1922 the population had dropped to 62,500, with 33,971 Jews. Compare these figures with Hebron. In 1880, that city had a population of 9,000, of whom 700 were Jews. By 1914 its population had reached 14,000, but only 1,000 of them were Jews, and in 1922 Hebron had increased to 16,000 inhabitants, but its Jewish population had fallen to 500.[102]

As the Ottoman regime drew toward its end, the populations of the villages surrounding Hebron grew. Villagers consumed more, and improvements in transport made it easier for them to get to Hebron. It was only natural for Jewish merchants in that city to establish business ties with the villagers. Jewish fabric wholesalers sometimes brought merchandise from as far away as Jaffa. Hebron's Jews pursued a variety of trades—there were goldsmiths, dealers in cloth, cobblers, and moneylenders. Most of them lived in homes they rented from Arabs. Shimon Hoisman managed a school for Jewish boys, lending money also to Hebron's farmers to cover their seasonal costs of sowing and planting vines. His son-in-law was Haim Hamburger, a member of a Jerusalem family that ran a small bank near Jaffa Gate. Hoisman enabled the Hamburger family bank to expand its business from Jerusalem to Hebron. Alter Rivlin and Eliezer Klonski dealt in cloth and made loans, and Levi Yitzhak, a Habad Hasid, did well in business.[103] Hebron's Jews did not engage in certain professions that were the specialties of Hebron's Arabs—viniculture, stone quarrying, and glassmaking. But they made honey and manufactured wine from grapes grown by the Arabs, highly valued then and today as well. Some of them peddled their wares in the villages, leaving home on Sunday and returning on Fridays. The Hebron community's rabbi, Haim Bagio, had a store in the village of Bayt Jubrin, and made visits to other villages. "Every day of the week," Menasheh Mani wrote, Hakham Reuven made the rounds "of the many Arab villages in the Hebron region ... selling his wares to the fellahs, lending them money, taking in lieu of interest chickens from their coops and crops from their fields."[104] In Hebron Arab–Jewish identity was stronger than Sephardi Jewish identity, in comparison with how Jews identified in Jerusalem. Mani recalled that "at weddings, as at every other opportunity for celebration, they would play songs and melodies in Arabic, a language everyone understood. In special cases, and by special request only, Ladino songs were played."[105] Hebron's Jews, the Ashkenazim included, spoke Arabic and read Arabic newspapers. "Almost no distinction could be made between Sephardi and Ashkenazi except by the hats they wore, because they spoke almost identically, since our Sephardim also spoke Arabic, and the Ashkenazim knew this language as well and did not even refrain from speaking it at home," Avraham Moshe Lunz wrote.[106] Jewish children played in the street with Arab children, running after tourists and asking for *baksheesh* (handouts). When the muezzin called Muslims to the evening prayer, Hebron's Jews knew that it was time for their own evening service. At the end of May, Greek and Russian Orthodox Christians would come to Hebron from Jerusalem and Bethlehem to celebrate the Festival of the Tamarisk (*'Eid al-Balutah*) to commemorate Abraham's encounter with the three angels, as recorded in the Book of Genesis. The ceremony was held at a tamarisk that, according to legend, had been planted by the biblical patriarch. Until they were forced to leave the city after the riots of 1929, many Jews would go to watch the ceremony each year.[107]

"Arabs would invite their Jewish neighbors to their celebrations, and in the summer lounged with them in the vineyards, under the vines and fig trees, eating, drinking, and sleeping with them. And vice-versa. There was no Jewish celebration at which Arabs were not among the most important guests," Menasheh Mani recalled. "Jewish peddlers lodged in village mosques, just like real Arabs, or in the home of the *mukhtar*. And when the villagers came to the city on Fridays to pray at the Makhpela Cave, they would stay in Jewish homes." Mani was not an outside observer. "My approach in these memoirs is not that of a scholar or regular teller of the Yishuv's history, but rather that of a man who feels the texture of that life in his bones."[108]

The author Yitzhak Shami also had this self-identity. Scholars of Hebrew literature argue over whether Shami was a Hebrew writer, an Arab writer who wrote in Hebrew, or an Arab–Jewish writer, and whether he felt himself to have a strong identity or was torn between different identities.[109] The question here is not about the works he produced but rather about the man himself. In his early days he felt conflicted between the two parts of his identity, which he felt unable to reconcile. Born in Hebron, his mother was a Castel, a Spanish-Jewish family that settled in the city in the sixteenth century. His father Eliyahu, a fabric merchant, was from Damascus. Like the rest of Hebron's Jews, Eliyahu lived much like the Arabs around him. He slept on the ground and ate rice and pita bread with his hands. His son, Yitzhak, was exposed to traditional popular Arab culture during his boyhood, then to the literature of the modern Arab enlightenment, which made its way even into conservative Hebron. His parents enrolled him in the Hebron *yeshiva* run by Rabbi Hezkiyahu Medini, but he found religious studies unsatisfying. No less dissatisfactory was his Arab–Jewish identity. Hebron was a small, traditional, and religious mountain town, not a cultural center. At the age of eighteen Shami left Hebron for Jerusalem, where he adopted a modern Western identity. He completed his studies at Ezra, a German teachers' college, learned German, met Zionists like the seminal Hebrew writer, Yosef Hayyim Brenner, and Yitzhak Ben-Zvi, and Ben-Zvi's wife, Rachel Yana'it. He joined the HaPo'el HaTza'ir party founded by young Zionists of the Second Aliyah and taught Hebrew in Zionist settlements and in Bulgaria. The next stage of his life was marked by an ability to integrate his Arab–Jewish identity and the tension he felt between tradition and modernity. He dedicated himself to Hebron, apparently with the goal of changing it. He returned to his hometown in 1920 as a mature person, working as a teacher, in both an Arab and a Jewish school. But he was not happy. He described himself as spiritually stifled, and the Arab city as hostile and confining. In 1928, after the death of his wife and his remarriage, he left Hebron, but remained emotionally tied to it. The massacre of the city's Jews in 1929 shook his worldview and identity. "Everything lost its value ... my very existence is a mistake," he wrote.[110]

Hebron was also difficult for the family of Rabbi Eliyahu Mani, the Jewish community's religious leader at the time. Like Yitzhak Shami, Rabbi Mani's son, Malkhiel, plus his grandsons Yosef and Menasheh, received traditional educations in the city, then went off to continue their studies and to work in other cities, where they joined the new Jewish Yishuv. But they preserved ties to the city of their birth and returned there to live for a time. Malkhiel attended a local *yeshiva*, but also studied, at his own initiative, Islamic official and common law under a *qadi* and *mufti*. At the end of the nineteenth century Hebron's citizens chose him to serve as a city judge, the first Jew to be given that post. In 1901, when he was forty years old, he moved to Jerusalem, where he worked as an attorney. Despite his lack of a law degree, Malkhiel Mani had an impressive career based on the complex identity implanted in him in Hebron. His clients ranged from Hebron Arabs to the Ottoman administration to Zionist establishment figures. He returned to the bench under the British, with appointments to the District and then the Supreme Court.

Yosef Mani also lacked formal legal education. He attended his grandfather's *yeshiva* and studied Islamic law with Hebron's sheikhs. As a talented and knowledgeable individual, he was eventually appointed to the local court. At the beginning of the 1920s he left Hebron and worked as a teacher in Jerusalem, Rehovot, and at the Herzliya Hebrew Gymnasium in Tel Aviv. Menasheh, unlike many members of his large family, had no interest in a legal career. He studied business in Jerusalem, then worked at the Hebron branch of the Anglo-Palestine Bank, and later at the Jerusalem branch. He returned to Hebron to serve as the manager of the branch there from 1919 to 1921, during which time he also chaired the Jewish Residents' Committee. When Habib Can'an, a policeman, visited Hebron in the 1940s, he liked to walk through the abandoned Jewish Quarter and listen to "the city elders' sentimental memories their Jewish neighbors, ... In every such conversation, over unending cups of *qahaweh*, the name of the Mani family was pronounced with special reverence ... and especially that the Manis had given the city exemplary justices."[111]

The community around the Slobodka *Yeshiva*, whose members arrived in Hebron from Lithuania in 1924–5, at first found it difficult to integrate into local society in the way the established Jewish population had. "The Arabs were hostile to the *moskubim* [as the Arabs called Jewish immigrants from Eastern Europe], who came to take over the city, rented the best apartments and raised the standard of living," wrote Haim Karlinski, a student at the *yeshiva*, in his diary in 1925, adding that "there were also cases of shattered windows and stone-throwing at the yeshiva, as well as attacks by hooligans on students, which the mayor quelled with a strong hand." On the eve of the opening of the Hebrew University in Jerusalem, rumors spread that Hebron's Arabs were planning "bloody riots" and that they would attack "the *moskubim* who had come to the city to take the Makhpelah Cave from them. *Yeshiva* students encountered hostile and contemptuous glances." They were frightened. "We had the bloody days in Ukraine and White Russia before our eyes and a great fear came over us." But the fears were unfounded and the rumors inspiring them were baseless. "The Arabs slowly began to treat the yeshiva students with affection and respect, friendships took form between the locals and the new immigrants, and many began to dream of a large Jewish settlement in Hebron."[112]

The *yeshiva* students' limited integration was a product of the suspicion with which they were treated by the Arabs. They arrived in the mid-1920s, when Jewish immigration was already viewed by the Palestinians through national and religious lenses. Karlinski adopted and employed Zionist claims—that the *yeshiva* helped the city develop and raised the Arabs' quality of life. The implication was that the Arabs were ungrateful and hated those who were doing them good. He called the students and their rabbis *'olim hadashim*, using the term for "new immigrants" that became part of Zionist parlance. Furthermore, some of the students dreamed that the *yeshiva* would serve as the nucleus of a large Jewish community in the city. But the lack of integration also had to do with the nature of the *yeshiva* as an insular institution that sought to protect its students from the vanities and temptations of the world outside. "It is too bad that I do not know how to speak Arabic, only a few words," another student, Binyamin Barkai, wrote in his diary in 1926 about a trip to villages in the region. But he presented himself to the villagers as a *hakham* (the title Sephardi Jews gave to their rabbis, and thus familiar to the local Arabs), and they treated him with respect. A year earlier, during the Purim festivities, Barkai had encountered a young Palestinian man from Hebron. "He proposed to teach me Arabic and that I teach him Hebrew. I considered his proposal favorably," and for a while they met twice a week. But that had not been enough for Barkai to learn to converse with his hosts in the villages. This encounter with a young Arab on Purim was not exceptional. "The Arabs were also caught up in the elation of the yeshiva students, and they danced as well," Barkai wrote of the Purim celebrations in 1926. "In many places Arabs danced the beautiful Arab dances together with the yeshiva students, and during the speeches an Arab offered a welcome in English, which was then translated."[113]

Yehudah Lev Schneersohn, from a family of Habad Hasidim that had settled in Hebron at the end of the 1800s, related that Sephardi and Ashkenazi Jews resided in the heart of the Arab city, but in two separate compounds. While many of the Ashkenazim lived off donations from Diaspora communities, the Sephardim worked for a living.[114] More than Elyashar and Yehoshua did in the case of Jerusalem, Schneersohn highlighted the friction between Jews and Arabs in Hebron, as well as the strain between the Sephardi Jews who had lived in Hebron for centuries and the Habad community. He would later join LEHI, an extremist Jewish underground militia, and his memoir was issued by the publishing house established by the movement's veterans. His book evoked sorrow rather than nostalgia. For him, the past was not something to be longed for, as it was in the letters of some of the Arab Jews of Jerusalem. The book was a lamentation. In this case, too, the author's background and ideology colored his point of view, but Hebron's Arab–Jewish milieu can still be glimpsed through this bias.

Eliyahu Yehoshua Levanon, a teacher and journalist, depicted Hebron in much the same way. "It is the only place in the Land of Israel that resembles a city of the Exile," he wrote. The small Jewish enclave was "almost on its last legs." The only Jewish school run under the supervision of Mizrahi, the religious Zionist movement, "was not worth much."[115] A few decades earlier the situation had been better. According to Lunz,

> Our material situation is not bad; a large part of our community trades with the Arabs throughout the region and earns a respectable living that way, and there are in our city people who were once miserably poor and who have grown wealthy. But being a small city [Hebron] that has no connection and communication with the cities of the coast, it will not progress a bit, and will always remain in its former condition, and its Jewish community will not only fail to grow, but will in fact diminish, because many of its inhabitants, and especially the Ashkenazim, have left recently, whether from a lack of livelihood or because

they have done so well—those who have made their livings and those who have gotten rich—they leave here and go to live in Jerusalem and Jaffa.[116]

The interaction between Jews and Arabs in Hebron, while profound, was less extensive than in Jerusalem. This was a consequence of the proportionately small number of Jews, the limited economic activity of an interior mountain city, and the conservative character of the Palestinian majority. The close ties between the city and the surrounding villages reinforced this traditionalism. In contrast, the Palestinian elite of Jerusalem did not own a great deal of property in the nearby rural area and its political power was not dependent on the socio-political networks in the villages. The Jerusalem elite instead owed its influence to its control of the religious establishment and the Waqf, its ties to the imperial capital, and the Western powers' growing interest in the holy city. Jerusalem opened to the West, whereas Hebron was not very open at all.[117]

As in Jerusalem, the Arab–Jewish identity that developed in Jaffa owed its origins to members of different classes. The children of the social elite attended integrated schools. Fakhri Jadai went to the French Collège des Frères along with Avraham Shlush, who would later serve as chief of the Tel Aviv police. There were also business partnerships—the father of Isma'il Abu Shehadeh (Abu Subhi) jointly owned a citrus grove with Yoav Zuckerman from 1945 to 1948. Malikah al-'Adasi said that her father's concrete-pouring firm was jointly owned with a Jewish partner. Khairi Abu Jabien recalled that he played with children from the Miara, Amzaleg, and Shlush families, and that his cousin 'Ali married a Jewish woman.[118]

Arab–Jewish identity in Jaffa had an additional dimension that was absent in Jerusalem's Old City and Hebron. Unlike the latter cities, Jaffa was a national, political, and media center. For the educated elite active in these areas, the Arab Jew was a textual fact as well. For example, over the decade from 1899 to 1909, Shimon Moial translated the rabbinic classic *Pirkei Avot* into Arabic, adding his own commentary.[119] He began work on this project in Egypt, with the assistance of Cairo's Ashkenazi spiritual leader, Rabbi Aharon Mendel, Hakham Eliyahu Hazan of Alexandria, Rabbi Mas'ud Hai, and certain wealthy Egyptian Jews. His purpose was to put the moral aspect of Judaism on display to readers of Arabic. In his edition, he presented the text, which is in fact a conflation of two different works from different periods, as characteristic of the Talmud. Yosef Meyuhas wrote for Jewish readers, seeing to convey to them the Arab spirit. Moial did the opposite, seeking to present Jewish ethics to the Arabs. In his remarks on the opening passage of *Pirkei Avot* he informed his readers that the Talmud was the product of an unbroken chain of transmission from Moses to the rabbis. In his comments on the most important links in this chain, Moial offered a brief summary of the Jewish scriptures and implied that the Jewish chain of transmission of the word of God was no less reliable than that of Islam. In 1914, Moial was among the founders of HaMagen, an organization devoted to responding to attacks on Zionism in the Arab press, to the translation into Hebrew of selections from Arabic periodicals, to awarding prizes to the authors of articles on Jewish–Muslim relations, and to filing lawsuits against journalists engaging in incitement. The organization's members hoped that their articles in Arab newspapers would convince the Palestinians that the interests of Zionism "not only do not oppose Arab interests but, on the contrary, offer the Arabs great economic and cultural benefit."[120] Moial named his son 'Abdallah Nadim, after a Muslim intellectual he met in Jaffa in 1890. His wife, the writer Esther Moial, called herself an Arab Hebrew.[121] They were part of a circle of Arab Jews in Jaffa that included their close associate, Nisim Malul, and members of Jaffa's Sephardi elite who were also active in HaMagen—Avraham Elmaliah, Yosef Amzaleg, Yosef Eliyahu, Ya'akov Shlush, David Moial, Moshe Matalon, and Yehoshua Elkayam.

In their writings, Malul and David Moial sought, in the face of the escalating national confrontation, to bridge the gap between Jews and Arabs by helping each side to better understand the other. And, in fact, the lines of the conflict were more sharply drawn in Jaffa than in Jerusalem, as will be seen below. Malul and Moial refused to accept this as an immutable fact. They believed that Arab hostility to Zionism was simply a misunderstanding. If so, it could be corrected by explanation and persuasion. They were invested in the effort to do so because it touched on their personal and collective identity. The Jews of the Arab world could serve, in their view, as a force for coexistence with Palestine's Arab inhabitants, in the face of the separatist and hostile nationalism advocated by both Ashkenazi nationalists and Christian Arabs. On the one side were those demanding Jewish independence and on the other those demanding Arab independence. Moial and Malul were advocates of Ottoman identity, and as such they did not grasp the potential of these nationalist movements. Like them,

Albert 'Antebi of the Jewish Colonization Association, an organization founded by Baron Maurice de Hirsch to resettle Eastern European Jews in agricultural settlements in various parts of the world, explicitly opposed political Zionism. He sought to expand Jewish immigration to and settlement in Palestine, but under the protection of the Turkish regime, and to further economic and cultural cooperation between Jews and Arabs.[122]

'Antebi, Moial, and even more so Nisim Malul felt an Arab–Jewish identity, but it was an identity distinct from that found in Jerusalem. In a eulogy for Moial, Elmaliah referred to that identity as Palestinian–Jewish,[123] but it could just as easily be called Arab–Zionist. Malul voiced this opinion in 1901–17 in *Haherut*, a newspaper that published both original pieces and translations from the Arab press. While it was printed in Jerusalem, its editorial offices and major writers worked in Jaffa. This says much about the paper's worldview and the heterogeneous readership it sought to appeal to: Ashkenazi Zionists, Sephardi Jews, and Muslim Arabs. Unlike the Zionist immigrants who had been preaching a doctrine of Hebrew labor and exclusive use of the Hebrew language since the beginning of the twentieth century, Malul maintained that Jews should learn Arabic in order to integrate into the country. If Ashkenazi Zionists, who were agents of Westernization, would only shed their alien stance and adopt the local language, integration could succeed.

But Moial and Malul did not just address themselves to their fellow Jews. They also wrote for Muslim Arabs, arguing that Zionism—which they defined as organized Jewish immigration and the purchase of land for settlement—was bringing progress and development to Palestine's inhabitants. Rather than speaking of the Zionists in political or cultural terms, they cast them as members of a geographical and demographic movement. They believed, whether naively or out of ideological blindness, that large-scale Zionist immigration and the creation of a critical mass of Jews in Palestine would not lead to the development of a separatist culture and community. Quite the opposite, they argued. The newcomers would be absorbed into the Arab and Arab–Jewish majority. This type of Zionism had to be pursued, Malul and his associates maintained, in the framework of an Ottoman Turkish state. They had no inkling that the Ottoman Empire was approaching its end. And they misapprehended something else as well—they labeled the Jews as agents of Westernization, while ignoring the fact that

Christian Arabs also played this role. They viewed Westernization as a positive process and its agents as benevolent. But they held a dim view of Christian Arabs. For Malul and Moial, the Christians advocated separatist Arab nationalism, rejecting Jewish–Muslim coexistence and cooperation in the framework of the multinational Ottoman Empire. The Palestinian Arab nationalists had their base in Jaffa and their mouthpiece was the newspaper *Falastin*, published by 'Isa al-'Isa. Malul and Moial thought it no coincidence that 'Isa was a Christian.[124]

But their views were not shared by all of the Sephardi elite. Haim ben 'Atar thought that Jews should only adopt Arab culture on a limited and utilitarian basis, in whatever measure was needed to counter Arab hostility. He thought that the budding Arab nationalism of the pre-World War I period was only a cultural phenomenon, and thus not a danger to Ottoman allegiance. In contrast, Haim Hasson viewed Hebrew culture as superior to Arab culture by any measure, and proposed that the Arabs adopt it. Eliyahu Elyashar advocated a middle way. He called for more modern Arab education. The adoption of a modernized Arab culture would open the eyes of the Arab masses and they would understand the benefits that Zionism was bringing to the country. Western secular education would turn the Muslim populace away from its clerics and restrain the primitive aggressive instincts that predominated among the ignorant. To achieve these goals, Hasson proposed the founding of a Jewish–Arab League in Tel Aviv and Jaffa in which educated members of both communities would study the languages and cultures of the other, laying a foundation for joint business initiatives that would raise the standard of living in Palestine and develop it for the benefit of all its inhabitants. But nothing was done to further this idea.[125]

The views of Jaffa's Sephardi elite were quite different from those of the Jews in Old Jerusalem. The texture of Jewish–Arab life in the latter city was traditional, religious, and egalitarian; that of Jaffa's Sephardim was elitist and manifestly secular. The Arab–Jewish identity of Jerusalemites was based on what the two national groups had in common. That of Jaffa created a hierarchy. It viewed secularism and the West as superior to ossified conservatism. In Jaffa, Arab Jews did not perceive Zionism as being fundamentally opposed to the modernization project. In their opinion, Zionism could only be realized in the framework of the Turkish state, not under the protection of the European colonial powers.

Jaffa's Arab Jews held the view that Ashkenazi Zionist activists did not know or appreciate Arab culture and the Arab way of life. Only the Arab Jews, who had come to Palestine generations before the Zionists, could find a way into the heart of the Arab masses. The Ashkenazi Zionists were exacerbating the hostility of these masses, incited both by Muslim clerics who opposed modernization and by Christian Arabs. The Zionist leadership was sabotaging the acceptance of the Jewish national movement by the country's Arabs by not including members of the Arab Jewish community in its leadership.[126]

This was an Arab–Jewish–Zionist outlook that grew up along the Jaffa–Jerusalem axis. It came into being before the Balfour Declaration and stood opposed to the goals of Herzl's political Zionism. Arab Zionism did not have a long life. The collapse of the Ottoman Empire and the promulgation of the Balfour Declaration turned this alternative approach into a footnote to history. Malul continued to work in Zionist institutions, as he had before the progress of history disappointed him. The Zionist movement's Palestine Office, headed by Arthur Ruppin, began to submit responses sympathetic to Zionism to Arab newspapers in 1911, and to fund its own Arabic publications. For the Zionist movement this was not a matter of identity, but rather public relations, a way of mitigating hostility and promoting Zionist political goals. The Zionist office funded both *Al-Akhbar* (founded in Jaffa in 1911), which Malul edited, and later *Lisan* (established in 1923). The office also paid Arabs to write articles taking the Zionist position in Arab-owned newspapers, which had much larger readerships than the Zionist-sponsored ones. In 1914 Malul established, with Zionist assistance, the Palestine Press Office, a news service that provided the Arab press with information and ostensibly objective articles on the Yishuv. Malul and the Zionist movement were also behind *al-Salam*, a newspaper that appeared after World War I. A total of eleven Jews, among them seven Sephardim, wrote articles for the Arab press.[127]

In the final years of Turkish rule, Jaffa, Jerusalem, and Hebron were thus charged with new energies. Modernism reached these cities and gradually changed everything—the physical surroundings and the look of residential neighborhoods and streets, education and ways of thinking, and national self-definitions. It would be a mistake to conclude that the inroads made by modernity created one-dimensional polarization that led only to the Jews isolating themselves residentially, and then to a national movement that became the only modernization movement in the country. The Jews, in this mistaken view, abandoned the backwardness symbolized by the Old City, along with their religious identities, before adopting nationalism and striding into the twentieth century, leaving the Arabs behind. But the truth is that a similar process took place in Ottoman Arab society even before Arab and Palestinian nationalism captured the hearts and minds of this large bloc of the region's inhabitants. Furthermore, the adoption of modern ways of living and thinking did not necessarily lead to the rejection of Arab–Jewish identity. Those who marched with the times and adopted modernity continued to hold on to their Arab–Jewish identities. Unfortunately, this identity was torn apart by another modern phenomenon—the escalating contention between Palestine's two national movements.

2

MIXED CITIES

"Jaffa is to Jerusalem as a nouveau-riche beggar is to a bankrupt tycoon," Yosef Klausner wrote after his visit to both cities in 1912.[1] Jaffa was never a holy city, nor had the spot been continuously settled since ancient times, as Jerusalem and Hebron had been. The man who seized the city from the Crusaders, Salah al-Din's brother, razed it in 1196. It slipped from history until the second half of the seventeenth century, when the Ottomans rebuilt the port so they could export the cotton being cultivated in central Palestine to eager French customers.[2] The Arab city that grew up there was, in local terms, more cosmopolitan, modern, and secular than the mountain cities of Jerusalem and Hebron. At the dawn of the nineteenth century its population was only 2,750, but by 1880 it had grown to 10,000, a tenth of them Jews. On the eve of World War I Jaffa had 40,000 inhabitants; in 1948, its population was 70,000.[3]

Jaffa developed much more rapidly than the other two cities. At the end of the 1840s it was a tiny walled village that covered only 7 percent of its subsequent area. By 1918 it had leapt into modernity, having become the second-largest city in Palestine after Jerusalem. In the 1880s a greater volume of goods was exported from Jaffa than from Beirut. Shipping and insurance agents and banks set up shop there. From 1889 to 1922 its population quadrupled and it became the economic and cultural hub of Palestine's Arabs. Improvements in transportation with the coastal plain and the foothills to the east enabled farmers in these areas to export their produce through Jaffa's port and thus make their operations more profitable. Jaffa's environs were home to 80 percent of the country's citrus production and 50 percent of its wheat crop. The country's largest and most important flour mills operated there, as did major factories producing cigarettes and tobacco products, as well as dozens of artisan workshops.[4] Jaffa was home to English, French, and Italian schools, two soccer teams, a boxing club that won the national championship, and a radio station. Three daily newspapers were published there, including *Falastin*, the largest and most important Arabic newspaper in the country until 1948. Cabs plied the roads from Jaffa to Damascus, Cairo, and Beirut. Young people rode them to take in Beirut's night life, and men and women came from Lebanon and Syria to work in the burgeoning city.[5] Jaffa's importance led the Jerusalem-based Hussayni and Dajani families to found their own newspapers and periodicals there, as part of their political rivalry. So did the Islamic societies that were a rising force in the early 1930s. Even the Zionists recognized that if they wanted to influence the Arab public, they had to do so from Jaffa. One way they tried to do so was through *al-Salam*, a newspaper that called for understanding and peace between Jews and Arabs, which Nisim Malul began publishing with Zionist funding in 1920. In 1939, the Histadrut, the Zionist labor federation, began publishing its own Arabic newspaper in Jaffa, *Haqiqat al-Amar*.

At the beginning of the nineteenth century there were hardly any Jews in Jaffa, but by 1914 they made up a third of the population. The growing Western interest in Jerusalem touched off development in Jaffa as well, since it was the port of entry and exit for Western visitors to Jerusalem, thanks in part to the rail link to Jerusalem that opened in 1895. Steamships facilitated the arrival of more cargo and larger numbers of tourists, businessmen, missionaries, pilgrims, and immigrants, and at a more rapid pace than in the past. Jaffa was thus a city traversed by a variety of communities and peoples. The Arabs came to call it *'Urus Falastin* (Bride of Palestine), *'Urus al-Baher* (Bride of the Sea), and *Um al-'Gharib* (Mother of Strangers), warmly welcoming all visitors. Most of these just passed through, but not before leaving a cosmopolitan imprint. But some liked what they saw there and stayed. Jewish immigrants, European merchants and tourists, Armenians, and Greeks settled in the city. By 1900, the latter two groups made up more than 10 percent of its inhabitants.

"I walked among the Jewish stores in Jaffa (in Tel Aviv there are no stores, thank God!), listening to the languages used by sellers and buyers," Yosef Klausner wrote of his visit in 1912. "I heard much Ashkenazi *zhargon* [Yiddish] and a lot of Arabic, a bit of French, Russian, and *Espaniolit* [Spanish or Ladino]. I heard only a tiny bit of Hebrew—when the buyer was a teacher or student from the Gymnasium, or in rare cases a laborer." Klausner came to Jaffa from Odessa, which was also a lively cosmopolitan port city that attracted Jewish intellectuals and Zionists. He could hardly avoid comparing the two cities:

> I entered a store owned in part by a man and his wife from Odessa who settled in Jaffa six years ago. The man knew how to *speak* Hebrew, because he'd known how to *read* Hebrew even before he left Odessa; but the woman did not speak Hebrew at all but *understood* what was being said, because when she left Russia she hadn't known or understood Hebrew at all. But what made me saddest was that in Jaffa she had learned to speak *Arabic*, which of course she had not understood when she arrived in Jaffa. Hebrew's luck is bad when faced with the language of the country. Is it just like us [in Odessa]? No, there's a difference. If you go into a store in Odessa and address its proprietors in Hebrew, they will not only not understand what you are saying but think you need to be sent to a mental institution; but in Jaffa and Jerusalem they'll understand you and won't think it at all strange, except that they'll answer you in *zhargon* or in Arabic, and sometimes might even answer you in Hebrew [emphases in the original].[6]

In other words, in Jaffa and Jerusalem the use of Hebrew, along with Arabic, reflected the city's cosmopolitanism—it definitely would not get its speakers committed to an asylum.

The first change wrought by rapid modernization was one of consciousness. Jews and Arabs both realized that they had to live differently from their parents, or from the way they themselves had previously lived. They gained a new perception of the space they resided in and of how they functioned within it. Beyond changes in the way they conducted their own and their families' lives, they developed new conceptions of collective identity and of its boundaries. They saw in a new light the sources of their and their parents' belonging to that collective and its territory, and gained a new conception, different from that of the past, of their relations to the Other.[7] The press, literature, and cultural–political clubs also served as important platforms for consolidating a local collective consciousness. In 1918 the Muslim–Christian Associations were established which sought to combine members of both faiths into a single Arab identity. A year later saw the establishment of al-Muntada al-'Arabi, the Literary Club, and al-Nadi al-'Arabi, the Arab Club. All these organizations were explicitly anti-Zionist.

Jaffa's development was no less impressive than Jerusalem's. "The city of Jaffa has changed much for the better since I was there six years ago, when I first trod on the soil of the Land of Israel," wrote a resident of Ekron in 1890. Ekron was a *moshavah*—a Jewish farming village—founded during the First Aliyah, the first wave of Zionist immigration to Palestine. "The Arab town I saw then has become a European city."[8] A new downtown area with modern buildings arose to the east of the Old City, along Butros Street. The city's wealthy inhabitants built large houses with sea views in two new neighborhoods, 'Ajami and Jabaliyya, to the south of the city walls, as well as in Nuzha, next to Clock Square. The Jews, as previously noted, left the Old City for new neighborhoods to the north, built between 1887, when Neveh Tzedek was founded, and 1909, when Ahuzat Bayit, Tel Aviv's first neighborhood, was built. In that latter year some 5,000 people lived in these Jewish neighborhoods.[9] A group of Yemenite Jews arrived in Jerusalem in 1882 and settled in the Arab village of Silwan, just to the south of the Old City walls. Yemenites who settled on the coast at the beginning of the twentieth century founded Kerem Temanim, another Jewish neighborhood on Jaffa's outskirts. While the Sephardi elite in Jerusalem still maintained its Arab–Jewish identity within the Old City, the Sephardim of Jaffa, such as the Shlush, Goral, Abulafiyyah, and Amzaleg families, preferred to move out of the Arab city. Along with Ashkenazi families, they founded a new neighborhood meant to be Jaffa's antithesis—Neve Tzedek. While Neve Tzedek viewed itself as not belonging to Jaffa, it officially became part of Tel Aviv only in 1923.[10] The precedent set by Neve Tzedek was a model twenty-three years later for the founders of Ahuzat Bayit. The Jews wanted not only a modern neighborhood but an entire city for themselves, diametrically opposed to and severed from Jaffa. They envisioned broad, straight, clean, quiet, and artificially lit streets where German or Russian would be spoken, instead of Jaffa's crowded and crooked alleys, full of sweaty men shouting in Arabic. In 1921 the British administration granted Tel Aviv its own governing council, but it was the Jews who decided to call it a city. Doing so was an ambitious act, one in which word engendered reality. In 1934 the Mandate officially granted Tel Aviv the status of city.

MIXED CITIES

Before 1914 Tel Aviv had never had more than 1,500 to 2,000 inhabitants, but during the 1930s the population of the first Hebrew city, as it was called, reached 75,000. Only a small number of these were Jews who had formerly lived in Jaffa. Most of the growth came from immigration. From the end of World War I through 1934, about 40 percent of the Jewish immigrants arriving in Palestine—about 60,000 people all told—settled in Tel Aviv.[11] But Jaffa did help Tel Aviv spread territorially. A good part of the land on which Tel Aviv grew in the early 1930s—the Florentin, Hatikvah, and Shapira neighborhoods—had previously been occupied by citrus groves that the Jews bought from Arabs. During the years 1930–5, a full 17.7 percent of all the land that Jews bought from Arabs in Palestine was in Jaffa. In size, it equaled all the land purchases that the Zionist movement made in the Jordan Valley, a region that was the focus of the Zionist labor movement's settlement activity.[12]

In the 1940s, about 5,000 Jews, out of the city's total population of 70,000, lived in Jaffa's northern Jewish neighborhoods and another 5,000 in the city center.[13] The Zionist utopia was in danger of shattering on Jaffa's streets, which looked nothing like the country that Jewish immigrants had been dreaming of when they landed at the port. It was on the streets close to the port that they had their first experience of Palestine. The immigrants wanted to live in a city modeled after a cultured European suburb and to continue to live by the norms of their countries of birth in their new land—their own Jewish country. What they found on their arrival contradicted the imagined Jewish renaissance that had attracted them to Jaffa's shores in the first place. As far as the Jews were concerned, Jaffa was a city that progress had not yet reached—dirty, teeming, and unhygienic. A stereotype of the Arabs as wild and violent coexisted in the minds of the newcomers with its opposite—Arabs as lazy and passive. In their imaginations, Jaffa included Salameh, an Arab village that had been circumscribed by Tel Aviv's municipal boundaries. It and other border neighborhoods were seen by Tel Aviv's Jews as places of degeneration and corruption that needed to be demolished, or as places only for penurious new Jewish immigrants to live. Those who resided there hoped to escape their Arab surroundings by quickly moving on. When Tel Aviv's first mayor, Meir Dizengoff, sent New Year's greetings to his counterpart in Jaffa in 1922, he could think of no better hope for the future than to express his wish that Jaffa would eventually become a European city like Tel Aviv.[14]

Jaffa's residents, for their part, believed Tel Aviv to be ruled by communists, and viewed it as a territory occupied by European invaders. As far as they were concerned, it was a city whose streets were full of morally corrupt and licentious people. The fact is that Jaffa was ahead of Tel Aviv when it came to modernity. The Arab city had Bauhaus buildings before the Jewish one did. Photographs taken between 1939 and 1945 by Miko Schwartz, who worked for the British administration, show well-tended modern streets in Jaffa's center and new neighborhoods. Tel Aviv's residents remained oblivious to this aspect of their neighboring city. To a large extent, Tel Aviv had to malign Jaffa in order to justify its separate status.[15]

Jews in Jerusalem left the city walls behind on a gradual basis. But Jaffa, which was more modern and cosmopolitan than Jerusalem, burst out of its old confines. The elites of both the Jewish and Arab communities left old Jaffa and each moved to new neighborhoods where they could live in more spacious houses. As a result, the line separating the two communities during the first half of the twentieth century did not coincide with the political border between the two cities. Jaffa had Jewish neighborhoods like Florentin, Shapira, Hatikvah, and Montifiore. While these areas were officially part of Jaffa, they received all their municipal services from Tel Aviv. But the Jewish city also contained Arab neighborhoods, such as Salameh, Sumayel, Jarisah, Sheikh Muwanis, and 'Arab Jamusin. The area where the two cities touched was a fuzzy zone. On Salameh Road and in Manshiyya, for example, an Arab market, Jewish workshops, and cafés with mixed clienteles stood side by side. An Arab-owned citrus grove stood in the middle of the Jewish Shapira neighborhood. The borders between the two cities, and between Jewish and Arab neighborhoods, were open ones. They could be crossed easily, whenever one wanted, for work or leisure. Jews who moved out of Jaffa continued to work and spend their spare time there. Before Tel Aviv managed to stand on its own two feet in the 1930s, Jaffa remained the urban center—the residents of the Jewish neighborhoods worked there, and the Arab city was home to the offices of a number of Zionist institutions. Jews went to downtown Jaffa to do business, and to shop for wheat, barley, tea leaves, and coffee beans at Ya'akov Hananya's store. They sat in Arab cafés in the border neighborhoods, like Café Baghdadi on Shabazi Street, which offered games of chance, hashish, and prostitutes. Moshe Matalon moved to Tel Aviv, but his office stayed in Jaffa. When he went to his office in 1924–5 he would put on a tarbush, removing it when he came back to Tel Aviv.[16] Jews worked as laborers and fishermen at the Jaffa port. Arabs from Jaffa worked in the post office and railroad offices run by the British in Tel Aviv, and Arab peddlers from Jaffa hawked their wares in Tel Aviv's streets. They sold lemonade and a tamarind-flavored drink, tahini, and dried apricots. They offered roasted chestnuts in the winter, prickly pears and watermelon in the summer, as well as dried peas, and sesame bagels sold with a newspaper cone of ground hyssop. For a penny you could watch an Arab with a dancing monkey. Before Tel Aviv's own ice factory was set up after the 1921 riots, Arabs also sold ice to the residents of Tel Aviv. Prior to the Passover holiday, Arabs, calling out in Yiddish, set up vats of boiling water for Jews to render their dishes and pots kosher for the holiday, when even a trace of leavened bread was forbidden. These hawkers were supplemented once or twice a week by soothsayers—card readers and fortune tellers who offered their skills in Arabic.[17] Arab laborers worked on the construction of the Tel Aviv port during the Arab general strike that accompanied the revolt of 1936–9. The soft border was also exemplified by the lifestyles of the Arab Jews who moved from Jaffa into Neve Tzedek. Aharon Shlush wore a *galabiyyah* his whole life. "In his daily life, he adopted the local customs ... the family was run in the same way that Arab extended families were run." Shlush decided what and where his sons would study, who and when they would marry, and after their marriage they and their families lived with him. The Shlushes slept on mats, not beds, ate the same food that their Arab neighbors ate, seated on the floor and reclining on cushions, in the oriental manner. Food was cooked and clothes were washed in the manner of Jaffa's Arabs, and when Arab Jewish family members were ill they were treated with folk medicine. Shmuel Moyal owned an Ethiopian slave whose only compensation was the family's leftover food and old clothes.[18]

Jaffa was a heterogeneous and lively city. Ben-Zion Amzaleg's family lived in a house in Manshiyya that had its own generator, at a time when most of the homes there had not yet been linked up to the electricity grid. Members of both the Jewish and Palestinian elite rented apartments in this neighborhood—the Shertok-Sharetts, Rokachs, and Levontins, as well as the Khalidis.[19] "My father maintained close ties with our neighbors. As an importer of lumber from Russia and Romania, he had commercial relations with Arab importers and they would partner in leasing cargo ships to carry their freight," Tziona Rabau recalled. "My father did not number among the city's well-off." So she was surprised one day to see movers bringing a piano into their home.

> It turned out that Mr. Houri, the rich Arab who imported lumber with [my father], had ordered himself a piano from Germany. Father was at the port when it arrived on a ship that brought lumber for him and the other merchants. Mr. Houri noticed the look of longing that Father cast on the piano and understood what he felt, and with the generosity characteristic of a man of the East he suggested that Father take it, and pay for it in appropriate installments.[20]

Arabs from Jaffa, including the mayor, were invited to Neve Tzedek's Hanukah ball in 1897—they were so impressed by the orchestra from Rishion LeTzion that had been hired to play there that a few even invited it to perform at Jaffa's Government House at the fete held in honor of the Ottoman sultan's birthday. A Jewish ensemble organized in Jaffa in 1905, Kinor Tzion, was frequently called upon to play at events sponsored by the city's Arabs, including its leading families. The Arabs also attended the classical music concerts organized by the group. The cinema run by the Eunides brothers in Jaffa sought to attract a Jewish audience in 1912 by screening films such as *The Beilis Trial* and *Haman and Esther*. Likewise, the Eden cinema on Lilienblum Street in Tel Aviv, which opened its doors in 1914, screened Arab films.[21] The Eden was so popular with Jaffa's Arabs that Tel Aviv residents petitioned the Tel Aviv Committee, the equivalent of the city council: "Who can guarantee that they will not seduce women and girls; you know the natives."[22] A group of Jewish and Arab merchants and artisans from Jaffa and Tel Aviv's southern neighborhoods petitioned the governor of Jaffa to take action against teenage Arab gangs that were harassing them and stealing their wares, and whose card games were setting a bad example for other young people. On occasion Jewish youths from Ahuzat Bayit would become involved in street fights with Arab youths from Jaffa.[23]

As the conflict intensified in the final years of the Mandate, hostility on the personal and neighborhood level increased. A defensive national consciousness gradually developed on both sides, with each viewing the other as a threat to the identity of the city and its surroundings. "I brought a few cases of grapes from my vineyard to sell in Jaffa, both to Jews and Arabs," Mohammad Mustafa wrote to Mayor Rokach of Tel Aviv on 18 July 1939. "Some of your young boys from the Jaffa–

Tel Aviv border came and poured kerosene on the grapes ... is this your hand [extended] in peace?"[24] Following the outbreak of the Arab Revolt in 1936, the residents of the Shapira and Florentin neighborhoods, who received their municipal services from Tel Aviv even though they lived in Jaffa, petitioned the Mandate government to sever their connection to Jaffa, "the nest of murderers," and annex their neighborhoods to Tel Aviv. But the British refused. The residents continued to press their case, and with the backing of the Zionist institutions founded a United Committee of the Hebrew Neighborhoods in Jaffa's Jurisdiction. In 1940 the Jaffa municipality agreed to the establishment of a "local council in the Hebrew neighborhoods," offering them a certain measure of autonomy. From then on, through the 1948 war, the two sides wrangled over the extent of the autonomy and over the budget for the local council, while the leaders of the two neighborhoods continued to demand that their ties to Jaffa be severed completely.[25] But even in these tense times the two populations maintained their ties. In the 1940s Arab peddlers sold oranges and milk in Shapira, and on Friday nights and Saturdays, the Jewish Sabbath when, in accordance with religious strictures, Tel Aviv's buses did not run, Jews from the two border neighborhoods hired horse-drawn buggies driven by Arabs to take them to the beach.[26] In the 1940s, Ahmed Hamami, who marketed citrus fruit from Jaffa, leased a large piece of land from the Jewish Citrus Growers Association, harvesting and exporting the fruit that Jews had grown there.[27]

The desire to make money and to break free of social policing impelled many Jewish women and girls to find work in Jaffa's cafés as waitresses, singers, and dancers—even during the Revolt. This occasionally led to liaisons between Arab men and Jewish women, as well as between Jewish and Arab homosexuals. At the same time, Tel Aviv's beach and the cafés that lined it attracted Jaffa's young men—but it was not just swimming that interested them: they also liked the freer atmosphere of the Jewish city, which gave them the opportunity to ogle Jewish women. Older, middle-class Arab men preferred to make friends with Jewish women at Jewish-owned cafés located on the seam between the two cities. The wealthier denizens of both communities patronized the Casino Café, on the beach, which offered live music. True to its name, the café housed a casino, and it sponsored weekly dance nights at which suits were de rigueur. Childcare was even provided for those parents who wanted to enjoy themselves undisturbed.[28]

Cafés were not always so civilized. On 11 October 1937, residents of Kalisher Street, on the edge of Manshiyya, submitted a complaint to the mayor regarding "Arab cafés that are always full, day, evening, and night. There are all sorts of dangerous elements: provocateurs, thieves, houses of ill-repute, prostitutes, and fairies with their shouts, their wild singing live, on gramophones, radio with loudspeakers at night ... gunshots and explosions in this deserted corner have become ordinary nightly events."[29] This letter is much like another one sent to the mayor in July 1936, in which residents of Neve Tzedek complained that the building at 24 Rokach Street contained "apartments of loose women from the underworld who have come from Jaffa ... recently, Arabs have also started visiting in the evening."[30] Notably, these letters were written during the Arab Revolt. These sources of tension remained even after the Revolt had ended, but this did not put an end to contacts. The Jews were frightened, their complaints focusing on security as well as public morals, noise, and quality of life. "Here the disturbances have come to an end," the inhabitants of the Brenner neighborhood wrote to the Municipal Security Committee on 13 November 1939, adding that Arabs "have begun visiting Tel Aviv freely—the same Arabs who only yesterday aimed the barrels of rifles and pistols at us are now sauntering through the city. Who knows what our neighbors are plotting ... will we leave the city wide open [to attack]? Will we forget the recent past?" The petitioners proposed that the Security Committee employ young Arabic-speaking Jews to track and keep watch over every suspect Arab in Tel Aviv.

Not only had Arabs returned to Tel Aviv in large numbers, but Jews had also returned to Jaffa. A few months later, on 14 January 1940, the city manager wrote to the mayor to inform him that his attention had been drawn "to the fact that, with the renewal of the sight of crowds of Jews walking from Tel Aviv to Jaffa and filling its streets and alleys, once again large numbers of young women from Tel Aviv are heading there dressed in shorts, with their shins bare." He suggested that this constituted a security threat. Jews who spoke Arabic had reported that they "had already more than once heard comments from Arabs that do not herald good tidings."[31]

From the perspective of Jaffa's Arabs, Jewish women who flaunted their sexuality posed a threat to Arab values and traditions. Whether or not they were prostitutes, such women were perceived as irresponsible seductresses who served the Zionist cause by staining Arab honor and causing them to waste their money on frivolities. In fact, Jewish prostitutes plied their trade in brothels along the roads connecting Tel Aviv to Jaffa, in Manshiyya and the Old City. Jewish and Arab pimps employed local women alongside girls they brought in from Lebanon and Syria. Jaffa was the place to which the Jewish communities of Jerusalem and Tel Aviv exiled women that they interdicted for sexual libertinism. The Ottoman regime had been aware of Jaffa's character and permitted the operation of brothels along the beach. The British closed these establishments. But it was hardly surprising that the port city's prostitutes continued to ply their trade, even in the absence of an officially sanctioned red-light district. Then, during World War II, the British revised their policy and decided that it was more important to ensure the health of the many soldiers who were spending time in Jaffa than to try to protect the city's appearance and reputation. The British army established licensed brothels for its forces, in which both Jewish and Arab women were employed.[32]

This is not to say that prostitution was unknown in the Holy City. During World War II, with increasing demand from British soldiers and the weakening of social strictures, the sex trade took off. Furthermore, romances sometimes developed between Britons and young women in Tel Aviv and Jerusalem. The Jewish underground militias fought this phenomenon, tracking and on occasion interrogating girls who socialized with British soldiers and civilians and with Arabs. Some were executed on charges of providing intelligence to the enemy.[33]

Arab Jews who moved from Jaffa to Tel Aviv received a hostile reception from the Jewish city's established residents who feared that their city would be "polluted," and that the Levantine character of the southern neighborhoods would infect Tel Aviv. Yosef Batito was an expert tailor with a shop on Butros Street, Jaffa's main thoroughfare. Arab rebels looted and burned it down during the Revolt. Batito and his wife moved to Tel Aviv, where they opened a café on Yehuda Halevi Street. A complaint from the neighbors was not long in coming. In a letter to the mayor dated 9 February 1939, they charged that "Under a sign [advertising an] 'Oriental restaurant' a Sephardi Jew, Batito, runs what looks like a restaurant but is really a brothel. In the greatest possible filth, with hands dripping with tar and the mud of the females from Jaffa, he fries the meat called *Shashlik* [sic]." Tel Aviv's citizens, inundating their mayor with complaints about noise from Jewish cafés, regarded Batito like the plague. They wrote that he was contaminating

Tel Aviv with Jaffa's filth. "He casts his grubby pants on the plates that the next day he gives to clients to eat on. The Arab music he needs to attract his clients booms throughout the area and disturbs us at our prayers ... He trades in live merchandise with the help of pimps and, at times, in full daylight."[34]

Tel Aviv's café proprietors cited Jaffa when they demanded that their city allow them to stay open later so that they would not lose their Jewish clientele to Arab establishments that stayed open late into the evening. Rabbis demanded that the Tel Aviv municipality enforce greater modesty on the beach, where, they said, Arabs from Jaffa eyed Jewish women. Such strictures would be good for Jaffa as well, according to the rabbis, since the Arab girl-watchers were violating Islam's strictures regarding women.[35]

To Haim Guri, a poet born in Tel Aviv, Jaffa seemed like an oriental city—alluring in its alleys, its aromas, the smoke of its nargilehs, its enticing music. But it also aroused primal fears of aggression and murder. "The Arab world was my milieu from childhood, it was the world I grew up in. Tel Aviv and Jaffa were two neighboring cities, and ever since then I have often written about this duality, about the seam between us and them. I have always written about living people; in my works Arabs have not been metaphors but living and breathing neighbors." Guri's depictions of Jaffa display his extreme ambivalence toward the city—it is seductive but deadly, a close neighbor but also an enemy. "I continue to write about Jaffa. Old Jaffa from the days of the prophet Jonah, the Oriental city generations old. Jaffa attracts with its sounds, tastes, and smells. It's the Jaffa of [the painter] Nahum Gutman. And there was also a frightening, menacing Jaffa, a Jaffa of the incitement in the sermons of the imams, the green flags of al-Jam'ah al-Islamiyyah, and hands bearing sabers. The memory of bloody riots."[36]

But another Hebrew writer, S. Yizhar, saw Jaffa in an entirely different way. He made much fuzzier distinctions than Guri did. In his account of the consequences of the 1921 riots, the Palestinian and the Zionist trade places. Sometimes the Zionist is the native and the Palestinian the invader, while at others the latter is the indigenous inhabitant and the Zionist an immigrant whose dreams, language, family, and emotions remain deeply implanted in the place that he left.

Jerusalem's residents sought out more spacious and modern dwellings. The Jewish population's exodus from the Old City, which had been the city's focal point, is reflected in the following figures. In 1880, about 2,000 Jews, some 12 percent of the city's Jewish population, lived outside the walls. Seven decades later, this was the number of Jews who remained in the Old City—constituting 2 percent of the city's Jewish population. By the end of the 1948 war, not a single Jew remained within the walls. The relative proportion of the Jews in the Old City also declined precipitously during this period, from 52 percent in 1880 to 6 percent just prior to the 1948 war and 0 percent after it. But this trend reversed dramatically after the 1967 war. Soon thereafter Jews began moving into the rebuilt Jewish Quarter of the Old City and into new Jewish neighborhoods built in East Jerusalem. Within three decades, half of Jerusalem's Jewish population lived in the formerly Jordanian side of the city.

Table 1: Changes in the Relative Proportion of Jews in the Old City as a Proportion of Jerusalem's Total Population, 1880–1948 (rounded figures)

	1880	1914	1922	1931	1939	1948
Jews in the Old City	15,000	15,000	5,600	5,200	2,000	2,000
Jews in the New City	2,000	30,000	28,400	48,500	78,000	98,000
Total Jews in Jerusalem	17,000	45,000	34,000	53,700	80,000	100,000
Relative proportion of Jews in the Old City to the city's total Jewish population	88%	33%	16%	10%	2.5%	2%

Source: Rami Yizraeli, The Jewish Quarter in Old Jerusalem During the War of Independence, in Mordecai Naor, ed., Idan 2, Jerusalem, Ben-Zvi Institute, 1988, http://lib.cet.ac.il/Pages/item.asp?item=12919.

Table 2: Jews and Non-Jews in the Old City 1880–1948 (estimates)

	1880	1914	1922	1931	1948
Jews in the Old City	15,000	15,000	5,600	5,200	2,000
Non-Jews in the Old City	14,000	20,000	17,000	20,000	31,000
Total Old City Inhabitants	29,000	35,000	22,600	25,200	33,000
Proportion of Jews among Old City Inhabitants	52%	42%	25%	20%	6%

Source: Rami Yizraeli, The Jewish Quarter in Old Jerusalem During the War of Independence, in Mordecai Naor, ed., Idan 2, Jerusalem, Ben-Zvi Institute, 1988, http://lib.cet.ac.il/Pages/item.asp?item=12919.

An interesting balance pertained in Jerusalem. The Jews were a demographic majority, but ownership of private land was in Palestinian hands. Of 19,311 dunams of private land within the city boundaries, only 4,830 were owned by Jews.[37] These figures indicate that the major change wrought by Israel in Jerusalem in the 1948 war was not a demographic one but was instead one of land and home ownership.

Following the wave of migration outside the walls, the period of the British Mandate saw the construction of the new Jewish neighborhoods of Rehavia, Talpiot, and Beit HaKerem. The architecture of the first neighborhoods outside the wall, those along Jaffa Street, preserved the closed courtyard structure of the Old City. But in the new neighborhoods built in the 1920s and 1930s the houses were freestanding. The Arabs also built modern houses in Sheikh Jarrah, Musrara, and to the north of the Old City. To the south, along the train tracks, they built Qatamon (today's Katamon), Talbiyyeh, and Baq'a (today's Baka). To the south of Talbiyyeh the Dajani family built a set of houses named after them. Jews also lived in these primarily Arab neighborhoods. Shulamit Laskov and her parents, as well as Keren Kayemet officials, lived in Baq'a. The Jewish *mukhtar* of Talbiyyeh was Reuven Mas, while the Arab *mukhtar* was Ibrahim Qabani. Each issued residential permits and birth certificates to the members of his community. Mas moved to Talbiyyeh in 1933, where he and his family were the only Jews in the neighborhood for two years.[38] For all intents and purposes, the 1948 war turned these neighborhoods into wholly Jewish ones, and in time they gentrified.

At the end of 1947, some 22,000 Arabs lived in south Jerusalem—9,000 Muslims and 13,000 Christians. About 550 Jews lived in the German Colony and Abu Tor, and another 1,230 in other southern neighborhoods. They constituted about 5 percent of Jerusalem's total Jewish population, while about a quarter of the city's Arabs lived in these neighborhoods. On the eve of the war the city's total population was 164,440—99,320 Jews, 33,680 Muslims, and 31,330 Christians. Most of the Christians, who included British subjects, Armenians, and Greeks, lived in the south.[39]

The Jews and their neighbors enjoyed friendly relations. One example of this was Ghada Karmi, whose family was friendly with their neighbor, Dr Kramer. Ghada also related how her older brother invited a Jewish friend from the neighborhood to visit her school, and that she paid a return visit to the Jewish school. The Karmi girls' father worked in the Mandate administration's education department along with a scholar of Islam, Professor Shlomo Dov Goitein. Goitein invited the father to a meeting of Brit Shalom, an organization of Jewish intellectuals who advocated reaching an agreement with the Palestinians even if it meant not achieving a Jewish majority and establishing a Jewish state. Karmi wrote that her father came home unimpressed by what he heard there.[40]

The south Jerusalem neighborhoods were populated by members of the middle and upper classes—college-educated professionals, senior officials, well-off businessmen, contractors, traders, doctors, architects, and lawyers like Khalil Sakakini, Mikhail Sansur, Sami Hadawi, the poet Fadwa Touqan, and the musician Tawfiq Jawhariyyeh. Their children attended multilingual private schools. Homes in Qatamon were lined with bookshelves containing works in several languages. The residents of the south Jerusalem neighborhoods were patrons of high culture—they heard concerts at the YMCA, and swam and played tennis there and at the German Colony's sports facilities. They lounged at cafés in Bayt Jala, vacationed in Ramallah, and visited the village of 'Ein Karem. Qatamon's single-family homes were surrounded by yards and small gardens. The neighborhood bordered on farmland cultivated by villagers who came into the neighborhood to sell their crops and work in the homes. The Karmis' maid came from Maliha, a village the Jews called Malha. Many of the neighborhood's inhabitants knew each other well. Several families owned cars. They dressed in the Western fashion but some of the men still wore tarbushes. Qatamon was also home to five small hotels, and the consulates of Iraq, Lebanon, Egypt, Belgium, and Poland. Four more consulates were located in Talbiyyeh, which was also the site of the Royal Air Force command center during World War II.[41]

The streets in Baq'a, Talbiyyeh, the German Colony, and the Greek Colony were named after famous medieval Arab and Muslim historical and cultural figures, as well as some who lived in the nineteenth and twentieth centuries—Sultan Baybars, the Islamic reformers Mohammad 'Abduh and Jamal al-Din al-Afghani, Egyptian Crown Prince Ibrahim Pasha, and the philosophers al-Farabi and Ibn Khaldun. In the Greek Colony the streets bore Greek names, commemorating, for example, the Byzantine monks St Artemius and St Nikoforos.[42] Following the 1948 war, Israel changed the names of Qatamon's streets to those of Israeli army units (Hayl Mishmar—the Guard Corps; Hayl

Nashim—the Women's Corps) and kibbutzim where heroic battles had been fought (Negba, Yad Mordechai, Be'erot Yitzhak). The main street that overlooks the neighborhood was named for the Palmach, the force which conquered Qatamon in a battle that quickly became part of Israeli mythology.

Its multicultural character was lost after the Palestinians left. The new inhabitants took pride in the streets that commemorated the Israeli military and Jewish valor. Israel imposed its culture in the nearby neighborhoods as well. Streets in the German Colony were named after non-Jewish Zionist sympathizers, such as South Africa's Prime Minister Jan Smuts. Talbiyyeh's streets were named after Jewish historians (Tzvi Graetz, Shmuel Klein) and, on the border between the two neighborhoods, Hebrew-language newspapers of the nineteenth century (Hatzefirah, Hamaggid, Hamelitz). Talbieyyeh's main street, initially named for Emir 'Abdallah, now honored Ze'ev Jabotinsky instead.

The move from the residential compound arranged around a common courtyard to modern separated family houses changed the nature of contact between Jews and Arabs. The intimacy and spontaneity involved in living together was lost; contacts between them now required deliberate visits or scheduled meetings. Such visits were shorter and planned in advance. They occurred primarily in places of business, work, and leisure rather than in homes. Still, for the most part they were as warm and friendly as they had been in the past. When the ethnographer Dr Tawfiq Can'an sought a wife in 1912, he asked his friend Miss Landau—that is, Hannah Yehudit Landau, a religious Jewish woman and headmistress of the Evelina de Rothschild school for girls—to find one for him. She prepared a list of eight Jerusalem women, some Arab and some European, and arranged introductions. But Can'an ultimately decided on a Jaffa-born German woman.

The Can'ans were next-door neighbors of the Schwartzes in Musrara, a neighborhood built on a northeast-facing slope adjacent to the Old City on its northwest side. His daughter, Mantura, was a good friend of Ruth Schwartz, who later married Moshe Dayan. Ruth's sister Reuma married Ezer Weizmann, who became commander of Israel's air force and later president of the country. The girls' mother, Rachel, taught at an Arab preschool in the Old City and took driving lessons with an Arab teacher. Other neighbors were Musa al-'Alami, 'Arif al-'Arif, and 'Awni 'Abd al-Hadi, all leaders of the Palestinian national movement, as well as Professor David Zvi Banet, the scholar of Islam, and Ya'akov Shimshon Shapira, who was Israel's minister of justice during the 1967 war.[43] However, the Arabs lived largely in the lower part of the neighborhood. Only one Arab home was built at the top, on the upper western side of Prophets Street—that of Amina al-Khalidi, on the corner of Chancellor Street, next to the Bikur Holim hospital. Menashe Hai Elyashar had been a friend of Jawad al-Hussayni ever since they attended the Alliance school together. They remained in close contact after completing their studies, and Elyashar visited his friend's homes in Jerusalem and Jericho. Elyashar and his wife Rachel went on a vacation in Tiberias with the families of Ragheb and Fakhri Nashashibi, and the Menashe Mani family and Shlomo Tusiyah Cohen were guests at the wedding of their colleague, Anwar Nusseibeh, with Nuzha al-Ghussei.[44]

The center of town and some of the workplaces (such as the British Mandate and the municipality offices), as well as some dwellings, had been integrated. After the British demolished the commercial center along the city wall near Jaffa Gate, businesses moved west. At the beginning of the twentieth century the Greek Orthodox Church sold a great deal of its property in Mamilla to the Zionist movement, which assigned Eliyahu Shama'a the task of building a commercial center there. Before the conflict intensified, it became a center for textile, fabric, and clothing stores. Most of these establishments were owned by Jews but had Arab and British clienteles as well as Jewish. According to a survey conducted in 1937, Arabs were regular customers in about a third of Jewish-owned stores.[45] Slightly to the west of Mamilla, Palestinians from Jerusalem's elite and upper-middle class, around the turn of the century, built houses to live in or rent out. Jews rented apartments there from the Meo, Hezbun, Saba, Albina, Qatan, Dajani, Nusseibeh, Habib, and Elias families, or lived as their neighbors in houses located close to the city's business, commercial, and entertainment center.[46]

The stand where the cabs to Jaffa clustered was located next to the Central Post Office and the Anglo-Palestine Bank, just to the west of Allenby Square, where the municipal building had opened in 1932. Barclay's Bank and Hotel Fast stood next to city hall. Safini's department store (which later opened a branch in the German Colony), Zanziri's household goods store, and George Lusidus's delicatessen were located in Mamilla next to Stern's store, Ludwig Meyer's bookstore on Princess Mary Street, and Tuchner's grocery store on Julian

Street. To their west, on Jaffa Street, two shoe stores owned by Arab-Armenians competed. Gaberdian's offered the most expensive and prettiest imported shoes in town. Cheaper shoes of local make could be purchased at Capelnian's.[47]

The British established their administrative center close by, including the headquarters of the uniformed and plainclothes police, courts, the Public Works Department, the offices of the district governor, and the income tax office. Since the public regularly visited these offices, it was natural for a commercial center to develop around them, overflowing from Jaffa Road on to adjacent streets—Princess Mary, Melissanda, and Ben-Yehuda. In 1931, the Arab entrepreneur Michael Sansur opened a modern office building at Zion Square, where Kupat Am Eretzyisraeli, a Jewish bank, operated alongside the Arab Othman bank. The Yishuv's legal elite opened offices on the square, among them the firms of Felix Rosenblit (later Pinhas Rosen, Israel's minister of justice), Moshe Zemora, and Yitzhak Olshan (later chief justice of Israel's Supreme Court). So did prominent Arab attorneys, such as Henry Qatan, George Salah, and 'Omar Salah Barghuthi. They all met at Café Europa, on the building's façade, where other lawyers also came to trade gossip and professional opinions. British officials and officers and Jewish and Arab intellectuals encountered each other at the Piccadilly, Kapulsky, Alaska, and Vienna cafés, each at a different corner of Zion Square. Halfway up Ben-Yehuda Street stood Café Atara, also an important social institution. Atara had the most staying power, remaining a major Jerusalem landmark long after the others had shut down. The atmosphere of the Jewish cafés in Jerusalem emulated that of Vienna's cafés, serving Sachertorte. The Jewish cafés differed from the Arab ones situated not far off, next to city hall, in that the former welcomed women and children as well. Only men sat at the Umayah, Jawahariyya, and al-Ma'aref cafés.[48] Arab developers built office buildings to rent out to Jews farther down Jaffa Road. The Qatan, Issa, Musa, and Hajj Mahmud buildings stood between the Mahaneh Yehuda market and Sha'arei Tzedek hospital. Like the cafés, the cinemas near the beginning of Jaffa Road—the Zion, Rex, Eden, Tel-Or, Edison, and al-Sharq—drew large crowds in the evening. The Rex was owned by a contractor, Josef Albina, and screened Arab films which both Arabs and Jews came to see. Not far away, at the YMCA, the Palestine Symphony Orchestra, including Jewish and Arab players, offered concerts. The audiences were made up of well-dressed members of the Palestinian, British, and Jewish elites. The King David Hotel, across the street from the YMCA, served as the elegant and exclusive place to be for Jerusalem's high society.[49]

Mamilla was the site of one of the most interesting partnerships of the period. In order to obtain the job of constructing the luxurious Palace Hotel, which the Supreme Muslim Council wanted to build on Waqf land that it administered, a Jewish contractor, Baruch Katinka, went into partnership with another Jew, Tovia Dunieh, and an Arab contractor, Josef al-Bina. Their professional reputation was not the only reason the partners received the contract to build the Palace Hotel. Katinka provided aid to the Haganah, the Jewish militia, and Dunya was Chaim Weizmann's brother-in-law. Al-Bina maintained close ties with Hajj Amin al-Hussayni. The council approved them for the job without any of the lengthy negotiation that usually takes place regarding such a large project. The same partnership constructed the YMCA building, which opened in 1932. When the foundations were dug, Muslim graves were discovered. After taking Jerusalem from the Crusaders, Salah al-Din buried his fallen soldiers in this area.

> Three meters down we found old graves containing many human skeletons. I was concerned that Arab laborers would inform the mufti that graves were being desecrated. I approached the mufti and told him about the matter. To my surprise, he told me not to publicize it and to keep it a deep secret between us. He would see to it that the Arab workers would not talk. He asked me to have the bones collected at the end of the excavation and to transfer them in secret to a special grave.

The mufti was worried that his rival, Mayor Nashashibi, would use the discovery against him—which indeed he did when it inevitably came to light. What did not come to light was Katinka's solution for the sewage produced by the hotel. The municipality, under Nashashibi,

> decided not to extend the sewage pipe to the hotel, and we faced a bad situation because no septic pit could take in the hotel's huge quantity of sewage ... The next day I went to see the mufti in his office. We sat in a room alone together and I told him that there was one way out of the complication but that I didn't dare propose it because he would be angry with me. Only after he promised me that no matter what my idea was he would listen to it seriously, I told him that, in my opinion, we should install two small electrical pumps in the building's basement. The pumps would pump the sewage out of our large septic tank into the [Muslim] cemetery of Mamila, which covered a large area. There we could arrange a network of septic pipes in the ground that would easily be able to absorb the sewage. I explained to the mufti that our large sep-

tic tank with a capacity of 200 cubic meters would purify the sewage to the point that what we would be transferring to the cemetery would be almost clean water. The mufti thought for a few moments and then asked me if I could carry out all this work without people suspecting it and without the matter reaching the municipality. I told him that I would take that responsibility on myself. All the work was done at night by Jewish laborers.[50]

In the 2000s, Katinka's recollections, and the construction of the Palace Hotel over the Muslim cemetery, became issues in a court case that sparked public controversy laden with religious, moral, historical, and national emotions. The Simon Wiesenthal Center of Los Angeles commenced construction of a Museum of Tolerance on a lot in the same Muslim Cemetery that had served as a municipal parking lot since the 1960s. The Muslim religious establishment went to court to try to stop the project, arguing that the building would desecrate Muslim graves. The developer submitted a legal opinion to the court based in part on Katinka's story and the mufti's sanction of the construction of the Palace Hotel on a part of the cemetery. The petitioners, for their part, submitted opposing expert opinions and rulings of Muslim religious courts claiming that Muslim religious law forbade the construction of buildings in cemeteries. The case pitted two historical and religious narratives, as well as opposing moral standards and political forces, against each other. Needless to say, what was at stake was not just the construction of the museum, but also the conflict over other holy sites in the city where Jews and Muslims staked opposing claims—a conflict that had grown more intense at the beginning of the millennium. The court accepted the Israeli–Zionist narrative that the museum's supporters had put forward and permitted the continuation of construction, with certain restrictions. The Zionist–Palestinian cooperation and understanding that had prevailed during the construction of the Palace turned, eighty years later, into a religious and national crisis.[51]

Katinka and the mufti trusted and understood each other. They were able to arrive at a deal that made it possible to hire a Jewish–Arab partnership to build the Palace Hotel, while ensuring that their solution to the sewage problem would remain confidential (or so they hoped). "We didn't set a price before beginning the project because we did not know what special outlays would be required," Katinka related. "At the end of the job I told the mufti that he had to pay us P£1,500 [Palestine pounds]. The mufti did not investigate or ask for details, just asked us, with a small laugh, if we would earn more than 50 percent on this part of the job. When I told him that the answer was yes, he ordered his treasurer, Hilmi Pasha, to pay me the sum." The mufti understood that he had to compensate Katinka well, and Katinka understood that he needed to repay the mufti for his generosity. "In one of my conversations with the mufti he told me that, despite his difficult job and high position, he was not at all wealthy and that he did not have the wherewithal even to finish the home in Sheikh Jarrah where he had laid the foundations two years previously. I asked the mufti to show me the plans for the house. After I examined the foundations I proposed to him that we would build his house for a low price, and that we would allow him to pay the bill over two years. Without signing a contract and without asking the price, the mufti gave us the job."[52]

The two men maintained a strong personal friendship despite the national sentiments and political opinions of each. "Since it was a time of tension and disturbances," when Katinka built the Palace Hotel at the end of the 1920s, he "included in the building two secret arms caches to hold weapons in case they were needed." But the personal relations continued until the Arab Revolt broke out in 1936. At that time the mufti fled the country in order to avoid arrest by the British. "From [the construction of the Palace Hotel] to the day the mufti left Jerusalem, I was invited each year as his private guest to the Nebi Musa procession and he also sent me a gift of leavened food on the night after the last day of Pesach—a large tray with hot Arab pita bread, cheese, butter, olives, and honey."[53]

The mufti gave George Antonius, the most prominent representative of the Arab national movement to the West, permission to reside in the house he built in Sheikh Jarrah. After George's death, Antonius's wife Katy conducted a political–literary salon there. She abandoned the house in 1947, and under Jordanian rule it became the Shepherd Hotel. When Israel took control of East Jerusalem, the house came under the authority of the custodian of abandoned properties. It continued to operate as a hotel for a few years after the 1967 war, but then the hotel closed. During the First Intifada, Israel's Border Guard began using it as a base. In 1985 the custodian handed the house over to a settler organization, which in July 2009 received from the Jerusalem municipality permission to build apartments there. The settlers view this as a historic victory over the mufti, a bitter enemy of the Jews who collaborated with the Nazis during World War II, and over the Palestinian national movement as a whole.[54]

The Palace Hotel opened in 1929 and served as the city's most luxurious place to stay until the King David was opened, not far away, in 1933. When the latter establishment, which was under Jewish ownership, began to draw away customers, the Palace was remade into an office building, with most of its space rented to the British administration. After the 1948 war the elegant building degenerated into the grim, neglected, and unimportant offices of Israel's Ministry of Commerce and Industry. Despite its age, the building's elegant façade remained as a reminder of its brief moment of glory. The Israeli government sold the building in 2006 to the Reichman family of Canada, which has constructed a plush new Waldorf Astoria hotel there, preserving the building's external appearance.[55]

Encounters between Jews and Arabs sometimes took place in neutral venues, in accordance with strict rules. The existence of such rules enabled the two sides to meet even at times of great tension between the two peoples. One such arena was the Palestine Oriental Society, a scholarly and professional organization that operated in Jerusalem from 1920 to 1948. The society brought together senior officials in the British administration, academic scholars, archaeologists, and Western clerics who worked in Christian institutions in Jerusalem and Palestine as a whole, as well as Jewish and Arab intellectuals. The society engaged in a wide range of activities, including studies of the Bible, culture, Semitic languages, and the customs, traditions, and folk art of contemporary Arab society. The society's meetings were of an academic nature and were conducted in English and French. It established a journal in these two languages in which the studies of its members were published. At the opening of its meetings the society's leaders presented an administrative report, which was followed by scholarly lectures. All its members held the local culture in high esteem and believed Britain to be an enlightened power. At the time the Palestine Oriental Society was founded its members had no doubt that British rule was a great advance over that of the Turks, and that the British would respect the country's heritage and protect the freedom of scholars to study it. The society was an elite organization, with its members drawn from the top echelons of their respective societies. Field Marshal Allenby and High Commissioner Herbert Samuel were honorary presidents. In order to join, a candidate had to be recommended by the society's administration and be voted in by a three-quarters majority of the members present at a general meeting.[56] From the Yishuv, members included figures such as David Yellin, Nahum Slouschz, Eliezer Ben-Yehuda, Arthur Biram, Haim Margaliot Kalvarisky, Hannah Yehudit Landau, Alter Levin, and Menachem Ussishkin. The Palestinian Arab members were a minority, and lacked the status of their Jewish colleagues. Elias Hadad, Tawfiq Can'an, Khalil Totah, Hana Stefan, and 'Omar Effendi Barghouti were not officials in the top Palestinian communal institutions. The members' motivations for studying Palestine's past varied—in some cases scholarly, in others religious (especially true of the Christians among them), and in still others national. Each of the members from each of the communities sought to use the study of the past as a way of strengthening his own and his community's connection to the country. In the past of their common land they hoped to find succor for the painful present and a way of building a better future. The Palestinian historian Salim Tamari has noted that the works published by the society's Arab members later enabled Palestinians of the generation recovering from the catastrophe of 1948 to fashion a response to the Israeli claim to have biblical roots in the land and thus exclusive rights to it. It was thanks to these studies that the Palestinians were able to renew popular local traditions and celebrations that hark back to the Bronze Age, such as the Canaanite festival in Qabatiyyeh and the Jebusite Music Festival.[57] These festivals were organized after the establishment of the Palestinian Authority in 1994, as part of an attempt to promote a Canaanite–Palestinian identity and in keeping with a desire to prove that the Palestinians had been in the country before the Israelis.

A Holy Site Chooses a City—A City Chooses a Holy Site

Nebi Rubin was a Muslim holy site chosen by the inhabitants of Jaffa, and they preferred to have it far from the city. At the beginning of the nineteenth century the port's development accelerated and its population grew more heterogeneous, consisting of merchants, middlemen, landowners, citrus farmers, exporters, and lawyers as well as seasonal workers, immigrants, and government officials. Pilgrims and tourists passed through it; journalists and publishers rubbed shoulders with political activists and social activists sat together with the owners of cafés and restaurants. And this is not to mention the fishermen and dock workers.[58] The dynamic city preferred a holy site that lay 9 miles south, the mosque in the village of Nebi Rubin, which tradition claimed was the burial place of Reuben (Rubin in Arabic, Reuven in Hebrew), the patriarch Jacob's oldest son. Nor did it need more than one holy site, which its inhabitants visited once a year after the orange harvest and the season of tending the citrus groves—sometime between July and September. The festivities lasted between three and four weeks. They featured a mixture of Muslim religious rituals such as circumcisions, prayer services, and supplications to the Prophet Rubin for male issue, along with other mundane as well as often quite sensual celebrations.

The event began with a celebration in the city, leading up to a procession from there to the holy site. The procession originally set out from Ramla, which was the major urban center on the coastal plain prior to Jaffa's rise in the nineteenth century. Once Jaffa established itself as the area's most important city, the procession to Nebi Rubin left from the port city, joined by people from Ramla, Lydda, Gaza, and their hinterlands.

Jews often took part as well. As Yair Hamburger reported in *Hamaggid* in 1867: "The Jews, too, can go in this month to that place without fear, and the Ishmaelites [Arabs] esteem the Jews and treat them with respect when they arrive there, and especially anyone named Reuven, and admonish them to come pray also at the tomb of Reuven, saying that he was one of the sons of your patriarch Jacob."[59] The Nebi Rubin festivities were of great interest to the Yishuv, as attested by articles depicting it that appeared in *Davar*, the daily newspaper of the labor movement, in 1928 and 1930.[60] The Jaffa riots of 1921 and the tension that preceded and followed the riots of 1929 did not prevent *Davar* from taking an interest in the festival and providing objective accounts of it; nor did the nationalist slogans and Palestinian flags that appeared in the processions from Jaffa to Nebi Rubin in the 1920s and 1930s.

Between 40,000 and 50,000 people took part in the Nebi Rubin festival during the first half of the twentieth century. The procession set out from Jaffa's Great Mosque, with the participation of entire extended families. Before cars and buses came into wide use, participants rode camels and pitched tents at the holy site, with the tents reflecting their social status. Huge ones were set up by the Jaffa municipality, which provided electricity, radios, music, and other entertainment on the hot summer nights. The Nebi Rubin holy site, owned by an Islamic trust (Waqf), covered 32,000 dunams (more than 12 square miles), most of which was leased out to farmers. The rent received from the farmers was used to set up a central kitchen to supply water and food. The participants ate freshly baked bread, rice, soup, meat, and fish. The Mandate government paved a road to the site, set up a water system and a bakery, and renovated the mosque. At its height in the 1930s and 1940s, the site boasted a kitchenware and clothing market as well as cafés, theaters, restaurants, and open-air cinemas (love stories were especially popular). The Muslim Ensemble Orchestra, with forty members, played there in 1933. It was such a hit that wealthy Jaffans began hiring it to play at private celebrations.[61]

On a November evening in 1934 two correspondents for *Davar* and two officials of Mapai, the labor party that was the Yishuv's largest, visited Nebi Rubin. "We passed by cafés in Jaffa and they were empty or half-empty, because most of their regular clientele had gone to Rubin," reported one of the journalists, Menachem Kapliuk. On their way they observed "city and village Arabs waiting for a car to take them to Rubin." The four Jews were hosted by a sailor from the port who had inherited the right to manage a café in the shrine's compound from his father. It was a time of the year when fishermen had little work and "they went out to Rubin, some for pleasure and some for business." In the host's café, "hidden behind a curtain," they found things the police did not allow: "those intoxicating leaves that are best not spoken of, the 'weed' [hashish]." Between 9 p.m. and midnight the market was open for women only. After midnight, when the women left and the market opened for men, the Jews arrived. They did not conceal their ethnic identity, and the hawkers tried "their tongues at Hebrew so as to win over the foreign buyers who had landed among them in the middle of the night."[62]

Each afternoon there were horse and camel races, as well as wrestling matches starring contenders from all over the country. In one match, Ya'akov Ben-Maimon of Jaffa defended his city's honor when he bested an Arab grappler from Ashdod.[63] In addition to the contests of strength, members of Jaffa's Boy Scout chapter paraded and there were music, magic, and dancing shows. In one tent a *hakawati* told stories to a rapt audience. He began with historical tales of heroism, followed these with love stories and moral preaching, and finished up with a satiric stand-up routine. In another tent Sufis—Muslim mystics—sought to attract an audience for a religious presentation of their own.

The card games, where erotic belly dancers entertained, ran through the night and attracted young Jews as well. One of them was Yizhar Smilanksy, then a boy living in nearby Rehovot. Later, under the pen-name S. Yizhar, he became one of the greatest modern Hebrew writers. One evening he accompanied his older brother and some of the brother's friends "to watch, in the light of campfires, flashlights, and all sorts of other illumination, even electricity, the dance shows, which included the gyrations of the dervishes, and the colorful stands of sweets." Smilansky stood with "the rest of the onlookers, watching the undulations of the belly of a gypsy woman, her navel bare, variegated scarves on her head, shoulders, and the curve of her waist, the gourd of her belly declaring her intentions, glistening with a glaring glow, shameless, giving the audience a sense-swallowing pleasure ... to the point that the breathing of those around us became horsey and heavier than their strength could handle." All this lasted "until the night's third watch, without any desire to break free and go back." When the group of Jews returned to Rehovot, "we could not shake off those voices, those poets of blows and wails ... fashioned with the sweet rot of the ardent, perspiring night that was nevertheless of a single hue, rising and falling, rising and falling without end."[64]

Between events, families got together, gossip and news was exchanged, business connections were established, and marriages were arranged.[65] The last of these celebrations was held in 1946. By the summer of the following year the impending war was in the air. And after the war, Israel confiscated the land where the festival was held and the mosque was demolished—but its minaret remained standing. At the beginning of the 1990s Haredi (ultra-Orthodox) Jews took over the tomb, rebuilt it, and began a tradition of pilgrimage in mid-December (the Jewish month of Kislev) to the tomb of "the saint Reuven ben Ya'akov [Reuben, son of Jacob]." The minaret collapsed soon after the Haredi pilgrimage began, which the Jewish devotees viewed as a sign from heaven that it now belonged to the Jews.[66] The new tradition gained considerable popularity during its first decade, but it still remains in its infancy, and the tomb's standing is still much lower than those of dozens of other Jewish holy men and women which have become pilgrimage sites. The expropriation of the site from the Muslims did not restore its former grandeur. The Muslims of Jaffa took its glory with them into exile.

Meanwhile, life in Hebron, an outlying provincial city, played out in a completely different way. Unlike Jaffa and Jerusalem, Hebron was not a major destination for Christian tourists and pilgrims. It was much smaller than the other two cities and was huddled close to the large compound that King Herod the Great built at the Tomb of the Patriarchs, the second-holiest Islamic site in Palestine, after al-Haram al-Sharif. It stood at the center, the reason for the town's existence. The city's Arabic name, al-Khalil, meaning "the friend," refers to the key figure buried there—Ibrahim, the name the Arabs give to the biblical Abraham, called Avraham by the Jews. In Muslim tradition, Ibrahim was the first believer, the spiritual ancestor of the Prophet Muhammad. Furthermore, Abraham was known for his hospitality, commemorated in Hebron by the Madafat Ibrahim, an Islamic trust that has provided food and drink to visitors since the ninth century and which continues to do so today, making it the oldest such organization in the Muslim world. Each important family in Hebron has a role in maintaining the site or in its devotions. There they conduct their family celebrations and mourn their dead.

During the British Mandate, Hebronites resented the Islamic establishment in Jerusalem for not granting them the representation in the Supreme Muslim Council that they felt the importance of their holy site entitled them to. They also chafed at the fact that, after the British creation of the Supreme Muslim Council led by the mufti, the Hebron Waqf became subordinate to that body in Jerusalem. Hebron's leaders charged that Jerusalem's religious establishment, controlled by the Hussaynis, was appropriating a large portion of the income from "their" Waqf. This sense of discrimination impelled most of Hebron's political elite to support the anti-Hussayni opposition, which was divided between a number of families, in accordance with the social and political breakdown of Jerusalem's Arab population. The opposition, which sought allies in their struggle with the Hussaynis, was impelled toward cooperation with the Zionists, helping the latter purchase land and providing them with intelligence.[67]

While there were occasional exceptions, as noted above, only Muslims had been allowed inside the Tomb of the Patriarchs since 1267, when the Mamluks forbade Jews and Christians to enter the compound—despite the fact that all three religions revere the patriarchs and matriarchs who are buried there. This only changed as a result of the Israeli conquest of 1967. Before that year, Jews were permitted to ascend only to the seventh step leading up to the entrance to the shrine. Jews prayed there, addressing their supplications to the patriarchs and matriarchs through a small hole in the building's wall. Interaction between the city's Jews and Muslims was restricted largely to commerce, but even there it was limited because of the small size and poverty of the Jewish population. Nor was there a pilgrimage festival associated with the holy site. Devotees visited it as individuals or families, as part of an annual public event. The public religious event that Hebron's Muslims participated in was one connected to Jerusalem—the pilgrimage to Nebi Musa.

Even though Nebi Musa lay in the desert, on the way to Jericho, about 12 miles from Jerusalem, its pilgrimage festival was very much a Jerusalem celebration. It helped place Jerusalem at the center of Palestinian identity. Jaffans left their city to visit Nebi Rubin. Jerusalem made Nebi Musa part of the holy city. The custom seems to have originated under the rule of Salah al-Din, who permitted Christians to visit their holy sites in Jerusalem after the defeat of the Crusaders in 1187. As a counterweight to the Easter celebrations in Jerusalem and to Christian visits to baptismal sites on the Jordan River, he initiated the Nebi Musa pilgrimage from Jerusalem to the shrine. That resulted in celebrants from outside Jerusalem arriving first in the city, then returning home via Jerusalem when their celebration was over. The Nebi Musa pilgrimage was not assigned a date on the Muslim calendar, nor was it associated with an agricultural season. It was held in accordance with the Orthodox Christian Church's calendar, so as to coincide with Easter. The Muslim festival began precisely a week before the Orthodox Easter and ended on the eve of Good Friday. Since it was both a counter-celebration and a Jerusalem–Muslim one, it could not escape a connection with al-Haram al-Sharif. Before descending the road to Nebi Musa and when they came back the pilgrims ascended to the al-Aqsa mosque.

The participants came from as far away as Hebron in the south and Nablus in the north—that is, the festival attracted the entire population of Palestine's hill country. These people celebrated in a different way from their coastal brethren. The former, especially those who lived in holy cities, preferred religious gravity. True, hawkers and peddlers worked the crowds at Nebi Musa, and horse races were held on the plateau where the mosque was located, but those were the only entertainments available. Otherwise, only religious dancing was allowed. Even the horse races had a religious rationale—according to tradition, they began when Salah al-Din resolved to display Muslim might for

Christian pilgrims. Nebi Musa was not a spring festival but rather a religious event and a show of power. The different atmosphere was not the only contrast with the Nebi Rubin pilgrimage. It was also a much briefer event—a week, as opposed to a month.

The Hussaynis were the primary patrons of the Nebi Musa celebration. The founder of the dynasty, 'Omar al-Hussayni, claimed as his family's founding father Sheikh 'Abdallah ibn Yunus, who had received from the Mamluk Sultan Baibars the post of overseer of the Nebi Musa Waqf, and the Hussayni family had managed it ever since. Income from Waqf properties paid for the costs of the festival. After taking the festival's green flag from the Hussayni family home, the mufti of Jerusalem would lead the pilgrims to the holy site in a procession that was both colorful and chaotic. Many of the participants waved swords and sticks in the air. The green flag was returned to the Hussayni home at the end of the pilgrimage. The fact that members of this family filled the post of mufti of Jerusalem and served in the city administration further enhanced the importance of the festival and Jerusalem's position as a focal point for all of Palestine.[68]

Jews did not participate in the Nebi Musa festival itself. As noted above, Arab Jews took a sympathetic view of the festival. Like many of Jerusalem's inhabitants, they watched the procession as it passed through the city's streets when the convoys of pilgrims arrived from the south and north. This was followed by an official reception to which the city's most important personages were invited, including the leaders of the Jewish community. Hakham Bashi (Chief Rabbi) Nissim Danon and other Jewish leaders took part in the ceremony in 1919, when Arab nationalism was already on display during the festivities.

The Nebi Musa celebration institutionalized Jerusalem's centrality and its relations with Hebron and Nablus and the villages around them. What had begun as a counter-Christian event was invested with new meaning as tensions with the Zionists and British grew and as feelings of Palestinian national identity waxed stronger. The national conflict co-opted religious identity. Religious contact between Muslim and Jews on the basis of a common residential compound or a holy tomb at which adherents of both religions worshipped became problematic, if not reprehensible. Nationalism penetrated the holy places, in particular the Temple Mount/al-Haram al-Sharif. The claim to exclusive rights to that site was used to rally national loyalties and public opinion on both sides, with each nation viewing the holy mountain as its exclusive birthright.

Coexistence Disturbed by Confrontation

Unlike many of his contemporaries, Khalil Sakakini was profoundly opposed to the marriage of nationalism and religious fanaticism. In the 1920s he taught that Palestinian patriotism and Arab nationalism did not have to be anti-liberal, fundamentalist, and devoid of universal values. He advocated an uncompromising national stance but at the same time respected his Jewish counterparts and maintained good relations with them. As an Arab patriot, Sakakini participated in the reception for the pilgrims returning from Nebi Musa in April 1920. He gazed out at the 70,000 countrymen in front of the Jerusalem municipal building and saw a political demonstration. Religious and nationalist tension hung in the air that Friday, which was both Good Friday and the eve of the Jews' Pesach holiday. The tension was caused, first, by what the Arabs viewed as Britain's betrayal of its commitments to Faisal and his Hashemite clan. The Hashemites had helped the British war effort by leading an Arab rebellion against Turkish rule. In exchange, as the Hashemites understood it, the British had promised to support their aspiration for a pan-Arab kingdom under their leadership. But when Faisal declared an Arab kingdom in Damascus, the British offered no help. On top of this, the British demonstrated that they were intent on keeping their promise to the Jews, made in the Balfour Declaration, to establish a Jewish homeland in Palestine.[69] The heated atmosphere prompted Sakakini to compare the singing of the Muslims to battle hymns and their flags to spears. He was right. Incendiary political speeches invoked anti-Jewish motifs from Islamic tradition. 'Arif al-'Arif, later a writer of history and mayor of Jerusalem (1950–5), then editor of the newspaper *Surriya al-Janubiyya*, declared: "Palestine is our land, the Jews are our dogs!"[70] The demagogic speeches fired up the Hebronites, who rioted and looted Jewish stores in Jerusalem. The fanaticism infected young people like 25-year-old Hajj Amin al-Hussayni, as well as his 67-year-old uncle, Jerusalem's Mayor Musa Kazem al-Hussayni, who had generally been one of the moderate voices in the Palestinian national movement. When reflecting on that day's events in his diary, Sakakini put his feelings succinctly: "I am disgusted and depressed by the madness of the human race."[71]

Tensions were so high that it took only one small incident to set off a large-scale confrontation. The Arabs claimed that a Jew had pushed an Arab who was bearing one of the banners, before spitting on him and trying to grab the flag away from him. The Jews said that Arabs had assaulted a Jewish passerby and had beaten the people who had tried to protect him. The Arab mob was then confronted by a local Jewish militia that had been founded by Ze'ev Jabotinsky, a junior officer in the British army during World War I who would later become the leader of the Revisionist Zionist Movement. The armed militia guarded the Jews making their way that day to the Western Wall, and its members apparently fought with the Arab mob. Jabotinsky had been a critic both of British policy in Palestine and of Chaim Weizmann, the president of the Zionist Organization. In fact, Jabotinsky had already predicted that violence would break out during the Nebi Musa celebrations that year, but Governor Storrs had not taken his warning seriously. Storrs did not prepare his forces for the possibility that the Arab leadership might ignore the admonition he had conveyed to them prior to the event. It took the British three days and a series of firm political moves to halt the cycle of mutual bloodshed and violence that left five Jews and four Arabs dead and 216 Jews and twenty-three Arabs wounded. Storrs ousted Musa Kazem al-Hussayni from the mayor's chair and appointed a member of the most important rival clan—Raghib al-Nashashibi—in his place.[72]

The violent confrontation of 1920 was a local manifestation of Arab nationalism, melded with religion, launched at a traditional ceremony, and intended to express opposition to the British, Jews, and Zionists. It was carried out in the name of Palestinian patriotism, while also expressing allegiance to Faisal as the Arab sovereign of Damascus. The confrontations of 1920 in Jerusalem and 1921 in Jaffa had repercussions in Hebron as well. "We had a few difficult days here, for two or three days we had to secure ourselves in holes and cracks and every nocturnal drum roll struck us with horror," Yitzhak Shami wrote from Hebron in 1921 to his friend David Avisar.[73]

In 1929 the disturbances bore a much clearer Palestinian nationalist imprint. Politically, they were centered on Palestine, not on Damascus. They were of a religious–political nature, but the focus was not Nebi Musa but the Temple Mount/al-Haram al-Sharif. Its geography was Jerusalem and it had a much tighter connection to Hebron than the previous round of violence.

The Zionist movement had an ambivalent position on the Old City as a whole and to the Temple Mount in particular. Zionists wanted to create a new type of Jew with an image that would supplant that of the traditional religious Jew. Zionism was a revolutionary, secular movement. It rebelled against the passivity that had been enforced by Jewish religious strictures, which preached to the Jewish masses that redemption would come only with the arrival of the Messiah at the end of days. To the horror of Orthodoxy, Zionism borrowed non-Jewish organizational templates and ways of thinking and proposed modern nationalism as a replacement for religion, or as a type of identity that contained religion but was of a higher order. Zionism did not replace religion entirely, but the Jewish faith lost its exclusive position as the organizing principle of Jewish society and a generator of identity. For Chaim Weizmann, Jerusalem symbolized the Jewish past. "The minarets and the bell towers and domes rising to the sky are crying out that Jerusalem is not a Jewish city," he wrote to his wife, Vera. During a visit to Jerusalem he likened the city to a swamp, adding that "It's such an accursed city, there's nothing there, no creature comfort," only filth, ugliness, and beggars. It was, he thought, humiliating, even sacrilegious.[74] Yet, at the very same time, Weizmann was angling to purchase the Western Wall for the Zionist movement and lobbied Ronald Storrs to that end.

Weizmann was not the first Jew to try to purchase the Jewish holy site. Others, as noted, had attempted to do so during the previous century. He spoke with Allenby and wrote to Lord Balfour in a style that reflected his cultural and political outlook. The wall, he told his correspondents, had been part of the Jewish Temple; it was in fact a retaining wall of the Temple Mount compound. He wrote to Vera that it had been neglected and was now decrepit, and "from the hygienic point of view [had been] a source of constant humiliation to the Jews of the world." The houses nearby, he wrote "belong to some doubtful ... religious community," his description of the Mughrabi Quarter built in 1193 by Salah al-Din for pilgrims from Morocco who wished to live close to al-Haram al-Sharif. The street that ran by the wall, Weizmann informed Vera, was "the haunt of Arab loafers and vagrants, whose presence and conduct do not tend to the peace of mind of the Jewish devotees ... [It] is painful beyond description."[75] Weizmann proposed raising a sum of £75,000 to evacuate the residents of the quarter and build them homes elsewhere. Weizmann suggested a political payoff to the British who would further the plan—the Jewish people would be grateful for the generous spirit of the British regime and would unite to support that country's rule in Palestine. As a British soldier says to his commander in A.B. Yehoshua's novel *Mr. Mani*, "As usual, sir, the Jews have little to offer except themselves."[76]

Balfour was not keen on the idea. He asked Weizmann to act with moderation and first to obtain the consent of the Muslims. But Storrs agreed to cooperate and negotiated with Arab representatives himself in order to obscure the fact that the idea had originated with the Zionists. But the latter did not have confidence in him and pursued their own talks. Arab opposition was not overcome in either of these channels.[77]

The British gently tried to divert Weizmann's energies in other directions. Weizmann indeed pursued these other ideas but did not give up his original goal. In May 1926, Gad Frumkin conducted negotiations with several of the owners of houses in the neighborhood, seeking to convince them to sell their properties. Frumkin wanted to buy the houses so as to open up a wider passage in front of the wall. He claimed that the Zionist leadership was in no hurry to raise the necessary money.[78] In his history of the Hussayni family Ilan Pappe claims that the Zionists offered P£70,000 to the owners of the Mughrabi quarter in return for evacuation, but that the Palestinian leadership prevented this.[79] In 1926, the head of the Jewish Agency's Political Department, Frederick Kisch, obtained a promise of P£5,000 for the purchase of the Khalidi family compound near the wall from the New York retail magnate and philanthropist Nathan Straus. Kisch subsequently presented Straus with a large-scale plan to buy more homes there for a total of $100,000, but at this point Straus suspected that Kisch was simply seeking to extract more money from him and withdrew his commitment.[80] Weizmann continued to seek funding. At Weizmann's behest, Baron Felix de Menasce, an Egyptian Jew, sounded out Muslim leaders in Jerusalem about the idea, but was rebuffed.[81]

The motives of Weizmann and his colleagues were not religious. On the contrary, they wanted to strip the Temple Mount of its religious significance. They saw it as they saw all of the Land of Israel—part of the political and cultural renaissance of the Jewish people as a nation of the enlightened and secular West.

This was not, of course, the only value reflected in the Zionist leadership, which included extremists who put the Temple Mount at the center of their version of the Jewish national movement. On the Passover holiday in 1928, the chairman of the Zionist Executive, Menachem Ussishkin, affirmed that "The Jewish People will not rest and will not remain silent until its national home is built on our

Mt. Moriah."[82] Others raised money and sought support from world Jewry with the help of postcards and posters depicting Herzl gazing out at Jewish crowds on his way to Jerusalem. At the center of a typical poster was a building with a dome that clearly represented the Dome of the Rock—with a Zionist flag waving over it. The Torat Chaim *yeshiva* raised money from overseas Jews by sending out a photograph in which the Dome of the Rock was adorned with the Star of David. The *yeshiva* had been founded in 1886 in the Old City with the express purpose of serving as the last stop for the Messiah as he made his way to the Temple Mount. The photograph was used by synagogues around the world to mark the direction to which worshippers should pray in order to direct their prayers to Jerusalem.[83] It clearly showed an Islamic structure, but one that had been Judaicized. The message was clear. It was understood quite well by the Palestinians as indicating Zionism's ultimate goal: the Zionists would not suffice themselves with establishing a Jewish state—they wanted to build a Third Temple on the ruins of Islam's holy sites.

Both Jews and Muslims did not easily distinguish between the Western Wall's symbolic aspects and its functional ones. The space in front of the wall was indeed tiny and narrow—just 16 or so feet wide and 92 feet long. Ottoman strictures forbade the Jews from placing benches or chairs by the wall for the elderly and infirm, or to erect a divider to separate men and women, as is customary in Orthodox synagogues. The Turks also forbade the blowing there of the *shofar*—the ram's-horn trumpet sounded ritually before and on the Jewish New Year. The purpose of these restrictions was to prevent the space from becoming a synagogue, which would change the symbolic status of both the site and of the Jews who worshipped there. The Muslims claimed that they were allowing the Jews to pray at a site that was sacred to Islam. They called the wall al-Buraq, after the name of the miraculous horse that, in their tradition, transported the Prophet Muhammad from Mecca to al-Aqsa, whence he ascended to heaven. According to this account, Muhammad left his steed by the wall before going up to the mosque.

Both sides occasionally violated the status quo at the beginning of the twentieth century. The Sephardi rabbi Hakham Hananiya, father of Ya'akov Yehoshua, persuaded the qadi of Jerusalem to place benches by the Wall. But the decision roused opposition and in December 1911 the benches were removed. In fact, the restoration of the status quo ante was supported by Leib Dayan, a representative of Jerusalem's Jews.[84] But the site's symbolic importance increased as the national conflict intensified, without regard to the functional aspect of the site as a place of Jewish prayer. Chairs, benches, and a divider were not seen by both sides simply as furniture but also as symbols of something larger, historical and metaphysical. The question of whether there should be places to sit at the Western Wall, and whether the *shofar* could be blown there, became matters of principle over which blood could and should be spilled. Small-scale confrontations over these issues, between Jews and Muslim and between Jews and the British authorities, took place several times during the 1920s.[85]

The Muslim figure who led the opposition to initiatives to assert Jewish rights at the Western Wall during the 1920s was Mufti Hajj Amin al-Hussayni, the leader of the Palestinian national movement. He sought to place Jerusalem at the center of Palestinian Arab national consciousness. He raised support and donations for the renovation of al-Aqsa and the Dome of the Rock, claiming that this work was vital in the face of the Jewish threat to these sites. And in 1931 he convened a large conference dedicated to protecting Muslim holy sites in Jerusalem. The zealous and sweeping propaganda campaign that he conducted in Palestine and throughout the Islamic world stressed that the Zionists were planning to seize control of al-Haram al-Sharif, where they would demolish the Dome of the Rock and al-Aqsa in order to build their Third Temple.[86] His claims fell on receptive ears. The Palestinian public was largely traditional in character. Its national sentiments and collective identity were tied up with Islam and its holy sites in Jerusalem.

The issue grew more acute as the decade progressed. On the eve of Yom Kippur, on 23 September 1928, a British officer, Edward Keith-Roach, noticed that the Jews had placed a portable divider in front of the wall. He ordered it to be removed, but the Jewish beadle there asked that it be allowed to remain for the night, or only be removed after the end of the fast day, the next evening. On the morning of the holy day, one of Keith-Roach's officers saw that the divider was still there and forcibly removed it himself. In response, Jewish fanatics tried to murder him on three separate occasions.[87]

In May 1929 Palestinian youths hurled rocks on Jewish worshippers at the Western Wall, beat up the beadle, and disturbed Friday night services by conducting a loud Sufi ceremony in al-Haram al-Sharif, on the other side of the wall. On 15 August 1929, on the fast of the Ninth of Av that commemorates the destruction of the two Jewish Temples, a large contingent of Jabotinsky's supporters arrived at the wall. They had received a permit for a demonstration, but violated its terms by making political speeches, singing the Zionist anthem "*Hatikvah*," and waving the Zionist flag. On the following day, Friday, the Muslims marked the prophet Muhammad's birthday by staging a counter-demonstration. Several Muslim worshippers descended from al-Aqsa, assaulted Jewish worshippers, and desecrated Jewish prayer books. The next day, near the Bukharian neighborhood at Jerusalem's western edge, a Jewish youth was murdered in a fight with Palestinians, and elsewhere in the city a Palestinian was murdered by a Jew. On the following Friday, 23 August, thousands of Muslims from the region showed up at al-Haram al-Sharif, many of whom were armed with knives and sticks. A preacher worked up the crowd, which then streamed into the city's streets and attacked whatever Jews they could find. They assaulted non-Zionist Haredi Jews in Meah She'arim, as well as residents of Yemin Moshe near Nablus Gate and Jews in Mamilla who were on good terms with their Arab neighbors. Jews also attacked innocent Arabs. But in other cases, members of each side protected and rescued members of the other. By the time the riots came to an end, eight Jews and five Arabs had been killed. Amram Blau, later the leader of the extreme anti-Zionist Neturei Karta Haredi faction, wrote that a family tradition says that Hajj Amin al-Hussayni ordered the rioters not to hurt members of the Blau family, permitting the rioters only to loot and damage the family's properties, including their home in the Nisan Bek compound in the Old City.[88] That compound, like other Jewish ones in the area of the Nablus Gate, was abandoned after these riots. At the time of writing, Israeli settler organizations and Israeli government offices are working to enforce Jewish property rights in these places. Eight settler families moved into houses in this area in 2010.[89] But their relations with their Palestinian neighbors are not like those that prevailed prior to the 1929 riots.

Hebron's Arabs mobilized during the 1920s in order to take part in the Muslim campaign against Jewish encroachments at the wall. During the riots of 23 August 1929, rumors reached Hebron and the surrounding villages that Jews were slaughtering Arabs on Al-Haram al-Sharif. Skirmishes took place between Jews and Arabs in the city's center. The British police commander in Hebron was new in his post and had not yet become familiar with the city. He only had three policemen at his disposal and had received no advance warning of the likelihood of disturbances. The next day, Saturday, masses of villagers flowed into Hebron and, together with Hebron Arabs, brutally attacked, massacred, and raped the city's Jews. Nevertheless, Arab families in the city saved many Jews and provided shelter to Jewish friends and neighbors. A total of 435 Jews, about half the members of the city's Jewish community, escaped harm by hiding in twenty-eight homes belonging to local Arabs.[90]

Musa Agima, a member of the Jewish community, related that "An Arab who worked for my father got us out. He put us on donkeys and took us to Jerusalem." Like other Arabs who saved Jews, this man did so because of the good relations between Agima's father and the Arabs who worked with him at the slaughterhouse he owned, which was used by both Jews and Muslims. "There was no Arab wedding that my father didn't do for them for free," Agima recalled.[91] The 1929 riots spread throughout the country, ending with 133 Jews and 116 Arabs dead; 339 Jews and 232 Arabs were injured.[92] The massacre, and the subsequent evacuation of Hebron's Jews, came as a profound trauma for the Yishuv. In 1931, Hebron's Jewish quarter was resettled by thirty-seven Sephardi families. "In general, a change for the better was evident in the attitude of the Arabs toward the returning Jews," wrote the journalist Ben-Zion Cohen, "and many of them even voiced regret and anger about the brutal massacre, or at least gave lip service to doing so."[93] But, according to Eliayhu Yehoshua Levanon, "the Jewish Yishuv in Hebron was like a battered willow branch" lacking all sense of personal and economic security and without related community services.[94] Cohen also wrote that the city lacked proper medical and educational facilities. Wealthy Jewish families were prepared to return to the city if the Zionist movement would help the Jewish community there get on its feet financially, as well as provide protection against a future massacre.[95] Ya'akov Ezra, a cheese maker, was one of those who returned to the city he so loved—in part because Arab friends of his pleaded with him to do so. He reestablished his dairy, which had been destroyed by the rioters. But when the Arab Revolt broke out in 1936 the British removed all the Jews from Hebron. Ya'akov Ezra was the only one to return afterwards, about half a year after the Revolt began. His Arab friends promised to guarantee his safety, and carried out their promise. He frequented cafés with them and shared celebrations and mourning with them. Sometimes he even walked Hebron's streets alone. But when the UN voted to partition Palestine in November 1947, his Arab friends could no longer keep him from harm, and he had to leave. Ezra died three days after Israel took control of Hebron in the 1967 war, without having had a chance to return to his city. The Jews evacuated from Hebron settled in Jerusalem, founding a synagogue of their own in Mahaneh Yehuda, where they shared memories. Only a few of them went back to visit Hebron after 1967, and those who did kept their visits short.[96] The Jews who fled Old Jerusalem's Jewish Quarter during the 1948 war also lived in its past. At the top of every letter he wrote from his new home in Jerusalem, Avraham Mordecai Weingarten inscribed the words: "From exile in Rehavia." He passed on this sense of living in exile to his daughter Esther Weingarten, but it was not felt by his granddaughter, who was born and grew up on the western side of the city.[97]

The violence in Jaffa came in a different guise. It was nationalist, not religious. It is hardly surprising that the conflict there took the form of a contention between rival peoples before it did in Jerusalem, and then in the rest of the country. The Zionist movement's Palestine Office, under the leadership of Dr Arthur Ruppin, opened in Jaffa in 1908. The city's Palestinian elite could thus closely observe Zionism's inclinations and goals. The most visible Zionists in the city were those of the socialist-nationalist Second Aliyah. The extraterritorial status enjoyed by Jewish immigrants who remained citizens of the European powers led Jaffa's Arabs to suspect them of being agents of Western colonialism and imperialism. Those who were less concerned about this aspect of the Jewish influx were nevertheless apprehensive about land being bought up by immigrants with a nationalist-Zionist ideology. In general, these two fears reinforced each other and were cited in tandem in the pages of newspapers such as *Falastin* and *al-Karmel*, both of which commenced publication in Jaffa in 1909. To impress on the Arab population the dimensions of the Zionist threat, in 1910 *al-Karmel* reprinted translations of selections of Theodor Herzl's *The Jewish State*, originally published in 1896, and of the resolutions of the First Zionist Congress, which convened in Basel the following year. As a counterweight to Jewish immigration, Arab Jaffans supported the incipient Arab nationalist movement, which first appeared outside Palestine. This was in contrast to Arabs in Jerusalem, who placed their trust in the Ottoman establishment, to which they sent waves of protests. Nor did the Jewish press remain silent. These newspapers, which adopted a patronizing view of the Arabs, were replete with preconceptions and stereotypes about the inferiority of the Arabs and their backwardness, in comparison to Jewish progress.[98]

The nationalist confrontation was accompanied by cultural and mental dichotomies. A Tel Aviv physician, Haim Hisin, wrote that none of his contemporaries "ever thought of taking a good look at the local way of life and needs. They looked on the Arabs as savages, with derision, with condescension. The first settlers felt themselves infinitely superior to the Arabs and saw themselves as bringing civilization to this backward country."[99] The Zionists who came from Russia violated local norms. "The immigrants from Russia," Mordechai Elkayam wrote, "wandered idly through Jaffa's streets and neighborhood, unfamiliar with the Arab mentality and without knowing anything about the religious customs and traditions of their new neighbors. Without meaning to, they breached conventions and sensitivities shared by both the Arabs and the local Jews." In reference to the Moroccan Jews who settled in the city in the mid-nineteenth century, he wrote:

The immigrants from the East wore the same clothes and spoke the same language, the elders with a Moroccan accent and the youngsters with a Jaffa accent. The women went out on the street modestly dressed, just like the Arab women. They wore scarves over their faces and black dresses, so that you could not tell a Jewish woman from an Arab one. Like the Arab women, the Jewish women did not go out to shop in the markets and certainly did not walk the streets. The men did the shopping and provided all the home's needs. In this way the two communities kept the peace. Relations between neighbors were thus relations of mutual respect. An Arab who saw a lout hassling a Jewish woman would reprimand and sometimes even strike him. There were exceptions to this harmony, but it was violated by the immigrants from Russia. What stood out was the sight of their women and girls walking the streets with their faces bare, dressed immodestly in a way that everyone could see. Their appearance provoked, angered, and roused the passions of the Arabs. Jaffa's Jews were also shocked. Most of them were very pious and opposed women publicly exposing parts of their bodies ... Young Jews who saw the "enthusiasm" of Arab youths and their groping of Jewish women and girls took up their cause and admonished the Arabs ... But talk generally did not work. On more than one occasion fights broke out between Jewish and Arab youths over the honor of Jewish women.[100]

This was the background to an incident on 13 March 1908, when some Arab toughs hassled a Jewish woman walking beside her husband. When the husband defended his wife, the youths beat him severely. "We decided to teach them a lesson," Avraham Krenitzi, leader of a group of Jewish socialists from Russia, wrote in his memoirs. Krenitzi had organized Jewish self-defense units back home and resolved to do so in Jaffa as well. Three days later a street fight broke out between Jewish and Arab youths, none of whom had been involved in the initial incident. While the Jewish newspapers reported that the Arabs were the first to attack, Krenitzi acknowledged that "we surprised them and with knives and clubs we beat them right and left. We broke into the store of one of them and trashed it. Nothing was left there." After that they proceeded to a large Arab café. "We were eight guys. We broke into the café, which was full of hundreds of Arabs ... The [Turkish] police also got it from us and fled." One of the Zionist attackers fatally stabbed an Arab with a dagger. "Dizengoff and Hisin, who lived in Neveh Shalom, tried to intervene and to calm us down, but it didn't work. We didn't stop until the whole place had emptied of both Arabs and police." The attackers fled into two hotels that served as centers of the labor parties that had been founded by the immigrants—the Haim Baruch hotel, headquarters of HaPo'el HaTza'ir, and the Spector Hotel, headquarters of Po'alei Tzion. In the meantime the family of the Arab who had been stabbed had called in the police, who arrived to arrest the Jews.

It was at this point that the incident took on international dimensions. In order to arrest the Jews, the police first had to receive the sanction of the Russian consul, because both the Zionists and the owners of the hotels were Russian subjects. Once the consul had given his approval, a contingent of Ottoman police, made up of Arab policemen under the command of Governor Mohammad Assaf Bey, entered the two hotels to make arrests. The Jews resisted, and fourteen were wounded in the fight with the police. Some of the assailants, Krenitzi among them, escaped and fled to the Jewish farming town of Petah Tikva. The five Jews who were arrested were identified in a lineup by young Arabs and were beaten by the policemen. The leaders of the Jewish community convened to protest against the governor's use of force. They enlisted the support of Jewish leaders from around the world who sent a protest to the Turkish capital. "With the lobbying of the JCA [Jewish Colonial Association], Dizengoff, and Shimon Rokach, the Turkish governor was dismissed, and the Russian consul was transferred elsewhere." The police commanders who led the force were transferred out of Jaffa and the five Jewish detainees were released.[101] Not every criminal attack in Jaffa, however, turned into a Jewish–Arab confrontation. Two similar incidents took place in June 1908. In one, Arab youths harassed a Jewish woman and injured her male companion, and in another a Jewish butcher was attacked in his store. But in neither case did these incidents lead to wider clashes.

Ten years later, the national battle lines were sharper and the opposition to Zionism was organized. The first Palestinian nationalist organizations appeared in Jaffa in 1918. These were the Muslim–Christian Associations, which protested against the celebration that Jerusalem's Jews had organized to mark the first anniversary of the Balfour Declaration. The Associations were founded at the initiative of officers in the British administration. Their purpose was to create a body that would articulate the positions of Palestine's Arabs against Zionism as a counterweight to the Zionist Executive, which the British administration had recognized as speaking in the name of the Jews. The Associations' members were drawn from the older and traditional Arab leadership. Young Arabs in Jaffa founded al-Muntada al-Adabi, the Literary Club. The latter's opposition to Zionism took the form of support for the Arab regime led by Faisal in Damascus. The Literary Club sought members in the high schools, sponsored athletic and musical events, promoted Arab culture, and worked to foster Arab national consciousness. The third group active in Jaffa at this time was al-Nadi al-'Arabi, the Arab Club, made up mostly of members and supporters of the Hussayni family. Yet another group was al-Kaf al-Aswad, the Black Hand (later al-Fiddaiyyah), an extremist group of young people who advocated violent resistance to the British and the Zionists. When senior figures in the British administration announced that they would implement the Balfour Declaration, this led to nationalist demonstrations being held in Jaffa in March 1920 during which an Arab mob attacked Jews and broke into their stores.[102] The disturbances in Jaffa were followed by riots in the following month in Jerusalem, though these were smaller in scope than those during the Nebi Musa celebrations. In contrast with the religious nature of the Nebi Musa incidents, in Jaffa the Arabs were motivated by nationalism.

The riots in Jaffa and Jerusalem worried Moshe Litvinsky, a manager at the Anglo-Palestine Bank in Jaffa and a native son of the city. He feared their possible consequences and, in response, published a small booklet entitled *Our Way Has Been Exposed!* He wrote in Hebrew, for the Jewish public. He was concerned that the Jews would reach the conclusion that "first, the Jews and Arabs are two opposite elements," and that, fundamentally, "they could never work together in friendship and brotherhood and, second, that the Land of Israel is the new Balkans, a volcano of flammable material." In a way typical of Zionists then, including Zionist Arab Jews in Jaffa, Litvinsky believed that the riots were caused by "a misunderstanding between us and our neighbors," as "the quiet and laboring Arab nation, which is not eager to riot for no reason ... understands very well the great benefit that the Jews bring to the country." But that understanding broke down, he said, in the face of incendiaries who told them that the Jews wanted to dispossess and conquer them. He saw no point in debating with the inciters. His goal was to transform the Jewish response so that it would not unintentionally impel Arabs to give credence to their community's demagogues. "Without in any way disavowing our nationalism ... we must quickly search for and reach a modus vivendi with our neighbors, members of our race, with whom we have come to bind our fate forever." No Jew wanted "to see the Arabs pack up their homes on their camels and leave the country," but "our utter self-isolation from them is what creates misimpressions" and, indirectly, the riots. Ending the Yishuv's segregation would be essential in order to create peaceful relations between Jews and Arabs. "Jews no longer keep themselves separate in any country and do not erect a Wall of China around themselves ... and why should such a thing be done in our land?" Letvinsky was thirty-two years old when he wrote these words. But he had not thought that way eleven years previously when he had been numbered among the founders of Ahuzat Bayit, the Jewish neighborhood that detached itself from Jaffa. Now he was touting the Arabs not only as neighbors but as racial kin and natives of the land just as he was. He looked at the problem as a native and it led him to the conclusion that the inhabitants of the country, Jews and Arabs, had to create common frameworks before utter hostility reined between them. His perspective also led him to another conclusion. "The center of gravity of our work must be in our land itself," not overseas. The Zionist movement had to cease debating sterile ideas. "Our politics need to be a practical and mundane politics, and need to be pursued natives of the country who are well-versed in its special conditions."[103] Although Letvinsky's call went unheeded, his fears proved to be well founded.

The worst riots came a year later. The date they began says much about the difference between Jaffa and the holy cities of Jerusalem and Hebron. In the latter places, disturbances broke out on dates of religious significance—on Passover or Easter, during the Nebi Musa celebrations, on the Ninth of Av. On 1 May 1921, a group of Jewish communist protestors, calling for the replacement of British rule with a Palestine Soviet, set out from Jaffa to Tel Aviv. In Tel Aviv they encountered their rivals, socialist Zionists of the Ahdut Ha'Avodah party, who sought to block the communists. The two left-wing groups clashed in the border neighborhood of Manshiyya, causing the police to intervene. The communists fled back to Jaffa, where they encountered an Arab crowd opposed to communism and which made no distinction between the pro-Soviet left and the Zionist left. In fact, the Arabs viewed Tel Aviv and Zionism as different parts of a corrupt communist monolith, as a threat that needed to be attacked. The clashes spread throughout the city. The Arab mob murdered, looted, attacked, and abused Jews. Among the attackers were Arab policemen whose ethnic-national identity was stronger than their commitment to the law and to their jobs. At the height of the disturbances, Yosef Eliyahu Shlush offered himself as a mediator between the Zionist leadership and the leaders of Jaffa's clans. When he entered the center of the city he was assaulted by an Arab from one of the surrounding villages. Luckily for Shlush, a Jaffa Arab saw the attack and shouted, "Take your hands off that man, he is a native!" In his meeting with the clan leaders, Shlush poured out his heart, berating them harshly for the murders committed by their people. "Who is guilty of all these disturbances if not those Bolsheviks of yours that you brought from Moscow?" they retorted.[104]

The number of casualties shows that the Jews and the British did not remain passive. Jews, including members of the Haganah, the Jewish militia, were among the attackers. They targeted Arab homes and stores in the border neighborhoods. A total of forty-seven Jews and forty-eight Arabs were killed, while 146 Jews and seventy-three Arabs were wounded. Several thousand Jewish inhabitants of Jaffa fled to Tel Aviv and were housed in tents until the disturbances quieted.[105] Most returned to Jaffa a short time later. But the clashes left a bitter taste for many Zionists.

The writer S. Yizhar was five years old when the riots broke out. In an autobiographical novel he portrayed Jaffa as it looked to him and his mother then, an image shaped by the fear the 1921 riots had instilled in him and his family:

What have we done to them? Why are they angry with us? Have we taken something away from them? It's hard to know anything. No one is saying anything. Just waiting and nothing is certain, nothing. Something strong, terrible and savage is stalking around free outside ... It's clear that Mummy is frightened ... Mummy never liked Jaffa anyway, ever since she arrived in July 1908 with her brother Joseph, when they landed excitedly from the boat that had brought them ashore from the ship, amidst the shouting and the crowds and the jostling and belongings plummeting down the side of the ship into the boat below, and among all those frightening big black rocks, and to the shore and even before we had managed to grasp that here we were in the land of our ancestors, and that this was our homeland ... we were already surrounded by the jostling and shouting, the stench and the filth ... already in a hurry to escape, to find a cart that would taken us while it was still daylight straight to the vineyards of Rehovot and the fresh air of its orange groves, freed from all these frightening Arabs, their crowd, their din, their filth.

Yizhar also portrayed the alienation he felt in the wake of a violent encounter between a Zionist immigrant and Arab natives on the streets of his own village of Rehovot, in the shadow of the riots of 1921:

Even though every morning it was they who filled the young settlement, the courtyards, the vineyards, and the orange groves, to leave each evening and return to their homes, out of bounds, far away, and we had no contact with them, until the morning when they come back again in crowds to the market and return to the courtyards of the houses crying their wares in Arabic Yiddish, their vegetables, their fruit, and their eggs, you had to bargain, with them firmly ... because you can't believe a word an Arab says, least of all when they swear, the only language they understand is deceit ... and one fine day they suddenly massed together and attacked the settlement in a wild screaming mob with ululating women ready to loot and plunder, a terrible, savage, uncultured, murderous mob, until finally after shots and shouts and the intervention of mediators they returned home, and the world was saved, the settlement like a little island surrounded by a sea of Arabs, or like a world of darkness around the little light.

Because who knew about the Arabs where she came from. Nobody had ever talked about them ... the Arabs were never there in any place or in any argument, in any consideration and certainly not in any songs, they simply did not exist ... because we want peace, Mummy claimed, and just to build the homeland, and what do they want from us all those desert Arabs, what have we done to them apart from bringing them medicine, enlightenment and a culture of cleanliness ... She, who was born and raised far away and has been here for twelve years, with all her heart and her dreams and all her loved ones still on the River Styr in Volhynia in the dark forests, and some ignorant Arab woman who was born and raised here and her parents and grandparents were born in this place, and the alleys of Jaffa have been the whole of her world for generations, are they really the same worth and can they really have the same rights, and can all their fear of each other somehow be transferred simply into good neighborliness with no fences?[106]

MIXED CITIES

The disturbances of 1921 did to the Jews of Jaffa and Tel Aviv what the riots of 1929 did to those of Jerusalem and Hebron. For Tziona Rabau they were "the heavy blow that caused the collapse of my naïve thinking about a life of friendship and equality and peace between Arabs and Jews."[107] The perception that this was a frontal and total confrontation between two national groups, with no compromise possible, penetrated the Zionist political consciousness and its institutions. It was against this background that the Jewish authorities sought to defend Arabs who had saved Jews in Jaffa and Jerusalem in 1921 and to prevent them from becoming the targets of vendettas. They issued documents certifying that the holder had saved Jews and that he was to be treated well and not hurt. Anyone who hurt him would be punished. The same was done with regard to Arabs who saved Jews in Jerusalem and Hebron in 1929. According to Tom Segev, in the 1920s Zionism's naïve period came to an end. The Zionists moved from viewing Palestine as a place for saving the Jewish people to seeing it as a national goal in and of itself—a place to which a good Zionist immigrated not to flee oppression elsewhere, but to fight for Jewish rights to the Jews' ancestral land.[108] At first this view was adopted by the Zionist leadership, and later it spread to the larger Jewish public. In the meantime, the populace at large, Jewish and Arab, continued to interact intimately.

3

LIFE ON THE VERGE OF THE FUTURE

A Large Problem in A Small Place

Palestine, a British statesman once said, has the size of a country and the problems of a continent.

– Arthur Koestler[1]

The Ottoman Empire's death throes were long and agonizing. Yet, as it hovered on the edge of life, its Palestinian province flourished. Although Palestine was prospering relative to previous years, it was on the margins of a declining realm. As Turkish rule waned, the empire's Arab communities waxed, those in Jerusalem and Jaffa included. Hebron remained a backwater.

The British conquest changed Palestine's political situation and that of its two major communities. Contention between the rival Jewish and Arab national movements ratcheted up, both in intensity and extent. Great Britain, an empire at the height of its power and glory, seized control of Palestine and put an end to the Turkish army's wartime predations of the local population. Furthermore, the national conflict between Jew and Arab, previously a local affair, now took on international dimensions. Each of the two communities now linked themselves to the British establishment via their political elites. In both cases, the elites were not entirely local. Young men from leading Palestinian families enlisted in the cause of the Hashemite clan of Arabia, which had become the vanguard of Arab nationalism. In 1918 the Hashemite Prince Faisal, leader of the Arab Revolt against the Ottomans, established an Arab kingdom in Damascus under British sponsorship. Arabs from Palestine filled key positions in his government. Zionism, for its part, was led by Chaim Weizmann and his colleagues who were headquartered in Europe. Both of these figures were supported by local adherents, who viewed them as their legitimate representatives. Each group had established a network of ties with the British during the Great War, and as a result both were overly optimistic that the victorious British would support their causes. High expectations were the rule—everyone, especially those in the national movements, believed that a new and better world would emerge from the horrors of the recent war. But, as always, such messianic hopes could not but lead to disappointment. The Zionists expected the British to keep, forthwith, the promise they had made in the Balfour Declaration of November 1917. The Arabs, for their part, demanded that the British rescind the Declaration and carry out their pledge to the Hashemites to incorporate Palestine into an Arab kingdom. This commitment to the Arabs had been made in an exchange of letters between July 1915 and January 1916, in return for Arab help against the Turks. As a first step, the Arabs demanded British support for Faisal's government in Damascus. They did not know that the British and French had already reached a compact—the Sykes–Picot agreement of May 1916—to divide the Levant between them. The agreement became public in 1917, after a copy was discovered by Bolshevik revolutionaries in the offices of the Russian Foreign Ministry in Moscow. In their letters to the Hashemites, the British had in fact indicated that their promises were subject to other obligations they had assumed, but the Arab leadership had not attended to this detail.

In February 1918, just three months after the Balfour Declaration, the Muslim leadership in Jerusalem expressed its concern that the Jews would take control of the city with the support of the British, who were about to carry out their commitment to the Zionists. The Palestinians took the Balfour Declaration as seriously as the Zionists did, who were now very much a presence in Jerusalem. The Zionist leadership was brimming with self-confidence, which the Palestinian elite, and the Hussaynis in particular, interpreted as arrogance and condescension.

The Zionists had high expectations of the Balfour Declaration. They pushed for the appointment of a Jewish mayor of Jerusalem and for at least half of the members of its city council to be Jews. They also demanded that invitations to the ceremony to mark the first anniversary of the British conquest be printed in Hebrew as well as in Arabic and English.[2] The expectations of one rival were the other's nightmare. On 2 November 1918, the Zionist movement held an enthusiastic celebration of the first anniversary of the Balfour Declaration in Jerusalem. Mayor Musa Kazem al-Hussayni conveyed to Jerusalem's British governor a protest petition signed by 100 leading Palestinians. The mufti, Kamel al-Hussayni, was favorably impressed by the modest goals put forth by the Zionist leadership—such as Weizmann's assurance that the Jews had no intention of establishing their own government. But that was not the reaction of his colleagues or the rest of his family.[3] The new Zionist immigrants tried to allay the Arabs' fears, but with little success. One reason for this failure was the sense of superiority and the insensitivity that the Zionists projected. Custom demanded that official visitors, as the members of the Zionist delegation were, call on the mayor. Elyashar managed to persuade Musa Kazem al-Hussayni to set aside protocol and pay a visit to Menachem Ussishkin, head of the Zionist Commission and the second most important figure in the Zionist movement after Weizmann. Ussishkin kept the two Arabs waiting in the corridor until they gave up and left in anger and frustration.[4] According to Gad Frumkin, Ussishkin's manner with the Arabs "was like the attitude of some gentile nations toward the Jews." Judge Frumkin and Yosef Eliahu Shlush were both appalled. "As far as the Zionist Commission was concerned," Frumkin wrote, "there was no Arab problem at all." Dr David Eder, the chairman of the Commission's Political Committee, Frumkin maintained, "saw his department's main job as smoothing out relations between the Commission and the British government."[5]

Following the disturbances of 1929, Shlush, who had worked to purchase land from Arabs for the establishment of Tel Aviv and who had come to speak in Zionist terms, nevertheless wrote indignantly: "We will state here the bitter and horrible truth, but the truth, that our managers and many of the builders of the Yishuv who came from the Diaspora to direct us did not in any way appreciate the great value of neighborly relations, of this fundamental and simple rule. Perhaps they did not understand or did not want to understand it, and in not considering this question they are much to blame for how the issue has gone so badly." In his view, the apathy, alienation, and disregard that the Zionists evinced toward the country's Arabs contributed to the failure to persuade them that Zionism would be good for them as well as the Jews. "I very much hope," Shlush wrote in 1931, "that the episodes in my book ... about the real and warm attitude of our Muslim neighbors will impel people to take up the question of our relations with our neighbors in a different way."[6]

Haim Arlosoroff, who succeeded Ussishkin as head of the Political Department, did not live up to Shlush's hopes. A breach opened with Jerusalem's mayor, Raghib Nashashibi, when the latter visited Arlosoroff's office to discuss conflicts between the Jews and Arabs in the municipality. Arlosoroff wrote in his diary: "His opinion is that were we to cease, finally, to think about Jews and Arabs, and we could start thinking about Palestinians [both Jews and Arabs], then he would not oppose having a Jew appointed mayor. Then perhaps an Arab could be a district governor, a Jew or Arab to be police chief, etc. His refrain is 'Palestinians,' not Jews or Arabs." Nashashibi was proposing to think in local categories and to count the Jews among the country's inhabitants. Arlosoroff, for his part, thought in ethnic and majority-minority terms. In his words, "We Jews perhaps should not want to create a precedent of majority rule, even though we are the majority in Jerusalem. We could support having two mayors, Jewish and Arab."[7]

Great Britain found itself caught between contradictory promises to its two local clients; its attempts to satisfy both the Jews and the Arabs were not successful. By favoring one and then the other side, it disappointed both. The Arabs in particular felt that Britain had misled them. Both sides sought to tip British favor in its direction, acting unilaterally to further its own interests. But the rivals were not equal in strength. The Zionists enjoyed much higher standing. For religious, cultural, and political reasons, senior British officials were openly sympathetic with regard to Zionism's strategic aims. Many of them viewed the Jews as agents of the enlightened West, assigned by God and history to bring culture to the Orient. That was also the way Weizmann and his Zionist colleagues saw it. Other top British officials believed that the Jews wielded huge influence in Berlin, Paris, and Washington, and that they were thus an asset to the British Empire. But the Arabs held the demographic lead in Palestine as a whole. They owned much more land than the Zionists, but they had a difficult time translating these advantages into political gains on the international stage. They were certainly unable to do so in the years immediately after World

War I. Over the course of the British Mandate, support for the Arab national cause from Arabs outside Palestine and the Muslims in India put pressure on Britain to tilt toward the Arab side in Palestine. But this was hardly sufficient for Britain to abrogate the Balfour Declaration explicitly.

Given these circumstances, it is not surprising that the conflict developed in the way that it did. The accelerating bloodiness of the Jewish–Arab conflict might well have been avoided had the British resolved in 1918–19 to establish an Arab kingdom under Faisal in Palestine. The Hashemite leader would have been compensated for the loss of his Damascus-based kingdom after the British ceded Syria and Lebanon to the French sphere of influence under the Sykes–Picot agreement. The British could have established an Arab kingdom instead of a Jewish national home, while providing the Jews with autonomy in Palestine. The Faisal–Weizmann agreement of 1919 recognized the Zionist right to settle the land and even included a provision stipulating that the Arab kingdom would "encourage and stimulate immigration of Jews into Palestine on a large scale, and as quickly as possible to settle Jewish immigrants upon the land ..." Clearly, such a Jewish autonomous entity could have grown into an independent state. In that accord, Faisal promised to recognize the Jewish nation, on condition that the Zionists help him obtain independence from Britain. Had the British endorsed this approach, the Jews would have placed their hopes less in Britain and in their own independent strength, and invested more effort in fostering good relations with the Arab majority and its political leadership.[8]

Britain later had a second chance. In 1921, Winston Churchill, then colonial secretary, awarded the part of Palestine to the east of the Jordan River to 'Abdallah, Faisal's brother. Rather than carving out this entity, Transjordan, from the territory of the Mandate, Britain could have offered 'Abdallah or Faisal an emirate of Palestine and Jordan, conditioned on them accepting provisions for Jewish autonomy. In both of these scenarios, Arab–Jewish identity could have played a key role in shaping Jewish–Arab relations. In choosing a different path, the British hampered Arab–Jewish identity with the burden of national conflict. As the conflict escalated, that identity eroded. A phenomenon that could have shaped the new society gave way to separate national-ethnic identities. During the Mandate period, the Palestinian Arabs were less successful than the Zionists in constructing modern political institutions, in consolidating their society as a step toward constructing a national entity. They were even less successful at gaining the support of foreign powers and building a fighting force that could stand against the Zionist militias. These fundamental differences pertain to this day.

Britain looked at Palestine from an imperial and patronizing viewpoint. The preconceptions that Mandate officials brought with them consisted of a mixture of attraction and revulsion toward both Arabs and Jews. This orientalist attitude led British officials to like the new Zionist Jew, and to admire the Jewish intellect that they saw in the religious Jews of the old, pre-Zionist Yishuv. But they also respected the dignity of Arab notables. At the same time, they were contemptuous of the non-productive Orthodox way of life of the Old Yishuv, and disliked the conceit reflected in the endless list of demands that the Zionists made of them. Jewish nationalists were never satisfied and always demanded more. But the British were no less disdainful of Arab inaction and fatalism. "There is a tendency among the British, and perhaps even more among continental Europeans, to regard the Arabs as a primitive people with, so far as Palestine in concerned, a cardinal grievance," wrote Richard Graves, a senior Mandate official and acting mayor of Jerusalem in 1947–8.[9]

Storrs described Jerusalem as a city with a tendency to become obsessed with the overpowering charm of a small and petty politics confined to two or three streets, yet girdling the globe and sparking the imagination. Jerusalem's scores of sects were constantly conniving alliances and betrayals, mixing piety with corruption, clad in variegated robes and festooned caps. Chaim Weizmann, who never hid his fondness for Britain, put it bluntly. Jerusalem, he said, was an accursed city that offered nothing, no creature comforts, only filth, unsightliness, and beggars.[10] Jerusalem was dismal, Storrs said, a city "where in times of anxiety the sudden clatter on stones of any empty petrol tin will produce a panic."[11] Storrs and Weizmann could both agree with the appraisal, in A.B. Yehoshua's novel *Mr. Mani*, reported by a British soldier to his newly arrived commander: "The population is extremely mixed, a hodgepodge of small, unsociable communities that are as indigent and ignorant as they are endowed with a messianic sense of superiority. As usual, there seems to be no relationship between the reputation of the place, which it owes to the great books written in and about it, and the sordid reality."[12]

LIFE ON THE VERGE OF THE FUTURE

The British administration in Palestine looked down on its two squabbling clients and tried its best to maneuver between the constraints and pressures that each exerted on it. Storrs commented that for "95 percent of my friends in Egypt and Palestine (as in England), the Balfour Declaration, though announcing the only Victory gained by a single people on the World Front, passed without notice; whilst the few who marked it imagined the extent and method of its application would be laid down when the ultimate fate of Palestine ... had been decided."[13] But due to the pressures exerted by the Jews and Arabs, the Balfour Declaration could not be disregarded or played down. Each side itemized its demands and submitted its expenses to the British government. In 1917 Storrs located his headquarters in the Fast Hotel. The Arabs demanded that the hotel be renamed the Sultan Suleiman, after the Ottoman sovereign who had built the city wall. The Jews demanded that it be renamed the King Solomon Hotel. The Zionists demanded that Jerusalem's Arab mayor employ Jewish workers in the paving of the city's streets, even though these workers required higher wages than Arab laborers. The Jews won recognition of Hebrew as an official language and printed maps that gave Hebrew names to Arab towns and cities. The Arabs took this to mean that the Jews were seeking to wipe them out.[14] "It was in fact a small place. A large problem in a small place," asserted Lord Martin Charteris, chief of British military intelligence in 1945–6.[15]

When the two ethnic groups plunged into violent conflict in 1936, the British reached the conclusion that the country had to be divided between them. But when the Mandate began, the British had hoped to erect common frameworks, for example government offices in which Jews and Arabs worked together. In this they succeeded. In the public works department that Graves headed, "the task was not a difficult one." There was an atmosphere of solidarity in the office and the families of the Jewish and Arab employees became friendly.[16] On the municipal level, the British hoped to construct a common political umbrella for the two autonomous communities. They divided Jerusalem into twelve constituencies, each of which had a clear ethnic majority—six Jewish, four Muslim, and two Christian. Each constituency elected an equal number of representatives to the city council. The two Christian and four Muslim constituencies created an artificial parity on the council, even though the Jews were a majority of the population—700,000 Jews versus 40,000 Arabs.[17] The British thus established the trappings of an egalitarian city, while they continued to award the mayor's chair to an Arab, as the Ottomans had done before them. The Jews griped that the system discriminated against them, and demanded a Jewish mayor. The demand was rejected. Instead, the British decided that the Jewish deputy mayor would be the senior of the two deputies (there was a Christian one as well). The mayor was also required to give special consideration to his Jewish deputy in matters relating to the Jewish community. Political alliances in the city council crossed ethnic boundaries when Jews and some Arabs shared the joint interest of countering the Hussayni family's dominance. While such cooperation for negative reasons is common in politics it differs from cooperation in everyday life, which is more often based on the positive motivation of mutual assistance and cooperation. In the case of Jerusalem, political cooperation went hand-in-hand with and supplemented contacts between Jews and Arabs in other areas of life.

The rivalry between the Arab aspirants to the mayor's post was fierce. On one side stood the Hussayni clan and on the other the allied Nashashibi and Khalidi families. Under Ottoman rule the Jewish vote had been unorganized, and in any case the Jews were not key players in Jerusalem politics. This changed when the British came. The Jews' ties to the new regime, Zionist organizational acumen, and the escalation of the nationalist struggle conferred on the Jews the balance of power in determining who would be the city's top official. In 1920 the Jews demanded the ejection of Musa Kazem al-Hussayni from the mayoralty because he had been one of the leading inciters of the mob that had attacked Jewish lives and property during the Nebi Musa celebrations. The British had appointed him upon establishing their rule in the city. He was replaced with Raghib al-Nashashibi. Nashashibi ran for a second seven-year term in 1927, facing off against 'Arif al-Dajani, who was supported by the Hussaynis. Just before the elections, the mufti offered the Jews a deal—if Dajani were elected with the help of the Jewish vote, the municipality would award jobs to the Jews in accordance with their share of the city's population, and municipal taxes paid by Jews would be allocated to the Jewish neighborhoods. These were the Jews' most central demands. In other words, the contest between the Hussaynis and Nashashibis was so intense that the mufti was prepared to grant the Jews much of what they wanted. The fiercely fought nature of the conflict prompted a huge turnout—88 percent of the eligible Jews voted, as did 85 percent of the Muslims and

75 percent of the Christians. In the end, the Jews supported Nashashibi in order to keep the Hussaynis out.[18]

In 1930 the Jewish members of the city council submitted their resignations and boycotted meetings because the mayor refused to award contracts to Jewish contractors and laborers in keeping with the Jews' proportion of the population. The British refused to support the Jewish demand, ruling that contracts were to be given to the lowest bidders, even if this meant that Arab contractors would win most of the tenders. After several months, the Jews withdrew their resignations.[19] Prior to the elections of 1934 the Khalidi clan transferred its support to the Hussaynis, in exchange for which the Hussaynis supported the mayoral candidacy of Husayn Fakhri al-Khalidi. The Jews suspended their support for Nashashibi, declaring neutrality, which led to his defeat. It was not that the Jews had any love for the Hussaynis, but they were fed up with Nashashibi's corruption and nationalist politics, and impressed by Khalidi's promise to act in the interests of all the city's inhabitants, without favoritism. But the promise was not carried out. The Jews felt they had been deceived, as well as being discriminated against despite being a majority in the city. Khalidi stripped his Jewish deputy, Daniel Auster (who would later serve as mayor under Israeli rule, from 1948 to 1951) of all his powers. And of the five municipal department directors under the new mayor, two were Arabs, two were British, and only one was Jewish. Only 28 percent of the municipality's employees were Jews. When city council votes, pitting Jews against Arabs, were tied, Mayor Khalidi, empowered to break the tie, voted with the Arabs. The Jewish council members demanded that the minutes of council meetings be issued in Hebrew as well as in Arabic (at that time, Jewish members who did not read Arabic received summaries in Hebrew, but only some time after the meetings). They demanded that council decisions and the municipal accounts be published in Hebrew as well, and that official letters to the city's Jewish residents and building permits granted to Jews be issued in Hebrew.[20] For these reasons, in addition to Khalidi's activity in the Palestinian national movement on the eve of the Arab Revolt of 1936, the Jews boycotted council meetings, preventing a quorum, so that no decisions could pass. The elected city government continued to operate in this hobbled fashion until 1944, when the British dissolved it and appointed a board to run the city.

Outside the city council, the Jews worked to help the anti-Hussayni opposition organize politically. In 1930 they approached the Darwish family of Maliha, the al-Khatib family of 'Ein Karem, the Abu-Ghosh family from Qaryat al-'Anab, and the al-'Az family of Bayt Jubrin in an attempt to establish a village front to stand against the Hussayni urban leadership, but the mufti sabotaged the effort.[21]

Outside the political arena, Jewish and Arab relations ranged between cooperation and ferocious rivalry. One example was a project promoted by Avraham Kantrowitz, a construction engineer who, in Jerusalem in the mid-1920s, sought "to found a company for developing the country and to establish mixed Jewish and Arab cities and villages." His plan was that "the Arabs would transfer all their land to the company in exchange for 20-year promissory notes, after which period the company would pay them the full value. On this land the company would build mixed cities and villages without any discrimination between Jews and Arabs." This might seem like the utopian dream of a naïve man, but that was not at all the case. "[Regarding] every citizen of these two communities able to purchase a home or plot of land and who pays its price, the company would be required to carry out the transaction without consideration of whether the majority of buyers were Jewish or Arabs (I knew in advance that the great majority of purchasers would be Jews, not Arabs)." In other words, Kantrowitz's project was not really egalitarian and binational. He ensured a Jewish majority in another way as well. "The company had to be composed of Jews and Arabs without consideration of the numbers of Jews and Arabs. But of course the price of a basic share and the initiative to dispense them would depend on the number of purchasers of these shares (I knew in advance that the greater number of share purchasers would be Jews and not Arabs). These estimates of mine were confirmed, as a majority of the shareholders in the company that was established were Jews, and most of those who leaped to buy land or a finished house from the company were Jews." But Kantrowitz's painstaking plan encountered a difficulty that he had not anticipated. "I founded the company and called it Binyan HaYishuv [Building the Yishuv]. The company's charter was published in the official gazette (the gazette is located in my private archive). But the company did not last. One of the Jewish members I brought in as one of the founders, R. Yosef Rivlin, who had come then from the United States, and was one of those daring and irresponsible speculators ... and as a result of this it went bankrupt." Kantrowitz succeeded in his manipulation of the Arabs, but fell victim himself to Jewish manipulation. "When the company was founded I set its policy, but after R. Yosef Rivlin brought his supporters into the company influence passed from me to him and, lacking influence over the running of the company I had no choice but to leave, and when left so did my brother Daniel and all the Arab members. I was extremely sorry that I was unable to bring to fruition the sublime idea because people I brought into the company erected obstacles to carrying out this important task." Still enthusiastic, Kantrowitz did not consider giving up. He made another attempt, proposing the establishment of a new firm with the same program. "The idea did not leave my mind and I thought of it day and night. At the time I revealed the idea to my brother Elazar, who was enthusiastic ... and composed pamphlets about the redemption that would come if my idea were to be carried out." But the Arab leadership was opposed and the Mandate administration refused to sanction the new company. "In his pamphlets he revealed the deep secret I revealed to him—that the intention of the idea was for the good of the Jews and not the good of the Arabs, and of course against British rule in the country ... Pamphlets that reached the hands of the authorities and the Arabs as well put an end to this important project. The founding meeting, to which I invited effendis and Arab notables and Jews, did not take place because both the authorities and Mufti Hajj Amin al-Hussayni warned the Arabs not to be taken in by the Jewish plot to steal Arab lands."[22] Kantrowitz did not blame the Arabs who joined his initiative for its failure. On the contrary, they remained loyal to him and left the company when he fell out with Rivlin.

Conflict as Routine

Both the religious–nationalist type of conflict that shaped Jerusalem and the national one that shaped Jaffa spread throughout the country in the 1930s. The Arabs protested against Zionist land purchases and immigrants, whose numbers grew significantly during this decade. They also opposed the ongoing British commitment to the establishment of a Jewish national home. Jerusalem and Jaffa were in the vanguard of the Palestinian Arab struggle in both these areas. In 1931 the mufti succeeded where he had failed in 1922—he convened an all-Islamic conference, for the protection of Islamic holy sites from the Zionists, attended by representatives of twenty-two countries. Under Hajj Amin al-Hussayni's leadership, a religious–nationalist militia grew up during this decade in the Jerusalem–Hebron region, Holy War (al-Jihad al-Muqaddas). It trained young men to fight the Jews and British.[23] The members of Holy War took part in the Revolt of 1936–9 and the war of 1948.

Not every mass protest turned into a riot and anti-Jewish violence. In October 1933, the Palestinian Executive Committee organized a demonstration and rally against Britain and Zionism in Jerusalem. According to the police, some 3,000 people participated; the organizers claimed 10,000. The permit confined the protesters to marching in the Old City and in the area of Nablus Gate, but they continued toward Allenby Square and Mamilla. The police dispersed them by force near the New Gate. Despite the heat of the conflict, the Palestinian leadership showed itself able to prevent the crowd from entering mixed and Jewish neighborhoods.[24]

It was no coincidence that the event that set off the Arab Revolt of 1936 took place in Jaffa. Jaffa and Tel Aviv were the most important cities for their respective national movements. True, the movements' national symbols and the places that provided them with legitimacy lay elsewhere—in Jerusalem for both Jews and Arabs, and for the Zionists in the kibbutzim they founded. But Jaffa and Tel Aviv were the largest population centers and the headquarters of political parties, communal institutions, and newspaper offices. Jaffa, aside from being the most important Arab city in Palestine, was the point of entry for Jewish immigrants. Jews fleeing Europe in response to the rise of anti-Semitism and Nazism then settled in neighboring Tel Aviv. The mixing of Arab and Jewish populations, which had given rise to Arab–Jewish identity, became a breeding ground for severe ethnic violence that created further mutual hostility. Tel Aviv developed thanks to the capital and urban-commercial culture that the immigrants brought with them. During these years the Zionist movement purchased larger tracts of better-quality land than they had in the past. The sellers included many of Jaffa's Palestinian elite. A full 17.7 percent of the land that Jews purchased from Palestinians during the first half of the 1930s was in the Jaffa area. This came up for public discussion at a gathering in Jaffa in March 1933, where the leaders of the Nashashibi camp were accused by the Hussayni party and others of selling land to Jews.[25] But the pursuit of personal financial gain over the communal interest and national ideology was not the only detriment to the Palestinian Arab struggle. The Arabs suffered from political discord as well, their community divided into parties based on the blood and family connections of the traditional elite and its loyalists. Such clan (*hamula*) divisions were the major source of the rivalry between the Hussayni faction and its opponents, as well as within the anti-Hussayni opposition. This traditional, now divided leadership was challenged by a younger generation that became politically active in the 1930s, and by extremist religious groups with power bases in rural areas and working-class neighborhoods on the edges of the large coastal cities. These young people, like the radical Islamic organizations, were more extreme than the traditional leadership of which they were so critical.[26] The success of Zionism, due in no small measure to British policy, along with the increasing extremism of Palestinian politics, changed the face of the conflict during the 1930s.

The conflict did not, however, penetrate the Mandate administration's police force. The British employed some 2,000 Jewish and 2,000 Arab policemen. They worked together, although in Jaffa and Jerusalem commanders often preferred to send Jewish or Arab teams into certain neighborhoods. At the beginning of the 1940s, police headquarters in Jerusalem would send the Jewish policeman Habib Can'an into Hebron every six months to test the Arab policemen there in spoken Hebrew—this despite the fact that, at the time, Hebron was home to only one Jewish inhabitant, and that man was an Arab Jew.[27]

In April 1936 Arab longshoremen discovered a Jewish arms shipment. That same month, following a clash between an Arab militia and the Jewish IZL (a nationalist underground force, later to be headed by Menachem Begin, known also as Etzel, the Irgun, or the National Military Organization), a rumor spread that Arabs were being killed in Tel Aviv. An Arab mob from Jaffa attacked Jews, killing nine and wounding ten. News of the clash spread rapidly through the country. The Arabs in Jaffa declared a general strike that was quickly taken up in other Arab areas. The strike crippled Jaffa's port but did not paralyze Tel Aviv, which had a population of 130,000 Jews; Jaffa, in contrast, had a total population of 70,000, of which one-seventh were Jews. Jewish farms were able to provide most of the food consumed by the Yishuv, and Tel Aviv responded to the strike by building its own port.[28] The Arab general strike lasted for 175 days, beginning in mid-April. Arab oversight committees enforced a boycott, preventing Arabs from entering Jewish commercial establishments and leisure centers, as well as forbidding the use of Jewish public transportation.

The Revolt lasted until 1939, and its outcome was a portent of what was to come in 1948. Hebron was cleared of Jews, while Jaffa suffered heavy physical and economic damage. In response to the disturbances of 1936, David Ben-Gurion wrote in his diary: "The destruction of Jaffa, the city and the port, will happen and it will be for the best. This city which grew fat on Jewish immigration and settlement is asking for destruction when it swings a hatchet over the heads of its builders and benefactors. When Jaffa falls into hell I will not be among the mourners."[29] Jaffa's destruction was commenced by the British. Arab attacks originating in Jaffa during the Revolt were aimed also at British government offices and military personnel. The attackers took refuge in the city's kasbah. In response, the British army took control of that area in a massive action in which they plowed new roads through the quarter's alleys, breaking from one house into another through their common walls. According to the British the action destroyed 300 houses, while the Arabs put the number at 800.[30] The same tactics were used by IZL in 1948 in its conquest of the Manshiyya neighborhood in April 1948.

The years from 1936 through 1948 were the formative ones for an entire Jewish generation. The poets Natan Alterman and Haim Guri served as the war generation's voices. Guri had been born in Tel Aviv. He was thirteen when the Revolt broke out and twenty-five when he served in the Palmach during the 1948 war. "And I already lived on rumor and fear was already in the air" when the disturbances of 1929 broke out. In 1936, he

> sensed the other who was suddenly an enemy ... I had been accustomed, after all, since childhood, to see the Arabs, the bell-ringing camel trains each day passing the shacks in the Nordiya neighborhood, proceeding south on HaCarmel Street on their way to Jaffa. So I already knew that something bad had happened. Afterward, a period of integrated neighborliness, without shouts, without daggers, returned for a time. I would walk with my friends to Jaffa on Saturdays, to the Basa field, to sneak in to watch soccer games. I also remember the Purim holiday, the carnival procession on Allenby Street and the cheering crowd, when *keffiyah* and tarbush-clad men were also among the spectators ... When we were young we would go to Manshiyya, seeking the aroma of the kebab grilled on coals, mixed with the scent of fish and oranges ... until a bloody day came in Jaffa on April 19, 1936, with its eighteen [*sic*] Jews killed. ... Now, in my twilight years, a feeling continues to dwell within me that history is repeating itself, that the east is far from tranquility, that they do not want us! And what has been, will be.[31]

LIFE ON THE VERGE OF THE FUTURE

Guri comprehends Jaffa, and its Arabs, via his senses. It does not appear in his consciousness and his memory as an advanced Western city. The Arabs are represented by camel caravans, as desert nomads, not as the builders of a modern city. Furthermore, he sees Jaffa as two-faced. It offers popular leisure activities—soccer games and roasted meat and fish, patronized by Jews and Arabs alike. At the same time, Jaffa is murderous, rejecting the Jews and not wanting to share its culture with them. The continuity he sees between the Revolt of 1936 and the present day testifies to the impact of the Revolt and of the 1948 war. In a similar way, the disturbances of 1921 made their imprint on S. Yizhar. He also saw Jaffa's Arabs as devoid of culture, primitive, violent, as deceitful attackers of the sons of light. But Yizhar differs from Guri in that his Zionist identity is complex; for Guri, the Palestinians, not his own identity, are problematic. But the difference between the two is not only personal. It has to do with the escalation of the conflict. Yizhar's ambivalence reflects the state of the conflict in 1921. By 1936 the conflict was much more severe, as seen in Guri's passage.

The escalation swept up Sakakini as well. In 1915 he had identified himself as a universalist, and in 1920 he had expressed his dismay at religious–national madness. But in 1936, when Palestinians attacked Jews emerging from the Edison cinema in Jerusalem, Sakakini saw it as an act of heroism expressing the spirit of his nation. The next day he filed an application for a gun license on the grounds that he needed a weapon to defend himself against Jews who attacked Arabs under government protection.[32]

During the disturbances of 1929, homes in the isolated Jewish neighborhood of Talpiot in Jerusalem were attacked and its inhabitants fled to the center of the city. Some of the houses were looted and destroyed. Life returned to normal a short time after the riots, and Jewish children from Talpiot once more walked over to the German Colony and Baq'a, and crossed these Arab neighborhoods on the way to the movie houses downtown. Adults soon did so as well. But in the 1930s Jewish stores near Jaffa Gate closed down one by one. The Arabs boycotted them during the Revolt. Jews stopped visiting Arab friends in their homes—it seemed too risky. In the 1940s, Tawfiq Can'an's family stopped buying clothes at Klein's shop on Zion Square. They also stopped traveling on Jewish buses because each passenger was charged a penny more as a contribution to the Haganah and two pennies as a contribution to other Jewish organizations.[33] At the beginning of the 1948 war Can'an left his home in Musrara and his extensive library was sent to the National Library in Jerusalem.

During the period from the beginning of the Revolt to the end of the 1948 war (with the exception of the World War II years, which were quiet), each side committed acts of terror against the other. The mixing of the two populations helped the terrorists. Arab transportation to the villages surrounding Tel Aviv went through the Jewish city. Jaffa, for its part, was surrounded by Jewish settlements—Tel Aviv to the north, Holon and Bat Yam to the south, the Hatikva neighborhood and Mikveh Yisrael to the east. The main road to Jerusalem passed through the Arab village of Yazur, and there were another four villages adjacent to Jaffa in which 40,000 Arabs lived. Migration from the country's interior swelled the port city's outer neighborhoods, which at that time bordered Jewish areas. These outer neighborhoods were inhabited by poor, low-wage, working-class Muslims of rural origin, who now lived at the edge of a cosmopolitan metropolitan center. Their worldview and ways of life were more conservative than those of Jaffa's original inhabitants. Their relations with the city's Christian elite were tense.[34]

Clashes between Jews and Arabs occurred largely in these peripheral neighborhoods and along the roads, the victims generally being people who crossed the lines for work or pleasure. In Jerusalem, murders of Jews from the Jewish Quarter who walked by the Muslim Quarter on their way to the new city prompted them to take the buses run by the Egged cooperative. The bus line to the Jewish Quarter left from Nahalat Shiva, not far from Jaffa Gate, passing through the Armenian Quarter to the Jewish Quarter.[35] Sometimes attacks were committed beyond the seam between the two populations. The residents of Shlomo HaMelekh and Kakal Streets in north Tel Aviv petitioned the municipality to raze a citrus grove from which Arabs had shot at Jews[36] emerging from the Edison cinema, which was distant from any neighborhood, on 16 May 1936, killing three and wounding two. Members of the three Jewish underground militias, the Haganah, IZL, and LEHI, attacked Arabs in Jaffa and Jerusalem. Between April and October 1936 around eighty Jews were killed and some 400 wounded throughout Palestine.[37]

The escalation of the conflict honed collective national identities, which were gradually adopted even by those who had not previously toed the hegemonic national line. "Even in the maddest hours, when personal contact was very difficult, there were Arabs who conversed with me and spoke openly. But later came times in which I refrained from getting into detailed conversations with our neighbors because I did not know what was going on in the hidden recesses of our inner circles, and I could not always defend their position," Justice Frumkin wrote.[38] Arab judges and lawyers were critical of the positions of their leaders, but Frumkin did not take that attitude toward the Jewish leadership. He did not agree with it but found himself emotionally incapable of speaking frankly with his Arab colleagues. He feared that his criticisms might be unjustified due to his lack of knowledge of the tacit assumptions behind the Zionist leadership's positions. While he did not follow his leaders blindly, neither did he feel that he had the right to criticize them to his Arab friends in the legal profession.

Nevertheless, segregation between Jews and Arabs was not absolute until the 1948 war. Jews returned to Jaffa after the suppression of the Arab Revolt. Beginning in 1936, the area of Tel Aviv along the beach, along with Allenby and HaYarkon Streets, developed as a zone of entertainment and leisure, an alternative to Jaffa. Cinemas, brothels, bars, and card parlors opened there. The process accelerated during World War II, when some 2 million British soldiers visited Tel Aviv. Yet, at the same time, Arab-style cafés, owned by Jews or by Jewish and Arab partners, thrived on the Tel Aviv–Jaffa border, in the Hatikva and Manshiyya neighborhoods. These establishments offered Jews, both Ashkenazi and Sephardi, as well as tourists, an oriental-style way to pass the time.

Following the lull brought on by World War II, the conflict returned to the path set in 1936. It was felt in particular in the border areas—Manshiyya and Salameh, on the Jaffa–Tel Aviv border; and in Mamilla, Talbiyyeh, Qatamon, and Musrara in Jerusalem. Armed British policemen and soldiers patrolled these areas, conducting identity checks and setting up roadblocks. But the British were not the only ones checking identity cards—the Jewish militias did so as well. When one of them learned from Layla Mantura's papers that she was an Arab, they humiliated her.[39] A group of youths from Jaffa unilaterally voided an unwritten agreement between them and a group of Jewish youths regarding the times when each group used a soccer pitch in the border area. The arrangement had been that the Arabs played there on Fridays and Jews on Saturdays. But when the conflict entered its final escalation in 1947, the Arabs prevented Jews from playing there, seeing the time-sharing agreement regarding the pitch as tantamount to consenting to the partition of Palestine between the two peoples. They took this step after one of their teachers told them: "The land is our land and no one else's."[40] In contrast, the Jewish and Arab members of the joint Tel Aviv–Jaffa Rotary Club continued to meet every Thursday afternoon, at a restaurant in Salameh, throughout 1947.[41]

The UN decision in November 1947 to partition Palestine into a Jewish and an Arab state set off a civil war. The very next day an Arab mob assailed the Mamilla commercial area, torching Jewish stores. By the beginning of December 1947, Arab snipers in Qatamon were firing on Rehavia, with Jewish snipers returning the fire. Haganah militiamen stationed in Tel Aviv shot at Arabs in Jaffa and IZL agents detonated a barrel full of explosives downtown. In January 1948, LEHI operatives blew up a booby-trapped truck in Clock Square. Jewish terrorists dealt a severe blow to the resilience of Arab civilians, and were a major factor in causing the collapse of Arab society in the city.[42] Jerusalem was also hit by terror. IZL men threw bombs inside Jaffa and Nablus Gates in December 1947; Arab snipers shot from the Old City walls at the Jewish neighborhood of Yemin Moshe, militants set off truck bombs on Ben-Yehuda Street in February 1948, and a month later another one in the courtyard of the Zionist institution buildings. The result was deepening animosity, suspicion, and fear. "Jerusalem is a difficult city to live in," Tzipora Porat wrote on 22 February 1948 to her family in the United States. "The Jewish sections are not exclusively Jewish, nor the Arab sections entirely Arab, nor the British zones strictly British. The hardest part is getting about from one section to another."[43]

The web of Jewish–Arab life unraveled not only as a matter of consciousness and identity—the very physical fabric of the cities also came apart. At the end of January 1947, the British established security zones in the mixed cities. These were surrounded by barbed-wire fences and their Jewish residents were ejected. Arabs residents were allowed to remain and those who did not needed permits to cross the security zones to get to their own neighborhoods without having to go through Jewish ones. The security zones in Jerusalem were situated around the British governing center on Princess Mary Street, the King David Hotel, the train station, the residence of the high commissioner, and around the areas in which British personnel lived—Qatamon, the Greek Colony, the German Colony, and Talbiyyeh. These areas were fenced off and their residents were issued entry and exit permits.[44]

LIFE ON THE VERGE OF THE FUTURE

The situation worsened in December 1947. The employees of the electric plant on Bethlehem Street in Jerusalem found it increasingly difficult to maintain their work routine. The few Jews who still worked there were brought in on a special transport through the British security zones. Within the plant, Jews and Arabs remained on good terms. The plant had commenced operation in 1930 and in its early years only Jews worked there as engineers and in management. But in time Arabs were also hired for these positions. During the Arab Revolt the Arab employees protected their Jewish colleagues when work had to be done in Arab neighborhoods. This partnership continued between December 1947 and April 1948. Jews and Arabs did guard duty together on the plant's roof, armed with hunting rifles. The Jewish employees never needed the arms smuggled in for them by the Haganah. But on 9 April they stopped reporting for work and stayed away until Jewish forces captured the plant a few weeks later.[45]

Following the UN partition resolution, Dr Kramer tried to persuade the Karmi family, his neighbors in Qatamon, to leave Jerusalem because of the danger. The Kramers themselves moved out of the neighborhood a few days later. Four months went by before the Karmis were finally convinced to leave, in April 1948.[46] The same thing happened in many other places. As violence grew, Jews left Qatamon and Baq'a, where they were a minority, and Arabs evacuated the Jewish neighborhoods of Makor Barukh and Romema. Jewish merchants and residents abandoned the cafés they ran and patronized on the edge of Jaffa and moved their businesses and patronage north into Tel Aviv.

The population adopted a mindset of total conflict, vigilant in the face of danger and seeking revenge. Jamil Toubbeh, the son of the *mukhtar* of Qatamon, was seventeen years old during the critical year of 1947, preparing to graduate from the Terra Sancta College high school at the edge of Talbiyyeh, on the border with Jewish Rehavia. One day at the end of 1947 he went through Jaffa Gate wearing khaki shorts—the informal uniform of Jewish pioneers. Arab passersby suspected him of being a Zionist and were about to lynch him when he was saved by a friend of his father's, who recognized him. From then on Jamil made a point of wearing a *khafiyyeh* when he entered Arab areas and a beret when he went into Jewish ones. He stopped wearing his khaki shorts. "Moving back and forth from predominantly Arab to predominantly Jewish sectors of Jerusalem, where a number of schools were located, became a game of Russian Roulette," Toubbeh wrote.[47]

His best friend was David, a blonde, blue-eyed Jewish youth from a family that had arrived from Germany in the 1930s. Both attended Terra Sancta, and they spoke Arabic together. "David was as much Palestinian as I, and I never thought of him or his family as otherwise," Toubbeh wrote. When David told Jamil that he wanted to go to a kibbutz—apparently so as to enlist in the Palmach, the elite Jewish strike force—Jamil asked if he could come along. "If indeed he had an enemy, I argued, his enemy would be my enemy, too ... when David told me that I would not be able to share his kibbutz dream, I was deeply hurt."[48] Jamil never thought that his best friend David would undergo so profound a change. It was not just youthful romantic innocence that had a head-on collision with bitter reality. The same thing that happened to David and Jamil happened to friends of all ages and in all mixed neighborhoods.

During the war's initial months, Arab peddlers from the Bethlehem area brought to Talbiyyeh food items that could not be obtained elsewhere in the city, including eggs; the Jews still living in the neighborhood benefited.[49] Until the conflict escalated, Max Hesse was able to keep Fink's, his downtown pub and restaurant, open. Fink's, a classy Vienna-style bar, had opened in 1932. Thick curtains hid the street outside from diners and muffled its sounds. Patrons ate Austrian goulash from mugs and drank fine liquor. It was a popular meeting place for Jerusalem's elite. Thanks to his good relations with Arab merchants, Hesse was able to obtain fresh produce and dairy products during the siege of Jerusalem, when other Jewish-owned restaurants, which purchased their food from Jewish sources on the coastal plain, had to shut down. While the Jewish side of the city was suffering from shortages, the Old City marketplace offered plentiful goods from local farms and from Jericho. One of Hesse's Arab contacts secreted crates of produce next to the ruins of the Rex cinema that IZL had blown up at the beginning of December 1947, a day after the burning of the Mamilla commercial center. Fink's chef collected the crates from the stash. The arrangement lasted until March 1948, when Hesse was compelled to shut down Fink's.[50] This was the state of the city on the verge of its partition between Israel and Jordan. When the war was over, Fink's opened again, offering newly provincial Jerusalem a little spark of the cosmopolitan flavor it lost in 1948. For the German Jews who lived in Rehavia, a short walk away, Fink's was a reminder of their European homes. Foreign diplomats, honored guests, and well-heeled tourists liked the Central European ambience, the aura, and the international standards adhered to by the restaurant. It closed down only in 2006. The bloody terror attacks of the Second Intifada dealt a heavy blow to Jerusalem's downtown, and in any case the European-born generation that had patronized Fink's was slipping away. A few years later Café Atara, on nearby Ben-Yehuda Street, also shut its doors. It had been another prime meeting place for European-born Jews, the most famous downtown café remaining after the closure of the Zion Square establishments during the Mandate.

Outbreaks of violence between Jews and Arabs toward the end of that period, in particular the cases of brutal murder, were surprising. How could neighbors who lived in common turn so viciously against one another? And how were such violent and vindictive persons able to live so politely and serenely with their next victims? One might suggest that the hostilities were carried out by extremists, and that the majority on each side was passive. In this view, the majority suffered because each side's extremists could not stand each other. But the ethnic conflict in Palestine was not one between marginal groups. The broad population took part at different levels, and at certain points was swept deeper and deeper into involvement in the civil war. Sixteen-year-old Nadi Dai'is was one example. He and his family were close to their Jewish neighbors in the Old City. But three days after the adoption of the UN partition resolution he was carried away by his emotions and by the mob and took part in the burning of the Mamilla commercial center. He felt that every Jew was an enemy who sought to rob him of his land and his soul. The next day he bought a pistol. A few nights later Nadi heard gunfire near his house. He rushed to his window and shot an entire magazine of bullets into the dark. Then he heard the Jewish woman who lived next door, for whom he had turned on the light every Friday night for ten years, shouting: "Don't shoot, don't shoot! ... Are we not neighbors since many years?"[51]

At around the same time, in Qatamon, Gibril Katoul told his Jewish friend who lived across the street that he would not be able to offer protection, as he had during the Revolt in 1936. At that time Katoul had hired guards to defend his neighbor's home. He said frankly: "We can do nothing to help you and you can do nothing to protect us. You are in danger here in this Arab quarter. You too must leave." Two days later both families in fact left, each to its own side of the city.[52] The breach between Jewish and Arab neighbors in Qatamon and elsewhere was not voiced publicly. Talk of leaving was conducted in private, each family making its own choice. As an Arab resident of the neighborhood later wrote, "Toward the end of 1947 and during the first few months of 1948 no one in Qatamon spoke of departure, even when departure was imminent. Indeed, children were aware of the need for absolute secrecy, for fear of being labeled cowardly."[53]

Palestine was not the only place to see such a sharp transition from close neighbors to sworn enemies. The phenomenon was a familiar one from ethnic conflicts in mixed areas around the world. When members of two communities live together, their personal relations with members of the opposite community do not necessarily guarantee them safety if conflict develops. In fact, close proximity and a lack of barriers enables each side to wreak havoc when an ethnic conflict spirals into violence, when there are no brakes on national and religious fanaticism. In the Middle Ages, religion and powerful rulers served as such brakes, placing minorities under their protection. In Mandate Palestine the ruler was a foreign power and, by the end of that period, it was already seeking a way out. A constitution and a legitimate elected government that provides equal civil rights for all groups, as well as a commitment to human rights, can also serve as brakes, but neither existed in Palestine. Jews and Arabs lived together, exposed to one another without protective walls. The lack of brakes also became evident later in the twentieth century in the wars between the Serbs and the Croats, between the Ukrainians and the Russians, and between the Catholics and Protestants in Northern Ireland. According to Michael Ignatieff:

In all three cases, essentially similar peoples, speaking the same or related languages, sharing the same form of life, differing in religions which few actually seem to practice, have been divided by the single fact that one ruled over the other. It is the memory of domination in time past, or fear of domination in time future, not difference itself, which has turned conflict into an unbreakable downward spiral of political violence.[54]

During this twilight period, ordinary people in all these places shifted back and forth between neighborliness and hostility. The time spent on the neighborly end of the spectrum grew shorter as the conflicts worsened. But not everyone involved surrendered to tribalism. Some continued to cooperate, coexisting in mutual respect. During the Jewish siege of Jaffa at the beginning of 1948, Jewish and Arab citrus farmers reached an agreement that the groves surrounding the city would not be attacked. They agreed to continue the harvest and to send the fruit to the port, and to export it to Europe.[55]

There were also those who lived in a bubble of their own, unaware that the earth was shaking around them. In 1948 Hisham Sharabi of Jaffa was about twenty years old. He later wrote:

I had never entered a Jewish house ... they were aliens for us and very strange. I didn't even register their presence in Palestine. Astounding, isn't it? Think of the fact that every summer I would travel from Jaffa via the area throughout which they had so many settlements, but all I saw on the way from Jaffa to Haifa were Arab towns, and if Jews appeared from time to time I simply did not notice them.

The rich Arab life of Jaffa and Beirut permeated the life of this young Palestinian Arab, who thought of himself as a member of a greater Syrian-Arab nation. The young Sharabi had succumbed to the charisma and ideology of Antun Saadeh, leader of the Syrian Social Nationalist Party. Saadeh maintained that Syria was the center of the Arab nation and that force would eject the colonial invaders and unite the Arabs.[56] Sharabi evinced no interest in the Jewish Other, which for him was totally alien. As aliens, they were transparent for him, even though they were physically present in his immediate environment and on the route he took as a teenager to visit his uncle and grandmother in Acre. Nor could Sharabi conceive of the possibility that these aliens would push the natives off their land:

I remember saying to a friend of mine when the troubles started, "the poor Jews, I wonder what is going to happen to them?" I was sure that if this continued they would be crushed. The last thing in my imagination was that we were about to be overcome by a force that was far better than anything that Arab or Palestinian society represented.[57]

Sharabi's bubble in Jaffa was the result of a type of blindness. In Jerusalem too, to live in a bubble required that one shut oneself off from the outside world. Educated, well-off, secular adults preferred to shunt the war into the background, to make it into a subject for political conversation, to view it through a protective glass—if not all the time, then at least during the brief periods that the Jews and Arabs in the bubble spent together. Lord Martin Charteris, chief of British intelligence in Palestine in 1945–6, recalled:

There were lots of parties in Jerusalem, and everybody always talked politics ... they were not interested in anything except for the Palestine question. What was beautiful in Jerusalem was that this was not just a colonial life with tennis and golf. Everybody talked politics with great intensity.[58]

The Jewish, Arab, and British elite maintained their connections while the conflict raged outside. They kept up social connections with the Other as the two ethnic groups spiraled toward civil war. They met at the King David Hotel's bar, at the YMCA tennis courts across the street, at the cocktail parties and teas that Katy Antonius gave at least twice a month, or those hosted by Henry Qatan. The guests included the journalist Nasser al-Din Nashashibi, Fakhri Nashashibi, Dr Tawfiq Canʻan, and Gabriel and Victoria Valero. They were joined by journalists who had come to cover the war, political exiles from North African countries that had been conquered by the Germans and Italians, and Arab statesmen taking vacations in Jerusalem because they could not travel to Europe, nor to Beirut, which was for a time under the rule of the Vichy regime.[59] "I ate at one of three places each night," Fuad Shehadeh related. "At the café that is now a department store, which was called Café Vienna; in a place that was called Café Europa and which is now a branch of Bank Leumi; the third place was called Atara and it is still there. One of the first places I went to visit after 1967 was Café Atara. I went to eat there."[60]

In the 1940s the Jerusalem YMCA had about 1,000 members. Half of them were permanent inhabitants of Jerusalem and the rest were staying in the city on a temporary basis—diplomats, journalists, clerics, and army and intelligence officers.[61] Katy Antonius's salon was the most celebrated of the places they met. The role of Mrs Antonius, Jerusalem's number one hostess, was tailored for her personality, so it was no surprise that her house became the center of the city's elite social life. She was curious, intelligent, and charming. She always dressed in the best of taste and was a wonderful conversationalist, chatting easily with everyone she met. After her husband died, she fell in love with General Sir Evelyn Hugh Barker, with whom she had a famous affair. She hosted formal dinner parties, serving the finest oriental dishes, and after dinner there was dancing.[62]

Katy Antonius was not particularly close to the Palestinian political elite, with the exception of one of its members, Musa ʻAlami. She preferred intellectuals like Walid Khalidi and Albert Hourani, later professors at Harvard and Oxford, who were among her prominent houseguests. She also carefully screened the Jews that she invited. The only two who met her standards were Gavriel Tzifroni, a German Jew who served as correspondent for the British newspaper the *Daily Mail* and also worked in the Mandate's information office, and Wolfgang Hildesheimer, another German Jew. Tsifroni, who invariably wore a three-piece suit, circulated in the Jewish, Arab, and British elites. As he liked to say, "The Levant has much charm, but the Jews have yet to discover it."[63] He was attacked twice by Arabs but this did not make him an Arab-hater. A charming raconteur of broad horizons, he was far from a typical Zionist. He termed himself a student of the King David Hotel.[64] Antonius's circle was made up of cosmopolitans who did not feel at home in Palestine, where there was ethnic conflict. He remained in Jerusalem, but Hildesheimer, Khalidi, and Hourani all left. In Hourani's recollection:

Jerusalem was a small town with small-town intellectuals, with small-town politics ... it was a special place for only a limited number, for that group that gathered there due to the war and the circumstances of those years of fragile tranquility. I had no doubt that it would end in tragedy. For us Jerusalem was a dream. It was too good to go on.[65]

Hourani did not look back nostalgically, perhaps because he moved to Europe, to what he saw as the real world. He went on to be the founder of the Middle East studies program at Oxford. It was men and women like him who remained in Jerusalem and who missed it as it was. For these elites the Mandate period was a golden age that would never return, an era in which they could feel, in Antonius's salon and the King David hotel, that they were in Paris or London. They were not entirely mad or mistaken to think that. These people felt that the worsening ethnic conflict, with its mutual bloodletting over every inch of land, was turning Jerusalem into another place, into a provincial and violent city, one that was not theirs. Some would say that they saw the future clearly.

PART II

CONNECTED BY FORCE

4

EXPANDING THE BOUNDARIES OF THE POSSIBLE

A New Land

The past is another country, but it has left its marks on those who once lived there.

– Eric Hobsbawm[1]

I had no idea, as I headed to school on the morning of Monday, 5 June 1967, that a new era in history was dawning. I boarded my bus without knowing that a war had begun. There had been tension in the air for the last three weeks. Everyone in Israel feared for the country's future, and I, fifteen years old at the time, was no different. I knew that Jerusalemites who lived through the siege of 1948 had stocked up on food and fortified the entrances to their homes and their windows with sandbags. But along the bus's route through the city I saw no sign that war was any closer than I had sensed the week before. However, by the time that I arrived at the tall hill in West Jerusalem where my school stood, my classmates and I could see the war raging in the distance, on the city's eastern side. We heard muffled booms.

At around two in the afternoon, I decided to go home. I walked down to the Mt Herzl military cemetery, on the main road, to catch my ride home. A bus was in flames. This was my first direct encounter with the war—a frightening though not a paralyzing sight. A passing driver offered to take me downtown. When I emerged from his car, I heard exploding shells and the crack of rifle fire. People told me not to walk up King George Street, which was in many places exposed to Jordanian snipers positioned on the Old City walls. So I made my way up silent side streets, holding my fears in check, intent on my goal of reaching my mother's office. When I got there, the few workers who remained in the building were huddled mutely in the basement, each sunk deep in his own fears. My mother was astonished to see me, but happy that I was safe and sound. She did not say anything. I do not know how many memories of Auschwitz passed through her head. Did she doubt, at that moment, her fierce belief that Israel was a secure haven against another Holocaust? Did she fear she would lose her son, just as she had lost her home in the world war and her family at the death camp? At 4 p.m. we decided that we would be more comfortable at home, which was just a short walk to the south. When we got there and I went to my room, I found that the war had paid a visit—and that it had been a good thing I had not been around when it did. My bed was covered with mortar shrapnel and stray bullets. I collected them and they sit on my desk to this day. Home was clearly unsafe, so we headed for the communal bomb shelter in our building's basement, where we would have to live for the time being. There, too, my mother kept her feelings to herself. The loud sound of the war outside rendered us all wordless and allowed us no rest. When, on Wednesday, I heard on my transistor radio that the Old City had been liberated, I liberated myself from the bomb shelter. A week later the road to the Western Wall was open to Israelis. It was the Shavu'ot holiday. I walked confidently, one of 250,000 Israelis, along the fenced-off path to the holy site. Two weeks later the entire Old City was open. Tens of thousands of Israelis swept through it with an intense curiosity undergirded by an upwelling of victorious pride.

The nerve-wracking period before the war had proceeded at an agonizingly slow pace. Now life sped up. Every day brought some new experience. On one it was the sight of Arabs from the formerly Jordanian side of the city making their way to the main downtown intersection of West Jerusalem, where Jaffa Road crosses King George. They had come to marvel at how a set of colored lights in a metal housing above was imposing discipline on drivers and pedestrians. It was the only traffic light on either side of the city. In East Jerusalem, traffic had been directed by white-gloved Jordanian policemen with whistles and energetic arms. The Jews of West Jerusalem observed the bewilderment of the easterners with humane understanding, much different in manner from the impatience and irritation so characteristic in Jerusalem today. With my school friends, I skipped classes again and again to take in the oriental *suk* and buy camels carved out of olive wood, fountain pens made in China, and Jordanian postcards, all items unknown in Israel until then. We were stupefied, trying to assimilate all the new sights. I personally experienced Jerusalem's opening to the East.

It was an incredibly intense experience for me. The transitions I had experienced were sudden and hard to digest—from a normal daily life to one of existential anxiety as the Arab countries placed Israel under siege; from a sense that we were on the verge of a Holocaust, filling sandbags to protect our homes and preparing public parks to be used as mass graves, to an inspiring military victory—of dimensions that Israel had not previously achieved (nor would it ever again). We had been living in a small country suffering from a severe recession; now we were citizens of a state that had acquired new territories several times larger than itself, a new regional power. Within a few months, the recession was over and the economy was thriving.

Our sense of helplessness had now been replaced by arrogance and the intoxication of power. The western, Israeli side of Jerusalem had been the nation's capital, but bereft of the major historical and religious sites of Jewish history and tradition, all of which had been on the Jordanian side. The new reunited Jerusalem could now reestablish its roots in the Jewish past. Uzi Narkiss, the general in command of Israel's central region in 1967, had in 1948 been a low-ranking officer in the Palmach force that broke through enemy lines and the Old City wall to relieve the besieged Jewish Quarter. But that operation failed; the Palmach withdrew and the Quarter's inhabitants fled or were taken prisoner. This time, Narkiss was determined to succeed. When the Israel Defense Forces retook the Old City, he lauded this modern Jewish army as superior to the Jewish forces that had rebelled against the Roman Empire in 70 and 125 AD. The Jews of that time had fought desperately and lost; the Jews of 1967 had won.[2]

Historically, the Jewish people had enjoyed few periods of independence and unity. The ancient Jewish kingdom of the biblical period was riven by rivalries between tribes and between the larger northern kingdom of Israel and the smaller southern monarchy of Judah. Foreign powers conquered and depleted both. Centuries later, a short-lived independent kingdom under the Hasmonean dynasty deteriorated into fratricide and the country was, in stages, brought under Roman rule.

To the extent that Israelis saw their newly enlarged domain as the restoration of the Jewish people's ancient glory, their reading of history was selective in the extreme. On top of that, it was heavily infused with religious–national sentiment. "We have returned to the holiest of our places never again to be separated from them," declared Minister of Defense Moshe Dayan at the Western Wall just a few hours after it was taken. Natan Alterman, the unofficial national poet, no longer viewed Jerusalem as a city alien to the Jewish national revival. The Western Wall, about which he had never before written, now became a national symbol for him. He insisted that secular Jews like himself had to recognize that the Jewish religion lay at the heart of the Jewish nation.[3] Among the most popular items in the summer of 1967 were Jewish New Year cards that overlaid images of the IDF and of its conquest of Jerusalem via pictures of the Western Wall and other Jewish symbols. A card bearing a photograph of Israeli soldiers at the wall, issued by the Palphot greeting card company, became the most popular Israeli postcard of all time, selling some 10,000 copies in September and October 1967.[4] The cosmopolitan Gavriel Tzifroni and communist Shimon Ballas, who had become deeply rooted in Arab culture as a young man in Baghdad, were swept away, too. Tzifroni evoked comparisons that were not Jewish. The Israeli victory, he proclaimed, was a historical turning point "like the British victory over the Spanish Armada or the Battle of Waterloo."[5] Ballas was moved to see the Israeli newspapers *Yediot Aharonot* and *Ma'ariv* on sale in the Old City. He took it as proof of the brotherhood of the two nations and of the possibility that Israeli could integrate itself into the region. But Ballas's unreserved optimism was tinged with naivety. Before Israel's integration on an equal basis with other countries, he thought, it would need to establish a system of enlightened rule over the Palestinian Arabs, so as to bring them into the modern age.[6] Optimism engendered euphoria. Israelis truly and simply believed that their victory had brought serenity and harmony to Jerusalem. Why shouldn't it? They returned home after the war to what seemed to them a rectified world.

The intoxicating feeling of victory, and of having embarked on a new era in Jewish history that harked back to the ancient Jewish kingdom, energized the leadership of the Jewish state. Even before the Israeli government decided officially to annex East Jerusalem, the Israeli part of the capital had penetrated the Jordanian city. It took less than six days for municipal workers, under the direction of Mayor

Teddy Kollek, to bury the Palestinian and Jordanian dead who lay in the streets and to connect the two water systems. Telephone wires that had been damaged in the war were repaired, and the police put up street signs on Jordanian streets. Israeli municipal officials perused the records of the Jordanian municipality and met with their East Jerusalem counterparts to fill in information that was not contained in those documents. Senior Arab officials, chief among them Mayor Rukhi al-Khatib, provided the Israelis with no little assistance.[7]

Hebron had not been a battleground in 1948, and in 1967 it fell to Israel without a fight. On the first day of the war, former IDF Chief of Staff Yigael Yadin urged Prime Minister Levi Eshkol to conquer not only Jerusalem but also Hebron. That would settle "an ancient account we have from the days of Abraham," who, according to the book of Genesis, had purchased the Makhpela Cave from an inhabitant of the city. Eshkol asked him whether he had given any thought to how Israel could survive with so many Arabs within its borders. "If you want to know, Mr. Prime Minister, I believe that by the time our forces enter, [the Arabs] will be in the desert," Yadin replied.[8] But the Hebronites did not flee—they waited for the Israelis to enter. The Jordanian army had withdrawn, which the locals took as a sign that King Hussein had agreed to hand the city over to Israel without a fight. Less than two weeks later, Deputy Prime Minister Yigal Allon proposed "to join to the state of Israel, in addition to greater Jerusalem, all of Mt. Hebron, with its population but without the refugees [from the 1948 war]. The southern part of the West Bank should be joined to Israel, including its Arabs, with a status like that of Israel's Arab [citizens]."[9]

Jewish communities around the world were euphoric. The establishment of Israel in 1948 and the war of 1967 had made the Jewish state a focal point of Jewish identity and an object of Diaspora love and admiration. In 1900 only one of every 100 of the world's Jews resided in the Land of Israel. In 1939 the figure was 3 percent of the 17 million Jews alive then, about 1 million of them in Islamic lands, and 2 million in the United States. In 1948, 6 percent lived in Israel; by 1967, Israel's Jewish population constituted about 20 percent of the world's Jews and by 2008 the figure was 42 percent.[10] The American-Jewish Holocaust survivor, novelist Elie Wiesel, heard on the radio an account of the 1967 battles from Mordechai Gur, commander of the Paratrooper Brigade instrumental in the conquest of the Old City, including the Western Wall. His story, Wiesel said, was an epic, a fulfillment of the prayers of

Jewish dreamers conveyed to him by the dreamers of redemption of all generations. He viewed Gur as the Jewish people's redeemer.[11]

A mystical-national encounter similar, if much less potent, to that which impressed itself on Israeli society in 1967 was experienced years earlier by Yosef Klausner: "I am in Jerusalem. Jerusalem, our holy city, treasure of all nations, sacred to all faiths, the heart of the entire world and the most dearly beloved and greatest hope of the Jewish nation," Klausner wrote, recalling, in Odessa two years later, how he had felt on his visit to Palestine in 1912. "And together with that, great sorrow disheartens me ... so much of the mundane, so much of the foreign." On his way to the Western Wall he passed "a number of streets and markets, so similar in their congestion, their lack of cleanliness, and their noise, to all Oriental 'bazaars' ... these streets are far from being clean. The Wall is located in the neighborhood of the Mughrabi (Moroccan) Arabs, who are conspicuous for their filth." So Klausner saw the Orient. He had expected to find diametric contrast between these miserable and neglected surroundings and "his" Jewish Western Wall.

> Where is the Wall? Why does it not appear? Haven't I been told that it is lofty and towering? ... Beggars from "every tribe of Israel" surround us and in different and strange jargons to ask for—or more accurately, demand—a handout ... if we even start giving they will not let us alone. We fortify our hearts and move forward. And suddenly, really abruptly, it is depressing, almost alarming ... my eyes are up against the Wall. Stones unimaginably huge ... and nails are stuck between one stone and another as a charm—a sacrilege without parallel in the world. Even our nation's most sacred site is used by us as a charm for prosperity and progeny.

Klausner's first impression of the wall was a mixed one—awe and the wretchedness of the beggars, who seemed to fit so well into the dilapidated surroundings. He was put off. But at second glance the picture grew clearer.

> It is precisely the wall's simplicity, its "crudeness," if one can say that, that makes every heartstring tremble ... Jewish men and women stand and kiss those stones, weeping and praying before these stones, without order and without restraint. A cluster on one side prays the afternoon prayer, another on the other side recites psalms, and a third busies itself with declaiming the order of the Passover sacrifice. These shout at the top of their voices and those pray at a whisper ... and this disorder—it in particular—is what most moves me ... rough stones with no majesty, prayers and supplications with no order, how appropriate all this is for an exiled and ruined nation! Jewish men and women approach the Wall and kiss each and every stone. And I watch this and wish

to do as they do, but the kisses have frozen on my lips. How can I kiss cold stones? ... Am I a fetishist that I should kiss stones? ... But I see a young Jew from the Caucasus ... tall and strapping ... lay his head on the hard stones as if it were a mother's bosom, bawling tears. Next to him is a Sephardi of middle age with a book of Psalms in his hand, and he cries out in a heartrending voice ... and I feel how from the recesses of my heart a stream of tears wells up into my throat and from there rises and breaks out from my eyes ... and a great light descends on my soul. The Wall is transformed in an instant ... millions of souls have been poured out on these stones for 40 generations. All those souls have become part of this Wall ... No, the stones of this Wall are no longer cold, they are warm, warm as the tears that have dropped on them for 2,000 years ... wet by the concentrated blood of a great nation ... I pushed my way through the crowd surrounding me, to the Wall, and I placed my two palms on the two largest stones I could find, and suddenly I felt that a huge and new force was flowing from the stones and flowing and passing into my inner soul, and at that moment I felt that my abstract faith that in the past we had had a Jewish state and my abstract hope that in the future we would have a Jewish state became as concrete as iron ... These stones are absolutely real ... they are testimonies to the vitality of what once was and in their tangibility they strengthen the hopes and the confidence of everyone who touches them in what will be ... the soul of the people permeates them and speaks from within them, and the people's soul sanctifies and reveres them when it embraces and kisses them ... I departed from the Wall purified and calmed.

Klausner's mystical-national experience includes a significant religious element. He imputed to the wall actuality and vital force, melding the Jews before it into an entity that merged with the stones. The stones were no longer stones, just as the people in front of them were no longer individuals. The stones were the embodiment of the nation. The mystical experience won out over his critical-rational approach and his revulsion at the people around him. But the potency of the experience faded when he and his wife walked away from the wall. "My wife opened her purse and placed a small gift into the first outstretched hand, but at that very moment all the beggars, men and women, assaulted her with shouts and shrieks." The beggars even tried "to wrench coins from her hand by force ... the entire feeling I had had before vanished like a dream. Only one thing remained—recognition of the Destruction. The rabbis and officials of Jerusalem, and the myriad Jews who come to visit the holy city, are unable to put in order even a little matter like alms-giving at the Western Wall in a way more befitting this most sacred site," he wrote.[12] His mystical-religious experience shattered entirely when Klausner experienced the repellent violence of the beggars. His revulsion renewed. Yet his experience at the wall remained part of who he was. His account demonstrated that the experience remained deeply etched in his psyche when, back in Odessa, he wrote of what had happened.

Klausner's nephew, the novelist Amos Oz, had a similar experience. Oz, too, imagined Jerusalem, and his dreams about the city also ran up on the shoals of what he felt was the bitter reality of June 1967. The Jerusalem of the boy Amos was the object of his dreams, a revered and beloved city besieged by cruel and powerful enemies. "I knew that Jerusalem was surrounded by forces that sought its death and my death … I saw it falling into the hands of its enemies. Feral warriors stalked its soul and Jerusalem had demanded, time after time, that its devotees accept martyrdom. In my childhood I was often told about besieged Jerusalem … I always belonged to the few who were under siege … we would die there," he decided to himself. Over the years this Jerusalem had preserved its alienating and "distant identity." Its inhabitants were "a silent people, acrid, as if always holding in an inner terror." For Oz, the city was "the dejected capital of a cheering country," a capital that never found its place in Israel. After his mother's death, the young Oz left his dismal city for Kibbutz Hulda, to be part of the joyful country. On 11 June 1967, at the climax of Israeli-Jewish excitement, Oz came to the city of his birth to see the Jerusalem beyond the lines. "I went toward places … and here they were the dwellings of human beings—houses, stores, stands, signs. I was dumbfounded. As if the dimensions within me had collapsed. The dreams were false." He had expected to find his imaginary and romantic city waiting for him, he who had redeemed it from foreign rule. But what was revealed to him was that "the constant terror had been nothing but a cruel and twisted joke. Everything was ordinary, common. My beloved and terrible Jerusalem was dead." Rather than a besieged city, he saw a wide open one. The Jerusalem he discovered was "mine and foreign. Conquered and hostile. Devoted and insular … people lived there and they were foreign." He did not understand their language, only the fact that he was foreign and unwanted. "Yes, the inhabitants were polite. Polite to the point of offense, as if they were perfectly happy to have been given the right and honor to sell me postcards or royal Jordanian stamps … and their eyes hated me, wished for my death, me the foreign and other."

Like his uncle, Yosef Klausner, Amos Oz fought an inner battle against his sense of alienation. "I sought with all my might to feel

Jerusalem as should a man who had overwhelmed his nemeses and returned to the land of his fathers. The Bible, too, shuddered and rose before me. Prophets. Kings. The Temple Mount ... I wanted to participate. To belong. If it weren't for the people. I saw hostility and rejection, flattery and astonishment and fear and affront and scheming." He wanted to reach "the city of my forefathers' and nation's yearnings," but he "was doomed to walk its streets armed with a submachine gun like one of the figures in my childhood nightmares. To be a foreign man in a very foreign city."[13] Unlike his uncle and in opposition to the uncle's collective Jewish encounter with the wall, Oz's experience was personal, not religious or national. The encounter with the past and with the place itself did not overwhelm him. It was the human beings he saw, the conquered presences, that shaped him. More than twenty years would pass before Israelis could identify with what Oz had felt. When Amos Oz wrote this account in September 1967, it was alien to the ears and hearts of his fellow Jews. Only after the Intifada of 1987 did Israelis start to wake up from their romantic dreams.

The new land was not born overnight. Between 1936 and 1939, and even more so after World War II, Zionists and Palestinians returned to fighting each other and the British, and the physical landscape changed. Checkpoints and roadblocks crisscrossed once open, inviting, and friendly urban spaces. Roads were blocked and British policemen and soldiers frisked passersby and searched their bags for weapons. The British erected barriers and fences and categorized the cities' inhabitants according to their nationality and ethnicity. Adults had to carry papers to prove what their nationality was. There were frequent curfews, lasting several hours or an entire night. No one in the Samuel family in Qatamon dared sit by a window in the evening unless the shutters were entirely closed. The door of the house was made of iron and was not opened unless a member of the family identified the visitor through a window first.[14] These physical barriers created for many a sense of national affiliation that replaced their previous identities. The identities of those who already put their national affiliation at the center were reinforced. On the street, at work, in schools, in the media, and at houses of worship, everyone talked about the burgeoning conflict. Rumors and secrets spread from ear to ear, along with news reports and official government announcements. Warnings about violent demonstrations and advice to avoid entering Arab areas on particular days were disseminated among Jews by phone and by messengers sent by the Jewish militias.[15] Everyone dressed and routed themselves in accordance with the danger that lay waiting on the side of the Other. Only a few people dared to go out for pleasure after dark. Cinemas and cafés were empty. No public events were held after sundown. Zionists and Palestinians conducted enlistment and propaganda campaigns in support of their militias and underground organizations. The British worked to arrest rebel leaders and to keep their own losses to a minimum. Even the sounds and sights on the streets changed. The armored cars used by British soldiers forced passersby to the side of the street and drowned out the city's usual sounds. Acts of terror committed by both sides made public spaces seem menacing. The authorities pasted up wanted posters on billboards. The reverberations of bombs and gunshots increasingly rang through the air as the conflict worsened.

But no previous stage of the conflict prepared the Jews and Arabs for what the 1948 war brought. It raged through the houses in Jerusalem and Jaffa. Even prior to 1948 Palestine was a small and crowded place. The confrontation between the two peoples made it even smaller and more intimate, as each side shut itself off from the other. Contacts between them grew more and more limited. The war was a personal trial experienced by every member of each community. Jewish Jerusalem felt it in its stomach as well. The siege of the city led to a shortage of water and basic food items. The Zionist blockade of Jaffa was shorter, but the collapse of that city's leadership and institutions created a paucity of food and municipal services. Both Jerusalem's Jews and Jaffa's Arabs lived in a state of panic. Jewish national organizations, and then Israel's provisional government, forcibly prevented Jews from fleeing Jerusalem for the coastal plain. This coercion was exercised in particular against Haredim, who were most anxious to leave. Haganah commanders stationed in the Old City opposed the wishes of the residents of the Jewish Quarter to surrender or flee to the western side of the city.[16] For many long months the war was everywhere. Newspaper headlines proclaimed it and it sounded in radio broadcasts. Long after it ended its traces were visible on the bodies of the wounded, and in scarred, abandoned, ruined houses. Every moment of the Palestinian refugees' days reminded them of the war and what they had lost.

Their loss shattered Palestinian society in cities, towns, and villages. It turned half of them into refugees and impelled members of many families to head for foreign countries to study or find work. National social and political networks started to replace local and clan ties. A generation of educated Palestinians who had lived through the 1948 war became rooted in their new locations and commenced social and political activity. But the tragic creation of the Palestinian diaspora had a positive aspect. The community's young members became agents of change and imbued Palestinian society with elements they absorbed in their hosting countries. Fatah, the Palestinian liberation movement, and the Palestine Liberation Organization (PLO) came to the fore with the intention of reversing the outcome of the war. Historically, that war was a dramatic and constitutive event. A short time later, the 1967 war impelled the Palestinians to refashion their national movement and unite around the PLO.

When the war ended in 1948, it became apparent that two nations had been born in the same place, on the same swath of the earth. One was a new land of defeated Palestinians and the other an independent Jewish state with its face to the future. The Arabs looked to a past life that had been expunged from the landscape. Most people who walked the land during the first half of the twentieth century are no longer alive. As they passed on, so did villages and neighborhoods, political institutions and social organizations. The British departed in a way that left no doubt that they had no intention of returning. The Jerusalem municipal bank account managed by the British at Barclay's Bank retained a balance of P£60,000. When the British left the city, the Mandate government divided the money equally, down to the last penny, between the Jews and the Arabs.[17] Half the Palestinians had been expelled or had fled. Israel did not allow their return and confiscated their property. At the end of the war only about 150,000 Arabs remained on Israeli territory, in comparison with the half million or so who were supposed to be there according to the UN partition resolution of November 1947. In that plan, Israel was to receive 55 percent of the territory of Palestine; it now controlled 78 percent. The rest was annexed by Jordan or, in the Gaza Strip, came under Egyptian military rule. According to the UN plan, Jerusalem was to be placed under a special regime (*corpus separatum*); instead, Israel and Jordan divided it between themselves. Israel declared the half of the city under its control to be its capital, an act which received a certain measure of de facto recognition from the international community. In the partition plan, Jaffa was to be an Arab enclave within the borders of the Jewish state. In fact, Jewish forces circled it, bringing about the collapse of its defenses and civil society. Its defenses collapsed in March–April 1948 and it surrendered in May. The rift between the land that had been and the one that would be was deep and unbridgeable. In the new country, a dominance of Jews over Arabs, of victors over defeated, came into being. From this point on, relations between the two peoples were conducted in the shadow of that ranking.

In June 1967, little was apparent to recall the war of 1948. The big differences between the two engagements lay in their duration and the relative number of casualties. In 1967 the war was not only immeasurably shorter; it caused far fewer deaths and injuries on both sides. The 1967 war lasted six days, but in Jerusalem only a day and a half, and in Hebron just a few hours. Jaffa was not a theater at all. The war was conducted in part on territory inhabited by Palestinians, but the Palestinians did not fight. The number of Palestinian refugees in 1967 was also far smaller than in 1948. Israelis and Palestinians thus distinguish between the two wars that so dramatically changed the face of the Middle East. Today, however, it looks as if these were not separate wars, but rather two rounds of the same war. In historical terms, the nineteen years that separated the two passed in little more than a blink of an eye. The farther we get from 1967, the shorter the distance between the two wars looks. In fact, twice as much time has passed between the 1967 war and today than passed between the wars of 1948 and 1967.

In many ways the years following 1948 were but a prologue to the chapter that would begin after 1967. The intimate pre-1948 society came to an end in the 1950s. People knew each other less, and the barriers separating groups grew larger. Every other Israeli had arrived in the country after the 1948 war, most of them from Arab lands. These immigrants brought with them cultures, languages, and skills that were entirely different from those of most of the Jewish immigrants who had arrived in Palestine before the war. Israeli society underwent a major transformation as its population became less ideological and more diverse, less ascetic and more consumer-oriented, looking less to Europe and more to the United States. The first supermarkets opened. The Israeli market opened to free purchase of imported automobiles and an inexpensive Israel-made vehicle was also marketed. Like their counterparts in the West, young Israelis discovered, thanks to the birth-control pill and greater permissiveness, the allure of sex and drugs and rock and roll. The latter was forbidden on Israeli radio, but it was not a problem to tune in to Radio Ramallah. In 1960, S. Yizhar, a Palmach veteran, scornfully referred to this younger cohort as the "espresso generation." True, Israelis did not have the money to live American lives, but their preferences were set during this period. While financial resources were limited, patterns were established that came into their own when prosperity grew after 1967. When that year's war expanded both Israel's boundaries and its economy, Israelis were able to buy more and more of the Western goods and culture they had come to covet.

The years 1948 and 1967 were high points in Zionist history and nadirs in Palestinian and Arab history. But most Israelis and Palestinians today need help understanding them. They had not yet been born when the battles were fought, or they were too young to experience them directly, or they were outside the country. Israeli society is an immigrant society. Between 1948 and 1955 the Jewish population doubled as a result of a massive influx. On the eve of the 1967 war only 41.6 percent of the population had been shaped by experiencing the land before 1948.[18] Today some 20 percent of Israel's population is comprised of immigrants from the former Soviet Union who arrived in the 1990s and after. Half of the Palestinians were displaced during the 1948 war or immediately thereafter. The disparity between their lives in the present and the way they lived before is enormous. Furthermore, theirs is a young society. According to 2011 figures from the Palestinian Central Bureau of Statistics, some 30 percent of the Palestinians living in the territories controlled by the Palestinian Authority are under the age of thirty. Almost 60 percent of those who are under thirty are under the age of fifteen.[19]

This new land issues "guidebooks" to the land that once was. It dictates the way in which each side views what came before. Israel and the Palestinian national movement employ diligent agents of memory who promote a glorious past used to explain the difficult struggle experienced by the current generation. Each constructs sites of collective memory and shapes idioms, language, symbols, and ceremonies that inspire and arouse identification. The national movements cannot dictate memories and identities to their peoples, who construct them, on both a collective and individual basis, by balancing those messages with their own needs and perceptions. These realms of memory were then privatized—during the 1990s in Israel and since 2000 among the Palestinians. In both societies, personal memories of those who died in the conflict are integrated into collective memory.[20]

Israelis tend to see Jewish history as teleological, leading inevitably to the establishment of a modern Jewish state. For the Palestinians, the teleology leads in the opposite direction, to a disaster caused by collusion between the Zionists and British imperialists, or the British and their puppet Arab states. Like the Israelis, the Palestinians see the past through the lens of the present. They envision the history of Palestine during the early twentieth century as a Zionist–British or British–Arab plot that brought on the *Nakba*, the catastrophe, their term for the 1948 war. For the Palestinians the realization of the Zionist dream is an ongoing nightmare. During the years in which Israel transformed its demography and geography, the Palestinians were preoccupied with survival and attempts to preserve their lost land, in memory if not in fact. It was impossible, even undesirable, to return to the past. While the Palestinians spoke about returning and imagined doing so, they did not mean a return to the Ottoman Turkish or British-ruled past, but rather of returning to a new land in which the Palestinians would seize from the Jews their standing as lords of the land. The real past awaited to be rediscovered, to be seen as a past and not a prologue to the future.

The 1948 war remained salient for many years after the armistice that ended it. The story was told and retold and people relived it in songs, ceremonies, and speeches. Those who had not experienced it personally identified with it as part of the collective identity of which they were part. The cost the war imposed on both sides was a heavy one. The death toll was about 6,000 for the Jews—around 1 percent of their population. Double that number were injured. The Palestinians suffered somewhere between 12,000 and 15,000 deaths, more than 1 percent of their population. We have no precise figures for the number wounded, but it was probably double that.[21]

In both wars, the new cities defeated the old cities. Jerusalem's Jewish Quarter surrendered to the Jordanian army in 1948 following a six-month siege. The attempts by Jewish forces to break through the Old City walls were weak and ineffective. The Zionist leadership had always concentrated its efforts in the Western part of Jerusalem, rather than in the religious Old City, and the Israeli state continued that orientation. When the government decided to found an East Jerusalem Development Company in January 1966, it did not intend to develop the Jordanian city. The East Jerusalem in question was the Israeli-controlled territory along the border with Jordan, from Allenby Square to Abu Tor, including the Hinnom Valley. The company's task, according to the decision, would be to turn this neglected area along the border into a tourist, entertainment, and leisure zone, with an artists' village and park. To make that absolutely clear, the government announced on 1 August of the same year that the purview of the company was development "up to the cease-fire line and also to develop other parts of the city, including Lifta, Malha [Manhat], 'Ein Karem, and their environs."[22] Israel wanted to erase the relics of Palestinian life found in the territory under its control, but not beyond that. In the lead-up to the war in June 1967, Israel sought to guarantee the status quo. It asked Jordan not to allow itself to be dragged into a war, but King Hussein responded with bullets. Israel then immediately changed its policy. It was guided by a sense of a historic opportunity, along with a sense of guilt and failure at having abandoned the Old City in 1948. Within two and a half days of the war's start, Israel's capital in West Jerusalem, with its 36 square kilometers (almost 14 square miles), had overwhelmed Jordan's "symbolic capital," which covered only 6 square kilometers (2.3 square miles). Already during the first day of the war, cabinet ministers Menachem Begin and Yigal Allon, along with the prime minister's adviser, Yigael Yadin, were pressuring Prime Minister Levi Eshkol to liberate Jerusalem and thus atone for what had not been done in 1948. They were joined by the ministers of the National Religious Party, Zerach Warhaftig, and Haim Moshe Shapira. The latter asked David Ben-Gurion, in retirement, what he thought. Ben-Gurion urged the government to conquer the Old City "and not miss the hour." That same evening the prime minister ordered Israeli troops to seize Jordanian Jerusalem. There were apprehensions. "I know that it will also be a political problem when the Old City is in our hands. If they come and propose turning it into an international city, that is the most they can propose to us, and I will agree to it," said Shapira, minister of the interior. "I favor the internationalization of Jerusalem." In this he was of one mind with Minister of Education Zalman Aran.[23] The ministers ended the meeting with a revision of a traditional Jewish greeting—instead of "next year in Jerusalem," they bid each other farewell by saying "next week in the whole Jerusalem."

Aran changed his mind within the week. At the cabinet meeting on 11 June, he said: "There needs to be an internal decision that, no matter what, this thing [the holy sites and Mt Scopus] will remain ours." In this spirit the government resolved to annex the Jordanian city quickly, before the United States imposed a withdrawal.

The next day a cabinet committee convened to discuss the details of the annexation. Minister of Justice Ya'akov Shimshon Shapira asserted that "the difficulty in terms of international law as I see it today in connection to Jerusalem is that, while with new Jerusalem we appropriated territory as if it were ownerless, not from an existing state" (when Israeli law was imposed on the western part of what was to have been the *corpus separatum*), "with regard to Old Jerusalem, Jordan was sovereign there from the point of view of international law, both de jure and de facto." In other words, East Jerusalem was occupied territory. The justice minister was frank when he said that "with regard to West Jerusalem—let's call it that—we have forgotten, and have done our best to make others forget, and perhaps also without really trying we have forgotten that it is occupied territory. Everyone knows that it is Israeli territory." But, he continued, "it goes without saying why we do not want to make Old Jerusalem into 'occupied territory.' All the more so because according to the [international law] compacts, [Israeli law] does not apply to a place that has been conquered from a sovereign country." East Jerusalem was captured territory, and in order to give it a status similar to that of the western side of the city Israel would have to proceed in a different manner than it had in 1949.

Three ways of doing this, all of which had been proposed at the previous day's meeting of the full cabinet, were discussed at this committee meeting. Menachem Begin, minister without portfolio, proposed drafting formal legislation that would unite Jerusalem de facto and de jure. Minister of Housing Mordechai Bentov proposed establishing only de facto annexation through administrative regulations. The attorney general, advising the committee, remarked that this approach could lead to myriad legal problems, and that legislation was thus required. In response, the minister of justice proposed a middle way. Instead of formal annexation, the Knesset would pass an act extending Israeli juridical and administrative law to an area, larger than Jordanian Jerusalem, that would be made part of the Israeli capital. In other words, while there would be a formal act declaring that Israeli law applied to this area, the word "annexation" would not be used, thus preserving a low profile. He termed it "entering Jerusalem securely but without drums and dancing." On 29 June, the Knesset approved the legislation proposed by the minister of justice.[24]

On 21 June, a new Ministerial Committee on Jerusalem Affairs convened and decided that the members of the Arab city's city council would, as individuals, be added to the Jewish city's city council. Mayor Kollek tried to persuade the committee to give the Jordanian city the status of a separate quarter, with the Arab neighborhoods to be represented on united Jerusalem's city council by the members of the city council of the Jordanian city. But the ministers rejected this idea, fearing that any form of collective representation for Jerusalem's Arabs could be interpreted as Israeli recognition of the Arab city's separate status. There was to be no arrangement that would cast any doubt on Israel's position that East Jerusalem was now part of sovereign Israel. The Jordanian city council was dissolved. Its members were offered seats on the Israeli council, but on an individual basis, not as representatives of their part of the city. None of them agreed to join.

On 29 June military police brought the mayor of the Jordanian city, Ruhi al-Khatib, and the members of the city council to the deputy military governor of Jerusalem, Lt Colonel Ya'akov Salman, and his aide David Farhi, in the Gloria Hotel restaurant, across the street from the Jordanian municipal building, to which the venue was moved when it turned out that the Israelis did not have the key to the building. Salman and Farhi read out to the mayor and city councilmen the decree dissolving the Arab council. Al-Khatib asked to receive the decree in writing and Farhi copied it out on a paper napkin. The officers had previously received an order from General Uzi Narkiss, chief of the army's central region command, to dismiss the city council members, but he did not tell them how to do this. Narkiss's order came after he had received a panicked call from Teddy Kollek, who feared that the annexation would be legally questionable so long as the Jordanian municipality existed. He had not taken into account the fact that the Jordanian municipality ceased to exist once the Knesset had passed the expansion law two days previously, rendering the entire ceremony pointless. The IDF did not show any consideration for the fact that al-Khatib had done much to enable an orderly transition of power. The Arab mayor had, for three weeks, taken action to reopen shops, remove debris and bodies, ensure the operation of the electrical grid and the supply of fuel, milk, and flour from the western side of the city. In radio broadcasts, he called on the city's Arabs to hand over weapons in their possession to the Israeli authorities. After being dismissed and humiliated, the mayor became a disappointed and bitter man. He began to work against Israeli rule in Jerusalem, as a result of which Israel deported him to Jordan in March 1968. He was allowed to return in May 1993.[25]

In December 1968 Israel decided, "for security reasons," to move the headquarters of its military government in the West Bank from Salah al-Din Street in East Jerusalem to an empty lot, owned by the World Lutheran Federation, across from the Augusta Victoria hospital in East Jerusalem. The real reason was to buttress the annexation and to place a wedge between East Jerusalem and the West Bank. The US government realized this and successfully pressured Israel to reverse the decision. But as the years went by, the need to cite security as a justification for Israeli actions in Jerusalem diminished. The United States did not in fact prevent such actions. In 1980, Israeli settlers bought a building next to the lot where they constructed the Beit Orot Yeshiva, which was intended to serve as the nucleus of a Jewish neighborhood. In 2010, the building of twenty-four housing units commenced.[26]

The US government came to terms with the annexation about a year later. On 23 June 1968, the Knesset enacted legislation requiring residents of East Jerusalem to register their businesses and companies in Israel. Washington took up the issue because King Hussein wanted to submit a protest to the UN Security Council on the grounds that the Israeli move made it less likely that his country could regain control of the city. But the Americans told Hussein that the protest would come at an inappropriate time. There was no way to persuade Israel to reverse its decision, Robert Neumann of the US consulate in Jerusalem wrote in February 1969 to Joseph Sisco, who had been appointed earlier that month to the post of assistant secretary of state for Near East and South Asian affairs. Neumann recommended demanding that Israel suspend the implementation of the decision for an indefinite time. Cables sent to Washington by the US ambassador to Israel and its consul-general in Jerusalem stressed that Israel would not retreat from its move because doing so would be detrimental to its annexation of Jerusalem and would also create a coalition crisis. The two Americans recommended asking Israel to put off implementation of the annexation law in exchange for a postponement of a Security Council discussion of the issue. Under pressure from the United States, Israel agreed to delay putting the law into effect for a few months. Foreign Service officers in the embassy in Tel Aviv and the consulate in Jerusalem reported that the annexation act of 1967 was, for Israel, irreversible. On top of this, in his contacts with the Americans, Mayor Kollek packaged the annexation decision in an attractive way that cast Israel's actions in a favorable light. "We have no intention of creating a unified city," he declared to the consul-general in Jerusalem on 14 January 1969. "There is no social integration ... it's a matter of two entirely different societies." Kollek advocated the creation of a Greater Jerusalem stretching from Bethlehem in the south to Ramallah in the north. When peace came, this large city would operate under divided sovereignty and joint administration, he said. But, Kollek added, this would not be achieved in the near future. Until then, Israel would not remain passive. Rather, it would build new neighborhoods for Jews in East Jerusalem. Jerusalem's Arabs preferred to see Israel leave, he acknowledged, but they would slowly get used to the Jewish state as a permanent fixture in their lives.[27] The consul-general did not ask how divided sovereignty in the future could be compatible with the far-reaching changes in its favor that a strong Israel intended to make.

The consulate closely tracked the progress of the annexation. It sent reports to Washington on joint Jewish–Arab business initiatives in Jerusalem and the expansion of the Israeli electricity grid into the West Bank. On 28 January 1971, in response to Israeli construction in East Jerusalem, then still small in scale, the consulate explained that annexation was not, as far as Israel was concerned, up for negotiation.[28] In recent years, the United States has expressed its displeasure with the expansion of Israeli construction in East Jerusalem, mostly when it occurred at times that seemed to be inappropriate from a US perspective. But in 2005 it exerted the full weight of its influence only to prevent civilian construction in the large area between Jerusalem and Ma'aleh Adumim. This did not stop Israel from building highways and its district police headquarters there. The municipal master plan for the area has now been completed and awaits an "appropriate time" in Israel–US relations to be put into action.

An Ambiguous V

Are you making a V for victory? asked the bureau director. Eshkol looked at him and his smile vanished. No, it's a V for *vi krichtmen arois*—how do we crawl out of here?[29]

Israel moved with great pride into historic Jerusalem in June 1967. This can be seen in the well-known picture showing Moshe Dayan, Yitzhak Rabin, and Uzi Narkiss striding through Lion's Gate into the Old City, helmets on their heads. The scene, which has become an icon of Israel's victory, was staged by Dayan and captured by Ilan Bruner, a photographer for the Government Press Office.[30] Crawling out of Jerusalem quietly and inconspicuously, as Eshkol seems to have wished, was not an option.

Israelis worried and Arabs hoped that the new boundaries resulting from the war would become but a short-term achievement. In living room conversations, newspaper articles, and political polemics, everybody speculated about what would happen next. The debate pitted fantasies against harsh physical facts, dreams of the future against the historical, demographic, and political constraints. "I have good will, a desire for peace and even a certain measure of appreciation for your project and sympathy for and good relations with the Jews. Just as you speak with Nasser and Hussein, speak to us as well," Anwar Nusseibeh, a former Jordanian cabinet minister and governor of the Jerusalem district, told Moshe Sasson, deputy director-general of the Israeli Foreign Ministry and Prime Minister Eshkol's emissary in talks with Palestinian Arabs.[31]

Sasson, born in Damascus, a diplomat and son of a diplomat, conducted lengthy talks with Palestinian Arabs from the end of 1967 through Eshkol's death at the beginning of 1969, and he filed detailed reports about them. These were not full transcripts of the talks but summaries in which he sought to convey to the prime minister as precise and objective an account as he could of the positions voiced by the Palestinians, even if these rejected the government's official policy and the program of Israel's coalition government.

Nusseibeh and Anwar al-Khatib, who in 1965 had succeeded Nusseibeh as governor of Jordanian Jerusalem and held that post until the war, sought to mediate between Israel and the leaders of Egypt and Jordan and conveyed to Sasson information about the real positions of President Gamal Abd al-Nasser and King Hussein. These West Bank figures did their best to convince Sasson that Hussein wanted peace and would conclude it in exchange for the return of his lost territories, and that Nasser would support this because defeat had made him a realist. But, in their estimation, the initiative had to come from Israel, the victor. Israel had to provide an advance promise of full withdrawal; after it did so, the Arab leaders would commit themselves to peace. Nusseibeh and al-Khatib also offered Sasson detailed surveys of internal political developments in Jordan and severely criticized Fatah, the Palestinian liberation movement. Sasson's reports show that they spoke with exceptional candor, and evinced no sense of inferiority, nor any fear of reprisal. But Israel opposed their offers of mediation. It did not want the help of the local leadership to pass messages to Arab rulers because Israel's leaders believed that the three "nos" that the Arab League resolved on at its Khartoum summit (no peace with Israel, no recognition, and no negotiations)[32] were more accurate expressions of Arab policy than oral messages conveyed by senior Jerusalem Arabs with access to the Jordanian royal palace.

As Sasson wrote in his account of these talks,[33] not all of the leading Palestinian figures were of the same mind. Each of them sought a just and honorable solution, but each also had his own version of what would meet those standards. They disagreed over when Jordan should enter the picture—immediately, or in the second stage, after the West Bank Palestinians took the first step toward an accord with Israel. Nor did they agree about what Jordan's role in the West Bank would be after Israel's withdrawal. On the whole, Sasson attributed internal dissension among the Palestinians to the fact that they felt weak and traumatized by the Arab defeat. He made no effort to help them unite. Israel did not take the initiative and did not help the local leadership consolidate itself. Instead, Israel responded, generally negatively, to ideas proposed by the Palestinians, but which were useless in the absence of a determined Israeli policy to disengage from the West Bank.

During 1968 there were many discussions of a Palestinian initiative to establish an Arab civil administration. West Bank leaders were divided over whether the administration would be established only in the Hebron area under the leadership of that city's mayor, Sheikh Mohammad 'Ali al-Jabari; whether it would also include Jerusalem, as Anwar Nusseibeh demanded but which Israel rejected categorically; whether it would cover the entire West Bank, an idea that Jabari toyed with but which aroused the ire of leaders in Nablus; or whether it would include only Hebron and Bethlehem, an idea that was unacceptable to Bethlehem's Mayor Elias Freij and his colleagues.

"The fate of this land will be determined by its present inhabitants; those who fled have no voice in the matter. There is no moral justification for continuing to leave the matter in the hands of the Arab countries that lost all of Palestine," Jabari told Sasson on 23 June 1968. He laid out a detailed, multi-stage plan of action providing for autonomy for the southern West Bank, proposing how it could be presented to Jordan and the Palestinian public ("Hussein will see that we reached an agreement and will want to join. The situation will turn around then—rather than him annexing us, we'll consider whether to annex him"). Jabari also spoke of his rivalry with the Nablus leadership. Five days later, on 28 June, his ambition had grown. He wanted to be governor of the entire West Bank and to establish his office in Jerusalem's Sho'afat neighborhood, or at Tel al-Ful on the northern side of the city, where stood the skeleton of a palace for King Hussein that had been under construction when the war broke out. If Israel were to reject the idea of having Jabari's office in Jerusalem, he would be prepared to compromise on Ramallah. He asked Sasson to arrange a meeting with Eshkol so that he could persuade the prime minister to permit him to extend his authority over the entire West Bank, although implementation would be gradual and would begin in the region of the Hebron highlands. Jabari, Sasson reported, would try to convince West Bank leaders to agree to this.[34] The Israeli diplomat made his own inquiries and found that the leaders of all the other areas opposed having Jabari placed above them. Nevertheless, Sasson did not want to cut off his talks with the man who was the most influential figure in the Hebron area. On 7 July he notified Jabari that the prime minister agreed in principle to the establishment of a civil administration for the entire West Bank that would operate under Israel's military government. He said the administration should be established gradually, and that Eshkol saw Jabari as the leader of the Hebron region. In response, Jabari reiterated that he would not be satisfied with just Hebron, and asked that at least Bethlehem be placed under his authority. Sasson agreed to try to persuade the public leaders of that city. In addition, Jabari sought real powers and a private fund from which he could make secret allocations. This was not an exceptional demand. At the end of 1967, Israel had "lent" money to leading Palestinians so that they could buy public support and serve as agents of Israel. When these leaders accepted the "loans" but did not change their positions, this program, in this blunt form, was ended,[35] to be replaced by more subtle efforts.

During July, Sasson and Jabari agreed that the inhabitants of Hebron and the surrounding region would petition the military governor to establish a civil administration "to be headed by a civilian governor from the region, who will be granted the civil powers now invested in the military governor" in such a manner as not to affect the question of the West Bank's future. The wording of the petition was agreed with Jabari and approved by Dayan. Jerusalem was not included in the plan because of Israel's opposition to anything that would impact negatively on annexation, while Bethlehem was not included because of the opposition of its leaders. On 12 August 1968, Eshkol and Jabari met, but the latter retreated from the agreements he had made with Sasson. He now wanted Israel to take the initiative, compelling him, as it were, to take over the civil administration. Furthermore, he asked that his authority extend over the entire West Bank.[36] Palestinian mayors and public figures outside Hebron were not alone in opposing Jabari's plan. So did Jordan. The kingdom was apprehensive that such a local initiative would diminish its influence in the West Bank. At this time, King Hussein still hoped to restore the West Bank to its prewar status as part and parcel of his kingdom.

Sasson's brother-in-law, Rafi Levi, then the Interior Ministry's Jerusalem district officer, conducted Israel's talks with church leaders, most of whom resided in Jerusalem. Like Levi, and his father, Eliyahu Sasson, Moshe Sasson was not an Arab Jew. The two ethnic identities were not of equal weight for him. He placed his Zionist-Israeli identity first; the fact that he was a scion of Arab culture was secondary. This ranking, along with the great Israeli victory of 1967, shaped his point of view. At the end of December 1967 Sasson visited the home of Anwar al-Khatib "to wish him a happy Ramadan." In a patronizing tone, Sasson later wrote that the rooms "were large and furnished with somewhat noisy replicas of the French style ... the children served coffee and cake, and he, despite the fast, joined us in drinking, without any discomfort at not fasting." Al-Khatib proposed that West Bank dignitaries be allowed to attend the next Arab summit to explain the circumstances under which they lived and to convince Nasser to back Hussein's desire for peace. "The Israeli reality needs to be conveyed to the Arab countries. [Al-Khatib] had, before the war, thought of himself as an expert on Israel. He regularly read the press and other material. Only now does he understand how weak and inaccurate his knowledge was," Sasson reported. Unlike his interlocutor, Sasson had no doubt that he understood the other side. When the West Bank's notables were permitted to assemble under a single roof, he replied to al-Khatib, they would begin to compete to take the most extreme position. Al-Khatib replied, correctly, that "The West Bank notables are not extremists."[37]

Nusseibeh was not playing the sycophant when he told Sasson of his positive attitude toward the Jews and his desire for peace. Israel's

National Archive has boxes of the Jerusalem lawyer's files from the Mandate period, and they show that he had many Jewish clients then. Nusseibeh was the most senior Palestinian leader in the West Bank. He had served as a member of the Jordanian Senate, as well as that country's ambassador in London and as governor of Jerusalem, and had been Jordan's minister of defense during the 1967 war. He was the most appropriate person to use to convey messages between King Hussein and the Israeli leadership. With Sasson's knowledge, Nusseibeh went to Jordan and met the king on 24 February 1968, some six months after the Khartoum summit. Upon his return, he told Sasson that Hussein saw no problem with accepting Israel in the region, recognizing it, and reaching a just peace agreement. Nasser, he said, shared this position and had given the king the green light to negotiate with Israel.[38]

At the end of 1969 Sasson asked the Greek Catholic Archbishop Hilarion Capucci to go to Amman and sound out his close friend, Jordanian Prime Minister 'Abd al-Mun'im Rifa'i, about his talks in Egypt with that country's foreign minister, Mahmoud Riad, and President Nasser. Rifa'i had gone to Cairo to discuss the diplomatic process in general, and specifically Egypt's position on the Jordanian aspect of the peace plan proposed by US Secretary of State William Rogers. The plan, first broached at the beginning of December, proposed a way to end the War of Attrition that had been raging between Israel and Egypt. Rogers hoped that, if carried out, it could be the first step toward ending the Arab–Israeli conflict as a whole. Sasson was at the time still deputy director-general of the Foreign Ministry, but Eshkol had died nearly a year before, so he was no longer the prime minister's personal envoy. "Nasser agrees to minor, inconsequential changes in the armistice lines, for example at Qalqilya," Sasson wrote to Prime Minister Meir.

> The principle, Nasser said, is that we return to the '67 borders with only minor changes. Jerusalem: Nasser rejects a solution of internationalizing only the Arab side of the city, while leaving the western side under Israeli sovereignty as Israel's capital. If the assumption is that Jerusalem is one, then internationalization has to apply to the entire city. Of course the city will in any case be open and it is also understood that the Western Wall will return to its owners [the Arabs]. Nasser also agrees that Israel will be granted a corridor to the Wall that will belong to Israel and which will pass through Arab territory ... all 1967 refugees will be returned to their places. Refugees from 1948 will have the right to choose between return and resettlement with reparations. 'Abd al-

Mun'am noted here that he estimates that 90–95 percent of the 1948 refugees will choose reparations.[39]

In other words, at least twice, at the beginning of 1968 and at the beginning of 1970, senior figures from East Jerusalem reported that Nasser's position differed from the final statement issued at the Khartoum summit. In fact, Nasser's reported position at this time differed little from proposals discussed by Israel and the PLO during their negotiations from the Camp David conference of 2000 through the Annapolis summit of 2008. The Palestinian position was and remains that the 4 June 1967 lines are the basis for any territorial accommodation. In both official talks and through unofficial channels, the Palestinians have stressed the principle of reciprocity. In their view, proposals for special regimes in Jerusalem must include at least some of West Jerusalem. The open city that Israel has so proudly advocated was acceptable to Nasser and it was not a subject of contention in Israel's talks with the PLO. Nasser's proposal about the Western Wall was a mirror image of one of the central proposals regarding the Temple Mount that Israel submitted to Arafat at the Camp David summit—that the site come under Israeli sovereignty while the Muslims would have free access and a corridor under Palestinian sovereignty that would link the holy site to the Palestinian state. Nor was Nasser's proposal regarding refugees much different from the Palestinian negotiating position throughout the PLO's contacts with Israel.[40]

"Our assumption is that we will rule Jerusalem, which will not be divided, but that a solution can be found to the problem of free and near-sovereign access to the holy sites ... this solution could even be quasi-sovereignty and include the raising of a Muslim flag over the Mosque of Omar [sic]," Moshe Dayan told Hamdi Can'an of Nablus and 'Aziz Shehadeh of Ramallah on 21 April 1968. Dayan related that he posed three questions about a peace accommodation to King Hussein, and that one of them related to Jerusalem: "Would you be prepared to agree to serious changes in the pre-June 5, 1967 status?" The Palestinian dignitaries expressed their willingness for a change with regard to 4 June 1967, inasmuch as Jerusalem would not be physically divided. But they insisted that Israel could not be the only sovereign in the city. "Joint sovereignty and a city open to all," they declared.[41] Restricting their authority to the operation of the Muslim holy sites under Israeli sovereignty was not an option, they told Dayan. Dayan, for his part, did not see an open city as that much of a change from the prewar status quo; and, as will be shown shortly, nor did Eshkol. Israel wanted to cement the principal achievement of the war and to change it only marginally. The Palestinians and Arabs wanted the opposite. The Israeli government, with pride in its great victory, did not entertain the possibility of responding positively to the Arab ideas. From its point of view, doing so would turn its victory into a defeat.

On 9 April 1968, Sasson met with Eshkol and reported to him that the Palestinian position was that Jerusalem had to be the capital of a Palestinian state or of a Palestinian–Jordanian federation that would include nearly all of the West Bank. "The prime minister responded that with regard to Jerusalem there was nothing to discuss ... except for some sort of status for al-Haram al-Sharif there was nothing to talk about ... They will have to become part of the Jerusalem municipality and that's it." One can almost hear Eshkol's thundering bass voice when Sasson paraphrases him. The prime minister's unequivocal position distressed Sasson, but rather than argue with the premier, he apologized. "I said that I was presenting the Arab viewpoint and that I had to confront him with reality as the Arabs saw it. With regard to Jerusalem, I was careful not to enter into any discussion or even to offer hints to any Arab [that the Israeli government might be willing to compromise on Jerusalem], so I could not know what Jordan could agree to." Sasson then offered an idea broached by Anwar Nusseibeh regarding a gradual solution that would begin by handing over responsibility for a number of areas in the West Bank, including Jerusalem, to Arab officials. Beyond Nusseibeh's idea, Sasson's report does not mention anything else. Eshkol said he wanted to think about it, but this may just have been a weary prime minister's way of ending the conversation.[42] On the face of it, Sasson had reached the end of his rope. How far he went at the end can be seen in his conversation with Nusseibeh ten days later.

Nusseibeh told Sasson about a proposition he had put together with Meron Benvenisti, the municipal official responsible for East Jerusalem under Kollek, and Fa'iq Barakat, the head of the East Jerusalem Chamber of Commerce. Benvenisti had proposed that he be commissioned by the Israeli army and, as an officer, serve as Kollek's aide responsible for liaison with the Arab sub-municipality, led by a reconstituted version of the Jordanian city council. Benvenisti constructed a plan down to the finest detail, including the furnishings in his office and its placement next to the office of the Arab sub-mayor.[43] The Arab municipality would once again function just as it had done under Jordan. Benvenisti's status as an army officer would create the appearance of there being a military governor in East Jerusalem, just as there was in the West Bank's other cities. Yet the annexation would not be abrogated. Benvenisti would, in this new guise, continue to serve as Kollek's adviser on East Jerusalem. Israel and Jordan would fund the Arab sub-municipality. Benvenisti would receive these funds and pass them on, as a kind of outsourcing, to the Arab municipality or to nongovernmental bodies, in accordance with the priorities and politics that he would set along with the Arab City Council. The Arab body would work together with the Israeli municipality to oversee all municipal functions, and they would establish a joint planning board to formulate a master plan for East Jerusalem. Unbeknownst to Benvenisti, his plan resembled the one Minister of Housing Bentov had earlier suggested to the cabinet committee on Jerusalem, charged with implementing the decision to annex Jordanian Jerusalem. It had convened the day after the annexation decision, on 12 June 1967. Bentov had proposed the appointment of a military governor over Jordanian Jerusalem who would "apply to the Jerusalem municipality on a contract basis and ask that it supply all the necessary services" to the inhabitants of the eastern side of the city. A subcommittee for East Jerusalem affairs, composed of the members of the Jordanian city council, would operate under the Jerusalem municipality.[44] Bentov's proposition was rejected.

Sasson was surprised by what Nusseibeh told him. With Eshkol's voice still ringing in his ears, he said that Jerusalem would remain annexed and that there would be no separate Arab municipality. An accommodation was possible only under those two conditions: "Nusseibeh tried to persuade me that Benvenisti's proposal was important," Sasson wrote, "and in the end he asked me not to interfere with but rather to promote it. I told him that there was no chance of that."[45]

Nusseibeh tried, on 9 September 1968, to persuade Foreign Minister Abba Eban to support the Benvenisti plan. He requested a postponement of the expropriation of land (on which the Israeli neighborhoods of Ramat Eshkol and French Hill would later be built) for three to six months so as to build confidence and to enable negotiations over self-government in the West Bank, including Jerusalem and the Gaza Strip, to be headed by apolitical Arab officials. He had no objection, he said, if Jews bought land in East Jerusalem and individual Arabs bought land in West Jerusalem on a piecemeal, individual basis, but he opposed government expropriations. Eban turned him down. There seemed to be no point in discussing the matter further, so they turned to a new subject. Nusseibeh declared that East Jerusalem had to be included under the West Bank self-governing arrangement. Eban rejected that as well. "If all hope of a political solution is lost, we will have to search together for consensual frameworks of coexistence," Nusseibeh told him, intimating a one-state option.[46] Eban did not respond.

The next day Nusseibeh drafted the outlines of a political solution. It included several possibilities—the internationalization of the city or two capitals, with the eastern part of the city serving as the capital of Jordan or Palestine and the western part as the capital of Israel. In the latter case, if in the future a Jordanian–Palestinian union were established, East Jerusalem would be the capital of the united entity. In any case, Jerusalem would be an open city with freedom of access and freedom of worship at holy places. With the consent of the world powers, UN headquarters would move to Jerusalem, which would become the spiritual capital of the world. But a precondition for discussing these ideas was a halt to Israeli land expropriations in East Jerusalem and the restoration of already confiscated land to its former owners. Nusseibeh asked Sasson to pass his plan on to decision-makers, but Sasson did not do so. On 26 September he told Nusseibeh why. Such ideas, he said, gave credence to the Arabs' illusions of regaining Jerusalem and caused Israelis, "who think in terms of positive solutions," to lose hope. Nusseibeh replied that "The truth is that I have reached the conclusion that you are not prepared to propose any plan on your own initiative. My intention was to spur you to make a counter-proposal." Sasson responded that "the time has come to be clear about where the winds are blowing and what the Israeli way of thinking is ... you need a solution much more than we do."[47] The thousands of hours of Israeli–Palestinian discussions over the future of Jerusalem in the years that followed were essentially repetitions of this dialogue and the principles voiced in it. "If there is no solution to the Jerusalem problem, then he, as an Arab, prefers full annexation with the grant of full rights to the Arabs in a democratic framework," Sasson wrote in a summary of Mahmoud Abu Zuluf, editor of the daily newspaper *al-Quds*.[48] In the 2000s, many of the inhabitants of both sides of Jerusalem would reach the same conclusion.

Many of these meetings between Israelis and Palestinians were held in the King David Hotel, as they had been during the Mandate. But the cosmopolitan atmosphere of that old Jerusalem was a thing of the past. The encounters were no longer between people of equal status who came to discuss culture and politics. Now they were between conquerors and the conquered. Furthermore, the King David lost its exclusive status in this regard—many such meetings were now held in East Jerusalem restaurants; at Sasson's apartment not far from the hotel, on 22 Lincoln Street; in Nusseibeh's home across from the American Colony Hotel in Sheikh Jarrah; and in al-Khatib's house in Beit Hanina.

At the same time that Benvenisti and Nusseibeh were doing their best to push their plan up the ladder, Benvenisti was asked by Israel's negotiators with Jordan to draft a proposal that would keep East Jerusalem under Israeli sovereignty while simultaneously providing for Jordan's interests. At the beginning of July 1968 Benvenisti proposed the creation of a greater Jerusalem composed of a number of quarters. The metropolitan region would be divided between Israeli and Jordanian sovereignty, with a single municipal administration under which two sub-municipalities, one for Arabs and one for Jews, would operate. In April 1971 the document was leaked to the press, torpedoing Kollek's intention of appointing Benvenisti, who had been elected to the city council, to the post of deputy mayor. Kollek disavowed the document, even though the idea behind it was not alien to him and was in fact quite similar to the plan he had proposed to the American consul-general about a year after the war.[49] The Benvenisti plan, it turned out, was way ahead of its time. At the end of the 1990s the Jerusalem Institute for Israel Studies, a think tank that works closely with Israel's political establishment, formulated several versions of the idea of a joint Jewish–Arab Greater Jerusalem. By this time, the Palestinian Authority, not Jordan, was the Arab party involved. As Jordan had, the Palestinians demanded that Israel forego annexation of the entire Arab half of Jerusalem, rather than soften its impact by wrapping it up in a metropolitan administration that would grant them only limited powers. This discussion of the 1990s did not lead anywhere.

Palestinian political leaders were not the only ones to offer plans for Jerusalem's future—religious leaders did as well. On 22 February 1968, Sheikh Yasin al-Bakri, the imam of the al-Aqsa mosque, approached Ya'akov Yehoshua, director of the Muslim Department of Israel's Ministry of Religions, with a proposal to establish a binational, triconfessional state under the name "the Government of Holy Palestine." To Yehoshua's surprise, al-Bakri had designed a flag for the new country. It showed al-Aqsa in the upper right, with a Star of David and crescent in the upper left. At the bottom right was an image of the Church of the Holy Sepulcher and at the bottom left Rachel's Tomb. Al-Bakri said he had not included a cross because Jesus himself had not made this a symbol of his faith. Jews and Muslims would alternate in the posts of president and prime minister; the foreign and interior ministers would always be Jews. In parliament, 40 percent of the seats would be awarded to Jews, 40 percent to Muslims, and 20 percent to Christians. If Jordan joined, the cabinet would include five Jews, seven Muslims, and three Christians. If his plan was not accepted, al-Bakri said, he would support the creation of a "Palestinian entity," the term then in use for an independent Palestinian state. Al-Bakri claimed that Ben-Gurion and Eliyahu Sasson took an interest in the plan, but that nothing came of it because Mufti Hajj Amin al-Hussayni demanded to be the first president, which was unacceptable to the Jews.[50] His claim regarding Ben-Gurion and Sasson is doubtful. While the plan seems delusionary, it nevertheless testified that a Muslim cleric acknowledged that the standing of the Jews had changed. Al-Bakri, who in 1948 had wanted to expel all the Jews from Palestine, was prepared after 1967 to have them as partners in a government and to invest them permanently with the tasks of representing his country to the world and of maintaining internal order.

But Israel did not seize the opportunity to explore any of these proposals. It rejected ideas that, in the perspective of time, later seemed to some Israelis like reasonable first steps. When Nusseibeh first broached with Sasson the plan he had drafted together with Benvenisti, Sasson thought it no less absurd than the plan that al-Bakri presented to Ya'akov Yehoshua. The question is thus not what might have been but rather why Israel's leaders did not seize the opportunity, why Eshkol did not have the courage to crawl out of the hole Israel was in. Neither a lack of political foresight nor a mistaken evaluation of costs and benefits seems like a sufficient explanation. True, Israel's leaders have, over the years, displayed much historical shortsightedness and faith in the military force they have built up and deployed so effectively. But something deeper lies behind this. This full or partial blindness and the euphoria of power have been fired by deep historical, emotional, and religious sentiments toward the land, sentiments that were fired by the country's stunning victory in 1967. Only a very small number of Israelis have developed mechanisms to regulate this euphoria. Most felt like the proprietors and lords of the land.

Jerusalem lay at the heart of this refusal to consider opportunities for accommodation. In accordance with instructions handed down by Prime Minister Eshkol, Moshe Sasson spoke on 19 November 1968 with Uri Avneri, a member of the Knesset and one of the most forceful and consistent critics of the government's policies toward the Arabs. Avneri had berated the country's leadership for not passing an explicit resolution favoring the establishment of a Palestinian state, and for not proposing the creation of such a state to West Bank leaders. He asserted that, when it looked as if Israel had no interest in such a state, important figures in the West Bank decided that there was nothing to wait for and resolved to take action to achieve this goal. "Without addressing the question of whether a Palestinian state is desirable or not, the question is whether the Arabs would want such a state if it did not include Jerusalem," Sasson told Eshkol about his conversation with Avneri. "Since we are not willing to return Arab Jerusalem, and since I do not know of any Arab who is interested in a Palestinian state without Jerusalem, the entire discussion of a Palestinian state is abstract and meaningless ... neither I nor Avneri can point to a single West Bank leader prepared to support the idea of a Palestinian state without Jerusalem." Sasson told the prime minister that, when he asked Avineri what the final solution would look like, Avineri said:

At this stage, in general and explicitly: "United Jerusalem is the capital of Israel, the capital of the common institutions, and the capital of the Palestinian state." Avneri agreed with me that the question of sovereignty over "the Arab capital in Jerusalem" is a central issue and he offered his opinion in light of his conversations with West Bank leaders that the general formulation he proposed would be sufficient to allow Palestinian leaders to open talks with Israel without being considered traitors, and he believed that during these negotiations a detailed formulation could be found that would enable Jerusalem to remain united and satisfy Arab honor. Furthermore, Mr. Avneri believes, also in light of the written documents he has received from West Bank leaders, that the Egyptian president would offer a tacit green light to such an initiative by the West Bank's leaders.[51]

Uri Avneri was not able to come down clearly in favor of a Jerusalem divided between Israel and the Palestinian state he so ardently supported. He hoped that his fuzzy and convoluted wording about a united Jerusalem and Arab honor would jumpstart a process that would lead to a joint capital, even though he knew that no Palestinian leader supported such a possibility. As already noted, Sasson's talks demonstrated that the West Bank leadership, along with Hussein and

Nasser, demanded Palestinian or Jordanian sovereignty in East Jerusalem. To extract the eastern side of the city from Israel, the West Bank leaders proposed incorporating the Arab city into an autonomous administration that would be set up in the West Bank. But Moshe Sasson and his superiors were not prepared to give up sole Israeli sovereignty in East Jerusalem.

5

LIKE OWNERS

No city arouses such a hunger for absolute possession, such cruel intolerance, as Jerusalem does.

– Simon Sebag Montefiore[1]

Transferring the Deed

When cease-fire agreements were reached in 1949, it turned out that the war had changed both the human and physical landscapes of Jaffa and Jerusalem. The lines separating Jews and Arabs had become institutionalized. The surrender agreement under which the Old City of Jerusalem's Jewish Quarter was handed over to the Jordanians explicitly defined the Quarter's Jewish inhabitants as prisoners of war, that is, as Israeli combatants. In consequence, they received the protection of the Red Cross and, after the armistice agreement was signed, they were handed over to Israel.

Some 10,000 Jews were to have remained as inhabitants of the Palestinian Arab state envisioned by the UN partition resolution. However, after the war not a single Jew remained in the Arab-ruled parts of Palestine, the West Bank and the Gaza Strip. In contrast, about 150,000 defeated Palestinian Arabs remained in the State of Israel, which granted them citizenship in the Jewish state but also imposed military rule over most of them. Jaffa's Arabs thus formally enjoyed equal rights. But, in practice, Israel treated them from that point on as potential security threats.² The few Arabs who remained in their homes in the villages near the city—Yazur, Tel al-Rish, Beit Dajan, Yahud, Salameh, Hiriyya, and Abu Kabir—were moved by the IDF to Jaffa, where they were resettled in a fenced-off and guarded compound in the Ajami neighborhood, along with the several hundred native Jaffans who had not fled. According to Israel's first census, altogether they numbered 3,647.³

The military government controlling Jaffa's Arabs was dissolved in 1949, but the Ministry of Minorities kept close track of them. Arabs who wanted to leave or enter Ajami, or to get jobs, needed to obtain a permit from the ministry. During 1949, Avraham Malul, its regional officer for Jaffa, Ramla, and Lod (the new Israeli name for Lydda), filed monthly reports on the reactions of Jaffa's Arabs to Israeli measures regarding the Arab population—such as issuing Israeli identity cards, international travel documents, and transit permits at Christmastime for Arabs who wished to visit holy sites that were under Arab control in Jerusalem and Bethlehem. The files residing in Israel's National Archives regarding these transit permits remain closed to the public. But there is good reason to believe that they document how the granting of such permits was conditioned on Arab collaboration with the Shin Bet, Israel's internal security service, providing it with intelligence. Malul also reported on Jaffa Arabs' attitudes toward Mapai, Israel's ruling party, and regarding political unrest in Arab countries.⁴

The Israeli government revised its oversight of Jaffa's Arabs in 1953. While those in Lod and Ramla remained under the purview of the Ministry of Minorities, those in Jaffa were placed under the Tel Aviv District Office of the Interior Ministry. Jaffa had been annexed to Tel Aviv four years previously and this administrative change brought national policy in line with municipal policy. The Interior Ministry did not, however, provide services to Jaffa's Arabs through the same office that served Tel Aviv's Jews. Rather, the ministry appointed a minorities officer who registered exits from and arrivals in Israel, as well as religious conversions between Islam and Christianity, and issued identity cards and birth certificates to Jaffa's Arabs. All the relevant government ministries, including education, health, and welfare, kept track of Jaffa's Arabs, while they were also controlled from behind the scenes by the Shin Bet. Nafa' Diab, from the village of Tamra, for instance, was not accepted by the Jaffa Arab teachers college for the 1960 academic year. To his surprise, however, he was accepted by the kibbutz movement's teacher training college, even though he was not fluent in Hebrew. He appealed the decision on the grounds that he preferred to study at the Arabic-language college in Jaffa, where he would understand his classes. The reasoning pertaining to his case can be gleaned from a marginal note written by Emannuel Yafeh, director of the Ministry of Education's Teacher Training Department, on a letter he received from Diab. Yafeh apparently had reason to think that Diab might be a bad political influence on the young Arab students in Jaffa. "There is an order: it would be undesirable for him to be among Arab students; at the kibbutz [college] at Oranim he can't do any harm."[5]

As the years went by this oversight was eased but not rescinded. In 2008, the Shin Bet vetoed the appointment of Sheikh Ahmed Abu Ajwa as imam of a mosque in Jaffa's Jabaliyya neighborhood, even though he was the only candidate to meet the requirements of the Ministry of the Interior.[6] A young Arab woman from Jaffa told a similar story: "I applied to nursing school. They did not want to accept me. The director said to me: 'I don't know [why]. I really don't know. I simply received an order.' ... The Shin Bet summoned me before that, when my brother got married, and they told me, congratulations, your brother is getting married, and we know that." It was the Shin Bet's practice to frighten Arabs by showing them how much they knew about them and their families. In cases like this one, the organization may well have been hinting that it could provide money to help her brother pay for his wedding in exchange for the woman's cooperation. She related: "For a while I didn't go to school out of fear. I lived in fear. But today when I think about [the fear], today I see that it was unjustified ... in the end I was accepted and I became an operating room nurse."[7]

The legal status of the Palestinians who remained in Jaffa in 1948 differed from those of the Palestinian Arabs of the part of Jerusalem that came under Israeli rule in 1967. So did their national consciousness. Citizenship was not imposed on the latter; rather, they were granted "permanent resident" status. The Jerusalem municipality incorporated East Jerusalem into the Israeli capital, making it part of Israel, but it did not do the same with its inhabitants, who did not receive citizenship. "To this day no clear and unambiguous policy has been pursued by the government regarding the Arabs of Jerusalem, who see themselves as inseparable from the inhabitants of the West Bank and claim that we have annexed only territory and not inhabitants, the proof being that they remain Jordanian citizens in every sense," Eli Amir wrote to his superior, Shmuel Toledano, in July 1968. Toledano held the office of the government's adviser on Arab affairs, a post that was created in 1956 and granted some of the responsibilities and authorities of the previous Ministry of Minorities, which had been dissolved in 1949. Consequently, "the people of East Jerusalem are not prepared to run for city council seats, neither on a party nor on an individual basis." Amir proposed conferring Israeli citizenship on the inhabitants of East Jerusalem. "The population will [then] finally understand that its fate is sealed, for better or worse, to be an inseparable part of the state of Israel. As an intermediate stage, in order to give them a sense that their interests are being represented democratically in the city council, I hereby propose declaring, in accordance with the Municipalities Order the establishment of [elected secondary] municipal councils" of East Jerusalem residents. The proposal to annex the Palestinians of East Jerusalem—that is, to grant them citizenship—had already come up in the cabinet. In March 1968, Minister of Justice Ya'akov Shimshon Shapira told Prime Minister Eshkol: "We should not speak about automatic citizenship for the residents of East Jerusalem; the Law of Return does not, of course, apply to them; [they] are not citizens by virtue of living in Israel because it speaks of living [there] from 1952 [when the citizenship law was passed]; they have no grounds for demanding citizenship by birth because [the citizenship law] speaks of people who were born with one or both parents being Israeli citizens." Nor could they be naturalized because "naturalization is at the discretion of the minister of the interior" and cannot be imposed collectively. Furthermore, "there are a number of conditions, of which they cannot meet at least three":

Three years out of a period of five years that preceded the submission of the application for citizenship; some knowledge of the Hebrew language; termination of previous citizenship ... the possibility of naturalization thus does not exist for the inhabitants of East Jerusalem at the current time unless the law is amended. Of course, if the law is to be amended, then it can be amended such that they receive Israeli citizenship automatically ... My advice is that you consider the question of whether the subject should be brought before the cabinet for discussion.[8]

In the initial years after June 1967, Israelis viewed the failure to grant citizenship to East Jerusalem Arabs as a liberal policy that demonstrated Israel's restraint. The policy was liberal, in their eyes, because it did not force the Arabs to accept something they might not want.

Furthermore, it was good for the Jews, since it neutralized the demographic problem of what would happen if the state suddenly gained a large number of new Arab citizens. The Arabs viewed it as evidence that the occupation of their city was temporary. Israel would withdraw and the catastrophe would end. "You'll leave here within two or three weeks, just as you left Sinai in 1956," Palestinians told Eli Amir. The world would not remain silent about the annexation and the demolition of the Old City's Mughrabi neighborhood, members of the Arab political and social elite declared at a gathering in Anwar Nusseibeh's living room.[9] Yet nearly two generations later, it is evident that the world did indeed remain silent about many actions Israel had taken to make clear that East Jerusalem was in Israel's hands permanently. The discrepancy between the status of the territory and its inhabitants increasingly revealed itself in the form of ethnic discrimination and violations of human rights. In terms of Israeli law and the courts, the territory was Israeli in every sense of the word. The fact that people who lived there were born in East Jerusalem did not give them civil rights. Legally, they were considered people who had come into Israeli territory from the outside.[10] In other words, before the law, Israel did not enter and take over East Jerusalem, as actually happened. Instead, East Jerusalem's Arabs suddenly appeared within Israel's sovereign borders. The gates open automatically to Jews who were not born in Israel, but Israel is prepared only to serve as host for Palestinian natives. For example, Marvin Arthur Hoffman came to Israel from the United States in 1967. As a Jew, he received citizenship immediately and, after a year of work on a kibbutz, decided that the country was not for him and returned to the land of his birth. His daughter Adina applied for Israeli citizenship thirty-five years later. An Interior Ministry official explained to her that she had already received Israeli citizenship automatically, having been born to an Israeli citizen who had not renounced his citizenship. As far as the official was concerned, the father had never left the country.[11]

The rules made by Israel had an extremely harsh impact on the Arabs, even though they did not shift the demographic balance in Israel's favor. The size of the Arab population, which made up 25 percent of Jerusalem's population in 1967, had risen to 36 percent in 2009, and this upward demographic trend continues today.[12] Israel has used bureaucratic methods to counter this. From 1967 through 2008, it revoked the resident status of 13,075 Arabs—about 45 percent of them in the years 2006 and 2008 (1,363 and 4,677 people, respectively). The sharp rise in such nullifications in 2006–8 resulted from a calculated reexamination of the right to such status by the Interior Ministry, the adoption of more efficient methods by the ministry, and instructions handed down from above.[13] Israeli and Palestinian NGOs estimate that, fearing the loss of their resident status (which required their actual presence in Jerusalem), some 10,000 Palestinians who had moved outside the city limits returned to the city during this period. The Muslim Quarter, the shoddy physical infrastructure of which can support no more than 17,000 residents, now contains twice that many people living in crowded conditions in the space of just 75 acres, slightly more than a tenth of a square mile. In parallel, the Jerusalem municipality and Interior Ministry have demolished structures they defined as illegal. However, only 4 to 8 percent of the 80,000 buildings designated as illegal were actually demolished before 2001.[14] According to the human rights organization B'Tselem, just 384 housing units were demolished for this reason in the 2004–11 period, leaving 1,500 people homeless.[15]

The disparity between the status of Jaffa's Arabs and those of East Jerusalem is also evident in the way the Arabs of both cities think of themselves and each other. Since 1967, the latter have condescended to the former. Jerusalem's Arab community has a larger and more developed elite. The community is better educated, and it has a much richer social and political milieu. During the decade following 1967, this attitude was accompanied by one common belief among Palestinian Arabs as a whole—that all of Israel's Arab citizens were little more than collaborators with the Jews.[16]

In 1948, many Arabs left their homes. In Jerusalem and Jaffa, they took few of their possessions with them. Most houses suffered considerable damage during the war. In the cities' poor neighborhoods, not much was left for looters. The situation was different in better-off neighborhoods. In Jaffa, Jews took whatever they could get their hands on, including windows and shutters.[17] In Jaffa's surrender agreement, the city's military governor wrote on 2 June 1948 to the minister of Arab affairs and police, "it was promised to the inhabitants that after they were identified etc. they would be allowed to return to normal life." "In the meantime," he protested, "there have been several cases of the confiscation of property and merchandise belonging to Arabs located there. An example is that of a juice factory that belongs to

Ahmed Abu Laban, in partnership with Jews, as well as other cases of property in stores belonging to local residents."[18] A few days earlier, on 26 May, the minister of police reported to the cabinet that Jaffa's first military governor, Yitzhak Chizik, wished to resign, "especially after the plague of burglary and theft has spread in an organized and unorganized way." The governor protested that soldiers had carried out "arrests and searches without orders, beatings and detentions and in particular killings of people. Up until yesterday, fifteen in number ... the city has been plundered and is breached and anyone who passes through would be ashamed at the sight of the disgraceful destruction ... you have no doubt heard of the cases of rape."[19] The value of goods looted in Jaffa was estimated by the military government at P£2 million. Collections of archaeological objects were taken from homes in Jaffa and from the Notre Dame monastery that lay on the front between East and West Jerusalem. Israel's custodian of abandoned properties took control of properties left behind by refugees from Jaffa. He first made this property available to the army, and what the army did not want was awarded to needy and handicapped Jews, the families of soldiers, and government officials. Whatever remained was auctioned off.

Looting and expropriation by the custodian also took place in Jerusalem. "Following the conquest of Qatamon," Meron Benvenisti wrote, "we manned roadblocks so that we could confiscate the plunder taken by Jews from Arab homes. We were ordered to store the confiscated furniture and rugs in the abandoned Park Lane Hotel, and we saw how 'authorized personnel' took this property for themselves, on various pretexts." Benvenisti also took some items from the Arabs. "My brother and I went into homes that were empty and open and we collected the food that remained in pantries and kitchens ... the food we collected helped us get through the siege without suffering from starvation."[20] On 14 June 1949, the custodian took a desk and four upholstered chairs from the Tanus family house. He sometimes took Jewish property by mistake. Y.H. Zeitlin filed a complaint just two days before this, saying that some garden chairs that he had stored in the stairwell of his home in Talbiyyeh had been taken by the custodian as abandoned property.[21]

Public and private libraries and manuscript collections were plundered. To put a stop to looting by individuals, the minorities minister set up a committee headed by Haim Ze'ev Hirschberg, an Arab language and literature specialist and director of the Ministry of Religion's Muslim and Druze Affairs Department, which collected and catalogued the books left behind by Arab refugees. To protect the books, the committee set up an Arabic library containing 4,500 volumes in the mosque in Jaffa's Nuzha neighborhood.[22]

In Jerusalem, Arabic books were collected in a more comprehensive and systematic way by professional librarians. Between May 1948 and the end of February 1949, the staff of Israel's National Library amassed 30,000 books, newspapers, and manuscripts from the homes of Palestinian refugees in Qatamon, Baq'a, Talbiyyeh, Musrara, the German Colony, the Greek Colony, and Abu Tor. Among the collections they acquired in this way was the ample one owned by Khalil Sakakini. A total of about 28,000 Arabs had been living in western Jerusalem just prior to the war, and many of them were educated booklovers who left everything behind. The librarians did not enter locked homes, only those that had been looted and left open. Most of the books collected in this way were in Arabic. At first, the books were catalogued according to the names of their owners, but they were gradually reclassified from the 1960s onwards under the catalogue designation "AP," abandoned property. The fact that the books were once privately owned is no longer acknowledged. While the librarians probably saved these books from destruction, they at the same time expropriated them from their previous owners and appropriated them for the National Library of the victors.[23]

Shulamit Hareven, later a novelist and in 1948 a soldier in Jerusalem, participated in taking over the beautiful home owned by Anton Awad, a well-off businessman. In her 2002 autobiography Hareven described what she and her comrades did, in the heat of battle, to the possessions the family left behind:

We opened refrigerators, cupboards, and ate our fill ... and since no water came out of the faucets, the boys began splashing vermouth over their heads ... we trampled through puddles of vermouth ... someone tried on one of Mrs. Awad's evening gowns. Menashe said that he could not stand the sculptured bust of a woman [that stood] on the stairwell between the house's two stories, and drew a moustache on it ... we found Anton Awad's and the family's shoe cabinet. There were dozens of shoes there. Mrs. Awad's embroidered sandals fit Moshe, who had small feet, so he wore them. Reuven put on high heels and the two curtsied to each other ... I went into the bedroom of Anton Awad's son ... a volume of Shakespeare was on the desk ... I took the Shakespeare with me.

LIKE OWNERS

Hareven felt remorseful about this in 1967, when the border that had kept her apart from the owner of the home she had broken into and had taken the book from disappeared. "When I saw Anton Awad's name in the telephone book, I could no longer tolerate having that Shakespeare for another moment ... I drove to see him" in order to "put things right," as she put it. She walked into his home in East Jerusalem and mentally compared it to his former home, the one she had been in. Anton Awad was no longer wealthy, and she found herself preoccupied with what had happened to him. When he greeted her, she found that she could say no more than "the winds of war brought me a book that your name is written in." Awad did not understand. More to the point, and without apologizing, she said: "I came to return to you something that was in my possession ... this book, it belongs to you and I want to return it to you ... it was in your previous home." The dialogue between them was broken, polite, and painful; their souls did not make contact. A barrier still separated them. Hareven did not ask about the family, some of whose secrets she had come to know that night in 1948 when, by candlelight, she read the diary of Anton's son, Joseph. *Julius Caesar* had been taken from a Palestinian to an Israeli home and was about to return to its owner, but not to the same house from which it had come and without the rest of the library of which it had been part.

My previous home?! His entire head suddenly flushed red. A rush of words emerged from his mouth. Don't want to hear. They should return everything. They looted property worth tens of thousands of pounds ... I don't need it. Tens of thousands of pounds they looted according to the value of money then and now they're returning one book. Is this supposed to be a joke? ... I suffer from nerves ... every time that subject is opened it's like opening a wound for me.

Awad rejected Shulamit Hareven's small personal gesture, the restitution of a tiny bit of his property. But was he giving up the book, or did he mean to say that he would accept it only along with the rest of his stolen belongings? In the end, she wrote, "the Shakespeare remained with me. My son is now using it to study for an exam on *Julius Caesar*."[24] Did she see the book as entrusted to her until its owner agreed to take it back, or did she believe that Awad had given her the book? Had he done it because his health worsened every time the wound of 1948 was probed, or because he had lost hope that Israel would act as he demanded, and therefore gave her possession of the book for her own son to use?

The Jews did not only take property from houses—they also took the houses themselves, and land. At first Jews squatted in Arab dwellings, without any prompting or oversight on the part of the central government. Afterward the state itself took over properties in a systematic way, via the custodian of abandoned properties, with the express purpose of housing Jews in apartments and houses that the Arabs had vacated. The custodian's first priority was to hand homes over to the Jewish Agency's Department of Absorption so that immigrants—Jews—could be settled in them. Second in line were the army and government officials.[25]

The houses were not only those of Arabs who fled, but also included residences belonging to Arabs who had remained in Jaffa. The IDF, in evacuating Arabs from their homes, provided them with a truck on which to load their belongings and sometimes pushed them to vacate quickly, without time to pack everything up. "Homes are not to be evacuated in a hasty and rash way and the Arabs are to be given enough time, to the extent that is possible," the minister of minority affairs ordered when he heard about this. "Within ten days the Arabs are to be evacuated from places in which Jews will be settled ... elderly and peaceful Arabs can remain in their homes with special permission from the governor, who can consider each case in point. Such people will be granted limited free passage permits."[26] Amin Andreus was one of those who was allowed to stay. He was a member of the National Emergency Committee that assumed leadership of Jaffa after the flight of the city's mayor, Yusif Haykal. The committee signed the surrender agreement of 13 May 1948, and worked to impose order on the abandoned city. Andreus refused to leave his home in Jalabiyyeh and move into the compound in Ajami. The army left him alone and his home was saved. But soldiers stole his car and the army expropriated a citrus grove he owned near the Lod airport. In June 1948, as the looting continued, Andreus submitted his formal resignation from the Emergency Committee. His three elderly daughters now live alone in the old house. They gaze out of the windows at the sea over which their friends and neighbors fled the closing Israeli siege, and at the closed-off, alienating Peres Center for Peace, built with green stones from somewhere else, and at the Muslim cemetery.[27]

The Arab homes were filled with immigrants, Jewish refugees from combat zones, and government officials who coveted these properties. By order of Prime Minister and Minister of Defense David Ben-Gurion, the top army command tried to preempt the squatters and the backing they received from local officials. But it was to no avail.²⁸ The custodian of abandoned properties, the Jewish Agency, and the army's Housing Department issued documents without any legal validity to soldiers and new immigrants that allowed them to break into and take over homes. The police did not accept the documents and ousted the intruders, who often resisted and generally succeeded in keeping the properties they had appropriated. "The custodian of abandoned properties has taken over a number of homes in Jaffa ... the military governor has taken I£3500 from Arab homes, and goods valued at I£30,000 have been taken from the Arab [National Emergency] Committee. People continue to remove furniture from Jaffa. At the time, it reached huge proportions ... a total of 395 suits were filed by unevacuated Arabs to receive back their property." But, reported Avraham Shlush, then a regional officer in Jaffa's military government, on 9 July "only 75 homes were released [back to their owners]."²⁹ According to one estimate, 1,500 rooms in the homes of Arab refugees were appropriated by military units, and by individual soldiers and members of their families.³⁰ What happened in Jaffa was hardly exceptional. Military and government personnel also took over the homes of refugees in Haifa's Wadi Salib neighborhood. They were protected by the army units that guarded the area, in violation of instructions from the Minority Affairs Ministry.³¹

About 23 percent of the land in West Jerusalem that had been owned by Arabs before the war became the property of the State of Israel, as did large houses in Qatamon and Talbiyyeh. Jewish war refugees from northern Jerusalem, the Old City, and the Etzion Block were housed in them, as well as army officers, government officials, and others who took advantage of the Arab exodus to improve their housing conditions.³² Israel's first ministers of labor, Golda Myerson and Mordecai Namir, both lodged in Talbiyyeh, in a house known as the Haroun al-Rashid Villa. Levi Eshkol, when he served as agriculture and then finance minister, lived in Qatamon, in the former home of 'Abd al-Ghani Kamleh. "After the war, my father was offered, thanks to his service in the Haganah, the opportunity to move into an Arab house in Talbiyyeh or Qatamon," Orna Ahimeir recalled. The offer caused a series of rare and acrimonious moral quarrels between her parents.

Mother thought about historical justice, retribution for acts of murder and theft by the Arabs that she had endured in Safed and which would have occurred in Jerusalem had we not won the war ... Father was unsure, but saw in his mind, so he said, the owners of the homes and their children and grandchildren returning to the home and demanding their property, and he knew that each day he lived in such a house their accusing eyes would pursue him ... even an enemy is a human being, he said. The argument between Mother and Father was conducted, as always, in hushed voices and in Yiddish, but was piercing nonetheless. At times he had the best of it and at times she did. There were also arguments over the subject of spoils. Carpets, pianos, and mother-of-pearl-inlaid Damascene furniture appeared, as well as radios and silver services, all taken from Arab homes. Father found this repugnant. Mother would enumerate the silver and household goods that the Arabs plundered from her parents' home in 1929, and repeated her claim that, now that we had the upper hand, we should pay them back. Father put an end to the debate by rejecting the offer and leasing an apartment for key money on Ben-Yehuda Street. Better to live in poverty than to live well on the ruins of others.[33]

Reuven Mass, the Jewish *mukhtar* of Talbiyyeh before the war, carefully recorded who entered which house, apartment, or room vacated by Arabs. He also preserved all the letters and messages he received from Israeli officials (one of them from Shimon Peres) regarding the assignment of housing to Jews. Mass issued the newcomers "housing receipt certificates," on which he recorded precisely which unit each one received. The new residents were required to care for the furniture in the home and keep watch over the closed rooms where the belongings the Palestinians had left behind were collected. The Jewish residents also obligated themselves on the certificate to vacate the property within one month if the legal owners so demanded. Mass also listed whether the person receiving the property was married and had children, his profession, and the number of people who moved into the property. In doing so, he was not only acting at the behest of the Situation Committee in Jerusalem (a body charged with putting the new state's governing apparatus in place) but also out of a sense of personal responsibility toward his Arab neighbors. "In keeping with the good relations that we had with the Arab population here, I demanded then that we preserve Arab property ... In every home we set aside a room and put all the belongings of the owner inside, with the exception of tables and chairs and beds, which we had to make available to the refugees," he recalled in 1974. "We closed up that room with wax and the family that moved in had to sign that they would not live in that [part of the] property ... we guarded these Arab belongings for three years ... three years later our government found itself in immediate need of rooms for additional immigrants and refugees, and government officials were sent to transfer all the belongings to warehouses. What happened to them in the end, I have no idea."[34]

According to reports submitted to Prime Minister Golda Meir in March and July 1969 by a group of experts headed by Professor Meir de Shalit of the Weizmann Institute of Science, about 18 percent of the households in East Jerusalem were refugees from the west side of the city. In addition, there were 1,700 such people in the Sho'afat refugee camp. UNRWA, the United Nations Relief and Works Agency, set up to aid Palestinian refugees, reported that some 23 percent of households in East Jerusalem received its support.[35] In August 1967, a joint Finance and Justice Ministry committee estimated that the value of the property that Arabs who were now living in East Jerusalem had left behind in 1948 was worth more than 320 million Israeli pounds— $579.55 million in 2012 dollars. The Finance Ministry made this estimate in the framework of the proposal, mentioned above, to grant full citizenship to the inhabitants of East Jerusalem. That sum of money would have to be made available, whether it was decided to restore the property to its owners or to pay compensation for it. The justice minister said that doing so would have far-reaching consequences: "Were we to decide to act in this way regarding the inhabitants of East Jerusalem, we would have to provide equal treatment for present absentees living in Israel today," he wrote. By "present absentees," he meant Arabs living in Israel who lacked citizenship or any recognized status under the law. Israel was not prepared to do this.[36]

For a short time it seemed to Israel's leaders that they could, in June 1967, repeat on a smaller scale what had been done in 1948. But circumstances had changed. Three armed and uniformed reserve officers with ranks ranging from captain to lieutenant colonel broke into Arab homes at the edge of Abu Tor, abandoned because of the war. The officers had a letter signed by a lieutenant colonel stating that the IDF did not oppose the officers' living in these homes. The former owners filed complaints with the police against the incursion, stating that they had been beaten by the officers. The police evacuated the intruders and arrested them. But the officers claimed that the homes had been given to them by the IDF and appealed to the Supreme Court. The court was highly critical. "I do not see where the army has the right to hand out houses ... the army has no rights to enemy property. The property belongs to the state and the army cannot hand it out," Justice Haim Cohen ruled. "Let them do it [expropriate houses] in Jericho, Sharm al-Sheikh, at the Suez Canal, or somewhere where there is a border," wrote Justice Binyamin Halevy, responding to the claim that the houses had been requisitioned for military purposes.[37]

Some 9,000 Jerusalem Arabs fled to Jordan in 1967 due to the eruption of battles near their homes. When the shooting stopped, Ruhi al-Khatib, mayor of Jordanian Jerusalem, submissive and defeated, went to the office of the Israeli military governor of the West Bank, Chaim Herzog. He asked that the families of Jordanian officials and diplomats be permitted to leave for Jordan so that they could reunite with their families. Herzog, along with Shlomo Lahat, the military governor of Jerusalem, and Defense Minister Moshe Dayan, were interested in thinning out Jerusalem's Arab population. On 11 June, the IDF made buses available, and each Jordanian official and diplomat signed a statement certifying that he was leaving the city of his own volition. At the cabinet meeting of 19 July, Dayan reported that about 1,000 Arabs were leaving the city in this way each day. A few days later, apparently as a result of the international outcry that this policy aroused, Herzog asked al-Khatib to sign a document stating that the initiative had been his.[38] But it was no use. The international community was not persuaded that these evacuations had been voluntary, and Israel was pressured to permit these people to return to Jerusalem. The same was true of other refugees from the West Bank.

As these buses were carrying Palestinians from Jerusalem to Jordan, the 135 homes constituting the Mughrabi neighborhood, adjacent to the Western Wall, were being demolished. The inhabitants had been forced out speedily during the night of 11 June and were not given time to pack up most of their belongings. One woman died during the demolitions. The evacuees were promised alternative housing and were in the meantime placed in empty apartments in the conquered city. They were alarmed and terrified by the Israelis, who carried out their task with mystical fervor. The members of the demolition crew believed themselves to be the emissaries of the Jewish people, charged with "purging" the site and demonstrating Israeli sovereignty. The functional explanation—the need for a large plaza in front of the wall that could contain large crowds, to replace the small alley that ran between the site and the Mughrabi neighborhood—was touted, ex post facto, as the principal reason for the action.

The demolition was decided on by General Narkiss, the regional commander, and Mayor Kollek, without sanction from Defense

Minister Dayan and Prime Minister Eshkol. When Eshkol learned of it, he immediately asked Narkiss why homes were being destroyed in the Old City. Narkiss played the fool and said he would look into the matter. In the meantime, the demolition was completed. In deciding exactly how much to demolish, Narkiss and Kollek consulted a historian, Michael Avi Yona, and an architect, Aryeh Sharon. The army preferred to remain in the background, so the work was done by the Israel Nature and Parks Authority. Building contractors speedily and enthusiastically sent in bulldozers, at Kollek's request. The next day, 12 June, at a meeting of the Ministerial Committee on the Status of Jerusalem, Minister of Justice Shapira asserted that "they are illegal demolitions but it's good that they are being done."[39] That same day a Muslim seminary built in the twelfth century, which also served as a mosque; the tomb of Sheikh 'Id; and the al-Buraq mosque were knocked down. The few structures left standing were those that experts said stood over a tunnel leading into the Temple Mount.[40] The demolitions were an impulsive act that wiped out an entire neighborhood in a single blow.

The potency of that encounter did not dissipate overnight. Following the demolition of the Mughrabi neighborhood, Military Governor Lahat and his deputy Ya'akov Salman turned to the Jewish Quarter. They acted on their own volition, perhaps with Dayan's tacit consent, without receiving authorization from the prime minister. At this time, about 5,300 Arabs were living in the Quarter's 1,500 structures. Most were poor people who had come to Jerusalem from Hebron. They had been preceded, in 1948, by refugees from the villages to the west of Jerusalem, such as Lifta, Maliha, and 'Ein Karem. In 1964 the Jordanians had evacuated these refugees from the Jewish Quarter as part of a development plan for the Old City prepared by a British architect, Henry Kendall, who had also been a city planner for the Mandate administration. The residents of the Quarter were transferred to the Sho'afat camp, to be replaced by the Hebronites.[41] Under the guise of mapping the holy sites, Lahat and Salman interviewed the inhabitants of the Quarter, asking where Jews had lived. Lahat knew that, in 1948, most of the homes there had been owned by the Muslim Waqf rather than by Jews, but he considered the Jews' historic ties to the site as more salient than formal legal title. Military personnel spread a rumor that it would behoove the residents to abandon their homes. To give them an incentive, houses were marked with paint as holy sites and their tenants were commanded to evacuate within three days, with a promise that they would be provided with alternative housing. Most left. But they returned when the municipality took over from the military government following the annexation on 29 June. In April 1968, Israel expropriated the area and commenced a long legal process of removing the 5,500 Arabs then living there. Over the course of a year and a half, 300 rooms in which 800 people lived were evacuated. Another eighty families were evacuated during this same period from structures that had once been synagogues. The expropriations included property belonging to the Waqf. Leaders of Muslim institutions and public figures sent letters of protest to Prime Minister Eshkol, claiming a breach of Muslims' rights to their holy places. But Israel did not relent—this was the Jewish Quarter, which the government viewed as an exclusively Jewish area.

The Jewish Quarter's unique status in Israeli eyes was demonstrated by the fact that the government did not display such determination in other places. Three months later, it set aside a plan to seize another Muslim site. In January 1968, Eshkol had approved the confiscation of the al-Maqased Hospital in al-Tur, even though the hospital was owned by a Muslim charitable foundation, so that the building could be used for a new police district headquarters. As in the case of the plan to install the military government's headquarters near the Augusta Victoria Hospital, the aim in placing the police building there seems to have been to create an Israeli wedge between the Old City basin, which the al-Tur ridge overlooks, and the West Bank. "On the day the expropriation is issued, there should be articles in the press about Arabs in Jewish hospitals in Jerusalem, as [already] agreed," wrote Adi Yafeh, director of the Office of the Prime Minister, to Yehuda Tamir, the man responsible for settlement in East Jerusalem. Rafi Levi, the Interior Ministry's district officer, presented himself to the hospital administration to inform them about the decision. He offered them an alternative building on the northeast side of the Old City. The management refused to agree and sent a letter of protest to top Israeli officials. The government backed down and the police headquarters was instead installed in a large structure in Ras al-Amud, not far away. Before 1948, this latter structure had been owned by the Bukharian Jewish community. A complex deal in 2010, involving that community's board, the Israel Lands Authority, the Israeli government, and an Israeli settler organization, put the building in the hands of Israeli settlers. The police headquarters moved to Area 1E, to the east of Mt

Scopus, the nucleus of a large construction project aimed at building up the entire area between annexed East Jerusalem and the suburban West Bank settlement of Ma'aleh Adumin (cooperation between settler organizations and the government will be discussed in detail below).⁴²

In 1978 Mohammad Sa'id Burqan filed suit in Israel's Supreme Court against the government's order that he leave his home in the Jewish Quarter. The Company for the Reconstruction and Development of the Jewish Quarter, the government-owned limited liability firm set up to carry out state policy in the Old City, acknowledged to the court that its policy was to allow only Jews of Israeli citizenship to live in the Quarter. The court saw nothing improper in this. "The need to reconstruct the Jewish Quarter in the Old City arose only because the Jordanian army invaded it and expelled the Jews and stole their belonging and destroyed their homes. The reconstruction naturally comes to restore the status quo ante of Jewish settlement in the Old City, so that the Jews will once again have, as they did in the past, a Quarter of their own, alongside the Muslim, Christian, and Armenian Quarters. There is no improper discrimination in the special nature of these quarters, each with its own community," wrote Justice Haim Cohen for the court. "To the extent that there is discrimination against Jordanian citizens who owe loyalty to the Jordanian kingdom (like said petitioner), this discrimination seems to me to be justifiable and acceptable: we bewail and protest against what the Jordanians did to us in the Old City, and we should not be expected to open the door wide to their return to the Jewish Quarter in particular. Both security and political considerations can explain and justify such discrimination." Justice Cohen did not see the petitioner as an individual, an inhabitant of Jerusalem, but rather as a bearer of Jordanian nationality. Nor did he see the reconstruction of the Jewish Quarter in municipal terms but rather in a national and historical context, as a national action by the Jews taken to right an injustice done to them by the Jordanians. In justifying his position, he added security to political considerations. In Cohen's view, the fact that the petitioner was a Jordanian citizen justified the sweeping application of these considerations to his case.

In a concurring opinion, Cohen's colleague on the court, Justice Meir Shamgar, also lent his voice to the view that each religious group had, historically, its own quarter in the Old City:

There is a basis for the view that residence in the Old City is divided into quarters by community, each community having its own quarter ... When the Old

City was liberated in the Six Day War, the government decided to restore the status quo ante, that is to reconstruct the [Jewish] Quarter and raise up its ruins and settle it with a Jewish population, so that it could once more take its place in the mosaic of the other ethnic quarters in the Old City, as was the case for many centuries until the expulsion of the Jewish population by the Jordanians in 1948.

According to Justice Shamgar, the resettlement of the Jewish Quarter with Jews was "precisely and fundamentally the reconstruction of a historical and national site—preserving its nature and identity—and, to no small extent, its re-creation."[43] But we have already seen that the court's claim that the Jewish Quarter had once been exclusively Jewish (and that the other Quarters had also been homogeneous) was not accurate. It was more a reflection of how Israelis viewed themselves in 1967 than it was a description of the Jewish Quarter as it had been in the past. In this, the justices were no different from the rest of Israeli society.

The Burqans, the last Palestinian family living in the Jewish Quarter, moved out in 1980, immediately after losing their court case. They resettled in a house they had built a few years previously in the far north of Arab Jerusalem, near Beit Hanina. Ironically, twenty years later, the Burqans again found themselves living in the heart of a Jewish area. The expanding Jewish neighborhood of Pisgat Ze'ev had engulfed the home in which they live to this day.

Houses from Within, People from Without

The city, however, does not tell its past, but contains it like the lines of a hand, written in the corners of the streets.

– Italo Calvino, *Invisible Cities*[44]

Two weeks after the end of the 1967 war, as tens of thousands of Israelis walked into the eastern side of the city, several dozen Palestinian Arabs walked west to see the neighborhoods and homes they had left there in 1948. Mayor Kollek called on Jews who had lost properties on the east side of the city in the 1948 war to declare these properties on a special form that the municipality had prepared. Without being asked to, some 100 East Jerusalem Arabs showed up at the municipal building to claim their properties on the west side of the city.[45] Additional Palestinian applications were filed over time, among them one from Mikhail Sansour, who demanded the restoration of his office and commercial building in Zion Square.[46] All these requests were turned down.

Ishaq Musa al-Hussayni, an author and historian, and Sheikh Jamal al-Dajani tried to get their homes back by reestablishing their personal ties to Ya'akov Yehoshua. The annexation of East Jerusalem fell under his purview as director of the Muslim Department in Israel's Ministry of Religions, and Palestinians viewed him as a person of influence in governmental circles. Al-Hussayni had been a childhood friend of Yehoshua's since 1921. They had studied together at the Anglican St George's College in Jerusalem in 1927, and then at Cairo University. They were separated by the 1948 war. "I put all my savings into the house and lost it all," Ishaq Musa told Yehoshua on 17 July 1968, hoping that his friend of decades could obtain a permit for him to return to Jerusalem and complete its construction. Yehoshua wrote noncommittally in his diary: "I sent him to Shmuel Yeshaya, the district officer." Yehoshua was no longer an Arab Jew, so he did not see his encounter with Hussayni as a meeting of friends. Yehoshua made a point of saying that he was a government official and that the defeated Palestinian was dependent on him. Thirteen months had gone by since the war, and Yehoshua, as did Israeli society as a whole, spoke as a proud victor settling historical accounts with a rival. Yehoshua offered Hussayni the lesson he learned from Jewish history in the Muslim world, and from his own experience: "It seems that you have not yet grasped the new concept of the Jew—the creature that you disdained in the past has become a brave warrior, a tank soldier, a pilot, etc. [Hussayni] replied that we had Maimonides among us. Apparently the honor [that the Muslims accorded to] a few Jewish scholars was [indicative not of real respect for of the Jews but rather of the Muslims'] strong position of wealth and power." Hussayni resubmitted his request to Yehoshua in August 1972. "I spoke about it with [the prime minister's adviser on Arab affairs, Shmuel] Toledano, and the chances are very small," Yehoshua recorded in his records. He was more gentle this time. "I am very moved by those asking for permission to come live in Jerusalem, and I stand helpless before them and do not know what to tell them and how to explain the government's refusal to them ... for me, it was a very tough moment."[47]

Dajani had first appealed to Yehoshua in December 1968. He asked that his family's residential compound, next to David's Tomb on Mt Zion, be restored to them, and that they be granted permission to be buried there and to rehabilitate their section of the Mamilla cemetery. In 1529 Sultan Suleiman the Magnificent had appointed the Dajani family as guardian of the tomb of the Prophet Da'ud—as Muslims call the biblical figure the Jews and Christians know as King David. The family claimed descent from Da'ud, and several of them lived at the site before the war. "All that I was able to do," Yehoshua wrote in his diary, as if trying to say that he had in fact done something for his old friend, "was to make the necessary arrangements to allow members of the family to come to visit their family's graves on the two holidays, 'Id al-Fitr and 'Id al-Idha, at the cemetery, which has been well cared for by the department."[48]

Homes in Jaffa and West Jerusalem that had housed Palestinian refugees were refurbished by the Israeli authorities as schools, synagogues, and health clinics. The new tenants built ugly additions, so that the houses not only lost their owners and original identities, but also their beauty. Israel claimed that it was holding the refugees' properties in trust, until a general settlement of the conflict, and in the meantime only leasing them. In fact, Israel acted as owner. The leases were granted for generations, and the tenants were not required to preserve the original appearance of the dwellings. In the 2000s the custodian of abandoned properties began selling refugee properties to private individuals and public organizations.

Constantin Salameh was one of the wealthiest men in Palestine during the Mandate. Like many residents of the Arab neighborhoods in southern Jerusalem, he fled his opulent home in Talbiyyeh in March 1948. Before departing, however, he signed a contract renting the house to the Belgian consul-general, with the provision that the tenant would keep up the building. While the Belgian consulate operated out of the structure following the war, ownership was transferred by Israeli law to the custodian of abandoned properties. In 1983, after the signing of the peace treaty between Israel and Egypt, Salameh applied to the Israeli government for compensation, based on his Egyptian citizenship. The government offered him only $700,000 for the mansion, and conditioned it on his signing an agreement that he would make no further demands regarding property he had abandoned during the war. He refused. In 2001, the government sold the house for $15 million to a foundation owned by David Sofer, a Jewish businessman from London. The sale contract stated that Sofer would not sue the Belgian government for its use of the house without approval of Israel's justice minister. In 2008 the foreign and justice ministers authorized Sofer to file suit in a Jerusalem court, after the Belgian government refused to recognize the legality of Israel's actions and turned down Sofer's demand for $2.66 million in rent for the time the property was owned by him. The court ruled that Belgium had to pay Sofer rent of $3.8 million.[49]

The Baramki family did not place its house in Musrara, on the street that would soon become the dividing line between Israel and Jordan, in anyone's care in April 1948. Had they sought to do so, they were unlikely to have found a person prepared to take responsibility for a structure that stood on the front line between the Jews and Arabs, no matter how nice a house it was. The Baramkis had purchased the land on which it stood from Hasan Tourjeman in 1930. The senior Baramki, a man of the Greek Orthodox faith who had studied architecture in Athens, built the house in 1934, combining the Arab and Greek styles. When the war started in December 1947, the Baramkis, with bullets flying over their heads, moved to the German Colony. Like other Jerusalem Arabs, the Baramkis panicked in April, after Jewish forces massacred Arabs in the village of Dayr Yasin, just outside Jerusalem. They fled to the town of Bir Zeit, a few miles north of Jerusalem. At the end of the war Bir Zeit was in the Jordanian West Bank and the Baramkis' home in Musrara was in Israel, inaccessible to them. Nineteen years later, after the 1967 war, they sought out their old home, bringing the key to the door. They were not allowed to enter. While it overlooked the border that ran through Jerusalem, it had served as an army outpost. The outpost had been called the Tourjeman House, however, not the Baramki house. It is unclear why it was given that name—whoever did so is unlikely to have known that it was the name of the man from whom the Baramkis bought the lot on which they built their home. Tourjeman was a common Moroccan-Jewish name and would have fit in with the North African population that settled in the neighborhood after the war. There was, of course, no way for the Baramkis to get their house back from the custodian of absentee properties. The custodian handed it over to the Jerusalem municipality, which opened the Museum on the Seam there in 1999. When the museum was dedicated in June 1999, Gabi Baramki, vice-president of Bir Zeit University in the years 1974–93, showed up and asked to enter. The guard at the door demanded that he pay an entry fee, but Baramki refused categorically. He was not a visitor, he said, but the owner of the home. After a long argument, during which Baramki refused to back down, the guard let him go in. Baramki went through the exhibit, which related how the house had been an army outpost in a divided and violent city. No mention at all was made of the house's builders and previous owners, the Baramkis.[50] That lacuna has been corrected—today, the museum's website states that the Baramki family built the house, but offers no further details. It states that "The museum is committed to examining the social reality within our regional conflict, to advancing dialogue in the face of discord, and to encouraging social responsibility that is based on what we all have in common rather than what keeps us apart."[51] The website is silent about the great controversy surrounding the homes of 1948 refugees and the city in which they lie.

"A celebration of architecture from all eras in renewed Jerusalem" was how Jerusalem Mayor Nir Barkat described, in 2009, "Open House," an event "entirely to honor and appreciate Jerusalem's builders and planners from all periods, and a tribute to world cultural assets in the city." As part of Open House—its Hebrew name translates as "Houses from Within"—ninety-seven homes and buildings were opened to visitors, but among them only seven in East Jerusalem. As in previous years, all the homes opened in that part of the city were public institutions—Brigham Young University's Jerusalem Center on the Mount of Olives; the Alhambra Palace reception hall on Salah al-Din Street; the Paulushaus and Schmidt's College opposite Nablus Gate; and the Austrian Hospice Hotel, the Franciscan Monastery Compound, the Russian Orthodox Palestine Society's Alexander Nevsky House, and the Christ Church Guesthouse, all in the Old City's Christian Quarter. Not a single private Arab home was opened to the public. Out of the 100 homes opened in 2007, only eleven were in East Jerusalem. Of these, three were Jewish sites on or next to the Old City walls. Five were Christian institutions, and only two were Arab—the American Colony Hotel and the Simon Cuba architectural office, in which a discussion was held about construction in the crowded eastern side of the city and about the Arab population's planning needs. No private homes were opened. Out of the eighty-nine sites opened in 2008, only five were in East Jerusalem, all of them public institutions—the Brigham Young University Jerusalem Center; the American Colony and Legacy Hotels, both in Sheikh Jarah; the Christ Church Guesthouse, near Jaffa Gate; and the Uzbek Center and home of the Sufi Sheikh 'Abd al-'Aziz al-Bukhari's in the Muslim Quarter (belonging to a non-Palestinian mystical Islamic sect).[52] Were Palestinians simply uninterested in showing their homes to Israelis, or were the Israeli organizers of the event deliberately overlooking the existence of a third of the city's population?

Tens of thousands of Palestinians lived full lives in West Jerusalem, in houses replete with cultural and historical value, but were forced to leave them in 1948. They left no few traces behind them. According to the booklet put out by the municipality for the 2007 "Houses from Within" exhibition, the home of the International Christian Embassy in Jerusalem was built in the 1930s and served as the embassies of Czechoslovakia and the Ivory Coast, and after that housed the Shalom Hartman Institute. The first embassy was housed in the building only in 1949. Its previous inhabitants might as well be ghosts—they are not mentioned in the pamphlet. The Baron Family House in the Greek Colony, renovated in 1985 and again in 2005, the booklet says, was built in 1937 by "an Arab family." No name is given. A walking tour in the Musrara neighborhood in 2008 was devoted to the Black Panther protest movement that emerged in the early 1970s from that neighborhood, one inhabited by both Arabs and Jews before 1948. The Rotem Family House in that neighborhood is described on the Houses from Within 2008 website as follows: "A Turkish Ottoman house—a Liwan house with a central Divan (a gathering hall), surrounded by living rooms. This house was kept in its original state and serves the family to this day. This is an example of how a traditional design can fit contemporary living needs." Note that the house's Palestinian history is skipped over in going back to the Turks. The Ruth Havilio House in Ein Kerem (formerly the Arab 'Ein Karem), exhibited in 2009, is described as "An Arabic stone house in the old part of Ein Kerem ... the building's foundations are made of ancient arches dating back to the Crusader's era. The rest of the floors are 90 years old." Here the Crusader period is followed by an era left unnamed and without identity, with only a chronological designation. With a little thought one realizes that this was the period in which Palestinian Arabs built homes and neighborhoods in new Jerusalem, outside the walls, but this is not mentioned. "The house underwent massive renovation—by altering the garden level, the house's small spaces could be harmoniously conjoined, creating a natural, organic connection between outdoors and indoors." This is the Shoval House—romantic but small. The Jewish renovation brought Jewish harmony to Arabic chaos.

The Houses from Within architectural tours in Jaffa sponsored by the Tel Aviv municipality do not ignore Arab homes, but their perspective is one that looks from the past to the future. One of the tours in 2011 was called "Old Jaffa Looks Ahead to the 21st Century." In other words, "Modern Tel Aviv Presents: This is How I Changed Jaffa." Arab Jaffa is presented as a substrate to be expunged by modernity. Another tour presents a Bauhaus-style home in the Ajami neighborhood as having originally been built for a "wealthy Arab physician," but modernized in 2006. The Casa Nova house, built in the mid-seventeenth century, is described as a hostel for pilgrims that subsequently served as a monastery; in the Israeli period it has become a set of exclusive apartments with arched windows facing the Mediterranean and high ceilings. It is located on Netiv Hamazalot Street, in the heart of the Arab city destroyed by Britain and Israel, but no mention is made of that. The home of Neta Peretz, according to Houses from Within, "was built in 1934," this laconic phrase omitting any indication that this was Jaffa's golden age, when it was the most important Arab city in Palestine. The text, written by the municipality, calls on visitors to take note of the "light shades of white and grey that convey a sense of softness and tranquility," and of the "artifacts that Neta brought with her from New York." The only event upon which the Arab past was explicitly mentioned, an exception that proves the rule, was a tour led by students from Tel Aviv University's school of architecture through the Dajani Hospital, a maternity facility founded by Dr Fuad Isma'il Dajani in 1933. Today it is the Zahalon Geriatric Center.[53]

Homes are not the only objects in Jaffa and Jerusalem that have been assigned new identities—the same also applies to the cities' streets. In April 1949, after Jaffa was annexed to Tel Aviv, the municipality began "Judaizing" the public space in Jaffa by giving Jewish names to Arab streets that, during the period of the military government in the city, had been identified by numbers. Ajami Street became Yefet Street, named for the son of the biblical Noah, who, according to a Jewish legend, founded Jaffa. The neighborhood of Jabaliyya became Givat HaAliya (Immigration Hill), because its residents were new immigrants. But official decisions to change names did not overcome old habits. The use of the old Arab names, even by the city administration,[54] continued into the 1950s; only thereafter did the new names take root. The erasure of former Palestinian ownership was sometimes accomplished arbitrarily. A central thoroughfare in the city, running from north to south, is called Jerusalem Avenue—a name more appropriate to a street heading east, in the direction of that city.

Jaffa is poor in Jewish history, so it had to be imported. The Tel Aviv municipality gave the streets of Jaffa names of important Ashkenazi rabbis, such as Hidushei HaRIM, HaMagid MiDubna, HaRabi MiKarlin, HaRabi MiKotzk, and Rabeinu Yeruham, as if Jaffa were an Ashkenazi Haredi area. Many streets have remained without names, designated only by numbers. Streets named 3071, 3852, and 3812 exist to this day.[55] No little historical ignorance and irony is involved. King Faisal Street was renamed Yehuda HaYamit Street, the name of a coin. According to the Jewish-Roman historian Josephus Flavius, the Romans defeated a small Judean fleet that engaged in piracy as a means of resistance to the Romans.[56] A coin imprinted with the words "Ivdaea Navalis" ("Naval Yehuda," or in Hebrew "Yehuda HaYamit") and bearing the head of the Emperor Titus, the conqueror of Jerusalem, was discovered in 1836 and declared to be a Roman one minted to mark this victory, alongside others minted to celebrate Roman suppression of the Jewish revolt of AD 70. In 1872 the coin was declared a forgery. Yet the Israelis who renamed the street liked the national message the name implied, even though the Judean kingdom was never a naval power and the fleet whose defeat was ostensibly celebrated by the coin was that of a crew of pirates and the event referred to was actually a defeat of the Jews, and the coin so named a fake.

In 1949, Mayor Rokach of Tel Aviv resolved that Jaffa street signs should offer the Arabic names as well, but this was done only in 1960 and only in those parts of the city inhabited by Arabs. In 2001, Israel's Supreme Court ordered the municipality to add Arabic names to all the signs in Jaffa.[57] Today it has some 400 streets, but only a handful are designated with Arab names. One is 'Abd al Gani Street, named after a Jaffa Arab who was killed by a Palestinian terrorist in March 1992 as he tried to defend a Jewish girl. Other streets are named after Rauf al-Bitar, Jaffa's former mayor, and the Muslim philosophers Ibn Sina (Avicenna) and Ibn Rushd (Averroes). At times Arab residents have asked the municipality to name other streets after Arab figures, but these requests have been denied. In a few cases, the municipality rejected the requests because it was found that the names proposed were those of people who had participated in the Arab Revolt of 1936–9. In November 2009, the municipality approved the naming of six small numbered streets after Arab figures. Most of these were writers—

Khalil Gibran, Naguib Mahfouz, Emil Habibi, and Ibn Khaldoun. Yet two years later the new signs had still not gone up—the reason offered by the municipality being that it had a problem proofreading the Arabic (they have since been installed).[58] In November of that year, the municipality sought to rename a street in Ajami after Shmuel and Sultana Tajir, two of Tel Aviv's founders. But residents of the neighborhood objected, as they wanted to name the street after Basam Abu Zayad, the popular imam of the local Mahmoudia Mosque, who had died in July 2008 and whose family lived on the street. The residents' request was approved in November 2010, and at the same time it was decided to rename a street in Ajami after Ya'kub George, who had been chairman of Jaffa's Orthodox Association.[59] At the beginning of 2012 the square next to the Zahalon Geriatric Center—the former Dajani Hospital—was named after the hospital's founder, Dr Fuad Isma'il Dajani, but six years after the decision to do so was made. The Tel Aviv–Jaffa municipality invited about twenty members of the Dajani family to the dedication. They arrived from Saudi Arabia, Tunisia, Jordan, Hong Kong, England, Switzerland, and the United States; Hebrew, Arabic, and English were used in the ceremony. The hosts took into account the visitors' sensitivities—an Israeli flag was moved from the square to a lamppost on the other side of the street so that the foreigners would not be criticized at home for participating in a ceremony in which this flag appeared.[60]

"Get rid of 'Abu Tor!' And 'Baq'a!' And the 'German Colony!' and 'Qatamon!'" the Jerusalem municipality was urged by the Names Commission, set up in the Prime Minister's Office in 1951. The commission refused to accept the city's excuse that it gave names to streets but not to neighborhoods, and its alternative claim that it had not yet managed to find Hebrew names for all the places that needed them. Deputy Mayor Paul Ya'akobi tried to mollify the commission in the summer of 1957: "In my humble opinion, every generation should know that Jerusalem had a non-Jewish period, and that our duty is to guard Jewish Jerusalem from losing its character again." A year later, as part of the celebration of Israel's first decade of independence, Musrara was renamed Morasha, Qatamon Gonen, and Baka Ge'ulim (in Hebrew: Heritage, Defend, Redemption, respectively). The German and Greek Colonies were renamed Emek Refa'im, Abu Tor became Givat Hanina, and Talbiyyeh became Komemuyot (the first two are Hebrew biblical names the last is Independence).⁶¹ In practice, the neighborhoods now have two names, used both by the city's inhabitants and on signs put up by the city. In most places the Hebrew name appears first, with the Arabic name following, side by side, in parentheses. But in the upper part of Abu Tor, which is inhabited by Jews, the sign says "Givat Hanina" above, with "Abu Tor" below, without any parentheses. This is not the only place Arab neighborhoods are shunted to secondary status. A sign next to Jaffa Gate points the way to the Western Wall and the Jewish Quarter, but not to the Armenian and Muslim Quarters, through which a visitor to the wall must walk. At the Pat intersection in southwest Jerusalem, a sign points to the Jewish neighborhood of Gilo, but there is none pointing to Beit Safafa, the Arab neighborhood that lies on the way to Gilo. On the northern side of the city, another sign points to Atarot, a Jewish industrial zone, but not to the adjacent Palestinian Beit Hanina neighborhood.

Angry citizens sometimes black out street signs. In West Jerusalem it is not rare to see that the Arabic name of a street or neighborhood has been splashed with black paint. In 1967, when the city named a street in the Arab neighborhood of Beit Safafa, formerly split between Israel and Jordan, HaIhud (Unification) Street, the signs were torn down by citizens who objected to the implied celebration of Jerusalem's, but not the neighborhood's, unification. The city later changed the name to Ihud HaKfar (Unification of the Village) and this sign was left intact.⁶² Palestinian activists in another Arab neighborhood, Jabal Mukaber, in protest against the municipality, put up nine street signs in Arabic and English, commemorating figures from Jerusalem's Arab history.⁶³

In East Jerusalem, Israel as a rule has changed only the names of streets that Jews often use. Tzanhanim (Paratroopers) and Hativat Yerushalayim (Jerusalem Brigade) Streets run past the west side of the Old City. But to the north, where the Arab downtown is located, the road that runs along the city wall on the outside is Sultan Suleiman Street.

Yesterday I visited, as I often do, my friend, Dr. Yitzhak Musa al-Hussayni, whose [family] has lived in Jerusalem for many generations, and who was my classmate in Jerusalem and at Fuad al-Awal University in Cairo, who lives in Sheikh Jarah, a writer and educator who has in recent years published books and pamphlets on matters pertaining to Jerusalem, and he told me in passing that the small street near his home had been named by the municipal Names Commission after Adam Smith, and he asked me in astonishment who this Adam Smith was and whether he was a well-known person in your circles,

Ya'akov Yehoshua wrote to the Commission on 26 September 1979. "Why does the Names Commission need to go to such lengths, when a man lives here whose forefathers were born in Jerusalem and did much for it?" He recommended renaming it Ishaq Musa al-Hussayni Street. The chairman of the commission replied that no street could be named after a member of the Hussayni family "because the similar sound might mislead people." He meant that Jews might think that the street was named after Mufti Haj Amin al-Hussayni.[64]

The Israeli government does not permit the commemoration of Palestinian settlements that were wiped off the map in the 1948 war, even though streets in West Jerusalem are named after Jewish settlements that were abandoned during that war, as well as after Israeli army units. A short time after the annexation, Israel removed the name of Palestinian leaders Musa Kazem al-Hussayni and 'Abd al-Qadir al-Hussayni from street signs; the latter had headed a Palestinian militia that fought the Yishuv and died in battle.[65] In the mid-1980s the city sought to rename several streets in Beit Hanina, an East Jerusalem neighborhood to which a number of Arab citizens of Israel had moved. One of these citizens, who was the chairman of the neighborhood council, prepared a list of names of Palestinian villages and cities that had been captured and largely demolished in 1948, among them Jaffa, Majdal, and Faluja. The municipality categorically rejected the list. It instead proposed the names of flowers and trees, or the names of Arab poets and cultural figures. A similar approach was taken in 2013, when the municipality approved renaming forty-three East Jerusalem streets. Most of the new names were innocuous, among them "Makom HaTatzpit" (Lookout Place); "HaSulam" (The Ladder), and "Giv'ol HaKash" (Stalk of Straw). In West Jerusalem most streets are named after people, but the only persons the city allowed to be commemorated in East Jerusalem were figures from the early Islamic period. With the exception of the Egyptian singer Um Kulthum, the city has not approved the names of modern Arab cultural figures, and residents have been told not to suggest such names.[66]

Palestinian memory does not cooperate with this Israeli project of obliterating the cities' Arab past. Palestinians in exile preserve the names of their lost houses as a family memory, fixed and unchanged by time. It has been transformed into an ideal dream house, an object of longing and a focus of emotional identity. "Jerusalem, the city we have inherited through imagination and loving memory, is not that war zone we see on the news, full of smoke and destruction. It is a serene place dominated by the golden Dome of the Rock ... Jerusalem is my mother's city, magical, luminous, bathed in holy light," writes Sahar Hammudah, a literary scholar and Palestinian refugee living in Alexandria, "frozen in time, it is motionless, and there, yes, there next to the *sabil* of Qaitbey [a fountain on al-Haram al-Sharif], I see a little girl with a heart-shape face and a silky fringe playing hopscotch ... wherever we live we remember that this house is our inheritance."[67]

Arabs who come from elsewhere to visit such a house, about which they have heard so much, must face up to a reality very different from the dream they grew up on, their family memory confronted with the real world. Reactions have differed. In 1977, George Bisharat, a law professor at Hastings College in San Francisco, paid his first visit to the house his grandfather built in Talbiyyeh in 1926. Its address today is 16–18 Marcus Street; his father called it Villa Haroun al-Rashid, after the Baghdad caliph who was a patron of the sciences and arts. Bisharat had grown up on his father's story of his childhood home and the fields surrounding it. His grandfather and grandmother had lost their fortune. They rented the house to British officers and moved to a smaller one in Baq'a. The 1948 war started while they were overseas, and the mansion was captured by Israel. Bisharat wrote:

Villa Harun ar-Rashid [*sic*] was divided into several flats. ... When I went to Jerusalem in 1977, I had only a photograph of the home and a general description of its location from my grandmother. It was summer, hot and dusty, and I paced back and forth through the neighborhood inspecting each of the houses, occasionally asking for directions. All the street names had been changed to those of Zionist leaders and figures from Jewish history, and the hospital that my grandmother had described as a landmark apparently no longer existed.

The family memory of the home, no matter how vague, softened for him the sense of alienation and disorientation that the present brought on,

As I was resting against a wall in the shade, I saw a home that resembled Papa's. As I hurried across the street, I could just make out the name in the title: Villa Harun ar-Rashid. ... I was immediately flooded with emotions—anger, sadness and most of all tension, tinged with fear.

The circle closed when he touched the house's stone exterior, connecting him to his family and its memory.

I walked through the garden toward the front staircase, putting my hand on the stone banister, as I knew Papa and my own father must have done countless times. I rang the bell. After a long wait, an elderly woman opened the door. I explained my visit by saying that my grandfather had built the home. I displayed my American passport and asked if I could briefly see the interior. Virtually her first words were: "The family (meaning my family) never lived here." Later I would understand this as part of the way of rationalizing the seizure of our property: It's easier to swallow, in moral terms, the expropriation of a speculative business investment by some rich absentee landlord than to contemplate the taking of a family's home. At the time I was speechless, as I had never had to confront this claim. When I recovered my wits, I was tempted to apprise her of the truth. But I feared she would deny my entry. The humiliation of having to plead to enter my family's home with this woman from I know not where in Eastern Europe, perhaps burned inside me.

We were soon joined by her husband, now-retired Justice Zvi Berenson of the Israeli Supreme Court, one of the drafters of Israel's Declaration of Independence. He permitted me to enter the foyer but no further, saying there was no need to see any more of the house as it had all been changed anyway. The couple insisted that the house had been in terrible repair, and that they had done much to fix it up, a claim I had no reason to doubt … The house was cold inside, and as I stood there, I tried to imagine the sounds of my father's and his siblings' voices, and the smells of grandmother's cooking. I left after no more than five minutes. Walking back out into the blazing sun, I felt no specific hostility toward the old man and woman living in Papa's home. But hospitality, such a strongly held value in Palestinian culture, is hard to uphold when guests become usurpers.

The encounter between the Berensons and George Bisharat was an extremely charged one. The latter felt himself to be the owner of the home, and to have historical truth behind him. At the same time, he acknowledged his inferior position and his need to play by the rules laid down by the controlling side to enable him to imagine, if only for a few minutes, the members of his family in the dwelling. Justice and Mrs Berenson wavered between total denial, fearing that Bisharat would demand the return of the property, and contrition about the changes they had made in the home. But behind the contrition lay the claim that the changes they had made had granted them the right to own the property. As the owners of the house, the Berensons decided that the Bisharats would not be allowed to see more than one room, the foyer. Bisharat returned to the house on another occasion with his family; the experience in some ways was similar, yet different.

In 2000, we made this same pilgrimage as a family. As we stood across the street, I recounted the story of Golda Meir's defacement of the title to my son and daughter. I was overcome. Instantly my little son embraced my leg, then my daughter huddled my waist, and finally my wife my upper body, and briefly we stood there, hugged together, tears streaking all our faces. Shortly, we composed ourselves, crossed the street and wound through the garden to the front steps. The front door swung open and a man smilingly offered: "May I help you?" Somewhat startled, I thanked him for his kindness, and he explained: "Many tourists come to see this house. It's included in walking tours of the city." The man, an American from New York, permitted us to enter and venture through more of the first floor than I had seen before. But when I said that my father's family had lived in the home, he was incredulous. This time, I was not surprised as he protested, still congenially: "But the family never lived here." He had gleaned this from a newspaper article, he maintained. Repeatedly, he insisted, it seemed a half-dozen times: "The family never lived here."... Recently I found my daughter lingering over photos of my father as a boy in his Jerusalem home. I know now that she and my son both are heirs of the truth about Villa Harun ar-Rashid.[68]

Such a memory is more than resistance to Israeli denial and obliteration of the past. It is a geographic toehold, a guide, when Palestinians visit their old neighborhoods. Hala Sakakini, Khalil Sakakini's daughter, arrived in July 1967, just a month after the war, to visit Qatamon, which she left with her parents in 1948. She began her trip in Mamilla, guided by her memories. In Mamilla she did not see what was then a dilapidated border region. Instead, her imagination showed her Abu Shafiq's delicatessen next to the Fast Hotel, Hamoudi's beauty parlor, and the Piccadilly Café. For a moment she was astonished to see that Mr Stern's store was still really there. Further up, next to the YMCA building, Sakakini recalled the concerts she had heard there, the athletics classes she had taken, and the tennis games she had played. In the German Colony she took note of Sayigh's pharmacy and Kaluti's butcher shop, but she did not see their current incarnations, Valero's pharmacy and Shoshani's butcher shop. She clutched the past, imagined it, and refused to give expression to the present, lest it grant legitimacy to the sharp change that took place in 1948. When she had no choice but to examine the homes of Emek Refa'im Street, they looked derelict and forbidding. At her school in the German Colony she saw that the clock that used to stand over the entrance had been removed.

In Qatamon, she had trouble finding her childhood home. Her memory had to open to the present and make use of it. It was then that she first made out the huge change in the landscape. New homes had been built on what had once been vacant lots, and ugly additions had been cobbled on to the homes that she remembered. She found one house that had not changed, the Talils' house; from there she knew the way to the homes of the Doumainis, Hournaisis, and Budeiris, from which she knew how to get to her house. When she found it, it gave her a cold welcome. The beautiful garden, full of jasmine, had withered. Passersby told her that the house was now a kindergarten. She entered and found herself in a large hall that had been created by removing the walls separating several rooms. From the direction of what had been the living room she heard children's voices. She was suddenly overcome with foreboding that someone would emerge and accuse her of trespassing. She had been told of such cases. Hala Sakakini knocked on the door of what had been her living room. Two women came out to greet her, and she told them in Arabic that this had once been her home. They did not understand her, nor did speaking in English help. Only on her third try, in German, was communication established, perhaps because the Jewish women spoke Yiddish. Sakakini could see that the Jewish preschool teacher was moved, telling her how she had lost her home in Poland. "As if I am to blame for what the Poles did to her," she thought to herself. She was invited to enter, and together they walked from room to room. Everything was like it had been, but very different.

It was no more home ... it is people that make up a neighborhood and when they are gone it will never be the same again. We left our house and our immediate neighborhood with a sense of emptiness, with a feeling of disappointment and frustration. The familiar streets were there, all the houses were there, but so much was missing. We felt like strangers in our quarter to me.[69]

Hala Sakakini found herself unable to accept this sense of alienation, and was not satisfied with memories.

Jerusalem in its present state is not whole ... give me back my home in Qatamon where I long to live, then only will Jerusalem be whole to me. Only when all children of Jerusalem live in it, when the property the Arabs own is restored to them ... will Jerusalem be whole.[70]

A similar potent sense of being a stranger at home was experienced in Jaffa by Hisham Sharabi, Salim Tamari, and the Hamami family. "I heard the honking of the cars and the voices of the hawkers and the street talk. But they were not the people I know and they were not speaking Arabic," Sharabi said when he visited the city together with a BBC TV crew in 2004.

The garden in the front of the house was the same and the jasmine plant from which my father used to pluck a little flower every time he left the house was in bloom over the same old wall. I learned that a Jewish family from Romania lived here. When the producer suggested that perhaps I should go inside the house I declined, I could not bear seeing the hall as I had known it, the dining room, the other rooms.[71]

The trips Salim Tamari and Rima Hamami made back to their roots in Jaffa in the 1980s left them disappointed and angry. They encountered a huge disparity between the Jaffa they knew as professional historians and the wretched look of the city that they visited, and between their memories as Jaffa refugees themselves (or, in Hamami's case, the children of refugees) and the shrouding of Jaffa's Palestinian past by Israel. No less painful was the sense of disaffection, bordering on hostility, with which the city's current inhabitants treated them. The real city rejected them and they rejected it in turn, making their visit into an imaginary journey to the city of the past, with its meals and foods, furniture, family celebrations. They visited not the Jaffa of the late twentieth century but their own rooms in their own homes, their front and backyards, the citrus groves that surrounded the city, and the sea, all as they had been but not as they were now. All these were abandoned in 1948. The "Via Dolorosa," as Tamari termed it, to the Arab fish restaurant in Jabaliyya, passed by the church where his uncle had celebrated his wedding, and Hana Domiani's soap factory, where Hebrew motifs and a Star of David had been added alongside the Arabic script that had been there before. "I always go to Jaffa with a sense of emotional trepidation and leave with diffuse anger and resignation. My final feeling on the way home to Jerusalem is generally that I don't want to go back," Rima Hamami wrote.

She made her first visit to the city in 1989, together with an aunt. They spent most of their time "circling and turning" in search of the family's house:

while my aunt pointed out Said Hammami's house, the Kanafani family's pink stone house on the adjacent corner ... Suddenly it struck her: the grotesquely ugly two-story pebble-brown Israeli building was actually *our house*, now concealed under a hideous façade of pebbled concrete. We got out of the car and she started crying "They've buried it! Our house is in a tomb!"... My aunt was too upset to go inside and got back in the car.

The name *Beit Nurit*, "House of Light" in Hamami's translation, was inscribed on the façade. Among all the additions to the building Rima made out a balcony with three arches. She felt "a sudden shock of recognition based on an old family photograph ... The photo had that slightly out-of-focus, dreamlike quality peculiar to old photos." But the reality was awful to her. She had not imagined how awful it could be:

> The gate was open so I walked in. I found myself in the large *liwan*, the womb of the house, which still had its columns and original Italianate tile floor. It was full of people who somehow didn't enter my field of vision: I was remapping the *liwan*'s formal reality, a process that excluded objects and people not part of the earlier moment. Then someone spoke to me in Hebrew and I was brought out of my dream. A woman in a white medical coat was asking me things I didn't understand. I looked around and realized that the *liwan* was full of retarded children. When I answered in English, the woman walked off and returned with a large blond Germanic looking matron, also in a white coat. She looked like the female jailer in *Seven Beauties* or a heftier Nurse Ratched from *One Flew Over the Cuckoo's Nest*. She asked me what I wanted, and I replied that this was my grandfather's house and I just wanted to look at it.
>
> For some reason I was surprised by her reaction, which was nervousness and agitation. She became very flustered and said variously that I must be mistaken, that it couldn't be true, and besides, how could I know it was my grandfather's house? I replied that my aunt who grew up in the house, was sitting right outside in the car. The woman told me that before I looked further she had to get the director. After a bit I was ushered upstairs to the director, ensconced in his desk and emitting an aura of deep and expansive self-confidence. "Sit, sit, come in, come in. Yes, yes, do come in," he said in that pushy way that Israelis seem to understand as warmth. "Here, I want to show you something." I followed him to the landing where he indicated an odd colored frieze on the wall. He asked me to look closely and then proceeded to explain with what seemed to be glee that the frieze depicted the return of the Jewish people to the Land of Israel and the creation of the Jewish state. He ended with a kind of hymn to the success of the Zionist dream. I was speechless at what I could only take as a form of sadism and mumbled something like: "Look, I just wanted to look around the house." Without waiting for an answer I proceeded to do so.
>
> On subsequent visits, the occupants changed from retarded children to incapacitated old people. This made the visits even more painful, since when I stopped visually excavating the place in search of the original structure I looked up to find myself surrounded by hunched up and drooling old men and women with unkempt hair lolling in plastic chairs as if sedated. I walked past them as if they didn't see me, like walking through a gallery of macabre statuary. Our house had become a dumping ground for unwanted people—God's waiting room. It occurred to me that in their earlier lives these pathetic souls may have played their part in making the victory frieze on the second floor possible.[72]

Rima Hamami moved in her mind between her family home as it had once been to the wretchedness of Jaffa today, between seeing the patients housed there as a metaphor for the Israeli people as a whole and seeing them as an allegory for Jaffa's current state. She did not want to go to Jaffa, but went back there, reigniting the anger that the city as it is now sets off in her. She could not deny what her own eyes told her, and she refused to fashion for herself a mythical city as a refuge from harsh reality. Nor was she capable of confining herself to memories of a lost Eden, because she had never lived in the city.

Rima returned to Jaffa for another visit in 1993, this time with her father, Hasan, as well as her mother and sister. Hasan Hamami did not recognize the city they entered. He had to dredge his memory in search of the Kishla and Saraya (the Ottoman army and police base and governor's mansion) as signposts and use them to orient himself in finding his old house, now an old-age home. The symbolism of the house where he had been born and lived, now serving as a shelter for people in advance stages of dementia, struck him just as hard as the stink in the air. The city was familiar but alien, especially the people there. Hasan Hamami searched desperately for someone who might recognize him and confirm to him that he was, in fact, a native in this place. He finally found an old-timer who rescued him.[73]

'Abd al Muhsan Qatan and his son, 'Omar, had a somewhat less painful experience in 1999. Jaffa's inhabitants greeted them warmly and accompanied them to their house in Jabaliyya. 'Omar described his father walking through Jaffa's streets and suddenly recognizing his house:

His expression conveyed a mixture of childish excitement and anxious sorrow. "This is it. I'm certain ... this is our house where my father died. Here is the sycamore tree, here is the school, there is the mosque, and that is the road that leads to the 'Shaba' Beach where we would swim. It's extraordinary. Here I am as if I am looking at it fifty years ago. But where are the other houses? The street used to be full of houses."

A different question ran through his son's head: why was his father's first memory of his house a memory of death?

I was soon filled with a feeling of failure and guilt. Had my father perhaps felt the same? Was it because we had both failed to secure our continuous existence on this land? Or was it something altogether more complex, where a father's death is at once a moment of terrifying loss, but also the source of a new courage and of that elated feeling that pertains to all new beginnings?[74]

'Omar Qatan wondered whether his grandfather's death and the loss of Jaffa were bound together in his father's mind, together engendering guilt, despair, and dejection. Did this perhaps mean that he, 'Omar, should rehabilitate his life and emerge from his loss with new strength? 'Omar preferred the second possibility. He returned to Jaffa in order to return to a new life.

After visiting the city several times from 1991 onward, Ibrahim Abu Lughud returned to Jaffa a final time, in May 2001, to be buried there. His daughter Layla had accompanied him on a visit in 1993. After her father's death she wrote an account of that trip and of her father's previous journey to the city. Like all Jaffa natives who no longer live there, she needed a foothold that could connect the city she remembered to the Israeli city she saw on her visits. She and her father oriented themselves using the Hasan Bek mosque and then strode excitedly along the road of their family's past. After finding her father's small factory, they turned to seek the school he had studied at, and then the café he had liked to sit in and flirt with European women. From there they went to the beach, his favorite place, adjoining the city. He asked some children if they knew where Faisal Street was and was happy to discover that they knew. At the post office he inquired whether his box had been kept for him, and was disappointed to learn that it had not. Abu Lughud regaled his daughter about the lost city, although he spoke not of loss but of a demand for his rights. Later, after his death, Layla regarded his mass funeral procession, which began in Ramallah and ended in the cemetery of the Ajami quarter, as a victory of Palestinian nationalism over Israeli denial. For her, the city welcomed him lovingly, and his death was a return from which there could be no further displacement. Layla Abu Lughud had no personal memories of Jaffa, only family ones, but those were not enough. As far as she was concerned, her father's death and burial in Jaffa were not the end of the road, but rather a starting point of a return of Jaffa's refugees to their old homes, some day.[75]

These visits by refugees to their former homes were individual and family initiatives. The encounters were potent because they were not confrontations between abstract entities or ideas, but rather the experiences of sensitive men and women visiting specific houses and discussing their past and future. The two sides are not equal in power, and each of them views the past, and its right to the houses in question, in a different way. When a Palestinian visitor introduces himself, her Israeli interlocutor generally feels discomfited, confused, and threatened. This is followed by explicit denial of Palestinian ownership, or implicit denial in the form of a claim that the Israeli's ownership is fully justified. The dramatic makeover of the neighborhoods, if not of the houses themselves, helps those who now have the upper hand to deny the past. Palestinian responses are not uniform. In some cases they adhere to the past, denying the Israeli claim to ownership. In other cases they accept the situation. In still others, they recognize that Israelis now own their homes but demand the homes back, seeking to recreate the Palestinian past. Sometimes, lacking any other option, the Palestinian accepts that the current situation will not change, but continues to declare his right to return, to remember the past, and to proclaim the injustice done to him.

Yusuf al-Tarhi visited his old home on Emek Refa'im Street in Jerusalem in 1995. He found it inhabited by Michael Bokovsky, who had emigrated to Israel in 1949 as a refugee from Romania. Bokovsky did not invite him in. He spoke with his Palestinian visitor through a window, exchanging memories of al-Tarhi's previous visit, in 1957. At that time, Bokovsky recalled, al-Tarhi had come with his father. "That's great that you remember," al-Tarhi told him. "He wore a red fez, right?" Bokovsky queried. He then softened up, comprehending al-Tarhi's pain, and asserted: "The government has to find a solution for this." In saying this, he laid the task of finding a solution at the government's door, while the Palestinian refugee found his solution on his own. "I understand that it would be difficult to remove these people from the homes they are living in," al-Tarhi acknowledged.

When Abu Nasser Nimri showed up at his old home in Talbiyyeh, on Dor Dor veDorshav Street, Aliza Bronsky, who had been born in Turkey, invited him in for a drink. Afterward she invited him to visit again, the next time with his family. She told Abu Nasser that she had purchased the home from a government housing company, Amidar. You have a right to compensation, she told her guest. The government should see to that.[76]

When Serene Hussayni Shahid went with her sisters and mother to visit their old home in Jerusalem in 1972, the result was a rare kind of human encounter. Serene and her sisters had first opposed their mother's proposal to visit the house in Musrara: "We had each felt that we could not bear to see our home, which was no longer ours, again. We knew it was occupied by an Israeli family. But Mother, with the authority of her eighty years, insisted on her wish to go." They knew how to find it, with no need of a landmark from their memories to guide them. Not much had changed. They were overcome by sorrow and old memories.

In our hearts we had each eagerly searched for it from the distance of Bab el-Amoud. Now as the car drew up outside the front door, none of us could move. Each of us tried to hide our tears, and our deep, silent, grief. Looking up at our former home apparently unchanged, with the same balcony, the same old tree, the same bedroom windows looking up to the Virgin and Child in the Dominican compound against the blue sky, I felt the years of separation and they set me trembling. Across the street was the site of Dr. Toufic Canaan's house, razed to the ground now, and newly planted trees covering the distance to Bab el-Amoud ... Now, Mother, the only one of us undaunted, got out of the car. Leaning on her cane, she walked up the three steps leading to the main door, and, with her stick knocked on the door three times. The door opened, and a middle-aged Jewish woman appeared. From the car, we heard Mother say politely but firmly "May I have your permission to see the inside of my house?"

"Your house?" the woman gasped. "But we bought it!" Mother said: "I did not sell it." The woman spoke with an Iraqi accent. Realizing what this sudden confrontation meant, she said: "Damn them. We had our own house in Iraq. We didn't have to come and face a situation like this."

The elderly Palestinian woman addressed the younger Iraqi Jewish woman politely, not in a demanding way. She was considerate of the fact that the Jewish woman lived in the house, but without giving up on her own claim to ownership. Later in the conversation, the Jewish woman did not deny that she was an immigrant. She expressed her empathy for the sorrow of the Palestinian woman facing her, and her own distress at having to cope with such an awkward claim. The two women were soon feeling like fellow refugees:

As the woman led the way into the house, Mother looked back for us, but none of us had the heart to follow her. The door closed behind them, and while we sat and waited for Mother to return, not one of us uttered a single word. Finally the door opened again and Mother and the Jewish woman emerged. Talking together as if theirs was the most normal kind of communication in the world, they walked slowly around the house, Mother following in the footsteps of the other woman.

The Jewish woman who lived in the house did not feel threatened by her guest, did not deny the latter's connection to the home, and did not limit the extent of the visit. The elderly Palestinian woman did not make a claim to legal ownership. They chatted about day-to-day life in the house, then and now:

> Finally, we heard Mother thanking her. She turned and very slowly descended the three steps down to the street. She stepped into the car and Najwa drove us away. None of us said a word. The charge of emotion in the car was enough to blow it up. At last one of us asked Mother what they had talked about and she recounted parts of the conversation. She had asked the woman if her family was alone in the house. "Alone!" the woman had laughed sarcastically. "There is a different family living in each room." "Where do you do your cooking then?" Mother asked. "Look behind you," the woman said, "on the window sill." ... The woman had asked Mother who had built the house. When Mother said her father had done so, the woman had wondered if it had been intended to serve a school. Mother told her that it had been built for his own family.
>
> As mother continued her account of the morning's visit, my deeply emotional state settled into a calm admiration for Mother's courage ... Her attitude became for us a model of courage ... sometimes with one or all of my sisters, sometimes alone, I set out to explore the city that I had loved so much, from which I had been separated for so long. At every turn we were confronted by the Israeli military occupation, and at every turn we were confronted by our memories ... Silence was our best defense. We also felt that we had no time to waste, that we had to soak up the precious memories and store them.[77]

Serene al-Hussayni Shahid learned from her mother to live with the past and not give it up, to accept the present, including its unpleasant parts, without papering over them, and without any illusion that the clock could be turned back.

Jews have also gone back to the houses that they or their parents left in 1948. Unlike Israeli settlers, such visitors do not present themselves as owners, demanding that the Palestinians leave forthwith, but as visitors. Aviva Sher joined her father, Eliahu Mizrahi, for a visit to the Old City after the border disappeared in June 1967. After visiting the Ben Zakai Synagogue, where they used to pray.

> Father insisted that we visit the family home. He led us through the alleys. He found his way as if there were not heaps of ruins and as if he had only recently been there. Without a single mistake and without any hesitation. We arrived at a house that looked like a wreck but remained standing, unlike the rest of the destroyed houses around. We opened the gate and entered the yard. Father was extremely emotional. Each corner of the yard reminded him of his childhood, and he relived boyhood experiences. The Arab inhabitants of the house were afraid of us. An Arab woman who lived there had known Father and was sure he had come to throw her out. But he reassured her. They hastily pre-

sented us with some sort of documents testifying to their rights. An old woman was the sharpest, declaring that she had paid rent to Hakham Elazar. We saw that it was over and done. Father spoke about the house's history and, as a man instructing his children, asked us to do all we could to redeem the house and return it to the family. A few months later, when we returned, we found no trace of the house nor of the poor tenant.[78]

The shock and fear of what the Israeli victory might bring impelled the inhabitants of the house to present the Mizrahis with documents that would purportedly allow them to continue to live there. They were fearful for their future, while the Jewish visitors were carried backward in time.

During those same days after the war, Yosef Meyuhas visited his former home in Silwan. When he introduced himself, Mohammad Gozlan, who lived there, was quick to show him the letter of thanks he had received from a Jew from Silwan whom he had saved during the disturbances of 1929.[79] The same sort of denial, brought on by fear, was evident in a Palestinian woman who was living in Menashe Mani's home in Hebron:

Menashe Mani halted at the front of one house in the center of Hebron and said: "This is the house. Here we lived, my wife and I, and here our son was born ... Let's go up to the house. A woman stood at the door. "Madame," we told her, "we have come to see the house. Mr. Mani lived in this house many years ago. We would like to look around." The woman was alarmed. "No, the man did not live here," she said. "Certainly not here. This is a different house. We don't know anything. We weren't here then—." Afterward, when she had calmed down and realized that we had come just for a visit, she smiled and invited us in.[80]

Menashe Mani had a hard time recognizing his city. Not only had his father's house and others disappeared. At the door of a café, "he stood and asked after his [old] friends, Hebron's notables and leaders. Almost all of them were dead, they told him." Mani felt that a much greater transformation had occurred in the city than just the change in the houses. "All the ancient majesty with which the city of my fathers had been anointed was not to be found. The city of Hebron had taken on the form of a modern city," he wrote six weeks after the war. The house he easily identified from the outside had changed considerably inside. It had been divided in two, one for the master of the house's first wife, the other for her co-wife, a woman who had been born in Jaffa. She could not hold herself back and grilled her guests about the city of her birth and about neighboring Tel Aviv.[81] Menashe Mani, who had come for a short visit to his past in Hebron, helped her revive her past in Jaffa.

The Jewish settlement that had been established in Hebron on the Passover holiday in 1968 did not raise Mani's spirits. The settlers had checked into a local hotel for the holiday, but then refused to leave and declared their intention of remaining in the city. When their intentions became clear, Mani asked: "How should we settle in Hebron?" He answered his own question. The Jews, he said, needed "to understand the city's inhabitants, to understand their mentality and to be considerate of their feelings." As far as he could see, the settlers had no intention of doing that. If the Jews did not establish friendly relations with the Arab population, "I do not believe that we can hold up among them." A settlement living by the sword did not seem sustainable to him.[82]

6

OCCUPATION, ASSIMILATION, OPPOSITION

A novel, of course, is not merely a book, a physical object of pages and covers, but a particular kind of mental space, a place of exploration, of investigation into human nature. Likewise, a city is not only an agglomeration of buildings and streets. It is also a mental space, a field of dreams and contention. Within both entities, people, individuals, imaginary or real, struggle for their "right to self-realization."

– Ian McEwan[1]

Jerusalem: A Bustling and Noisy Place

An intoxicating sense that history was in the making fanned Israelis' excitement about going to, touching, and being in the Old City. Jerusalem was the heart of the matter for Israelis and Israel. The Jewish Quarter had been a symbol of the pious, poor, and weak old Yishuv; now it would become an icon of Israeli power. Both within the government and outside it groups and individuals involved themselves intensively in the newly liberated part of Jerusalem. "You said that it isn't running away and that Jerusalem will be ours forever. The truth is that the soil under our feet is on fire and any delay may defer the Messiah's coming," Levi Eshkol wrote to Housing Minister Bentov about a year after the war.[2] This sense of urgency came with a feeling that we, the Israelis, were managing history. But there was no overall planning, no organized staff work. Rather, institutional and a variety of other interests collided during the initial years after the annexation.

Immediately after the conquest of Jordanian Jerusalem, the Office of the Prime Minister began registering institutions and individuals who sought to return to and reside in the Jewish Quarter. Dozens of the former and thousands of the latter signed up, putting pressure on the government to allow them to commence construction of their buildings or houses immediately. The government, for its part, took some time before accepting the municipality's proposal that the state expropriate all the homes in the Quarter, in anticipation of negotiating compensation with those who held the rights to the houses. In the meantime, several *yeshivot*, whose leaders were impatient, set up house in the Quarter on their own initiative, without receiving permission, establishing facts on the ground.[3]

Israeli law had no sooner been imposed on all of Jerusalem than intensive archaeological work began in a search for Jewish roots in the Quarter (1969–82). Excavations also commenced along the Western Wall and its continuation, the southern retaining wall of the Temple Mount, during the first decade following the war. These digs uncovered Roman, Byzantine, and Muslim objects, but most scholarly and public attention was given to Jewish artifacts. The Arab presence in the Jewish Quarter was obliterated and buildings from the Mamluk period destroyed. The Nea Church, built in AD 543 and second only to the Church of the Holy Sepulcher in importance to Christians, was in poor condition. The Church of Theotokos and other Crusader and Mamluk sites were not conserved.[4] In the Jewish Quarter, the symbolic center of Jerusalem, now stand archaeological artifacts from the city's Jewish acme, the period of the Second Temple. Some of these items are currently on display in the Jewish Quarter in two small museums, with the purpose of justifying Israeli sovereignty over the Old City. The message is that the Jewish people have returned to their home, taken from them by foreigners from Titus to the Arab Legion. The museums exhibit the magnificence of the Quarter during the reign of King Herod and contrast it with the devastation wreaked thereafter by the Romans.[5] Three other small museums operate as memorials to Jewish life in the Quarter before 1948, and as chroniclers of the destruction wrought by the Jordanians. In November 1967, the Ministry of Religion quickly granted its imprimatur to the identification of the remains of a synagogue founded in the Quarter in 1267 by the great Spanish rabbinic scholar and commentator Nachmanides (in Hebrew, RaMBaN). The synagogue was quickly rebuilt to serve as a place of worship, to complete a saga that had begun 700 years earlier and which reached its climax with the Israeli conquest of the Old City. Historians would later challenge this hasty identification, which was motivated less by study of the evidence and more by overenthusiasm brought on by contemporary events.

The Ministry of Religion took the side of religious organizations and individuals who, in 1968–71, demanded a return to the Jewish Quarter to rebuild it in its original splendor as a hallowed district replete with *yeshivot* and synagogues. The Company for the Reconstruction and Development of the Jewish Quarter in the Old City of Jerusalem Ltd (JQDC), a government-owned corporation established in September 1968, resolved that the Quarter should be almost entirely residential. For the most part, the JQDC, which has directly administered the reconstruction, has had its way. Nevertheless, the religion minister and figures in the National–Religious (modern Zionist Orthodox) and Haredi communities did not give in. They continued to push to make the area primarily a religious preserve; they accused the company of shunting aside religious Jews who wanted to return, and demanded that the cafés and art galleries that had sprung up in the Quarter under the JQDC plan be removed. They failed. More precisely, their success was delayed by twenty-five years.[6]

The Hurva Synagogue, built in 1864 in the Jewish Quarter, had been the largest and most magnificent synagogue in Palestine. Destroyed in 1948, it was not rebuilt immediately after 1967. In contrast, a complex of four Sephardi synagogues desecrated by the Jordanians was restored. A plan to reconstruct the Hurva as an opulent modern synagogue was set aside. For those who waxed nostalgic for the old Hurva, the new blueprint was not grand enough. Furthermore, the planners of the rebuilt Quarter did not want it to be inhabited solely by Orthodox Jews. A stone arch, not too high, was built on the Hurva site to symbolize the former structure's prominent dome and to commemorate the destruction of the Quarter by the Jordanians. The synagogue became a memorial site.

But the Israeli government changed course in 2002, when it resolved to rebuild the synagogue itself. The decision was in large part the product of a notable change in the population of the Quarter. The new neighborhood had initially attracted a heterogeneous population. Both religious and non-religious Israelis were drawn to the Old City's charms. Among the purchasers of homes in the Quarter were Yigal

Allon, formerly a kibbutznik and commander of the Palmach, who held the post of minister of education at the time of the reconstruction; and Yitzhak Neventzal, a modern Orthodox Jew from Germany, then state comptroller. Not far away from their residences stood Porat Yosef, a Sephardi–Haredi *yeshiva* founded in 1923, which had now returned to its original location; and Yeshivat HaKotel, a National–Religious seminary founded in August 1967 in response to the victory. The Hebrew Writers' Association ran a Writers' House there, which sponsored writing workshops and evening seminars on literature, history, and archaeology. By the 1990s, however, most secular individuals and organizations had moved out. In the 2000s, about 90 percent of the 6,000 families that today live in the Quarter were Orthodox Jews, many of them on the extreme end of the religious and nationalist political spectrum.[7] In other words, the Quarter was once again for the most part inhabited by observant Jews, as it had been in 1948. The difference is that then the Quarter's population was Haredi and thus had little connection with the greater part of the Yishuv and its Zionist institutions. In contrast, the religious Jews who today inhabit the Quarter are closely tied to the Israeli establishment and provide it with ideological energy. "The Hurva once more raises spirits and glorifies Jerusalem's skyline," boasts the JQDC Hebrew website.[8] Before the reconstruction of that synagogue, the Old City skyline had been dominated by the Dome of the Rock, al-Aqsa Mosque, and the Church of the Holy Sepulcher. Now the Hurva rivals them.

The excavations carried out in the Quarter unearthed the Cardo, the main road of Roman Jerusalem. Right by this reconstructed ancient street stands the Temple Institute, devoted to raising consciousness of the importance of the Jewish Temple and preparing the items that will be required for a renewal of the sacrificial service in a rebuilt Third Temple.[9] The institute encourages religious Jews to visit the Temple Mount. Traditionally, religious law forbade Jews from setting foot there, and most Haredi and some national–religious Jews still abide by that ruling. But, since 1967, many mainstream national–religious rabbis have ruled that Jews may and should visit those parts of the Temple Mount that were not part of its sacred precinct. The institute's website provides a long list of rabbis who take this position.[10] The institute has also placed a reconstructed golden *menorah* (candelabrum), intended for use in the new Temple, next to the stairway leading to the Western Wall plaza. It is situated exactly opposite the location it is intended to occupy on the Temple Mount. Nearby, on a roof of a building that offers a view of the Temple Mount, the Aish HaTorah Yeshiva installed, at the end of 2009, a model of the Temple. Built of stone, marble, and gold, its purpose is to enable viewers of the Mount, now occupied by the Dome of the Rock and al-Aqsa Mosque, to imagine that they are gazing at a new Jewish Temple.[11]

Planning and construction in East Jerusalem proceeded at a feverish pace, impelled by a sense that a new historical era had begun in June 1967. The Arabic Department of the Public Affairs Center in the Prime Minister's Office was quick to organize conferences and tours, as well as to issue propaganda. The office of the prime minister's adviser on Arab affairs, Shmuel Toledano, encouraged Israeli organizations and media to extend their services to East Jerusalem and to set up chapters and offices on that side of the city. One of the most important of these was the Histadrut labor federation.[12] Meron Benvenisti, Mayor Kollek's adviser for East Jerusalem affairs, wrote that the municipality should seek "integration of all parts of the united city, aim to equalize all service, equalize all working procedures and modes of operation, and maintain a level of service befitting Israel's capital." At that time, 60 percent of the households in the Old City lacked running water, depending on some 6,200 cisterns in which rainwater was collected. There was no central sewage system and refuse was carted away by donkeys. Many homes were not connected to the electricity grid. Benvenisti warned that:

There is a danger that parts of the [Old] City will be commercialized and their character blurred. ... We should see to it that the neon signs on business establishments in the Old City are removed, and that standards for business signs established to replace the glaring and ugly signs on some of the city's most beautiful streets. The installation of television aerials should also be prohibited, and telephone and electrical wires should be placed underground ... the facades of residential building also require renovation and cleaning. ...

A considered and deliberate policy of thinning out the populations of the Old City's poor quarters [should be instituted], involving the construction of appropriate public housing in new neighborhoods to be planned and constructed outside the [Old] City, in its immediate environs.[13]

Benvenisti also asked for money to purchase two Arabic typewriters. They arrived, and from that point on every letter issued from his office was written in both Hebrew and Arabic, side by side. Other municipal offices also issued letters in both languages, but on separate pages. In 2011 most of the forms used by the municipality were translated into

Arabic, and the new master plan for the Old City is currently being translated so that residents of the Old City will be able to study them and file objections. But a Jerusalem resident who wants to appeal a parking ticket or file some other complaint still receives a response in Hebrew alone. Israeli government offices have discriminated against Jerusalem's Arabic speakers much more severely than the municipality does. Arab students from Jerusalem enrolled on auto mechanics courses sponsored by the Ministry of Labor and Welfare study in Arabic. Yet until 2000 they had to take their exams in Hebrew—the exam questions were not translated into Arabic even though it is an official national language. (The exam was available in Russian, even though that is not an official language.) In one representative case, a resident of East Jerusalem employed as a practical nurse in the French Hospital and who wished to take the exams to become a registered nurse had to wait for a year because the Ministry of Health did not want to translate the exam into Arabic, even though it offered the same exam in English.[14]

Israel developed East Jerusalem for Jews with the express intention of making the annexation a permanent fact. At the end of 1971 Teddy Kollek urged Prime Minister Golda Meir "to assign five percent of the public construction [funds allocated] by the Housing Ministry in Jerusalem to Arabs, on terms more or less equal to those given to similar cohorts among the Jews." Kollek proposed that the Israeli public housing initiative focus on the Old City, because of the huge disparity between the Muslim Quarter, "where 20,000 people live in substandard conditions" and the adjacent modern and pleasant Jewish Quarter. "The necessary investment for the non-Jewish part of the city should be about fifteen percent of the state's investment in the development of the Jewish Quarter," Kollek added. But he feared that Meir would think that even this very unequal division gave too much to the Arabs. To convince her, he warned that "We must take this action, or we will walk with our eyes wide open straight into an explosion a few years from now."[15] But the prime minister rejected his plan nonetheless. Israel built tens of thousands of housing units for Jews in East Jerusalem, but not a single one for Palestinians. In 1992, less than 6 percent of the municipal budget was allotted to the Arab neighborhoods, even though a third of the city's population lived in these areas. In per capita terms, the city budgeted $900 for each of its Jewish residents and only $150 for each Arab resident.[16]

OCCUPATION, ASSIMILATION, OPPOSITION

Nevertheless, the little that the Arabs received from the municipality was considerably more than they had under Jordanian rule. Many other aspects of life changed as a result of Israel's energetic entry into East Jerusalem. The city's Arabs bought four times as many television sets and washing machines in the years following the annexation than they had in the years just prior to the war. They also earned more money than before, thanks to the large increase in tourism and the considerable investment in infrastructure that Israel made.[17]

In the euphoria after the 1967 war, the power that Israel had displayed and the trauma that the Arabs suffered gave Israelis the impression that the Palestinians were gradually accommodating themselves to the new situation. Israel dealt harshly with the few signs of rebellion and protest, worried that such phenomena could nevertheless set off a broad popular uprising.[18] In September 1967 Palestinian militants staged their first terror operation in Jerusalem following the war, but the terrorists had come in from the outside. They were not seen as representing the will of the local Arabs. Immediately after the annexation, dozens of Arab municipal employees—people who had worked for the Jordanian municipality and who had been moved into the Israeli one—were sent on courses to learn Hebrew. At the end of 1967 the Hebrew University opened two centers in which the city's Arabs could study Hebrew. It also sponsored tours and other cultural and social activities in which Jews and Arabs could meet and get to know and like each other.[19]

The Histadrut moved into East Jerusalem right after the annexation. The 20,000 people who made up the area's workforce had at that time no labor union tradition and no class consciousness. The Israeli labor federation's East Jerusalem branch was headed by Ghazi I'lm al-Din, who had previously served as foreign editor for the Jordanian daily newspaper *al-Difa'*. Only 3,500 residents of East Jerusalem joined the Histadrut, but more than 13,000 took part in cultural activities sponsored by the organization during the first year and a half after the war. In 1968, for example, ninety young people enrolled in Histadrut-sponsored Hebrew-language courses, while 300 East Jerusalem teachers visited the Hebrew Gymnasium High School in Rehavia to meet officials from the Histadrut's Department of Arab Teachers, which wanted to bring them into the Israeli teachers' union. A year later, forty East Jerusalem Arabs went to Kibbutz Givat Brenner to work there for a day. The Jerusalem Workers' Council founded a 22-member Arab dance troupe in East Jerusalem, Kochav Yerushalayim, directed by a Jewish Israeli, Ayala Goren. The troupe participated, along with other municipal dance companies, in the 1968 Israeli Dance Festival at Kibbutz Dalia. In August of the same year, this and the Jewish municipal dance troupe toured Germany, France, and Italy, where they performed and appeared at youth gatherings.[20]

In February 1968 the Grand National Hotel fired three employees who had been among the first Jerusalem Arabs to join the Histadrut. The labor organization supported their cause and the strike that the hotel's employees had declared in response. The management agreed to a compromise. A year later much the same thing happened at the Intercontinental Hotel on the Mount of Olives. In March 1968 the Histadrut supported the lawsuits filed by twelve drivers employed by an Israeli bus company. The drivers demanded that they receive the same work hours, days off, and overtime pay given to Jewish drivers, as well as social benefits. The bus company tried to replace them with Arab drivers from the West Bank, but the latter refused. With the Histadrut's support, the drivers' grievances were rectified. The Histadrut's support of Arab workers' committees at places of employment in East Jerusalem led some 40 percent of the area's workers to join the labor organization. The Histadrut worked to raise its members' salaries and for East Jerusalem Arabs to receive tenure and the social benefits that Israeli workers were entitled to. Arab waiters, carpenters, locksmiths, electricians, and auto mechanics learned their trades in courses sponsored by the Jerusalem Workers' Council. However, non-organized Arab workers did not benefit from the Histadrut's protection and were often exploited by their employers—building contractors, storeowners, operators of stands in the open-air market in West Jerusalem, and truckers. Nor did the government enforce its own labor laws when it came to East Jerusalem workers. Israeli employers took advantage of this to save themselves the expense of paying social security, severance pay, and the legal minimum wage. Arab laborers could receive unemployment compensation only if they registered with the Ministry of Labor's Employment Service, as 2,000 residents of East Jerusalem did. The service was supposed to refer these laborers to jobs, but employers did not want them because unregistered workers were 50 percent cheaper.[21]

Efforts at Jewish–Arab economic cooperation often ran into problems. The leaders of the Jerusalem Small Business Association wrote to

OCCUPATION, ASSIMILATION, OPPOSITION

Minister of Labor Yigal Allon in December 1969 asking that he extend them financial support on the grounds that they had agreed "to government and public proposals ... and established a branch of our organization on Ibrahimiyya Street in East Jerusalem." The goal was "to strive for economic cooperation with the capital's Arabs, while maintaining the economic positions of proprietors on both sides of the city against mutual trespass. We made sincere efforts to establish cooperation with the Arab Chamber of Commerce in Jerusalem. We realized, however, that this Arab Chamber of Commerce is not interested in the capital's economic development and prosperity, but rather in political subterfuge," because it rejected the unification of Jerusalem. "Given this approach, and after consultations with the Adviser for Arab Affairs in the Prime Minister's Office and other public officials, we commenced a wide-ranging operation of organizing Jerusalem's Arab proprietors in the Israeli organization. Within a month after this decision, 500 proprietors joined the organization." The manner of the Chamber's operation in East Jerusalem differed from that in the rest of Israel. "As you know," the Israeli association's leaders wrote to Allon, "the Arabs do not distinguish between economic-sectoral problems and their personal problems." The association was thus compelled to deal "also with problems of identification cards, problems of family reunification, the visits of relatives from Arab countries," and to resolve issues growing out of the differential status of East Jerusalem, where Israeli law applied, as opposed to its economic hinterland in the West Bank, where Jordanian law applied and a military government ruled. The Small Business Association, which in Israel operated as a civil organization that looked out for the economic interests of its members, functioned in East Jerusalem as an arm of the government. The authors of the letter did not note this contradiction, just as they saw no problem in condemning the political objectives of the Arab Chamber of Commerce as subversive, even though they themselves were promoting a no less political goal, that of reinforcing the Israeli annexation. With the Public Affairs Center in the Office of the Prime Minister, "we organized integrated social trips [together with Israeli Jews] throughout the country, visits to manufacturing plants, in Hebrew settlements, research and scientific institutions, etc. In this way we imbued the Arab street with an awareness of Israel." The Public Affairs Center and the Small Business Association's Jerusalem chapter brought "dozens of groups of tourists from overseas, including

English-speaking countries" to meet "Arab businessmen for conversations and an exchange of views." As they saw it, the heads of the Chamber of Commerce were people with good intentions who wished to do well for the Palestinians in Jerusalem and to change their view of Israel. They were convinced that, thanks to their efforts, the annexation would be good for the Arabs of East Jerusalem. Their guiding principle was much like that of the Zionist settlers at the beginning of the twentieth century: "The Arab and Jewish businesses are not competitors but rather partners in Israel's economic prosperity." The authors of the letter to Allon were certain that their work "gave us prestigious standing in the 'Arab' street, and even the Arab Chamber of Commerce has no choice but to admit that."[22]

Jerusalem's Palestinian consumers had no alternative to asking for help from Jewish institutions and officials. The contacts between them were formal and hierarchical, which took both sides several years to adjust to. Arabs had to obtain from Israel identity cards, building permits, and permission to travel to Jordan, as well as to provide the Israeli authorities with documents proving that they lived in Jerusalem. Palestinians felt uncomfortable dealing with Israeli officialdom and displayed a high degree of sensitivity to anything they viewed as disrespectful treatment. In large part, Jewish officials were oblivious to these feelings. They did not take into account parameters that were salient in Palestinian society, such as family pedigree and social status. Palestinians were insulted by this and viewed the Israelis as arrogant occupiers. The officials acted as bureaucrats do—they expected people to show up on time, to send their letters and applications to the appropriate person, and sometimes to set up an appointment in advance. They saw one person at a time and the interviews were businesslike and impersonal. Jerusalem's Palestinians were not accustomed to such treatment. They were used to speaking with officials in groups in which each person spoke favorably of the others, and they were also unaccustomed to the convention of first come, first served. They did not make appointments in advance, or arrive at a set time. Bureaucratic processes were beside the point, in their view—personal interaction was the only way to solve problems. They would thus end up waiting for hours each day for no other reason than to obtain a brief opportunity to speak to an official personally. When the municipality and the Interior Ministry began issuing numbers to make lines more orderly, a new business arose among the Palestinians—fixers came early to take numbers, selling them afterward to latecomers. The Israelis tried to keep order in line by installing benches and roped-off lines to prevent such transactions, but the Palestinians kept finding ways around it. When an official told a Palestinian that he would receive an answer to his request by mail, the latter would insist on a personal and immediate response. Sometimes an impatient Jewish bureaucrat would tell an applicant "come back tomorrow" just as a way of getting him out of his office, but the Palestinian would take this literally and show up the next day, only to be disappointed. Jewish civil servants, trained and expected by their superiors to deal with requests objectively, impersonally, and efficiently, did not like it and felt uncomfortable when Palestinians attempted to develop personal relations and trust by telling their stories and presenting their cases at length. Attempts to verify a petitioner's claims insulted and infuriated Palestinians, rendering communication impossible.[23]

Palestinians found that myriad officials processed their requests and made decisions about them. They observed that senior government figures had close personal relations among themselves, and that Israeli Jews often got around red tape by making use of personal connections with officials. These factors, along with their aversion to cold bureaucratic treatment, prompted Palestinians to make personal appeals to anyone they thought could help them circumvent the bureaucracy. Many requests for family reunification, travel permits to Jordan, and transit permits from the West Bank into Israel, necessary for East Jerusalem Palestinians whose Jerusalem residence status has not been recognized, were submitted directly to senior figures, rather than to the lower-ranking civil servants who were supposed to handle them. Records of such end-runs are preserved in Israel's archives and illustrate how Palestinians in Jerusalem, finding themselves suddenly under foreign rule, coped with a new set of power relations.

On 19 October 1972, Yehoshua Palmon, Mayor Kollek's adviser on East Jerusalem affairs, wrote to Colonel David Farhi of the Judea and Samaria Command ("Judea and Samaria" is the official Israeli term for the West Bank). He asked Farhi to issue a permit to a cousin of Ahmed Zuhir al-'Afifi to resume residence in Jerusalem. The cousin, he said, was slated to receive a job in the municipality or as a manager in the East Jerusalem Electric Company.[24] The city's director-general, Aharon Sarig, wrote on 3 September 1989 to Yosef Tov, deputy director of the Interior Ministry's Population Registry, asking him to permit Samir

Hasan Abu Hajla, a 47-year-old Jerusalem native, to be granted the status of a Jerusalem resident. In 1967, Abu Hajla had accompanied his father, who had fled to Jordan out of fear that he would be in danger from the Israeli authorities because he had served as a Jordanian official. He had lived in Jordan since that time. In 1972 Abu Hajla married a woman from Jerusalem. Their four children had been born in Jerusalem and were listed on his wife's Israeli identity card. His wife and children, as well as his mother, all lived in Jerusalem. But Abu Hajla's application was not for family reunification. His mother was ill and needed her son to care for her. Sarig asserted that Abu Hajla would not be an economic burden (presumably meaning on Israel's social services). He said he was a successful businessman and could support himself.[25] During their talks with Moshe Sasson over a possible accommodation in the West Bank and about local politics, Anwar Nusseibeh and Sheikh Jabari asked Sasson to obtain approval for family reunification requests of relatives of theirs.[26] Gabriel Stern, a journalist, was approached by Ahmed Mohammad Khalil al-Hussayni on 6 October 1968 with a request that he see to it that al-Hussayni, his wife, and his three children be allowed to return to Jerusalem and receive resident status.[27]

On 31 May 1968 Israel officially appointed thirty-one men in East Jerusalem to the post of *mukhtar*, that is, local representative of the Israeli government, to serve as intermediaries between the Arab population and the authorities. The post had originated under the Ottomans and was retained by the British and Jordanians. *Mukhtars* were selected by Israel from the second and third tiers of the traditional elite—members of the first tier would not agree to serve in this capacity. Each *mukhtar* was given a certificate, an official municipal stamp, and 30 Israeli pounds (IL) (about $54) a month for "personal expenses." The sum was small, but the *mukhtar* gained prestige and the ability to open doors for his personal gain. Jordan certified as *mukhtar* those who had been appointed by Israel. Representing members of their families and residents of their neighborhoods, the *mukhtars* signed, for example, requests for building permits and for home construction or renovation loans. Until the early 1980s, the *mukhtar* also brought the mail from the central post office on Salah al-Din Street to his neighborhood, placing the bundles of letters at the opening of a neighborhood grocery store. *Mukhtars* were invited to official ceremonies and to receptions where city officials wished to demonstrate to foreign visitors how pleased the city's Arabs were with Israeli rule. The army and Shin Bet also made use of them.[28]

Even with the *mukhtars* in place, Palestinians continued to send personal appeals to Israeli figures. On 1 June 1970 Mahdi Mohammad Yehiya Da'is wrote to Mayor Kollek (with copies to the prime, interior, and police ministers and to Meron Benvenisti): "During the Six Day War my house was destroyed by shells fired at the Old City. The house I lived in on Harat al-Sadiyya Street (the private house) was destroyed and I have nowhere to sleep because I am married to a second wife after the death of my mother. I was compelled to move to Hebron to live with my aunt until my father could fix the room in which I lived all my life." He also complained about his dealings with the Israeli bureaucracy:

While I was in Hebron there was a census in the area of East Jerusalem. My father explained to the census takers that he has a son who is in Hebron right now for the above-mentioned reasons. The census takers promised him that there would be no problems and that as soon as I return from Hebron I should report to the Interior Ministry and receive an identity card like the rest of my family. I could not return to Jerusalem at the time of the census because a curfew was imposed on East Jerusalem. When the city was opened I returned to Jerusalem and I thought that my father had registered me as his son. I went to the Interior Ministry to receive an identification card and they gave me a temporary slip and to this day, for three years, I come and go and the matter has still not been arranged. I am afraid to go out on the street because the police make problems for me ... I have been detained several times and then released because I do not have an identity card. PS, I can produce for you the documents that confirm that my house was destroyed during the war and we received from the government compensation of IL 1,800 to repair the ruins of the house. I have a birth certificate from the Mandate showing that I was born in Jerusalem and that my father is Mohammad Yehiya Da'is who is listed in the East Jerusalem population registry.

A person living under foreign occupation would not ordinarily send letters to such top officials. The use of the term "East Jerusalem" and the correct, if stilted, Hebrew of the body of the letter over his signature in Arabic indicate that Da'is was helped by an Israeli. These were some of the most salient signs of the occupation in its early years.[29]

Israeli officials formulated one plan after another for East Jerusalem, often setting off controversies among their colleagues and the public. Minister of Education Yigal Allon was motivated to fashion his own program by his service as commander of the Palmach during the 1948 war and his long political and personal rivalry with Minister of

Defense Moshe Dayan, whose decisions often had an indirect impact on the government's Jerusalem policy. In August 1967, at Allon's prompting, the government decided to instruct schools to halt the use of the Jordanian curriculum and to replace it with that used by the schools that served Israel's Arab citizens. The Ministry of Education banned eighty-one Jordanian textbooks on the grounds that they contained anti-Israeli material or Palestinian nationalist incitement, and ordered that the Hebrew language be taught in Arab schools. These decisions were met with a public outcry in East Jerusalem, the West Bank, and Amman, because of the expectation that the territories would eventually return to Jordanian rule. In his decree, Allon went beyond what the military government in the West Bank was prepared to agree to. The latter examined the books that the Education Ministry had banned and found that the material the ministry had found objectionable was simply an account of centuries of Arab history, and that many of the passages cited by the ministry as incitement were legitimate expressions of national sentiment. Furthermore, the military government had no interest in taking aggressive measures that would push Palestinians into the arms of nationalist activists fomenting rebellion. It thus rejected the ministry's directive.[30]

But East Jerusalem fell under the purview of the ministry, not the military government, so Allon's policy, rather than the army's, was instituted there. In the meantime, the Palestinians had staged a school strike to protest this policy and the academic year began one or two months late (depending on the school). Many parents transferred their children from city to private schools, where the Education Ministry had no say. This trend accelerated when, at the end of the 1967–8 school year, only four out of ninety-six seniors at the Rashadiyya high school passed the Israeli graduation exams; 70–80 percent of the school's seniors had generally passed the Jordanian graduation exams before the war. In the 1969–70 school year, Benvenisti decided to circumvent the ministry and to allow East Jerusalem high schools to offer additional lessons to students who wished to take the Jordanian exams. Since Israel's diploma was not recognized in the Arab world, it was of no use to a young East Jerusalemite who wanted to continue his studies at a university in an Arab country, or to benefit from one of the generous scholarships that Arab states provided to Palestinian students. Enrollment in the public high schools recovered slightly after Benvenisti's move.[31] In the 1972–3 academic year the Jordanian curriculum was given equal standing with the Israeli one, but students found it difficult to meet the demands of both curricula simultaneously and, during the mid-1970s, East Jerusalem public schools were again allowed to teach solely according to the Jordanian curriculum.

When the Palestinian Authority was established in 1994, it adopted Jordan's curriculum and gradually began to issue its own textbooks. It also took over Jordan's role in overseeing the curriculum of East Jerusalem's public schools. Israel exercised only loose oversight of Palestinian education during the Authority's early years. A Jerusalem municipality sticker was placed over the Authority logo in the textbooks issued by the latter. But at the beginning of the 2000s Israel began, in accord with the policy of the Likud government that was then in power, to assert authority over textbooks and education. According to a report issued by the Knesset's Information and Research Center, "The Jerusalem Education Administration submits the books received from the Palestinian Authority to a careful reading by an external examiner who marks all passages in which there is incitement against Israel and the Jews. The books are subsequently sent for reprinting without the proscribed passages. This is done both with new books and books issued in new editions. At the same time the Education Administration provides clear instructions to all public schools in East Jerusalem that they may not use Palestinian textbooks purchased on an independent basis."[32] The censored items included a picture of a Palestinian flag, a passage about the arson attack on the al-Aqsa mosque by an Australian fundamentalist Christian in 1969, sections on the history of the Palestinian national movement, a photograph of the PLO chief and Palestinian Authority President Yasser Arafat, and Palestinian population data from the Palestinian Central Bureau of Statistics. At the end of 2011, many parents sought to replace their children's censored textbooks with the original versions. Moshe Marzuk, a former intelligence officer who vetted the books for the municipality, retorted: "Censorship? On the contrary. We see it as a preventative humanitarian measure. The system operates in self-defense, to prevent incitement to violence."[33] But for some Israelis, even censorship was not enough—they wanted to adopt Yigal Allon's policy. On 12 April 2011, the Knesset's Education Committee debated a proposal by its chairman to require all East Jerusalem high school students in municipal institutions to be taught the Israeli curriculum, in keeping with Israel's sovereignty in the city.

Israeli textbooks were also subject to careful scrutiny. "Who is a Jerusalemite?" asks a typical homeland and social studies textbook intended for fourth-graders. The question is posed by three fictional Jerusalem children, Yaron from Musrara, Yael from Kiryat Yovel, and Rami from Ramot. No Arab children from East Jerusalem are included—say, Mohammad from Silwan or Taisir from Sho'afat. The Jewish children go for a journey through "urban Jerusalem" and discover, as one might expect, that a Muslim minority lives in their Israeli–Jewish city. The textbook quotes Jerusalem's mayor, Ehud Olmert, saying that these children have a right to "freedom of choice and freedom of religion, so long as they obey the laws of the state and treat others with respect."[34] Olmert's version of religious freedom is not presented as a conditional, not an absolute, right. The Israeli state grants freedom of religion in exchange for obedience to its laws—which by implication includes the law that annexed East Jerusalem to Israel. The chapter that addresses the city's neighborhoods offers eight photographs, only one of them of an Arab neighborhood, al-Tur. This is the only Jerusalem neighborhood outside the Old City that is mentioned. Palestinians in Jerusalem are, in this picture, confined to certain places and kept to a low profile. The book expresses this in three additional ways. First, the expansion of the city outside the Old City walls is referred to only with regard to its Jewish inhabitants, without reference to the establishment of neighborhoods like Sho'afat and Sheikh Jarah. A map of the Arab neighborhoods in pre-1948 Jerusalem disregards the fact that there were large Arab neighborhoods on the west side of the city, among them Malha, Lifta, Qatamon, Bak'a, 'Ein Karem, and Romema. Second, Jewish life in the city before the 1948 war is depicted as meaningful and full—in terms of synagogues that operated in the Old City, but no more than that. Third, in its depiction of the city's places of employment and business centers, no mention is made of the East Jerusalem downtown that extends from within the walls at the Jaffa gate to Nablus Gate and outside it to Salah al-Din Street. In other words, both Arabs and religious Jews are presented as stereotypes, not part of the city's urban fabric. The Arab population, as depicted in the book, lacks an urban center just as it lacks a national, as opposed to a religious, identity and with no mention of its history or roots in Jerusalem.

Five children, all Jewish of course, set out for an adventure in Jerusalem, relates Asi Weinstein in a book for preschoolers. An elderly

Arab man tells them how he was treated by the famed ophthalmologist Dr Albert Ticho. Here is a frail Arab in need of Jewish assistance, in need of succor from a kind and educated Jew who helps everyone. These are not the book's only stereotypes. Dr Ticho, it says, did not stop caring for Arab patients even during the Jewish–Arab clashes of 1929 and 1936–9. In the book, he is stabbed by a young Arab, despite the protection that Avi, the narrator, tries to provide. In this story, all Arabs are violent, with one exception, and Jews are always victims. According to the story, "The Muslim Arabs, who had never considered the Western Wall important, invented a new legend. They said that their prophet, Mohammad, hitched his magical mare, al-Buraq, meaning lightning, to the Wall before he ascended to heaven … my grandmother told me that the Muslims used to bring their garbage and dump it in front of the Wall."[35] Is it any wonder, then, that when the book tells about a trip to the excavations by the Wall by five children, they only encounter artifacts from the Second Temple and know nothing about the Muslim periods in Jerusalem's history?

Other such books observe that there are Muslims and Christians in Jerusalem—but no Palestinians.[36] In practice, there is every reason to believe that schoolteachers do not teach only what is in the books. And, of course, students' minds are not only shaped by their formal educations but also by their daily encounters with the Other on Jerusalem's streets and on television and computer screens. The textbooks do not, therefore, reflect the way Israeli students think. But they do depict the Palestinians in the way that Israeli educators and leaders wish them to be seen by young people.

Shmuel Toledano told Eshkol in December 1968 that government ministries were circumventing him, the prime minister's adviser on Arab affairs, and that the result was a "lack of coordination among the actions of government ministries" in East Jerusalem. Eshkol replied that "the same rules that apply to Israeli Arabs apply to the Arabs of Jerusalem, and that interministerial coordination is the responsibility of the adviser on Arab affairs." But this directive was not carried out, as is proven by another letter Toledano sent at the beginning of 1972 to Eshkol's successor, Golda Meir. "We must make every effort … to effect maximal integration of Jerusalem's Arabs with the Arabs of Israel and to detach them as quickly as possible from the Arabs of the administered territories. Our office is working in this direction on all levels."[37] Toledano here reiterated the position he had taken since June

1967. Ya'akov Yehoshua, formerly an Arab Jew, thought the same. In 1967, Yehoshua had sought to impose heavy censorship on the Friday sermons given by imams in al-Aqsa, just as was done with the sermons of Israeli Muslim preachers. Meron Benvenisti, Teddy Kollek, and David Farhi took the opposite view, with the support of Moshe Dayan. They argued that Jerusalem's Arabs were different from Israel's Arab citizens. Israel controlled the latter with an iron hand, using a divide-and-rule strategy that involved favoring some clans over others. Jerusalem's Arabs had a high-level of political awareness and strong institutions, meaning that this method could not be applied to them. Farhi, the adviser on Arab affairs to the military government in the West Bank, was assigned the job of overseeing Muslim sermons in Jerusalem. He did so with great leniency and consideration for Muslim sensitivities.[38]

The same rule applied to the East Jerusalem daily newspaper *al-Quds*. When, in 1968, Mahmud Abu Zuluf received a license to put out the newspaper, it was conditioned on the publication being subject to Israeli censorship. But the Israeli authorities realized that this put him in a difficult position and thus accepted with understanding the newspaper's first editorial, which called for an end to the Israeli occupation and annexation. "Under our guidance, the Jerusalem Arabic-language newspaper *al-Quds* acted to keep tempers down [after the arson attack on al-Aqsa by a Christian fundamentalist] in an exemplary way—it described the disaster as a fire in a part of the mosque; refrained from printing any references to *jihad* ... [and] gave prominent play to government statements."[39] On 17 February 1969, Moshe Sasson and Shin Bet operative Eliezer Tzafrir met with Abu Zuluf to reprimand him for an editorial they read as supporting an independent Palestinian state of the type the PLO supported, without balancing this with a call for coexistence with Israel. They "made clear to him what they expected of him." Abu Zuluf promised that the next day he would publish a clarifying article in which he would address the issue of how to establish a Palestinian entity. But the next day no such article appeared, to the displeasure of Sasson. In the end it appeared the following day, two days after the original piece. Sasson thought that Tzafrir should take Zuluf to task for not keeping his promise. Abu Zuluf's article asserted that the majority of Palestinians believed that a Palestinian entity would be based on humanitarianism, democracy, and peace. This was not the formula the two Israelis endorsed, but they let the matter pass.[40]

OCCUPATION, ASSIMILATION, OPPOSITION

Meron Benvenisti, Kollek's assistant, was the prime implementer of Israeli policy in Jerusalem in the initial years following the annexation. "I began my involvement in Jerusalem affairs as a pragmatic participant. I believed in the power of process and I had no well-defined goals except to alleviate suffering, reduce tensions, and foster coexistence. All I saw before me were the symptoms of the conflict, which were sufficiently severe to leave no time to draft 'permanent solutions,'" he wrote of himself. It was neither easy nor simple. "My Zionist–Israeli ideology, my professional training, and my liberal approach clashed with each other time and again. But the contradictions did not confuse me. I addressed each problem on its merits without considering how a particular action contradicted a previous action and might contradict one that would come later." At times he acted as a Zionist patriot; at others as a compromiser who sought a common denominator between rival groups. At still other times he was a technocrat who took no interest in, or disregarded, politics and ethnic conflict. He supported, for example, the demolition of the homes of terrorists, but also permitted them to be rebuilt. He approved the construction of a memorial to fallen Arab combatants, but then ordered it razed. "I wanted to keep options open," he said, but as the years went by options closed. "Now that years have passed and turned into decades, I wonder how much I contributed to the legitimacy of the status quo," which became fixed. "But how could I have acted otherwise?"[41]

Thanks both to his personality and mode of operation, Mayor Kollek became the symbol of an enlightened Jerusalem. Kollek was an impulsive man of action who spoke his mind. He identified with his job to the point of erasing his private persona. The Vienna-born Kollek radiated humanism and liberalism and he displayed sincere concern for Jerusalem's Arabs. He was a man of the center, an advocate of pragmatic compromise, dialogue, and restraint, who did his best to prevent friction between ethnic and religious groups. Yet he was a complex person. On the one hand he ordered the demolition of the Mughrabi neighborhood that lay next to the Western Wall. On the other hand, in the following year he saw to it that the bodies of the 366 Arabs who had been killed during the 1967 war, and whose bodies had been buried at various sites throughout East Jerusalem, were moved to a central resting place next to the northeastern corner of the Old City wall, and approved the erection of a memorial there. The memorial replaced the plaques that Palestinians had placed at the locations of the temporary graves, just as the friends of Jewish combatants had placed plaques at places where soldiers had fallen in battle. Kollek stood his ground in the face of outrage from the Israeli public, who saw this as a reward for the enemy and a threat to Israeli rule of the city. Kollek also condemned the humiliations that Jerusalem Arabs suffered at the hands of Israeli soldiers and policemen and fought to increase government allocations to Jerusalem's Arabs. On the other hand, he gave up on a plan to move the auto repair shops out of Wadi Joz so that neighborhood could be developed, on the grounds that it was too expensive. He preferred to raise money for small projects, such as the establishment of a health clinic in Sheikh Jarrah. These funds were channeled through the Jerusalem Foundation, an independent body he set up and ran. Kollek knew how to use the media to gain much play for the few things that he actually did for Jerusalem's Palestinian inhabitants. These highly visible micro-initiatives, Kollek hoped, would minimize the probability of an outbreak of Palestinian protest.[42]

After 1967, Jerusalem became a noisy place. The racket of construction and development filled the air. Thousands of buses deposited tens of thousands of tourists at the Old City gates and took the city's residents from one part to another of the growing city, which soon doubled in size. The booming economy made family cars, formerly a luxury, affordable for the middle class, filling the city's narrow streets and polluting its air. Jerusalem's fabled mountain air became less breathable, but Israelis did not care—they inhaled history. When the initial euphoria was institutionalized and routine took over, policy became systematic and planned. The sense that Israel's victory in 1967 was a decisive historical moment that set history on a new path was replaced by anxiety that the new Israel was a passing phase. To fix the historical moment, policy-makers concluded, the city's physical and demographic landscape had to be changed. Jerusalem's rapid expansion following the 1967 war evinced an architectural style different from what had previously characterized the city. The international–universal style that had preceded the war was replaced by the adoption of Palestinian motifs. The building plans for Ramat Eshkol, a new Jewish neighborhood in East Jerusalem, had actually been originally intended for West Jerusalem. When the decision was made to build, as quickly as possible, such new neighborhoods in the perimeter surrounding the formerly Jordanian city, as a way of fixing the annexation in stone, architects took the existing plans and added arches to make the construction feel more local, native, and authentic. The model set by Ramat Eshkol was then copied in other new East Jerusalem neighborhoods. More and more modern apartments went up, most of them sporting oriental curves, courtyards, and domes. Jewish architects sought to commandeer Jerusalem above the surface just as archaeologists were doing under the surface. But these Israeli homes are in no way similar to the Arab houses in Qatamon, Tabiyyeh, and Sheikh Jarrah.[43] Unfortunately, this style influenced the Palestinians as well. Many of the new apartment buildings they built in northern and eastern Jerusalem are similar to the homes in the Jewish neighborhoods in East Jerusalem. They can be told apart only by the black water tanks that stand on the roofs of the Arab houses, signs that they, unlike the Jews, are not connected to the municipal water system. In contrast to the beautiful Arab neighborhoods that were built in the early twentieth century, these are functional blocks of concrete faced with stone. The Palestinians seek to maximize the number of housing units they can build on each small lot, whereas the Jews seek to maximize the number of people living on each large piece of land taken from the Arabs. Palestinian homes were constructed without any master plan, without any overarching concept of how a neighborhood should look, and without any thought to preserving Palestinian architectural and esthetic values. The glorious architecture of the past was abandoned.

Kollek oversaw this massive building boom and accelerated development, marketing Jerusalem as a multicultural city, a mosaic of ethnic groups and minorities living side by side. Sometimes, he acknowledged, there was tension between the different parts of the mosaic, but there was no unbridgeable gap between them and the Israeli sovereign. According to Kollek, politics would not decide whether the unification of Jerusalem would be maintained over the long term, but coexistence within a single city. The acceptance of Israeli sovereignty by the Arabs of East Jerusalem would happen gradually, he maintained, a grassroots process in which the Palestinians would slowly come to accept Israeli rule and enjoy its benefits.[44]

The Intifada that began in 1987 knocked the Arabs of East Jerusalem out of the mosaic. Kollek's doctrine that coexistence would determine the future could not contain the contradiction between coexistence and Israeli superiority. The right-wing city government from 1993 and the national government from 1996 took off their gloves. Guided by a historical-religious ideology, the national–religious right has acted to impose symbols of Israeli sovereignty and rule. Kollek's successor, Ehud Olmert, declared that the government had to "take our side with determination, and to make it clear that there will be no political and diplomatic compromise about the status of the entire city as Israel's capital." The government should work to "bring about a dramatic improvement in the quality of life of the Arab residents."[45] A healthy dose of improved daily life, he thought, would mitigate Palestinian pain at Israel's deep incursion into their territory. In practice the right-wing government also broadened the Jewish hold on the eastern part of the city and widened the gap and the conflict between the two populations. The expansion of the Jewish hold in East Jerusalem is based on a Jewish right to the city, whereas the equalization of municipal services for the Arabs is based on the inhabitants' universal rights. The two approaches contradict each other. Meron Benvenisti now declares sadly:

We thought that people like us—people with good hearts and esthetic tastes who believe in coexistence—could create an apparatus with which they could manage the city and its surroundings. What happened? They [Jews with an insatiable appetite for land and power] grabbed it all away. It breaks my heart to see what romantic idiots my I and my friends, Teddy and others, were when we thought that we would always be in power. Now we sit here, miserable old men watching it and saying: how could we have thought that we could let the genie out of the bottle without the genie consuming us in the end?[46]

The attempt to tame the genie, which succeeded for a few years, was made by a group with a common language, mutual understanding, and a consensus on policy. Even though Moshe Dayan did not directly involve himself in Jerusalem affairs, he helped set overall policy and was in contact with those who did make decisions in the city. In December 1967 a bomb went off at the Fast hotel and in October another was discovered before it went off at the Zion cinema in West Jerusalem. Both were laid by agents of Fatah, the militant Palestinian organization. In response, the IDF demolished the home of a member of the organization, Nimri Kamal, in Wadi Joz. Insufficient care was taken and other houses were also damaged. Benvenisti invited those whose property had been damaged to submit receipts for repair costs to the city. In August 1968 the municipality paid out IL42,921 to forty-five people. The funds came from the Defense Ministry and were approved personally by Dayan.[47]

Eli Amir, who worked for the office of the prime minister's adviser on Arab affairs, and Rafi Levi, the Interior Ministry's Jerusalem district chief, had sharp senses. Levi had been born in Hebron, grew up among Arabs, and spoke their language. He served in Haganah intelligence and after 1948 was the Interior Ministry official responsible for the Mandelbaum Gate in Jerusalem, the transit point on the border with Jordan. Following the victory of 1967 he was appointed district chief, serving as Israel's liaison with the Christian churches whose holy sites Israel now controlled. He found a way to bridge between the two worlds that were his own two worlds—the Orient and Zionism—by putting Zionism first. Neither he nor Amir were Arab Jews of the pre-1948 generation. They represented Israeli rule. They generally displayed sensitivity to the feelings of the Palestinians who now found themselves under Israeli occupation, and worked hard to find openings in the Israeli establishment's general impermeability to such sentiments. Amir had been born in Iraq and grew up on a kibbutz. The Arabs called him "an Arab native" (*mawlad 'Arab*), "not Ashkenazi" (*mush Musqobi*), and "a son of Arabia like us" (*ibn 'Arab kathayna*). Rafi Levi says that he made sure to make it clear to those he spoke with that Israel was in charge. The Zionist and Israeli ruling class was no place for Arab Jews to develop. "Our approach was to offer humane treatment, to treat them like human beings with a right to fair treatment in exchange for recognition of the Israeli ruling hierarchy," Levi said. He and his colleagues would solve the Arabs' routine problems so long as they acknowledged Israel's authority and, in practice, made their peace with it. The idea was "to give them a good feeling a feeling that they had something to lose."[48] Arabs who cooperated with Israel found it easier to get licenses and identity cards. "We wanted to help them as if they were new immigrants, as those who would be our neighbors for the rest of their lives," Amir said, to treat them "reliably and honestly. I spared no effort to help them, including those without a pedigree, ordinary people, to be an intercessor for them, to speak in their name and to listen, to understand and feel their frustration and hope that we could live together."[49] In handling the Arabs on a personal basis they were considerably aided by their direct contacts with senior implementers of policy and with Jerusalem's Palestinian elite. Matters were resolved through ad hoc telephone calls and decisions, without bureaucracy. "The sense was that we had come into an important business, a historic one, and that we had, with our combined strength, to push it and do the best we could. We wanted to have nice faces."[50]

That was indeed something to strive for. A survey ordered by the municipality in mid-1968 showed that Jews characterized Arabs as hypocrites, cowards, and primitives, as people who did not wash regularly and who were always sick. On the positive side, Jews valued Arabs as diligent, and believed that there were no few educated people and advocates of peace among them. According to the survey, 55 percent of Jerusalem's Jews did not want their children to go to school with Arabs; 62 percent were not willing to work under an Arab boss, and 75 percent feared that the unification of the city would raise the number of intermarriages. Eshkol was not pleased with these results and ordered all but two copies of the survey to be destroyed.[51] The unflattering results, he worried, were liable to crush Israeli optimism that unification could work.

Israeli rule seemed to have a promising future in East Jerusalem during the first years after the war. The East Jerusalem cinema Alhambra advertised in what was then Israel's largest newspaper, *Ma'ariv*, highlighted the fact that it was open on Friday nights, when the Israeli cinemas on the western side of the city were closed for the Sabbath. The Shepherd hotel, located in Mufti Hajj Amin al-Hussayni's former home, where, after that, Katy Antonius had resided, offered Jews, on the first Rosh Hashanah holiday after the war, "a wonderful holiday vacation in a pleasant and brand new hotel." The Bob restaurant on Suleiman Street and the Semiramis night club invited the Jewish public to dine, and the Arabesque restaurant on al-Zahara Street, next to the al-Quds cinema, announced that it was opening under the joint ownership of Avraham Gil and 'Adel Kamala.[52] Israelis flocked to East Jerusalem's restaurants, cafés, and discotheques. The area of Nablus Gate was especially popular. Young Israelis and foreigners crowded into the tiny cafés near the gate, whiling away the night on the Old City walls. Jewish students rented rooms in the City Hotel on the east side.[53] East Jerusalem dentists did a brisk business with Jewish patients, and the East Jerusalem garages repaired the cars of West Jerusalem drivers. The elites on the two sides of the city established personal relations, Israeli movers and shakers becoming friends with leading East Jerusalem Arabs. Rafi Levi, Meron Benvenisti, and their friends spent weekend vacations in Jericho with the Nusseibeh, Nashashibi, and Barakat families.[54] Arab workers found jobs in West Jerusalem, reporting to work even when the Palestinians staged general strikes on the east side of the city. Jewish employers protected their Arab workers, driving them home when Jewish toughs threatened them following terrorist attacks.[55]

Sari Nusseibeh, Anwar Nusseibeh's son, first met Israelis on an airplane, when he returned from Oxford to Jerusalem in August 1967. He thought them impolite, loud, and badly dressed. In other words, they were flesh-and-blood human beings with weaknesses. On the other hand, his mother, born to a family of refugees from the coast, thought that Jews were cultureless hooligans—they had, she said, looted her family's house during the 1948 war. When Sari got home, he saw that a barrier no longer separated his house from the Jewish houses across the way. "Defeat had given me back my homeland," he wrote.[56] Sari crossed the former no-man's land, near the location of the Mandelbaum Gate, and gazed at his house from the Israeli point of view. He tried to imagine what they had thought when they saw an Arab boy looking at them from the other side of the border. Sari Nusseibeh spent that entire summer trawling through West Jerusalem so as to get to know it closely. He had a hard time deciding whether he reviled those who lived there serenely in the homes of refugees. But he was furious when he saw that the Mughrabi neighborhood had been razed, including the two twelfth-century mosques that he had loved. He visited the Knesset, Israel's parliament, and volunteered at an archaeological dig at al-Aqsa—an excavation his father, a former governor of Jerusalem, had condemned. He also worked as a volunteer on a kibbutz, where he was deeply impressed by Israeli idealism and humanism. At the same time he saw the limits of that humanism, which refused to include the Palestinians and to acknowledge the price they had paid. Sari hung out at West Jerusalem cafés with left-wing Jews and made note of the crude lines contained in Palestinian propaganda. His father, and even more so his mother, did not approve of his disdain for the attacks committed by Fatah and the PLO—they admired their attempts to oppose the Israeli occupation. His mother took part in demonstrations, was clubbed by the police, and told Sari that Israel would give way only by force.[57]

But Israel's optimism soon ran aground. Only two Jewish stores operated within the walls in February 1969, and only a handful of Jews had entered into business partnerships with Arabs from East Jerusalem. The students who had found rooms in East Jerusalem soon returned to the western side of the city, after encountering hostility from the Arabs. A bomb exploded in Shlomo Levy's electrical supply store at Herod's Gate, which he had rented from the Waqf.[58] The Israeli public flooded Arab stores in the Old City, buying everything they could lay their hands on, making the Palestinians realize that these were not the same Jews they had known in 1948. Those Jews "had high breeding and modesty," but these Jews were greedy.[59] Shopkeepers in the *suq* and restaurant owners took advantage of the Jews' enthusiasm and raised their prices. The Arab middle class was not willing to pay such prices at restaurants and cafes, just as young Arabs were not willing to do so at discotheques. The Palestinians behaved graciously, but hidden behind their polite demeanor was fear and a lack of trust, as well as a hope that the occupation was temporary. The Jews, for their part, were proud, and Mizrahi Jews—those with roots in the Islamic world—made every effort to distinguish themselves from the Arabs and to demonstrate their superiority. The Jews who filled East Jerusalem's restaurants were frequently rude and arrogant. A group of young Mizrahi Jews showed up at the Jerusalem Grand restaurant in June 1967 and tried to force the pianist to play "Jerusalem of Gold," a popular song that had become the unofficial anthem of the 1967 victory. A brawl was prevented only by the arrival of the police. In many respects, the city remained divided. Today, the average income for Jews remains four times as high as that of an Arab, population density and illiteracy are more than twice as high on the Arab side of the city than the Jewish side, and there are only a fifth as many university graduates among the Arabs as among the Jews. Prices in East Jerusalem are lower than in West Jerusalem, but higher than in the West Bank, so East Jerusalem Arabs generally go shopping in the nearby West Bank cities. One place where cooperation between Jews and Arabs flourishes is in the criminal underworld and the illicit drug business. Hashish parlors operate in the Old City, and in Arab cafés the drug is mixed with the tobacco used in water pipes. At the end of the 1960s hashish easily made its way into Israel from East Jerusalem and Hebron, and was often smoked at parties.[60]

Religious and social mores weakened under Israeli rule. In May 1969, rumors spread through Jerusalem and Hebron that a group of young Jews had gotten drunk in the cavern under the Dome of the Rock, and that a similar act of sacrilege had taken place in the Tomb of the Patriarchs (Muslim leaders said the stories were untrue).[61] "It is hard to walk down the street and see the white legs that look like lumps of white sugar ... if I were young, that would be more dangerous. I saw a young woman almost entirely naked. It's too bad that I'm not young. You people have freedom of prostitution," complained

Sheikh Yasin al-Bakri, the imam of al-Aqsa to Ya'akov Yehoshua on 8 July 1968. He added that Jerusalem had turned from a holy city into a city of debauchery and licentiousness in which women walked bare and intoxicated and harlots filled the streets. "It won't be long before you show your private parts as well," predicted Sheikh al-'Abd al-'Mu'atazim al-'Alami to Yehoshua on 26 July 1969. He "told of the prostitutes in Jerusalem and their prices, and it's true that in recent months young women have flooded Jerusalem's streets and gone to cafés with Arabs; its new merchandise for these Arabs."[62] The Christians were no less disturbed by the way Israelis dressed and behaved. "The number of bars and places of entertainment is much larger than the number of churches and houses of prayer. The hoots of the whores and drinks ascend together with devotions and prayers," asserted an article in *al Salam wa-al-Khair*, a religious Christian publication. "Tourists do not come to Jerusalem to spend their time in bars ... tourists want to see Jerusalem as a city of prayer ... the tourist does not want to see half-naked bodies walking the same road that the Messiah trod bearing the cross ... every stone in Jerusalem will cry out bitterly and every grain of dust will shout, restore me my sanctity."[63] Under Jordanian rule, when food was served during Ramadan it was always done behind a curtain, and alcohol was sold only under the table. Now both were freely available. Israel forbade the sale of alcohol only on the streets around the Temple Mount. The immodest dress of Israeli women and tourists, their miniskirts in particular, aroused the ire of conservative Arab society and had a negative influence on the status of young Arab women. Under Jordanian rule, traditional families only allowed young women to go out once a week with a brother or cousin as chaperone. Now traditional families forbade their daughters to leave the house at all, out of fear that they would be swept up by the permissiveness of surrounding society. In many cases young women did not want to be seen in public anyway because they felt that they would not look modern enough in their traditional modest clothing.[64]

This change in norms discomfited religious Arabs and their institutions. On 21 July 1968 the chairman of the Supreme Muslim Council wrote to Prime Minister Eshkol requesting that he "take action to shut down lewd establishments" in which liquor was served in anticipation of "orgies." On 8 August, Christian and Muslim leaders met to protest "the decline of moral life in East Jerusalem, especially in nightclubs."

They called on the police and the Ministry of Religions to help them. Aharon Bar Eliezer, an Education Ministry field man in East Jerusalem, submitted a detailed report to the religion minister on the differences of opinion at that meeting. The Muslims wanted to use force against the owners of clubs, as well as to involve international bodies and the media. The Christians favored asking Israeli officials to shut down the establishments. The Muslims opposed this because it could be seen as acknowledgement of the annexation. But Muslim leaders were not really consistent. Just a day before they had presented a petition on the same subject to the Israeli military governor of the West Bank; the first signatory was Mufti Sa'ad al-Din al-'Alami. On 11 August, a letter signed by sixty-three women was submitted to the prime minister, protesting the "corruption and moral depravation" that had followed "the opening of clubs and immoral places of entertainment ... prostitution and drug addiction in the Old City, without shame." The women who had signed the letter came from the city's most prestigious families, among them Amina al-Hussayni, Shaira al-Hadi, and Lina al-Khalidi.[65] Eshkol asked the chief of police for the Jerusalem district to prepare a detailed report on the issue. The chief, Shaul Rozolio, wrote that, under Jordanian rule, shows had not been presented at the Old City's sixty-three cafés, no licenses for the sale of alcohol had been issued to Muslims, and that seven brothels operated in violation of the law. Outside the walls there had been seventeen establishments that sold alcohol under the counter. No new cafés had opened since the war, but seven new bars had appeared, some of them jointly owned by Jews. Two of them offered strip shows and belly dancers. "Today there are no more brothels than there were under Jordan," Rozolio wrote. "However, nearly all the prostitutes from West Jerusalem, about 100 in number, now operate in East Jerusalem. Furthermore, an average of ten prostitutes from other cities visit the city every day." These women sought out clients in bars and on the street, and the police were acting to restrict their activity. The police would operate against streetwalkers, but "we should not seek publicity for operations to halt prostitution." The unification of Jerusalem tied the hands of the police, Rozolio explained: "The prevention of strip shows on the eastern side of the city is liable to create a precedent regarding such shows on the west side."[66]

During the first twenty years of the annexation relations between the two sides of Jerusalem ranged from good neighborliness to the sense that an invisible boundary separated Jews and Arabs. Meron Benvenisti lived for years on the border between the Jewish and Arab sections of the Abu Tor neighborhood. The son of one of his neighbors, Abu Zohir, was convicted of planting a bomb in the yard of one of the neighborhood's Jewish homes, about 100 yards from Benvenisti's home. His children were out playing on the street when the charge was set to go off, and they would probably have been hurt had an Arab gardener not found the bomb in time. Abu Zohir's son was sentenced to a prison term. When he was released, Benvenisti visited his neighbor to congratulate him. Benvenisti had been the official who gave Abu Zohir a permit to rebuild his house after it was destroyed during the 1967 war. Benvenisti had invited his Arab neighbors to his son's bar mitzvah and the Benvenistis had been guests at the wedding of Abu Zohir's son.

But these friendly relations had their limits. Benvenisti's family never invited his Arab neighbors to visit their *sukkah* (the booth or temporary structure Jews build to live in on this holiday), nor did Abu Zohir invite him to the celebration he held when he returned from his pilgrimage to Mecca. In another case, when a *sulha* (reconciliation ceremony) was held by the Arab families in the neighborhood, all the men who lived there were invited, but not Benvenisti. The son of another neighbor was released after a long prison term and the family held a party. But, in lieu of an invitation, the released prisoner's mother sent Benvenisti's wife a cake. Benvenisti's wife sent a cake in return. On Israel's Independence Day, the Benvenistis always flew an Israeli flag over their home, even though they knew it would anger their neighbors—and that if their neighbors were to fly a Palestinian flag, they would be arrested. There was hardly a young man in the Arab part of the neighborhood who did not spent at least a night in jail during the First Intifada, yet the Benvenisti family continued to patronize the Arab-run corner grocery store, and with their Arab neighbors they signed a petition sent to the municipality complaining about a lack of garbage collection and faults in the supply of electricity. Benvenisti and Abu Zohir exchanged advice about gardening, drank coffee together, and played backgammon, trying their best to set aside their disagreements. Such complex relations were sustainable among the adults, but had no analogue in the younger generation. The Benvenisti boys did not invite their Arab compatriots to their parties. They had no Arab friends.[67] Ten years later, when the First Intifada began, neighbors on the seam between Jewish and Arab Jerusalem and Jews and Arabs who shared workplaces found it difficult to maintain their previous cordial relations. Violence first appeared in these borderline areas. In October 1998, young Jews and Arabs from Abu Tor fought over the use of the local community center's basketball court. A Qur'an and Islam class at the community center was shut down on the orders of the Shin Bet. Jews from the neighborhood wrote to the mayor to claim that Arab youths were vandalizing their property and harassing their girls.

When dozens of Arab children from the Arab neighborhood of 'Isawiyya started playing at a playground in French Hill in 1998, a Jewish neighborhood on the east side of the city, the park turned into a battleground between Jews and Arabs. In May 2000 the French Hill neighborhood administration announced that it would henceforth permit only people bearing a certificate of residence in the neighborhood or the nearby Jewish neighborhoods of Givat HaMivtar and Ramat Eshkol to enter playgrounds in French Hill for free; Arabs from 'Isawiyya could use the facilities but only after paying an entrance fee of five shekels (about $1.40).[68] Arab women visiting a public clinic on Hebron Road in the Talpiot neighborhood were accosted by a Jewish woman who shouted at them "You dirty Arab women, go get treated in Gaza, dirty smelly Arabs, we'll smash your faces in."[69] A writer for the British newspaper *The Guardian* witnessed a similar outburst from a Jewish settler woman in Sheikh Jarrah. It was aimed at an 88-year-old Arab woman, Ribkah al-Kurd, who lived in a tent next to the house from which she was evicted. "Beast!" the settler shouted at her. "Shut your mouth, you whore!"[70]

Israel pursued a policy of "Judaizing" Jerusalem and cutting it off from the West Bank, as will be described in detail below. One result was that middle-class Palestinians in the city began to develop a survival strategy in 2008, after the end of the Second Intifada and in the wake of the decline of the Palestinian Authority and the diminishing prospects for the establishment of a Palestinian state. In the past, Palestinian high school students in the city overwhelmingly preferred to take the Jordanian high school graduation examinations and continue their studies at a university in the West Bank or the Arab world. Now more are opting to take Israel's exams and pursue higher education in Israel. Likewise, increasing numbers of East Jerusalem Arabs are applying for Israeli citizenship. In absolute terms, no more than 2,500 of Jerusalem's 200,000 Arab residents were naturalized between

OCCUPATION, ASSIMILATION, OPPOSITION

2008 and 2013, but this is a significant increase from previous years that indicates that the mood in East Jerusalem is less tense. The Israeli government has also displayed increasing willingness to grant such applications, after previously subjecting Arabs to procedures that deterred them from applying. Furthermore, in recent years the municipality has worked to open more post offices in East Jerusalem and to connect more homes to the city's water supply. This improved atmosphere has encouraged more Palestinians to frequent shopping centers, places of entertainment, and parks in West Jerusalem. Yet it is still the case that only 13 percent of the city's budget goes to East Jerusalem, even though its population is 40 percent of the city's total.[71]

When conflict between Israel and the Palestinians flared up once more in 2000, it destroyed cooperation between two feminist peace groups and, to a lesser extent, between other Jewish and Palestinian organizations in Jerusalem. From 1967 onward, Jerusalem had become a place in which civil action groups from both sides met, and the headquarters of organizations that reported and acted to find a solution to the Jewish–Palestinian conflict in general and in Jerusalem in particular. At first, optimism prevailed. But when the expectations of each side were not met, bitter disappointment set in. The two women's organizations, the Israeli Bat Shalom and the Palestinian Jerusalem Women's Center, severed their ties after the failure of the Camp David summit of 2000 and the beginning of the bloody Second Intifada. The Palestinian group demanded that Bat Shalom recognize Israel's responsibility for creating the refugee problem; such recognition, the Jerusalem Women's Center maintained, was, according to UN decisions, a precondition for any solution to the conflict. The Israeli organization refused. Some of its members agreed to the center's demand, but others argued that such a declaration would be detrimental to the organization's standing among the Israeli public.[72] But there were also other reasons for the parting of ways, beyond this declaration. A member of Bat Shalom, Dafna Golan-Agnon, wrote about this to Sumaya Farhat-Naser of the Jerusalem Women's Center:

The relations between us were so asymmetrical and so loaded that we spent most of the time trying to define our joint agenda, without much success ... The number of Palestinians was usually smaller than the number of the Israelis. We Israelis would always arrive first. Almost all our meetings took place in East Jerusalem, in the last building on the outskirts of the city, close to the West Bank. They were always late, always with good reason: the checkpoints, the roads, they were members of a lot of committees and worked very hard ...

The meetings usually began with a description of the events of the previous week and included criticism of us, the Israelis.[73]

Golan-Agnon was seeking to understand what happened. She suggested that the reason why relations between the two groups were never ideal was the asymmetry she described. But that, she felt, could not be the only reason. In June 1997 the two groups organized a week of culture and politics in Jerusalem under the title "To Live Together in Jerusalem: Two Capitals for Two States." No art gallery agreed to host the exhibit the organization had put together for the event, because the idea that Jerusalem could be the capital of both Israel and Palestine was then considered illegitimate by both sides. The Irish singer Sinéad O'Connor was scheduled to close the week with a concert at the Sultan's Pool, an outdoor theater just below the city walls, but she cancelled the event after receiving death threats. Furthermore, Golan-Agnon wrote, the difficulty of marketing the idea of a common city was not the only problem:

There seemed to be no subject over which we did not argue, from the name of the event to the location of the jazz performances to whether Israelis and Palestinians should appear together on the same stage. The Israelis always wanted more things to do together, and the Palestinians wanted fewer.

They even fought over the invitation:

How much tension, how much violence, how much anger and misunderstanding can be contained in sticking peace dove stickers on an invitation to a week of events proposing shared life in this city? It was as if generations upon generations of hostility had found expression in our inability to formulate one joint invitation in three languages to a different life in this crazy place. Some of the tensions between us derived from more than suspicion grounded in national conflict. Even though the status of women is subordinate to that of men in both societies, the role of Palestinian women in their society is even more problematic than in our own ... the Palestinians faced harsh criticism both for their feminist positions and for their cooperation with us.[74]

The Palestinians were furious at Golan-Agnon for writing an article condemning a terror attack in the Mahaneh Yehdua *shuk* in West Jerusalem, in which thirteen people had been killed. Her article appeared a short time before a final meeting to draft a common program for Jerusalem's future. But she failed to mention the IDF's demolition of Palestinian homes in Jerusalem or the killing of Palestinian civilians by the IDF. For her part, Golan-Agnon found herself troubled by other questions. "We could eat together; we could be frightened about our children's future; we could struggle together for peace. But you tell me—not yet ... If we—Israeli and Palestinian women—cannot eat together, then this is not the way I want to work for peace."[75]

The breach hurt her counterpart, Farhat-Nasser, as well. She recalled with great pain how each side was nearly unable to rise above its fears and stereotypes about the other. But, unlike Golan-Agnon, she did not seek personal friendship. For her, the national asymmetry needed to be reflected rather than fudged in their common work:

As long as [there is] an enormous asymmetry ... [one] "occupier," the other "occupied"—it remains unacceptable to address you as "friend" ... It is not possible that you can enjoy living in your society and at the same time make demands on Palestinians as if we were part of your society ... And it is your state and your people who are responsible for the misery imposed on the Palestinian people ... Do you know the enormous sacrifice we are making when we say we want only East Jerusalem? What about West Jerusalem home for generations of Palestinian families, until it was taken by force by the Israeli forces in 1948? ... You expect us to pretend normalcy when we are trapped in a surrealistically abnormal situation. Were we to do so, it would mean we accept the imposed "contra-normal" situation, and that we view it as normal.[76]

Farhat-Nasser's emphasis on the asymmetry was a type of protest and resistance displayed by the weak against the strong, even if the latter felt extremely uncomfortable about the imbalance and sought to eliminate it. Farhat-Nasser did not view Golan-Agnon as an equal partner in the struggle against the occupation, but rather as a representative of the Israeli side:

Each Israeli citizen bears a responsibility for the consequences of this and all other crimes committed against the Palestinian people ... I wish that a deep and honest feeling of guilt would find its way into the Israeli people. This would be a powerful first step towards a genuine future reconciliation ... Many women in the peace movement have experiences of coming together and then having that meeting misused for personal political reasons, often leading to difficult consequences for the individual involved [because she will be blamed for cooperating with the enemy and violating social norms].[77]

This was now the lay of the land. There were no more Arab Jews. Ya'akov Yehoshua offered this account of his encounter with the other side of Jerusalem following the 1967 war:

When we encountered them on the streets of the new Jerusalem [after 1967] and when they met us in the Old City's alleys, we did not know or recognize each other ... We gazed on them with a sense of strangeness and astonishment, just as they gazed on us. Only the elders among us, the veteran inhabitants of Jerusalem [both Jews and Arabs], would halt for a moment to shake the hand of a man they had known during the Mandate period ... About 75 percent of Jerusalem's residents, those who are of Hebron descent, never saw the figure or face of a Jew.

Most of the Arabs he met were strangers. He realized that this was a new state of affairs, but tried to make the best of it. He concealed the fact that the response of the Israeli government, which he represented, to the requests of the Palestinian "veteran inhabitants of Jerusalem" was limited in the extreme:

> But we, the Jerusalemites of many generations, both Jews and Arabs, asked and interrogated each other. We recalled from the depths of oblivion those common memories we had of the past. When we met them in homes and government offices, we tried to give them a feeling of good friendship, to provide them with all the information we had available, to use all our connections with important people and institutions to, as it were, "atone for our sins" for having conquered their Jerusalem and united it with our Jerusalem. Our past acquaintances and friends found in us a kind of psychological crutch for their troubles. They spoke to us in the Arabic language that we and they spoke in the past. It was a free and open exchange with us, the veteran inhabitants of Jerusalem ... and through us they did their best to submit their grievances and troubles to the authorities and other offices. And we responded willingly to their requests. We remembered the good many of them had done and we forgave many for both the slight and serious injury they had caused us. We took upon ourselves to give them a good feeling.

The encounter between Yehoshua and his old friends was no longer a meeting of equals. Their common identity had been replaced by a hierarchy in which the Arabs were dependent on the Jews. The Jews displayed their power in a generous but patronizing way, while the Palestinians reacted with flattery, cooperation, and profound frustration at the reversal of their fortunes and the humiliation inherent in the new situation. As the years went by, Yehoshua wrote,

> the old and new people of Arab Jerusalem no longer need the backing of the veteran inhabitants of Jerusalem ... that romanticism, those ties of friendship and brotherhood that pervaded us in the distant and more recent past have passed from the world, and both of us have become more practical, with no trace of a dream. Harsh reality has and continues to slap us in the face.[78]

Jaffa: Abandoned and Attractive

Israelis walk and with them walks their shadow—the Palestinian people; they beat the shadow with a big stick but it doesn't leave them alone.

– Meron Benvenisti[79]

OCCUPATION, ASSIMILATION, OPPOSITION

Unlike Jerusalem's rapid and enthusiastic spread eastward, Tel Aviv's expansion to the south took place slowly, without euphoria, and in contentiousness. In June 1967 Jerusalem shifted its symbolic center of gravity to the territory it had just occupied. True, no government ministry moved into the Old City, and the few that moved into East Jerusalem stayed close to the old boundary. But the Old City and its surroundings were seen as the long-lost kernel of the real Jerusalem. Tel Aviv, for its part, did not see Jaffa as a new center for the city. Instead, it was considered a heavy burden. Ever since many of Jaffa's Jews left the Arab city behind them in 1909 and established a Jewish city to its north, the inhabitants of Tel Aviv have viewed themselves as living in a hygienic, modern, healthy, and quiet European city, the polar opposite of lazy, wild, polluted, and noisy Jaffa, more a desert caravanserai than an urban center. Up until 1948, the two cities indeed mixed, but Tel Aviv's inhabitants generally preferred to live in denial of that fact and to adhere to their self-image. The war destroyed the fabric of common life and reinforced the stereotype. Tel Aviv was the city in which Israel had declared its independence on 15 May 1948; Jaffa was the defeated aggressor.[80]

Jaffa's defeat opened up new possibilities for Tel Aviv. The Jewish city cast its eyes at the border area. The municipality wanted to demolish most of Manshiyya and Abu Kabir, both of which had suffered heavy damage during the war, and to appropriate the land on which they stood. In particular, it wanted to uproot the citrus groves that Jaffa's Arabs had left behind and turn them into residential neighborhoods. The municipality also demanded custodianship of abandoned Arab property in Jaffa. All these steps required the approval of the national government, as did the municipality's request that the government fund the reconstruction program it planned for Jaffa.[81] The cabinet vociferously debated which city would annex which, and approved only some of Tel Aviv's demands. At a cabinet meeting on 4 October 1948, Interior Minister Haim Moshe Shapira proposed that Jaffa be absorbed by Tel Aviv. Ben-Gurion supported this in principle, but thought that, for historic reasons, the united city should be called Jaffa. "Jaffa existed 4,000 years ago," he explained. "Historically, it is important to stress that it is a Hebrew city and that it is now in our hands." By calling the city Jaffa, Ben-Gurion sought to provide the new Hebrew city with legitimacy and historical depth. Most of his cabinet colleagues could not fathom his position. They did not want to do away with "white" Tel Aviv and adopt a "black" name. Finally, as a compromise, they resolved that the city would be called Jaffa–Tel Aviv. Tel Aviv choked on the decision. "[The name] Tel Aviv evokes the ongoing rebellion against Jaffa," Mayor Rokach wrote to the interior minister in August 1949. Two months later he added: "The name Jaffa has no right to be preserved, not in our hearts and not on our lips, because that city played a despicable role in our nation's history."[82] Some nine months later, on 28 June 1950, the issue was brought before the cabinet once more. Shapira explained the Tel Aviv municipality's opposition to the inclusion of Jaffa in the city's name. The most municipal leaders were willing to do, he said, was call the city Greater Tel Aviv. Shapira offered the compromise name of Tel Aviv–Jaffa, thereby placing Tel Aviv first. Ben-Gurion, for his part, insisted on reaffirming the previous decision. The only change he was willing to consider was simply renaming the city Jaffa. The cabinet conducted four votes between Shapira's and Ben-Gurion's proposals, each of which resulted in a tie. Only on the fifth round did a minister from Ben-Gurion's camp switch his vote. Tel Aviv won first place but Jaffa remained part of the city's official name.[83] It was not just a decision about what to call the city—it set the basis for policy.

The government's policy on Jaffa has been more consistent than its policy on Jerusalem, and easier to carry out. The small number of Arabs remaining in Jaffa made it a simpler case, and the national government was not all that interested in what happened in Tel Aviv's backyard. Unlike Jerusalem, Jaffa had little Jewish history, so the winning side consistently neglected it. While Jaffa's Arabs make up only 4.5 percent of Tel Aviv's population, they comprise 20 percent of the population affected by the municipal neighborhood renovation program. A third of those receiving assistance from welfare offices and about a third of the one-parent families in Tel Aviv–Jaffa live in Jaffa, and Jaffa's population, Jews and Arabs together, makes up 13.5 percent of the city's population. In 2003 Jaffa's Arabs received 0.9 percent of the city's budget.[84]

The conquerors of Jaffa in 1948 did not view themselves as returning to a beloved city that they had previously been barred from, but rather as victors in a war. They behaved accordingly. After being taken by Israel, Jerusalem was full of the clamor of construction. After its conquest, Jaffa was full of the din of destruction. In August 1950 the government decided to raze its Old City so as to prevent the return of refugees. At this point in time, Israeli planners and officials had no romantic attachment to Arab buildings and no interest in preserving structures of historical and architectural importance and, in general, not mosques, either. They were motivated by a conception of urban development based on a worship of modernization. It was also in the victor's interest to establish irreversible facts. The person swimming against the current was Shmuel Yeivin, director of the Israel Department of Antiquities and Museums. He asked Ben-Gurion to halt the demolition of the Old City. He was supported by the artists Marcel Yanko and Reuven Rubin, both of whom had direct contacts in the government and ruling party. They proposed that partial demolition was enough, and that the remaining buildings should be left in place and an artists' quarter be established in the Old City. The government agreed.[85] In the 1970s the municipality, under Mayor Shlomo Lahat, initiated a new wave of demolitions. Some 3,700 Arab houses in Ajami and Jabaliyya were marked for destruction, to be supplemented by reclamation from the sea and replaced by a park, promenade, and low-density apartments not intended for the inhabitants of the destroyed homes. The plan was halted by two resident groups, a liberal Jewish group called Yafo Yefat Yamim and Al-Rabita Liri'ayat Shuon 'Arab Yafa (Society for Jaffa's Arabs), founded in 1978 by educated young people who wanted to preserve Jaffa's Arab character. Between 1960 and 1985 Manshiyya was entirely leveled, houses were demolished in Ajami and Jabaliyya, and about 70 percent of the structures in the Old City were destroyed.[86]

As noted, some 4,000 Arabs were confined to Ajami in 1949, and they were required to remain in their homes at night. The curfew was gradually eased during the 1950s. Army bases and public institutions moved into the homes of Jaffans who had left the city, reminding the remaining Arabs who was in charge. Some 80,000 Jews, most of them immigrants from the Balkans and North Africa, were moved into houses south of the Old City that had not been destroyed, with the intention that they forever replace the former Palestinian inhabitants. Ajami degenerated to become a crowded and derelict place inhabited by indigent Jews and Arabs. As soon as they could, its Jewish residents moved into the housing projects that went up in central and eastern Jaffa, and then later moved on to better housing in the surrounding Jewish cities. They were replaced in Ajami by Arabs from the Galilee and Little Triangle, the latter a region of Arab villages in central Israel.

Immigrants to Israel from the former Soviet Union also settled there, and the Shin Bet placed in the neighborhood the families of Palestinian collaborators from the West Bank and Gaza Strip who needed a refuge. Arabs from the heart of Jaffa whose economic fortunes improved followed the Jews, moving eastward and also north to the area around Clock Square and Jerusalem Avenue. Those who could not afford the prices there moved to the Arab parts of Ramla and Lod, mixed Jewish–Arab cities to the east. By the early 2000s, Jaffa was home to about 30,000 Jews and 15,000 Arabs. Ajami and Jerusalem Avenue were tense mixed neighborhoods.[87] In the meantime, Jaffa gentrified as wealthy Tel Avivians moved into new luxurious apartment dwellings and renovated Arab houses—and thus changed the character of the city. On its website, one of the new apartment compounds, Andromeda Hill, is described in pastoral terms:

> Andromeda Hill is a kind of city within a city, surrounded by a wall and guarded 24 hours a day. Its open spaces and byways are constructed of natural stone; it is lush with authentic Israeli flora and ornamented by original light and water elements. The parking spaces and machinery are located on a subterranean level to prevent noise, smells, and esthetic blemish. Andromeda Hill was planned for you, so that you may sit at home, gaze out on the sea, enjoy its beauty, and hear only the murmur of the waves.[88]

The development towers over its surroundings to a height of seven stories, and its architecture is eclectic, including Arab, Italian, and international elements. It seeks to be Mediterranean, to express authenticity and historical roots. But, in reality, it is an Israeli citadel, modern and alien from its environment. Yussif 'Asfur posed a question about it:

> We thought that the Jews would strengthen Jaffa. But that's not what happened. The Arab areas have been neglected more and more, and the Jews built magnificent residences on the line with the sea view. But even then we did not imagine that they would build fortresses with walls, real settlements, under our noses ... Why must they come to Jaffa of all places to build this sort of closed precinct, closed in particular to Arabs? If they want to build in Jaffa, they should build in our style. Here they have constructed something in an entirely alien style. And how are we supposed to feel when we are forbidden to enter? The only Arabs who go there, go there to, excuse me, clean up the Jews' crap, we go there only to clean it. In my view, it's a mini-occupation.[89]

Veteran and young Jaffans were outraged by the project not only because of its overbearing nature but also because the project blocked passage from Yefet Street, Jaffa's main artery, to the sea. In August 2007 a magistrates' court order accepted a petition by the Jaffa Association for Human Rights and the Society for Jaffa's Arabs, ruling that the guards at the gates to the complex allow anyone who wishes to pass through to do so between 8 a.m. and 10 p.m.

The Israeli establishment exploits its power in the free market to change Jaffa. Huri Sh'aya, a Greek Orthodox priest and leader of that community, built his home in Jaffa in the 1920s. But in 1950 he and his family were forced to evacuate the house and were moved into refugee dwellings. The house was transferred to the custodian of abandoned properties under the terms of the law governing Arab holdings—even though he and his four sons lived in Jaffa. When Sh'aya died in 1963, the sons claimed the house. The custodian recognized the sons' rights to only 60 percent of the property, and the custodian transferred the rest to the Israel Lands Authority (ILA). The sons tried to purchase that portion but the ILA refused to sell it to them. Later, the ILA offered to sell, but at a high price beyond the family's means. The two sides continued to fight over ownership and money. In June 2007, the ILA filed suit to dissolve its partnership with the family in the property—tantamount to a demand to eject them from the house. The Abandoned Property Law of 1950 granted protection to the homes of refugees in Ajami, but the right to remain in such houses as protected tenants could be transferred only once. In other words, under the terms of the law, the priest's grandchildren, who continued to live in the house, were illegal squatters in the house in which they had been born. The ILA and the Amidar public housing corporation took advantage of this provision to throw hundreds of Arabs out of their homes and to change Jaffa's character.[90]

Old Jaffa was never restored to its former glory. The Old City is no longer the vibrant and important port it was in 1948—now it is Israeli Jaffa. The ruins of the Old City are covered by the spacious Pisga Park, which displays ancient archaeological remains uncovered in the excavations conducted there since 1948. An archeological museum located underneath the park documents important dates in the history of modern Jaffa. The chronology it offers celebrates the period leading up to the establishment of the Israeli state. It marks the establishment of Jewish guest houses in 1750 and 1820, and the arrival of the Bilu immigrants in 1881 is accorded the same importance as Napoleon's conquest in 1799, while both are portrayed as stepping stones toward 14 May 1948, when the city was liberated by Jewish underground militias.

In 2007 the derelict port began undergoing a facelift. Restaurants and galleries opened and it became a site for open-air concerts and dance performances. Clearly, the new port is nothing like the historic port of Arab Jaffa. Rather, it is an extension of Tel Aviv, just like the big city's crushing incursion into Manshiyya. That formerly Arab neighborhood is now covered by the spacious Charles Clore Park. Next to the park stands a museum devoted to the IZL underground militia, which attacked Manshiyya in 1948 as part of the offensive against Jaffa. In 2010, the old Jaffa train station facing the museum was transformed from a clutch of abandoned buildings into a mall with upscale restaurants, cafés, and brand-name fashion stores. Clock Square and the Jaffa flea market are also in the process of becoming part of modern Tel Aviv. Another park is situated south of the Old City. Its lawn and picaresque promenade lie over the dumping ground for the ruins of Arab Jaffa, which for more than sixty years blocked access to the beach from Ajami.

At first, the Hasan Bek mosque, the last Manshiyya structure to remain standing, was slated for inclusion in the modernization project through which Tel Aviv was to expand into Jaffa. In Palestinian memory, the mosque was the focus of religious life for Jaffa's Muslims, but Israelis recalled it as an enemy stronghold from which Arab snipers targeted Jewish homes in the 1948 war. After the war the mosque was transferred to the custodian of abandoned properties, who in turn transferred the deed to the Jaffa Waqf, a body whose members were appointed by the Israeli government. The Tel Aviv municipality occasionally used the mosque as a youth center, but most of the time it was abandoned. People dumped refuse there and it became a haunt for drug dealers and prostitutes. At the beginning of the 1970s the municipality drew up a plan to make the mosque part of a projected shopping complex, tourist site, and commercial center. A number of senior Israeli figures were involved in the initiative. Gershon Peres, brother of Shimon Peres, was awarded a lease on the mosque. Some of the members of the Waqf board, which was composed entirely of Arabs, cooperated with the initiative. But the proposal was shelved thanks to the opposition of other members of the Board, who made common cause with the Islamic Charitable Society (al-Maqased al-Khiriyya al-Islamiyya), a religious welfare organization founded in 1975. Some years later, al-Rabita Lir'ayat Shuon 'Arab Yafa (Society for Jaffa's Arabs), founded by young Jaffan Arabs in 1979, turned the mosque into a symbolic site of resistance to the erasure of Jaffa's historic Palestinian identity. The latter organization, together with the Islamic Movement, completed a renovation of the structure in 1988, and it is currently under the control of the Islamic Movement's northern wing, headed by Sheikh Ra'ad Salah. Most of the city's other mosques are controlled by the more moderate southern wing of the same movement. Many of Jaffa's Muslims stay away from Hasan Bek, a mosque so central to their history.[91] In the end, the structure was saved, but it remained physically isolated. It is surrounded by Charles Clore Park, a luxury hotel, office buildings, and expensive restaurants, large roads, and an upscale mall. However, its isolation from today's Jaffa and its marginality for the city's Arabs have not dispelled its symbolic significance for the Jews. On the contrary, it stands out as alien to its surroundings, making it all the more threatening to some Jews. A Palestinian terrorist blew himself up in the midst of a crowd of Israeli teenagers outside a discotheque across the street from the mosque on 1 June 2001. The next day Jewish demonstrators surrounded the mosque, seeking to destroy it and threatening to lynch the Muslims defending it from inside.

After 1948, Jaffa was a place of poverty for Jews and Arabs alike. Their common plight brought them together in a way reminiscent of Jerusalem in the late nineteenth century. Both Jews and Arabs in Jaffa had lost their old homes and settled in new ones, and both felt neglected by Israel's rulers. "In Jaffa I feel at home ... Three different women nursed me and were like mothers to me, Arabs and Jews," wrote Shimon Amar.[92] Isma'il Abu Shahadeh recalled that he and other Arabs learned to speak not only Hebrew but also the Bulgarian and Romanian spoken by many of the Jewish immigrants.[93] "I could walk into and sit down in any home I wanted to. Even the homes of the rich [refugees] ... Jews and Arabs all went into [each other's homes], there was no conflict," related Subhiyya Abu Ramadan.[94] Rabbi Avraham Bachar, who arrived from Bulgaria and was assigned living quarters in an Arab house whose owner was now in exile, wrote that "relations between Jews and Arabs in Jaffa were always good." But not always good. "There were never really good relations," he added, contradicting himself.[95] Avraham Shlush, an officer in the Jaffa military government, wrote in a report he filed in October 1949 that, next to Jaffa's Great Mosque, "a gang of Moroccans has squatted, and every Saturday they curse the worshippers emerging from the mosque, all Muslims, the Muslim religion, and Mohammad. I requested that the police assign a guard to the site." A rumble between Arabs and Oriental Jews broke out at a ball sponsored by the Israeli Workers'

Alliance. "They take vengeance on Israeli Arabs for persecutions the Jews suffered," explained another officer, Avraham Malul, in a report he filed on 1 March 1951. The municipality's demand that Arab merchants close their stores on Friday nights and Saturdays, the Jewish Sabbath, unless they applied for and received special permits, aroused the ire of Jaffa's Arabs.[96]

Neglected Jaffa pulsated with life. Its inhabitants developed their own cultural institutions, which served as alternatives to those in Tel Aviv. Arab cafés, ethnic restaurants, and nightclubs opened in Ajami and in the Artists' Quarter. Drug dealers, prostitutes, and thieves also plied their trades in the ruins. "There's nothing like Jaffa at night," the Theater Club Quartet sang, a French chanson melody with lyrics by Tel Aviv bohemian Haim Heffer, a Palmach veteran. The Jaffa nights in Heffer's song were spent womanizing, drinking beer, playing cards—and robbing a bank. Heffer and Dan Ben-Amotz, a writer and entertainer who lived in the Artists' Quarter, ran a nightclub called the Hamam in what had formerly been Jaffa's central bathhouse. At the end of the 1950s, the Ariana club, built on the ruins of an Arab building not far from the Hamam, began to host Aris San, a Greek vocalist who had moved to Israel as a boy. San introduced Greek music into Israel, making it into a popular genre that would become a major influence on Israeli pop music later in the 1990s. In the 1970s, Menachem Talmi published a series of stories about Jaffa in the daily newspaper *Ma'ariv*, which were later issued in two volumes and were adapted into a television series in the 1990s. Talmi's Jaffa was an alluring, powerful, and colorful city where drugs, violence, and crime rubbed shoulders at fish restaurants and cafés frequented by warm and decent people, most of them Jews. Here and there these people stumbled into crime, but with no evil intentions. They were bound together by a common destiny and mutual responsibility, which sharply contrasted with the anonymity and alienated individualism of Tel Aviv.[97] It was not the Jaffa of people who struggled to make a living during the day, but rather that of those who spent their nights there. For the most part, it was Jaffa as imagined by Jews who lived to its north, in Tel Aviv. For such people, Jaffa was foreign, enthralling, violent, passionate, and hospitable.

Amram Ben-Shimon lived in Ramat Aviv, at the northern end of Tel Aviv, but spent his nights and days at Clock Square, near the "big area" he had once ruled as a pimp. "A lot of Israeli Arabs live here. We see them every day. They grew up with us over the years ... they are good people. Not all of them. Some hate us. But they don't hate us here. They hate the government." Still, "You can't trust them ... they hate us because we conquered them ... that's why we suffer from them ... I don't have any Arab friends and I'll never have any Arab friends." He sent his children away from criminal Jaffa in order to protect them.[98] Musa Agima, born on Shabazi Street on the edge of Arab Jaffa, also lives in northern Tel Aviv. His father was born in Hebron and was saved in 1929 by one of his Arab employees. "In Hebron, Arabs live on my father's land ... What can you do? Cast them out on the street? No way. As of now, I'd never return to Hebron." He drives to Jaffa every day to hang out with his friends, some Arab and some Jews of Lebanese and Syrian extraction. "This is home," Agima declares. And he adds: "I'm like an Arab." His wife is a Moroccan Jew, but culturally "an Arab born to Arabs" who cooks only Arab food. All his children understand Arabic, "and I listen only to Arabic music."[99] But Ben-Shimon and Agima are not Arab Jews, as their fathers and grandfathers were. In a restricted way, they integrate Arab elements into the fabric of their lives and their identities as dominant (Ben-Shimon) or patronizing (Agima) Israelis.

Nor are Jaffa's Arabs like those of previous generations. Jaffa's identity, as well as that of its inhabitants, Jews and Arabs, changed in 1948. Sisters Su'ad, Widad, and Layla, the daughters of Amin Andreus, returned to Jaffa in 1950 under the aegis of the Red Cross. "We went back to [the Scottish] school. It was the same school, the same building, but the people were different. There were Iraqi Jews, Jews from Romania, Jews from Bulgaria." They worked in the British embassy and their social circle was made up of diplomats, foreign correspondents, and Jaffa residents. Their niece Robin feels much more Israeli than her aunts. Her Hebrew is fluent, she pursued film and communications studies at Tel Aviv University, and her social circle is Israeli in every way. But ultimately, the majority Jewish–Israeli society does not really accept her because she is an Arab. So she keeps her distance.[100]

In Jaffa, compassion is not a sentiment felt toward the entire human race—it is felt toward one's tribe and family. This can be seen in the film *Ajami*, written and directed by Scandar Copti and Yaron Shani, a Palestinian and an Israeli Jew, respectively. The film portrays how violence reigns within and between the social groups that comprise Jaffa. The city's Arabs are trapped in cycles of poverty and drugs, and live on the margins of the big city. But the Israelis who rule over them are also trapped in the violent milieu that they impose on the Arabs. Even well-intentioned Israeli Jews misunderstand the codes of Palestinian society. Some want to replace Arab mores with Jewish ones, but the attempt to do good ends in tragedy and Palestinian rejection.

Jaffa's young people are rootless and their identities are vague, says Ayman Siksak, a young Hebrew-language author born to a Muslim family in Jaffa. Tel Aviv tempts them and they seek refuge there from the neglect and filth of their own city. They speak Hebrew on the Tel Aviv beach, attempting unsuccessfully to hide their origins. Jews immediately suspect them of being terrorists. In Jaffa they speak Arabic, but use it to talk about the Hebrew poet Chaim Nachman Bialik, whose works they studied at school, and suffer the rebukes of Jaffa old-timers upset by the fact that they do not recognize the Palestinian author Ghassan Kanafani. Arab children enthusiastically celebrate Hanukah in their preschools, while at the same time the *mu'ezzin* call the faithful to prayer and teenagers sell jelly donuts, traditional on the Jewish holiday, in Arab bakeries. None of them knows anything about the Prophet Muhammad's birthday, which in 2004 fell during Hanukah. They hear about the significance of the day for Muslims not at home or at school but from day-laborers from the Israeli Arab city of Um al-Fahm. The dream of young Arabs from Jaffa is an Israeli bourgeois one—a plush apartment facing the beach and a Mercedes in the parking garage below. But Israel rejects them for being Arabs, so they are left alienated and without a foothold.[101]

In contrast, young Arabs and Jews of meager financial resources but full of ideals are laboring to preserve the city's Palestinian identity and to turn it into a site of coexistence. Their hangout is Café Yafa (Yafa is the Arabic form of Jaffa) and Arabic bookstore, a small family operation that also sponsors Arabic lessons, literary and musical events, lectures on the city's Palestinian history, and tours of the city's Palestinian heritage. Members of an organization called Ayam–Recognition and Dialogue have set up a website where they post interviews with Jaffans,[102] and Yafa Action takes down the stories of the cities elders and creates bridges between individual and collective memory. The city's young Arabs speak a pidgin of Arabic and Hebrew, exploiting the initiative and ambition they have acquired from Israeli Jewish society to reinforce their weak Palestinian identity in the face of the stronger Israeli identity.

OCCUPATION, ASSIMILATION, OPPOSITION

Jaffa is increasingly coming to resemble East Jerusalem. In 2007 several national religious Jewish families moved into Jaffa as an organized group and, a year later, established a *yeshiva* and seminary for girls in the middle of Ajami. An Israeli flag flies over the *yeshiva*, as one does over the settler outposts in Jerusalem's Arab neighborhoods and Hebron. Its website proclaims: "The yeshiva's goal is to return Judaism to the city of Jaffa and to strengthen it ... In the city of Jaffa we connect with the Jewish people's ancient roots ... The yeshiva's activity in the city instills steadfastness and faith among the Jewish inhabitants and injects forces of Jewish growth and renewal."[103] These settlers do not view the city's Arabs as people to conduct a dialogue with. Their goal is to make Jaffa Jewish and to supplant the Palestinians. According to the director of BeEmunah, a company that builds homes exclusively for the national religious Jewish population, "For the settlers, the lesson of the disengagement [from Gaza in 2005] was that they need to begin a dialogue with Jews inside Israel to persuade them that a settlement in the West Bank is no less legitimate than one in Jaffa." It began by building twenty housing units in Jaffa, a synagogue, another *yeshiva*, and a commercial and service area. In November 2010 Israel's Supreme Court rejected an appeal by Jaffa's residents against the decision of the Israel Lands Authority to grant one of the last reserves of land in the heart of Ajami, land that was under Palestinian ownership before 1948, to BeEmunah.[104] "Settlers Out!" "Jaffa is not Hebron!" shouted graffiti on the city's walls. In 2013 the company put out a new tender for the construction of forty housing units on this land.

Jaffa is dynamic, varied, and turbulent. But it began to seem more and more like Hebron at the beginning of the Second Intifada in October 2000. Arabs from Jaffa, like those in Galilee, the Triangle, the West Bank, and the Gaza Strip, took to the streets. These violent demonstrations led Jews to view Jaffa as a threatening, dangerous place. Some called on their fellow Jews to stop visiting the city, and to boycott its restaurants, bakeries, and butcher shops.[105] When the tension subsided, material interests bridged the widening gulf between Jew and Palestinian, but the gulf still remained. In March 2008, for the first time, Jaffa's Arabs marked Land Day, an annual day of protest against Israeli expropriation of the land of its Arab citizens, long observed in the country's other Arab areas. Jaffa Arabs had long kept their distance from the revival of Palestinian national identity that been underway in

Galilee and the Triangle for some time. Later that year, during the Israeli army's Cast Lead incursion into the Gaza Strip, stones were thrown at Jewish buses and cars driving through Jaffa. In 2009 the windows of the Peres Center were smashed, street signs and signals were knocked down, playgrounds were vandalized, and anti-Israel graffiti was sprayed on walls.[106] Social tension turned into national conflict and relations between Jews and Arabs worsened. In the summer of 2008 Jewish parents in one Jaffa neighborhood discovered that a preschool where Jewish children had always been the majority would, in the coming year, turn into an Arab-majority school. The Jewish teacher was replaced by an Arab. Many of the Jewish parents then transferred their children to a different preschool where only Jews were enrolled.[107] Once every two weeks that same summer the residential committees of some Jewish neighborhoods in the city rented a local pool for the day and allowed only Jews in. The reason they offered was that Arab children attacked Jewish ones when swimming was mixed.[108] In October 2011 Jewish extremists desecrated Muslim and Christian graves, spray-painting "Death to the Arabs" on headstones. They also set fire to an Arab restaurant and covered its walls with anti-Arab slogans. One of them was "Price Tag," the same slogan used by extremist Jews in campaigns of revenge against Arab attacks and against Muslim and Christian religious institutions and holy places. Arab extremists responded by throwing a Molotov cocktail at a synagogue.[109]

Hebron and Jerusalem: The Force of History

In the seed of the city of the just a malignant seed is hidden, in its turn: the certainty and pride of being in the right—and of being more just than many others who call themselves more just than the just. This seed ferments in bitterness, rivalry, resentment; and the natural desire of revenge on the unjust is colored by a yearning to be in their place and to act as they do.

– Italo Calvino[110]

When Israeli soldiers evacuated the few Arabs who remained in Jaffa from their homes in 1948, they did so at the point of the victor's sword. Jaffa has no real significance in Jewish history. It does, however, play a major role in Zionist history, having served as the Zionists' port of entry into Palestine, their transit station before they left to found separate Jewish neighborhoods and cities. The conquest of Jaffa, Palestine's commercial, social, and intellectual hub, was perceived in Israel as part of the Zionist destiny of subjugating the country's Arab past and constructing a new society. In Jerusalem, the encounter with history occurred in 1967, when the Old City and Hebron were taken. Israel overwhelmed the Palestinians and was simultaneously overwhelmed by Jewish history. When an Israeli Jew knocks on the door of a Palestinian Arab in Jerusalem or Hebron, he does so with the force of history.

"Here it all began," is how the El-Ad (Ir David) Foundation introduces visitors to Silwan. The Jewish people's history and mythology are all there is. The starting point is the conquest of the Jebusite city by King David, who arrived from Hebron to expand his kingdom. "Here it all began" means that at that point in time Jerusalem first became Jewish. Jerusalem has no other beginning and no other meaning than being Jewish. One of the features on the organization's website is a panoramic photograph of Jerusalem taken from the Mount of Olives. Jewish sites and neighborhoods are tagged but not Arab neighborhoods or Muslim and Christian holy sites, which are all prominent features in the landscape. The El-Ad Foundation is devoted to strengthening Israel's hold on the valleys and ridges that circle the Temple Mount. The website also offers a timeline of Jerusalem's history, but one that is completely oblivious to the Muslim and Christian presence in Jerusalem, as well as its rich Arab history. The only exception is a segment called "The Early Arab Period," which, like the descriptions of all the other periods, focuses largely on Jewish settlement in Jerusalem. The chronology begins with the biblical Patriarchs and the story of Abraham's binding of Isaac on Mt Moriah, and ends with the rebuilt City of David.[111]

Archaeologists and historians agree that a part of the Arab neighborhood of Silwan is built on the slope that was the site of ancient Jerusalem. For that reason, the site has been subject to excavations since the nineteenth century, and since 1967 such excavations have been undertaken by the Israel Antiquities Authority. Israel has declared it a national park. What is anomalous is that this national park is presented to the public by a private organization with a clear and explicit political agenda. According to many scholars and experts, El-Ad deliberately misrepresents the excavations to the public and, since it also works to bring Jewish settlers into the neighborhood, it uses the archaeological site in its campaign to Judaize Silwan. One archaeologist who has worked extensively at the site on behalf of the Antiquities Authority, Professor Ronny Reich, related that "I found a Byzantine water pit. They [El-Ad] said it was Jeremiah's pit. I told them that was nonsense. But for a long time the guides would tell the tourists that this was the hole Jeremiah was thrown into."¹¹²

In the initial years after 1967, Israel sought to empower the Jewish–Zionist narrative over the Palestinian historical narrative. While it did not seek to hide the Palestinian story, it placed that story in a subordinate position. Beginning in the 2000s, El-Ad and similar organizations have worked with the Israeli authorities to ensure that the Jewish historical narrative is the only one salient in Israeli public consciousness. A response has been provided by a different organization, Emek Shaveh. In contrast with El-Ad, which uses history and archaeology to tell an exclusively Jewish story, Emek Shaveh presents archaeology as a bridge between the peoples and cultures that share a land that belongs to all of them.¹¹³ But the two organizations are not equals in influence and financial resources. El-Ad is well endowed and enjoys close cooperation with the Israeli government. The IDF and the Ministry of Education regularly send soldiers and schoolchildren to tour the site under El-Ad's guidance, some of the nearly 500,000 visitors to the site each year. Israeli's Nature and Parks Authority has granted El-Ad a franchise to manage and operate the site.¹¹⁴

It all began modestly. On 9 January 1968, Finance Minister Pinchas Sapir appointed a committee to purchase land in the valley and on the ridges surrounding the Old City. He gave it a budget of IL 2 million (about $700,000 at the time, according to the official exchange rate). According to the documentation for this decision, "No encouragement will be given to the purchase of land in East Jerusalem by private elements." But as of July of that year the committee had not been able to find a single Arab willing to sell such land, so the committee was disbanded.¹¹⁵ In March 1973 the Israel Lands Authority set up a division named Igum to purchase homes in the Muslim Quarter. Igum purchased Palestinian homes through straw men who presented themselves as private individuals. The ILA's plan was to use the buildings purchased to house the offices of Jewish organizations and institutions rather than as residences, in keeping with the policy of the Labor-led government and of Teddy Kollek's administration in Jerusalem that Jewish and Arab residential areas should be separate. Igum had only limited success. The Likud governments that ruled Israel beginning in 1977 turned this policy around in the early 1980s, using the same methods pursued by Igum to settle Jews in Palestinian areas. And, instead of using a public body like the ILA to do so, it granted aid and authority to private organizations.[116]

A large number of national and municipal bodies were involved in this policy, requiring the establishment of a Committee to Coordinate Activities in the Muslim Quarter, chaired by Efrayim Shiloh of the Jerusalem municipality. In March 1984, the committee met to discuss the question of which of two rival organizations should receive its support—Atara LeYoshna, founded in 1979, or another organization that split off from the first, Ateret Cohanim. Representatives of the former appeared before the committee and presented the properties it had purchased in the Muslim Quarter. They declared that their goal was "to purchase every possible property in the Muslim Quarter so as to create a physical link between it and the Jewish Quarter." Ateret Cohanim was not represented at the meeting, so the committee heard only a report about it. This organization was described to the committee as being extremist and as having the goal of establishing a Jewish stronghold on that part of the Temple Mount that, according to its interpretation of Jewish law, it was permissible for Jews to enter. Atara LeYoshna was depicted by Shiloh as a moderate and level-headed organization, and in keeping with that the committee awarded its support to that organization. But the committee did not authorize it to settle Jews everywhere in the Muslim Quarter. "From the point of view of security and Jewish interests, housing in Jewish-owned buildings is favored ... along the principle arteries leading to the Western Wall, along HaGai, David-HaShalshelet, and Beit HaBad Streets. The purchase for residential purposes of homes bordering on the Temple Mount is not to be encouraged. Private developers are to be discouraged from purchasing, without government approval, homes for Jewish habitation in other areas in the midst of dense Arab population," Shiloh wrote in his summary of the meeting and its decisions. "The committee will ask the Ministry of Construction and Housing to accept itself or to assign to a company connected to the ministry the responsibility to allot financial assistance for the evacuation of non-Jewish residents to homes outside the Old City, and recommends to the Ministry of Construction and Housing to continue to assist in the renovation of buildings and apartments under Jewish ownership and to accept the assistance of one of the private organizations involved in this matter."

Following this meeting, on 1 June, Yehuda Ziv, Jerusalem district chief for the Ministry of the Interior, submitted a proposal to his ministry's Jerusalem Committee. He recommended that Ateret LeYoshna "act as the government's principal agent in everything regarding the policy of purchasing and populating Jewish properties in the Muslim Quarter." Representatives of the ILA, the ministry, and the Office of the Custodian of Absentee Properties would be added to Ateret LeYoshna's board. The organization would be given the purchased Arab properties for the purpose of renovation, habitation, and upkeep. Money for renovation would come from the ministry's budget for aid to home buyers who met ministry criteria. In accordance with Ateret LeYoshna's goals, preference would be given to properties lying along the roads leading from the Nablus and Jaffa Gates to the Western Wall. "In the current circumstances, we should prevent to every extent the law permits aid to the housing of Jews in the vicinity of the Temple Mount if it seems reasonable that the purpose is to create a jumping-off point to the Temple Mount," Ziv wrote. Although his wording lacked clarity, the intent was plain enough—the two organizations, both Ateret LeYoshna and Ateret Cohanim, were to be prevented from obtaining a foothold on or near the Temple Mount. On 17 September 1984, Ziv's proposal became government policy.[117] Ateret LeYoshna was dissolved in the latter part of the 1980s. Its place as the organization with which the government works was taken by Ateret Cohanim. This organization switched its goal from gaining a foothold on the Temple Mount to purchasing residences in what it called the "renewing Jewish Quarter," meaning the Muslim Quarter. At the same time, the Israeli authorities revised their approach to push for Jewish settlement everywhere in the Old City and in the valley surrounding it, including sites adjacent to the Temple Mount. In organizational terms, the method was changed from purchase by Igum to outsourcing or semi-privatizing the purchase of property. As its agent, the government chose an organization that had the explicit goal of actualizing Israeli sovereignty in Arab Jerusalem, a goal motivated by a messianic religious theology.[118]

In 1992 a government committee of inquiry known as the Klugman committee found that, by the beginning of the 1990s, the government had transferred $8.2 million to private organizations for the purpose of seizing control of homes in East Jerusalem. In 1985, another $12 million were allocated for the renovation of homes purchased in East Jerusalem by settler organizations. These were properties that were not purchased but were rather declared to be abandoned properties under

Israel's Absentee Properties Law, which meant that ownership passed to the custodian of absentee properties. Such determinations were made on the basis of information submitted by settler organizations. The Office of the Custodian did not check the truth of these claims, did not visit the sites, and did not take an interest in whether Jewish settlement in these properties would require the expulsion of Palestinian families living in them. Furthermore, representatives of the settler organizations took part in the meetings in which decisions were made to allot them government funds and powers.[119]

"The heart of Jerusalem calls us—six properties, all registered, are now offered for sale. The properties offer the prospect of augmenting the Jewish community in the Old City with 22 more families, which will raise the number of Jews living in the Old City, not including the Jewish Quarter, to about 1,000," declared a pamphlet sent by Ateret Cohanim to its donors in September 2009. "At a time when the United Nations and countries around the world are plotting to take Jerusalem and its holy sites from the Jews by force, a stable and strong Jewish presence in the Old City has become critical to our capability as a nation to preserve and control our spiritual center. Ateret Cohanim and you will make that happen." Each of the homes in question was given, prior to its purchase by a donor, a Hebrew name evoking the Jewish past, such as Herod's Gate House, Miracle House, or Sacrifice House. According to Ateret Cohanim's chairman, Matti Dan, "Our activity is part of a natural process of the Jewish people's return to its country, to the place from which it was expelled. It is a divine command and the word of the prophets. There is nothing political here; the construction of Jerusalem is this people's national identity."[120]

The Israeli government handed over properties for which it had assumed ownership under the terms of the Absentee Properties Law to Ateret Cohanim, El-Ad, and similar organizations. Originally, that law transferred to the state ownership of the property of Palestinians who, after the 1948 war, ended up outside Israel's borders. The application of the law to East Jerusalem was delayed from 1967 to 1977, and then was suspended in 1992 by Israel's attorney general because, in the case of East Jerusalem, it was questionable whether the owners of the properties in question could be defined as absentees who had left Israel. East Jerusalem had been annexed to Israel, but the owners lived in the Occupied Territories—that is, they were outside Israel's borders as defined by Israeli law, but under Israeli rule. At the beginning of the

2000s the law was invoked to take control of properties in Sheikh Jarah and Silwan that had been owned by Jews before 1948. The homes of Jews that the 1948 war had turned into refugees had been appropriated by Jordan's custodian of enemy properties, which housed Palestinian refugees there. When East Jerusalem was annexed, Israel's general custodian, who assumes ownership of the assets of Israeli citizens who die intestate and other properties that come into possession of the state by law, assumed ownership of these properties. According to Israeli law, the general custodian was required to release these properties to those who had owned them before the Jordanian occupation. Under these terms, in 1977 land and homes in East Jerusalem were returned to Jewish organizations that had been their owners before 1948. These organizations transferred the properties to settler organizations, and in the 2000s legal methods were devised for expelling the Palestinian residents of these properties. Following a long legal battle, the Gozlan family was compelled in 2005 to leave its home in Silwan, after a court determined that the house had been sold in 1923 to Baron Rothschild, who transferred the deed to the Jewish National Fund, which in turn transferred it to El-Ad. "Munificent God can be trusted to recompense all those who do good," the Jews of Silwan wrote to the head of the Gozlan family, thanking him for saving their lives during the 1929 riots.[121] The State of Israel and the settler organizations did not do justice to the family.

The principle that Israel has established in East Jerusalem is that every property that belonged to Jews before 1948 is to revert to Jewish ownership, while no Palestinian property in West Jerusalem is to be so returned. The Palestinians can, if they wish, receive compensation for their property on the west side of the city, but that compensation does not accord with its current value but is instead paid in accordance with its assessed value on 29 November 1949. If the sum is a large one, the payment is spread out over fifteen years. According to a study by 'Adnan 'Abd al-Rasiq, about a third of the property in West Jerusalem was owned by Palestinians before the 1948 war.[122] Furthermore, a Jew can buy a property or home anywhere in East Jerusalem, but a Palestinian from East Jerusalem cannot do the same in the west. Israeli law permits foreign citizens to purchase property on Israeli soil only if they are Jewish under the terms of Israel's Law of Return. In other words, Israelis, and Jews around the world, have a right to buy property in the country even if they were not born in Israel. But a

Palestinian has no right to return to the home in which he was born, even if he lives only a mile or two away.

The settler organizations see Jerusalem as a theater of military-messianic operations. In describing their actions, Dan uses terms like "urban warfare," "redemption of Jerusalem," "this place is the nation's heart," "the war in Jerusalem is over every centimeter," "one sees divine providence in the alleys."[123] Ariel Sharon, a non-religious Jew, preferred to use security and historical arguments. "There is no dense Arab population in Silwan," Sharon wrote while serving as housing minister in an affidavit submitted to Israel's Supreme Court in 1991. Sharon was speaking of a section of Silwan in which El-Ad was seeking to settle Jews but which was home to 5,000 Palestinians. Sharon continued:

The place is close to the Old City wall and the Jewish Quarter and can become well-integrated into the areas of Jewish settlement around it. I am personally acquainted with the area, the places, and the homes in question, and have visited there. On the basis of my acquaintance with the area in question, and based on my wealth of experience in security matters, acquired during my long service in the IDF as well as in the framework of my service as an Israeli government minister (including as minister of defense), I maintain that the settlement of Jews in homes in the City of David, as requested by the petitioner [El-Ad], would be a considerable contribution to the security of the entire area. A Jewish presence in this place aids the security services in their activities, provides sympathetic and convenient lookout points, intelligence collection, and daily assistance to the security forces. This is especially true given the specific location of the houses in question and the integration of a Jewish presence in the place with the adjacent Jewish settlement ... It is clear to me that the necessary guard and security arrangements needed in the City of David are much easier and simpler than those required to secure the Jewish residents in their homes in the Muslim Quarter and Christian Quarter of the Old City.[124]

Violent clashes between Jews and Arabs have become a daily occurrence in Silwan since the arrival of the settlers, and on more than one occasion they have resulted in injury and death. Palestinians are arrested by the settlers' guards and by the police that patrol the neighborhood. The settlers act like lords of the land, using fear to rule the neighborhood. They benefit from state-funded private guards and from direct contact with the police and the Border Guard, who are quick to intervene in their favor in any dispute. They stonewall and stymie Palestinian complaints about violence on the part of settlers or their security guards.[125]

At times, however, a different sort of attitude can be seen, one that is more humane. One snowy night 'Adel, a resident of Sheikh Jarah locked in a legal battle with the settlers because he lived in a house that they coveted, heard a loud knocking on his door, followed by a voice pleading "Let us in! Let us in!" 'Adel opened the door and found himself facing the two security guards who had been stationed by his house by the settlers who were seeking to evict him. Their tent had collapsed from the weight of the snow and they were freezing. He let them in. His neighbor, Rima Hamami, was shocked when he told her the story a year later: "'Adel, you let the guards into the house?" she said in astonishment. In her account, he replied:

> "Only that one time. What's a person to do—let someone freeze to death?" I know what I wanted to say but kept my mouth shut. He went on, "You know, they're not all the same, the Jews. One of the guards, Max, I swear to God he's *maski'in* [wretched], just like us. He's Iraqi. Well, I mean his parents were from Baghdad, the Jews tricked them into coming here. There they had a big house and servants and everything and here what was he—a guard! He had no choice, it's the only work he could find. He doesn't believe in Israel and settlers and all that crap but he has a family to feed."[126]

The violence that always lies just under the surface in Silwan and Sheikh Jarah, and which breaks out from time to time, makes Jerusalem much more like Hebron than it has ever been before.

Like Jerusalem, Hebron is rich in Muslim and Jewish history but not in Zionist history. The Arab Jews who lived there were not Zionists. Yet the city became a powerful symbol for Zionists after the bloody anti-Jewish riots of 1929. The Arab massacre of Hebron's Jews was part of a week of bloody riots that swept through not only the two holy cities but also Zionist cities and farming towns. The Jews of Hebron inadvertently became part of the Zionist struggle and the city's Arabs were labeled as murderers. Even forty years later, in 1967, the massacre remained the first thing that came into Israelis' head when they thought of Hebron.

On 12 June of that year, just after the war, Michael Sassar went to Hebron. The Arabs in the city's street looked to him "like rioters ... 'murder in their eyes' was no mere expression when you looked at their faces." A month later, on 9 July, he returned to the city as the military government's press secretary to participate in the opening of the first post office in the West Bank. Nothing of his initial reaction remained when he saw the post office standing empty. His reaction this time was typically Western: "The Arabs apparently don't write many letters, and overall it seems like we think in Western terms that do not always apply to them."[127] It could be that his close work with Moshe Dayan changed his perceptions. Dayan did not associate Hebron solely with the massacre of 1929 and did not think that Jews should settle in the city as revenge. He ordered the removal of the Israeli flag that had been placed over the Tomb of the Patriarchs by the Israeli force that took the city, recognizing that the site had served as a mosque for the previous 1,300 years. He did not, however, have the courage to shut down the synagogue that the IDF Chief Rabbi Shlomo Goren had inaugurated in the mosque immediately after Hebron was conquered. In fact, Dayan ordered that Jews would not have to remove their shoes before entering the Tomb, despite its status as a mosque. But he did not allow the consumption of wine or food within the building, which the Muslims would view as sacrilege, nor did he permit Jewish ceremonies that involve the drinking of wine to be held there, such as circumcisions and weddings. In consultation with Hebron's mayor, Sheikh Ja'abari, and with the mosque's top Muslim cleric Sheikh Mustafa Tahboub, Dayan granted the Jews one of the prayer spaces in the Tomb and issued a schedule that ensured that Jews and Muslim did not hold their devotions at the same time.[128] Dayan fashioned this fragile coexistence agreement for the site on the assumption that he could control the demons of history and hold in check the settlers who sought to cast off the restrictions he had imposed and to gain full control of the site.

His success was only partial, and temporary. As long as he remained defense minister he personally dealt with all violations of the rules he had set and forbade Rabbi Goren to have any direct contact with the heads of the Waqf that governed the site or to enter the cave that lay below the sanctuaries where prayers were held. Dayan likewise forbade Rabbi Goren to pray on the Temple Mount or to have any contact with the Waqf there. In May 1969, the cabinet's Security Committee approved Dayan's proposal that Jewish prayer services in the Hebron shrine on the Shavu'ot holiday be coordinated with Mayor Ja'abari. Wine would not be brought into the Tomb. He vetoed a Jewish plan for a procession and dancing in Hebron's streets, and ruled that Jews who were not residents of Kiryat Arba, the Jewish city that had been built next to Hebron, would not be allowed into the shrine that night.[129] But the defense ministers that followed Dayan, along with most other Israelis, were swept away by the enthusiasm of the settlers and the politicians who supported them. Dayan's restrictions were steadily whittled away.

Dayan himself was not always consistent. The shrine in Hebron is built over the cave where, according to both Jewish and Muslim tradition, the biblical patriarchs are entombed. The upper building has three prayer chambers, one each for Abraham and Sarah; Isaac and Rebecca; and Jacob and Leah. A large tombstone in each chamber lies over the location, according to tradition, of the actual burial spot and gravestone of these patriarchs and matriarchs. The Jews who settled in Hebron were eager to see the holy graves. Dayan, hardly a religious man but an amateur archeologist, was no less curious to know what lay down there. While he forbade the settlers from descending into the cavern, in October and November 1968 he sent thirteen-year-old Michal Arbel, daughter of the West Bank Shin Bet chief, down into the cave. She took photographs and, after being brought up, drew pictures of it as well. What she saw was a small room, about 10 feet by 10 feet, with a high ceiling reaching, at places, a height of 13 feet. There were only three gravestones, rather than the six marked in the shrine above. Only one of the three bore an inscription, a verse from the Qur'an. On the southern side of the cavern there was a *mihrab*, a niche in the wall found in all mosques, indicating the direction of prayer. Another expedition into the cave was made a short while later. A thin soldier was let down into the cave to examine the possibility of creating a subterranean Jewish prayer hall under the halls above. Dayan thought that this could be a good way of dividing the site between Muslim and Jews without creating friction—Muslims on the upper level and Jews in the cave below. But the results were disappointing. The lower space was too small.[130] Jews and Arabs would have to pray in adjacent halls up above, and come into constant contact and conflict with each other.

Ten years after Dayan formulated this arrangement, not much remained of it. In October 1968 the settlers of Kiryat Arba demanded that Dayan lift the ban on wine and allow them to conduct celebrations involving its use. They also wanted to be allowed to pray every day of the week and at all hours. Furthermore, they demanded that a Jew be appointed to run the site, instead of the sheikh appointed by the Waqf. Dayan did not give in. They reiterated their demands in April 1969 and October 1972, each time meeting with refusal. But the settlers were not deterred. Despite the rejection they had met with, they violated the rules. Such incidents took place, for example, in December and June 1970, in May and June 1974, and in 1975. Fights broke out between Jewish and Muslim worshippers, with each side desecrating the sacred books and objects of the other. Following the incidents in May and June 1974, Rabbi Moshe Levinger, a Kiryat Arba leader, acknowledged to the IDF's West Bank commander that the atmosphere among the settlers was tense because of their spiritual objection to Muslim management of the Tomb. He expected further incidents, he said. The only way to prevent them was to remove the sheikh from his post.[131]

In 1975 Shimon Peres, who was then the minister of defense, permitted Jews to conduct ceremonies that involved the consumption of wine and to repartition the shrine. "The effect of the decision," Teddy Kollek wrote in a personal letter to Peres on 10 August 1975, "does not lie in the fact that the new arrangements are less favorable to the Arabs than the previous ones ... bur rather in our, the Israeli government's, willingness to violate a given status quo that we ourselves put into place regarding the holy sites, and in fact to retreat from it." That status quo, Kollek said, "granted no little measure of stability ... in our relations with the Arabs we are interested in obtaining a similar stability, the importance of which I need not explain. It could be that, eight years ago, we should have established the arrangement that has now been put in place in the Tomb of the Patriarchs. But once the arrangement was made then, it must not be changed now." Kollek feared that any change in Hebron would have implications for the Temple Mount and its environs.

Against the background of the archaeological excavations we are carrying out and the unfortunate fire in the al-Aqsa mosque, we have yet to allay the fears of the Arabs regarding our intentions on the Temple Mount, and now comes this matter of the Tomb of the Patriarchs, which has reinforced and rekindled those fears of theirs. Nothing we can do will gain us the Arabs' favor ... I believe, nevertheless, that under certain circumstances that we can attain what the entire Jewish people wishes for—to live with the Arabs in relative quiet. I believe that the decision about the Tomb of the Patriarchs cannot be considered one of those deeds that move us forward toward the situation we aspire to. The opposite is the case.

Peres replied four days later:

The truth is that [the rules] established for the Tomb eight years ago were not, in practice, followed during those eight years. Furthermore, the corrections and changes made over eight years, with the government's approval, were not laid out in clear language. The alternatives, in my opinion, were to rely on history [to work things out], which led to clashes and tensions; or to sum up the experience acquired in the Tomb, while respecting the feelings of the members of all religions, in a clear and updated document that will enable peaceful coexistence even in this holy and sensitive place ... The Tomb cannot be filled with soldiers and policemen to keep order.[132]

Peres did not enforce the rules Dayan laid out on the settlers; instead, he changed them in their favor. In fact, the changes in the prayer arrangements at the site did not, at the time, worsen Jewish–Arab relations on the Temple Mount, but they did set a precedent. In 2012, right-wing members of the Knesset submitted a bill to apply the prayer arrangements of the Tomb of the Patriarchs to the Temple Mount.[133] The proposal was that Israel unilaterally, by force, revise the centuries-old arrangement according to which Jews pray at the Western Wall and Muslims above, on al-Haram al-Sharif. Furthermore, the changes in Hebron led to even more clashes between the city's Jewish settlers and Palestinians. "Sometimes the tension is held back, and at times it breaks forth and rises," declared the national commission of inquiry established to investigate the massacre of Muslims in the shrine by a Jewish settler in February 1994. "Since the city's life revolves around the Tomb, every clash left its impression, not only within the walls [of the shrine] but in the entire city."[134]

In August 1967, the former residents of Hebron's Jewish Quarter asked Prime Minister Eshkol for permission to resettle in the city, and in October the head of the Hebron Yeshiva, which moved out of the city in 1929, requested to be allowed to move the seminary back to the city where it had been founded. Eshkol was favorably disposed, and in January 1968 Deputy Prime Minister Yigal Allon proposed to the cabinet the establishment of a Jewish neighborhood within the city.[135] The cabinet formed a Committee for Hebron and Etzion Block Affairs, these being the two locations, other than the Jewish Quarter in Jerusalem, where Israel had asserted a right of return. "We must not accept the fact that, because of a deadly pogrom in the summer of 1929, we at our own volition will turn Hebron into a city cleansed of Jews," Allon declared when he notified the Knesset of the establishment of Kiryat Hebron, the Jewish settlement adjacent to the Arab city, later renamed Kiryat Arba. "It does not set policy in any way," he added to mollify his critics both inside Israel and overseas.[136] Most likely, he did not believe his own words. But the Israeli government was united in perceiving Hebron in this way. Every objection and restriction imposed by the government was seen by the settlers and their supporters as a betrayal of the victims of 1929 and as aid and comfort to those who had killed them.

OCCUPATION, ASSIMILATION, OPPOSITION

Neither Hebron nor Jerusalem's Jewish Quarter had any Zionist history, but in Hebron Israel used Jewish history to justify or impel the creation of a new reality as it did in Jerusalem. Hebron lies distant from Israel's sovereign territory and there is no large and strong Jewish city alongside it that can serve as a wellspring for expansion, containment, or control. The settlers of Hebron and Kiryat Arba refuse to accept this situation and struggle against both the government and the city's Palestinian inhabitants to change it. The lack of Zionist history and Hebron's distance from Israeli cities magnifies the sense of isolation felt by Kiryat Arba's 7,000 Jewish settlers and Hebron's 700, who face off against some 35,000 Arabs. To overcome this sense of isolation, novelist Naomi Frankel found succor in mystical experience. "I returned to stand facing the destroyed homes, everything was different and I was quiet. My spirit and soul ignited, and the spark that began to burn within me was stronger than any fear. In one pure moment I was rewarded with something that would never fade. The sunlight broke through the haze of the summer heat, and it was to me like a rainbow, like a token of covenant between Hebron and me."[137] Frankel left Kibbutz Beit Alpha in 1982, moved to Kiryat Arba, and became religiously observant.

Those who do not have mystical experiences evoke Jewish history and the bloody account Hebron's Jews have constructed with regard to the Palestinians. Hebron's Jews have constructed a story of continuous Jewish settlement over thousands of years that was cruelly severed in 1929. For them, Hebron is a place of eternal struggle, without routine and without serenity. The Book of Genesis tells how Abraham bought the Makhpela Cave from an inhabitant of Hebron so that he could bury his wife Sarah there. For the settlers and their supporters, this constitutes a legal document, a precise historical account, and a divine imperative. A covenant of blood and land was made between the Jews and Hebron when Abraham, the first Hebrew, established it as his burial place. The settlers view themselves as emissaries of God, of Abraham, of King David, and of the Zionist movement. In their view they are the heirs of the Jewish settlement in Hebron that came to an end in 1929. The Tomb stands at the center of their public life and rituals, which is circled by memorials to settlers who were murdered in the city—Erez Alley, Yehoshua Square, Shalhevet Outlook, to name but a few. The dead are constantly present in the life of the settler community, and the settlers believe they have a duty to avenge them by enlarging their presence. The cycle of blood that has enlarged over the years empowers the identity of the city's Jewish inhabitants, who feel that they are poised between life and death, between Jewish redemption and Arab brutality. Hebron thus becomes a higher place, a point at which the physical land of Israel links up to the heaven where the murdered Jews and the nation's founding fathers and mothers reside. In their minds, the real Hebron is but a pale reflection of the mythical city, a fundamental point of connection between each and every Jew and the Land of Israel and the Zionist enterprise. In Hebron the father of the Jewish nation set out on the path of faith, the first Jewish grave was dug, and King David was crowned king of Judah before conquering Jerusalem. Hebron preceded Jerusalem in time and importance and heralded its role as Judaism's holiest city. "Hebron conquers Jerusalem," Naomi Frankel said. "Without Hebron, my city, the Land of Israel is not the Land of Israel."[138] In this view, the Arabs are foreign invaders, brutal murderers, not natives. In a museum they founded to commemorate the massacre, the settlers recount the event in vivid terms ("Rabbi Zvi Dravkin was slashed by daggers and his intestines poured out ... his fingers were cut off. Baker Noah Imerman was shoved into his blazing oven"). There are graphic photographs. According to this account, the Arabs have yet to pay for the massacre. To this debt of blood and history the settlers add the construction of the city's *suq*, garbage dump, slaughterhouse, and public toilets over the ruins of synagogues and Jewish houses, and the desecration of the Jewish cemetery. The consciousness of the Jewish settlers alternates constantly between activism and displays of power on the one hand and lamentations over Jewish weakness and victimization on the other. Their mottos are "removing an ancient disgrace"; "annulling the evil degree and removing the curse"; "planting life and sowing light in a place of darkness and the shadow of death"; "vengeance on the nemeses and murderers, a vengeance of construction, resurrection, and return, a vengeance of the spirit."[139]

The Palestinians of Hebron counter the settler mythology with one of their own. The ancient Canaanites were the first Palestinians, the natives of the land and tillers of its soil, while the Israelites were foreign invaders, maintains Dr Yunes 'Amro, dean of the literature faculty at Hebron University and an inhabitant of the city.[140] Mohammad Hasan Shirab goes even farther. In his account, all the ancient nations of Palestine were Arabs, and "Canaanite" was simply the collective name for all of them. The Jebusites, Moabites, Ammonites, Amorites, and Arameans were all ancient Arabs who spoke ancient Arabic, a language that spread from Palestine into the Arabian Peninsula's Hejaz region. The Canaanites of Hebron were also known as Anakites, a people who lived in the territory extending from Hebron to Jerusalem. The Anakites built a city called Arba' that was later renamed al-Khalil (the Arabic name for Hebron). Abraham was an Arab who wandered from Babylonia, an area of Arab habitation, to the Hejaz and Palestine, where the al-Aqsa mosque was already standing. Shirab rejects the Jewish traditions about King David, as the Jewish Bible is the only text that speaks of a King David who reigned in Hebron, and the Bible was written by Jews who deliberately falsified history. The Prophet Daoud—the Arabic name for David—was simply one of the many prophets who lived in the Arabian Peninsula. The Tomb of the Patriarchs is an Arab and Islamic site that was stolen by the Jews. The Jews who now live in Palestine, Shirab maintains, are foreign invaders from overseas. The Arabs under Jewish rule are in an ongoing state of war with the Jewish people, because the Jews seek to empty Palestine of all its Arabs.[141]

Since 1967 no other place has seen such bloodletting between its Palestinian and Jewish residents, and in no other place have relations between the two peoples become so ugly and hateful. Murderous climaxes by Jewish perpetrators were reached in the Jewish Underground's attack on the Islamic College in July 1983, in which three Palestinians were killed and thirty injured; and in Baruch Goldstein's slaughter of Muslim worshipers in the Tomb of the Prophets in March 1994, which left twenty-nine dead and 125 injured. Palestinian perpetrators took their bloodiest tolls in two shootings of settlers, one in May 1980, killing six and injuring sixteen, the other in November 2002, killing twelve and injuring fourteen. According to the Israel–PLO agreement on Hebron, signed in 1997, when people still thought that Hebron could remain an open city, "Both sides reiterate their commitment to the unity of the City of Hebron, and their understanding that the division of security responsibility will not divide the city." In January 2007, the legal counsel for the West Bank Civil Administration reached the opposite conclusion:

It seems that the basis of the opinion [of the security experts], whereby it is possible for Palestinians to live a normal life in the area alongside that of Israelis, is inconsistent with the principle of separation that underlines the security forces' plan to safeguard the space ... Would anyone think it possible to protect the Jewish residents in the area of the Jewish neighborhoods when these neighborhoods are isolated from each other and between them is an area in which Palestinians live a regular and routine life? How is it possible to prevent friction in the space encompassed by these neighborhoods when on their doorstep (and in most cases, even under or alongside them) regular Palestinian commercial life is taking place?[142]

When a choice has to be made between interfering in the lives of the Palestinians or the settlers, the Israeli authorities come down on the side of the settlers. Security cameras are operated by the army rather than by the police because such intelligence, when collected by the army, cannot be accessed by a Palestinian who submits a complaint to the police about settler violence. Only 8 percent of the cases in which Palestinians have complained about Israeli soldiers using unjustified violence against them have resulted in indictments. Notably, in cases of police violence 12 percent of such complaints lead to indictments, which suggests that army control over the footage makes it harder to convict soldiers than policemen.[143] The security forces are not neutral. They operate in symbiosis with the settlers. "What do you expect, for my people to inform on their friends? The fact is that most members of the Border Guard Unit [in Hebron] are residents of Kiryat Arba," a Border Guard commander responded in April 1979. He had been asked why he had not prevented settlers from cutting down hundreds of Palestinian grapevines in an area between Hebron and Kiryat Arba.[144]

The old *suk*, once the center of Hebron's Old City, had constituted the Jewish Quarter until 1929. Most of the Palestinians who lived there or who had shops in the area are no longer to be found there. About 42 percent of the residents and 76 percent of the proprietors were compelled to leave, and heavy restrictions on movement were imposed on the Palestinians who remained—making life nearly impossible for them and prompting even more to depart. The area is now controlled by national–religious settlers and is surrounded by soldiers, fences, and roadblocks. Settlers have moved into some of these abandoned homes, squatting in a room or store and then breaking down walls and floors to expropriate more property. The traces of conflict and violence are apparent in every house. Stars of David are spray-painted on the closed shutters of Palestinian stores in order to mark them, in a way reminiscent of how Jewish stores in Central Europe were marked as Jewish at the beginning of the twentieth century. Throughout the city's old commercial center Hebrew graffiti is scrawled on the walls: "Death to the Arabs!"; "Where there are Arabs, there are mice!"; "For every settlement evacuated we'll kill 100 Arabs!"; "Arabs to the gas chambers!"[145]

Jews and Arabs of all ages are combatants in the conflict in Hebron. The Cordoba elementary school is located across the street from the Beit Hadassah, where settlers live, and the only entrance to the school is from the street they share. The school's pupils were constantly getting into fights with settler children, leading the principal, Rim al-Sharif, to decide that the school day would begin and end at times that would prevent the two groups of children from encountering each other. As a result, Cordoba's school day begins at 7:30 a.m. and ends at 1:30 p.m., before the Jewish children leave for and return from their school. Cordoba is closed on Saturdays because on that day the Jewish children do not go to school and remain at home. The safety of the 116 Palestinian children enrolled in the school is ensured by an escort of agents of the Temporary International Presence in Hebron (TIPH) and of other international welfare organizations.[146] In 2011, both Jewish and Palestinian schoolchildren from all over Israel and the West Bank began to make pilgrimages to the Tomb of the Patriarchs in order to show that the site was their exclusive birthright.[147]

In the settlers' view, the debt of blood created in 1929 sets the contours of their actions. Some campaign for the apparatus of the Israeli state to take action to return Jews to the city. The government generally acts as the settlers wish, if not immediately, then after a time. This was how the Jewish presence in Hebron began. In April 1968 a group of Jews took rooms in the Park Hotel, a Palestinian-owned establishment in Hebron, ostensibly to celebrate the Pesach holiday in the city. Once there, they announced that they were not leaving and intended to settle in the city. Deputy Prime Minister Allon supported them, as Central Region General Uzi Narkiss seems also to have done. Both helped the settlers establish a fact. But Minister of Defense Dayan opposed a continued Jewish presence within the city itself. A compromise was reached in the cabinet—a month later the settlers were moved to an army base next to Hebron, which was then transformed into the settlement of Kiryat Arba. After Dayan left the Defense Ministry the settlement then served as a base for the settlers to establish outposts in Hebron itself.[148]

In the summer of 1968 the settlers demanded that the ancient Jewish cemetery in Hebron be fenced off, and that Jewish properties abandoned in 1929 be handed over to them. Within a month the army had erected a fence around the cemetery, but Jewish homes were not handed over to them. The settler leaders in Kiryat Arba continued to pressure the government to allow them to settle in Hebron's Old City. In 1979, a group of settler women and their children entered the Beit Hadassah and squatted there. Their presence eventually received retroactive sanction from the Likud government, following the murder of a *yeshiva* student, Yehoshua Saloma, in Hebron the following year. At the same time the Palestinian Osama Ibn al-Munqaz school was evacuated from the nearby Romano house, another Jewish-owned property, and its place taken by a *yeshiva*.

Those settlers who work through state channels maintain a symbiotic relationship with the government. "In the final analysis, army officers are a tool in the hands of the settlers," admitted a commander who served there. When Hebron's mayor, 'Abd al-Nabi Nathshe, was dismissed by Defense Minister Moshe Arens in 1983, the reasons that Arens gave for the move, as presented by the army spokesman, were taken directly from letters he had received from a prominent Kiryat Arba settler, attorney Elyakim Haetzni. When the army issued orders to soldiers at the beginning of the Second Intifada in 2000, they copied, nearly word for word, a set of recommendations sent by Hebron's settlers to the commander of the army regiment responsible for the Hebron region.[149]

But there is another group of settlers, a group who could perhaps be called the avengers. They believe that the 1929 massacre and subsequent Palestinian attacks grant them a license to use force against the Arabs, on the grounds that the government's hands are tied. Rather than appealing to the government, they take direct action against Arabs. They include the Jewish Underground that operated in the early 1980s and others who have desecrated Islamic sacred books and objects in the Tomb of the Patriarchs. When a settler funeral procession was fired on by Palestinians, the avengers took out their rage at Arab stores and homes. In other cases they have attacked Palestinian homes and vineyards in order to force out their owners so that these properties could be taken over by settlers.[150]

A typical example of an avenger is Ben Zion Tavger. Tavger emigrated from the Soviet Union in 1972 and settled in Kiryat Arba. From the start, he treated every Arab in the city as if they had personally participated in the massacre of 1929. This even included Arabs who, following investigations by the settler community, had been found innocent and thus acceptable to work with. One such Arab was Sheikh Ja'abari, with whom Elyakim Haetzni maintained a working relationship. Tavger charged that the methods used by the military government and other state bodies in the city were typical of a Diaspora mentality and were not befitting proud owners of their own country. These methods, he said, often humiliated the Jewish nation. When he refused to leave the Tomb of the Patriarchs during the hours set aside for Muslim devotions, he was evacuated by soldiers. He called them leftists, and claimed that anti-Jewish IDF officers had sent them to carry out this mission. When Palestinians held nationalist demonstrations, Tavger termed them "riots." During the First Intifada, he and his friends conducted violent patrols in Hebron so as to demonstrate Jewish power and sovereignty. Without having received any authorization from the army, they used weapons to compel Arab passersby to dismantle piles of stones that Palestinian youths had placed in the streets to block traffic. They checked the papers of Arabs and enforced a curfew. When Tavger asked an Arab to give him a drink of water, he forced the Arab to drink from the bottle first to make sure that it was not poisoned. Tavger's henchman, Eliezer Breuer, liked to wave a hatchet at passing Arabs, as well as to beat them and knock over their stands in the *suq*. Tavger claimed that he treated Arabs "like one neighbor to another," and that he was certain that Arabs were "interested in having good connections with me, good neighborly relations." This, he claimed, was why they obeyed his commands. They did not, in contrast, obey Israeli soldiers because the soldiers were foreigners who had arrived "from Tel Aviv" and were not local natives as Tavger was.[151]

In 1975–6, Tavger was a central figure in excavating the ruins of the Avraham Avinu Synagogue and the desecrated Jewish cemetery. Under Jordanian rule, Hebron's Jewish quarter, including the cemetery and the sixteenth-century synagogue that had served as the Jewish community's religious center, was demolished and replaced with a *suk* and bathhouse. Part of the area was turned into a garbage dump that was also used by a nearby slaughterhouse. After 1967, the military government paid a half-blind Arab named Hussein, more than sixty years old, to watch over the remains of the graveyard. In Tavger's account, when he had his friends arrived at the cemetery, Hussein realized that everything was about to change. Without any authorization from the military government, Tavger uprooted the vegetables and cut down the grapevines that Hussein cultivated in the cemetery: "I took the leaves from him, stepped on them, and said to him: 'Do you grow grapevines in Arab cemeteries?' He did not answer me but his expression became grave. I, at any rate, knew that this crafty old Arab understood everything very well and didn't require any further explanation."[152] Hussein helped Tavger tear out the roots of the vines, and Tavger uncovered some graves, filling his daily quota. Tavger threw the pieces of metal, rags, and old shoes he found in the cemetery into the yards of nearby Arab homes and "taught" Hussein to do the same. In this way, he said, he developed friendly relations with Hussein and the neighbors agreed to take it upon themselves to collect the refuse from the cemetery, so that it would not get cast on to their property.

Tavger also began clearing the refuse off the roof of the Avraham Avinu synagogue, with the purpose of preparing the site for reconstruction. But, since he had received no permit to do so, the police arrested him. In response, his friends beat up the Arab they suspected of informing on him. "He very quickly grasped what he was being told and in short order we could discern his full loyalty," Tavger wrote.[153] Tavger employed Arab boys to evacuate the garbage because, he said, they were less nauseated than he was by the awful stink of animal carcasses. The boys, he claimed, were willing to do this for meager pay, enough for them to buy a few pieces of candy. Adults also helped uncover the synagogue, but "my principle was not to pay [them] because the Arabs are to blame for everything that happened to the synagogue."[154] One day he was approached by an Arab who presented him with a contract signed by the military government that permitted him to use the site over the ruins of the synagogue. He demanded to be compensated for the damage he had suffered as a result of the excavations. Tavger asked him to come to Kiryat Arba to discuss the matter with his lawyers. When the Arab showed up for the meeting, he was attacked and beaten by a group of Tavger's buddies. They seem to have believed that he deserved to die. The next day he asked some other Arabs whether, according to the laws of Islam, the man should be sentenced to death for his nefarious deed of having used a synagogue as a goat pen. Tavger said that he had actually treated the man mercifully, since he ought to have been killed. The Arabs agreed, Tavger wrote.[155]

The boundary between the avengers and the settlers who work through the state apparatus is a porous one, and there is movement between the camps. The most prominent figure in Kiryat Arba and

Hebron, Rabbi Moshe Levinger, has moved from one side to the other on numerous occasions. Like the avengers, Levinger declared that he and his associates "help them [Hebron's Arabs] break free of the aspirations to annihilate [the Jews] on which they were raised; we cleanse them of an atmosphere of murder and accustom them to an atmosphere of peace."[156] "Blood, blood, blood!" Levinger demanded in February 1983, after a stone thrown at a car killed an Israeli soldier, Esther Ohana. He declared that the members of the Jewish Underground who killed three students and wounded thirty others at the Islamic College in Hebron in July 1983 had carried out a sacred task.[157] In September 1976 he demonstratively ripped up an order restricting his movement that had been issued by Hebron's military governor. The order was issued against the activities he conducted as an advocate of government promotion of and aid to the settlement project, such as holding prayers on the ruins of the Avraham Avinu synagogue in the center of the Old City. The number of worshippers became larger each day, blocking the nearby main road during the 7–8 a.m. rush hour when Arabs were hurrying to work. Military forces were sent to defend Levinger and the prayer service turned into a political demonstration. The military governor asked the settlers to desist from holding the prayer service at the site, but they refused. When soldiers attempted to evacuate the settlers, they forcibly resisted. Ten years later, Levinger was convicted of attacking a solder at the Tomb of the Patriarchs.[158] In April 1979, Rabbi Levinger's wife led the group of fifteen mothers who, with their children, broke into and refused to leave Beit Hadassah. "The local residents are raising their heads in a troubling way, both in the Makhpela Cave and on the streets of Hebron," Rabbi Levinger cautioned, speaking for the Kiryat Arba Committee, in a telegram he sent to Prime Minister Yitzhak Rabin and Minister of Defense Shimon Peres on 2 July 1975.

Here are a few examples: on the eve of the Shavu'ot holiday, the cloth covering the table on which the Torah scroll is read [in the Jewish sanctuary in the Tomb of the Patriarchs] was found slashed with a sharp instrument ... an additional arson attempt was conducted at the Settler Restaurant ... the curtain [of the Holy Ark] in the Hall of Abraham [the Jewish sanctuary in the Tomb] was found deliberately soiled ... On the two most recent Sabbaths, during the Friday night service, an overflowing and loud service was deliberately held in the Hall of Isaac and Rebecca [in which Muslims worship] in order to disturb our devotions ... there have been arson attempts at the post office in Hebron and at Bank Leumi in Hebron.

Levinger demanded that Rabin and Peres take action:

> I have no doubt that the Muslim Arabs are encouraged by the slow development of Kiryat Arba, by the lack of enforcement against Arab construction in the area designated for Kiryat Arba ... by their sense that the [military] government still views Jews as guests and second-class citizens ... We would therefore be grateful if you would take care of all these matters more energetically, as befits the Jewish nation returning to its land and inheritance, to the city of the Patriarchs, the city of the beginning of the Davidic dynasty's reign.[159]

Up until the settlers' penetration of Hebron's Old City at the end of the 1970s, relations between Kiryat Arba's Jews and Hebron's Arabs were reasonably good. The military government and Defense Minister Dayan also had good relations with the Arab public. Mayor Ja'abari spoke regularly with Israeli leaders and turned over terror suspects to the Israeli authorities. Hebron's merchants notified the military government when a commercial strike was planned and allowed it to make the necessary arrangements. In return for such information and assistance, the military government helped Hebron's senior figures build up or preserve their status as leaders. If an Arab in Hebron needed something from the military government, he would submit his request to a local intermediary, who would pass it on to the mayor, who would submit it to the Israeli authorities. When the military government responded to such a request, it was perceived by the Palestinian applicant as being addressed to the mayor or some other intercessor, rather than as a direct response to a person in need from a governing apparatus that owed him a response by virtue of his being a citizen. Hebron businessmen invited the military governor to their homes for lunch or dinner. In contrast to the time of Hebron's Arab Jews, however, the Jews did not host Arabs in their home. As Zvi Barel, who served as deputy military governor in the early 1970s, explains: "When a conquered person hosts [the conqueror], it is a gesture of courtesy and respect, but when the defeated person is the guest it reeks of corruption. Being hosted is work, whereas hosting is perceived as recreation. Recreation is forbidden during the work of occupation."[160] To avoid any suspicions that they were making personal gain from their positions of authority over the Palestinians, officers working in the military government were forbidden to buy goods in Arab stores.[161]

Arabs from Hebron worked in Kiryat Arba, mostly in construction and service industries. They used the post office and bank in the settlement and often helped out settlers whose cars had stalled. Haetzni, the

OCCUPATION, ASSIMILATION, OPPOSITION

Jewish attorney from Kiryat Arba, represented Arabs from Hebron, particularly in cases in which an Israeli party was involved. Settlers shopped in the Hebron *suq* and in its commercial center. Hebron's prices for food and services were lower than Kiryat Arba's, so settlers took driving lessons, had their hair cut, filled prescriptions, and had their teeth cared for in the Arab city. Hebron merchants accepted settler checks written in Hebrew, dated according to the Jewish calendar. Hebron Arabs went to Kiryat Arba to buy goods they could not find in their city, such as liquor. In a small number of cases real friendships developed, relations that went beyond mutual respect and connections of commerce and employment. A branch of Israel's Bank Leumi operated in downtown Hebron, as did an Israeli post office, patronized by both populations. Occasionally, Jews and Arabs went into business together. Not even the most extreme of the settlers boycotted Hebron's Arabs or refused in principle to buy goods and services from them. Their hostility was directed at the Arab collective, not at the individuals they met on the street. Settlers rode to Jerusalem in Arab buses and shuttle taxis, unarmed and often alone. For a small additional fee, a driver plying the Jerusalem–Hebron shuttle route would detour to Kiryat Arba to let off a Jewish passenger and then continue to Hebron with his Arab clients.[162]

While life in Hebron and Kiryat Arba was mostly routine, there were occasional misunderstandings and incidents. When the original Jewish settlers at the Park Hotel declared in April 1968 that they intended to stay and settle in the city, Sheikh Ja'abari asked Dayan to take responsibility for them, expressing his hope that someday both Palestinian refugees and Hebron's Jews would return to their homes. He said the same thing to the settlers when he invited them to meet him. They interpreted this as a green light for their settlement, not as a conditional statement meaning that they would have to wait until the Palestinian refugees could also return.[163] A month after the settlers were given permission to move into an army camp next to the city, in May 1968, a settler delegation led by Rabbi Levinger walked into Ja'abari's office and informed him that "the city of Hebron has been a Jewish city for thousands of years and has not returned to Israeli rule. We will settle in it whether or not you maintain friendly relations." Ja'abari was infuriated and asked the military governor "to take the necessary steps to put an end to such intolerable behavior."[164] The military government informed the settlers that they were forbidden to have direct contact with the Hebron municipality and could deal with it only through the Israeli authorities. The military governor told the city's leaders that all complaints about settler behavior should be addressed to him and the minister of defense. At the beginning of June, Dayan met with a delegation led by Ja'abari. The defense minister expressed his regret for the settlers' discourteous behavior. He explained that "there is lots of infuriating talk and were we to jail everyone who spoke in an irritating way we would not have enough jails to put them in ... we will take action against anyone who incites the use of force and violent acts, just as we act against anyone who acts contrary to the law ... we hold back when it comes to speech and are well able to distinguish between speech and deed, among both Arabs and Jews."[165] During the period that the settlers were lodged at the Park Hotel, no Palestinians patronized it, nor its restaurant.[166] Even after these correct relations came to an end and were replaced in large measure by confrontation and violence, there have been exceptions. For example, at the end of 1995 a foreign volunteer in Hebron observed a Kiryat Arba settler of American birth treating Palestinians with respect, to which they responded warmly.[167]

West Jerusalem offers more opportunities for positive relations in the context of daily life. For the most part, it is Palestinian Arabs who cross the lines from their neighborhoods to the Jewish side. Cab drivers, construction workers, cooks, delivery men, garage workers, and movers from East Jerusalem spend long hours on the west side of the city. During periods when there are no terror attacks or exceptional tension between the two peoples, many Jerusalem Arabs go shopping at nearby Jewish shopping centers, or at Malha Mall. The latter offers a wealth of stores, cafés, and leisure activity, patronized by Palestinians as well as Jews. But Jews do not shop at the Palestinian commercial center in East Jerusalem. When they visit the *shuk* in the Old City they feel like foreigners and tourists. The Jewish settlers who live in East Jerusalem's Palestinian neighborhoods and walk through the Arab *shuk* on a daily basis wear expressions on their faces that make clear their sense of alienation and disgust at the Palestinians around them.[168]

Palestinian organizations in Jerusalem and Hebron have adopted Israeli tactics to halt the settler incursion into their territory. They lack the backing of a state apparatus and do not have the financial resources that Israel has. Their achievements are commensurate with their modest budgets. Beginning in 1995, with financial aid from overseas, some of it from Saudi Arabia, the Welfare Association, registered in Switzerland, has rehabilitated 364 housing units located in historic buildings in Jerusalem's Old City. Since 2003, the same organization has rehabilitated another sixty-two Arab structures functioning as public buildings that serve and strengthen the Palestinian community—preschools, clinics, and community centers. Most of these sites are located in the Muslim Quarter, a central area of settler expansion, but some are in the Christian and Armenian Quarters.[169] Thanks to mediation by UNESCO, Israel consented to turn a blind eye to such financial transfers from overseas sources, while the Welfare Association has taken care to keep a low profile. After 2003, during the Second Intifada, the election of a new and less amenable Israeli government caused the Welfare Association to bring its activities to an end.[170]

Similar work has been accomplished since 1996 in Hebron's Old City by the Hebron Rehabilitation Committee (HRC). This is a project of both preserving the city's heritage and defending it against the settlers. When Israel took possession of Hebron, its Old City had a population of about 7,500; by 1996 only 400 Arab inhabitants were living in this area, which includes 1,200 old houses. Most of those who remained were one-parent families, old people, and people with physical disabilities. Drug addicts and other marginal types had squatted in the abandoned houses. The HRC's goal was to rehabilitate and repopulate the Old City's homes. It enjoyed political and financial support from the Palestinian Authority. The organization was headed by 'Ali al-Qawasma. Qawasma, the Palestinian Authority's minister of transport, lives in Hebron and comes from a family that has dominated the city's political life since 1976. With a staff of thirty-seven and 400 laborers in its employ, the HRC drew up plans based on a survey conducted in the 1980s by students at Hebron's Polytechnic College, with the guidance of overseas experts. In addition to Palestinian Authority support, the organization received funds from Arab countries and Spain.

The first houses to be rebuilt and resettled were those closest to Jewish homes, the goal being to prevent them from being taken over by settlers. Its second-stage goal was to create a link between the homes in the Old City and the Arab city. By 2000, work was completed on about 60 percent of the 1,225 structures designated for rehabilitation. The renovation turned the houses from structures appropriate for extended families to ones tailored for nuclear families. Facades were preserved but major changes were made in the interiors, including the addition of kitchens and toilets. Hebron's Arabs took a great interest in the work and demand for the renovated homes was high. Within three years, between 300 and 400 people moved into the Old City, most of them in the project's first stage. Most of these tenants were Arabs who had moved to Hebron from the surrounding villages and who lived beneath the poverty line. Before they were permitted to enter the renovated homes they underwent a security clearance to ensure that none of them intended to harm the settlers. For the first five years, their rent was paid by the HRC.

The project encountered a number of difficulties. The renovated homes' nearest neighbors were violent settlers, and as a result most of the Arab shops in the area had closed their doors. The inhabitants thus had to do their shopping in downtown Hebron, where there were no settlers. Another problem was social. The residents of the project and Hebron's Arabs were separated by a social, status, and economic gap from the city's native Arabs, who did not welcome the newcomers. In response, HRC expanded its activity so as to boost the new inhabitants of the renovated homes. The HRC built schools, preschools, and opened vocational courses for women and the unemployed. It organized afterschool activities for children and sponsored lectures on Hebron's history. It brought schoolchildren from other Hebron neighborhoods to tour the rebuilt homes of the Old City.

Israel tried to halt the renovation project. In January 1997, it arrested 416 workers involved in the program and issued six work stoppage orders. After the Second Intifada broke out in 2000, Israel imposed heavy restrictions on the project. The Old City's population was physically cut off from municipal services and the Arab city; as a result, the tenants of most of the renovated homes moved out. The army took over or demolished the homes adjacent to settler homes, and the Palestinians who were allowed to stay have suffered harassment and violence on the part of the settlers, who are seeking to push out these remnants as well and take over their houses.[171]

EPILOGUE

Leiden, Holland. Early October 2011. The city is celebrating its liberation from Spain in 1574, as it does every year. The city center has become a place of street parties, parades, amusement parks, food stands, and music. I stand facing a small and quite unassuming bridge. But it was over this bridge that the provisions that saved the besieged city from starvation had arrived. At the end of the sixteenth century, Leiden was one of the Dutch provinces that rebelled against Spanish rule and, after their victory, formed the independent state of The Netherlands. But that is not the only reason the bridge is important. A year after breaking free of its Catholic overlords, the city founded Leiden University, where I have been invited to serve as a scholar-in-residence and where I have completed writing the second half of this book. The university's buildings stand close to the bridge and serve as a concrete expression of the two sides of independence—political freedom, and the freedom of the human spirit. It marks the beginning of Holland's liberal and tolerant society. According to the sign next to the bridge.

From 1608, Leiden offered refuge to the Pilgrims who had fled religious persecution in England. William Brewster established the Pilgrim Press, printing the books that were banned in England ... In 1620 they left the town ... they boarded the Speedwell and later transferred to the Mayflower. They then sailed to America, where they would lay the foundation of the United States.

Independent Holland granted freedom of religion not only to the Pilgrims but also to Spanish and Portuguese Jews who had been compelled to convert to Christianity, as well as to Ashkenazi Jews who fled persecution and harassment. Free Holland was one of the sources from which the United States drew its liberal principles and spirit of toleration.

In 1658, fifteen Jewish families descended from a ship docked at Newport, Rhode Island. They were the descendants of Portuguese Jews who had been forced into Christianity and who had fled to Brazil a century earlier, where they established a flourishing Jewish community. In the middle of the seventeenth century, Portuguese forces prepared to conquer the city from the Dutch, who had ruled the city for nearly a quarter of a century. The Jews fled. Some of them went to Holland and others to Dutch colonies in North America. But New Amsterdam, the Dutch colony on Manhattan Island, would not allow the Jews to build a synagogue, only to worship in a private home. So they set out again, this time for more tolerant Rhode Island. About a century later, in 1759, the grandchildren of these immigrants laid the cornerstone of the first synagogue in what would later become the United States, Yeshuat Yisrael. It still stands. When President George Washington visited Newport in 1790, he promised the Jews there, and all American citizens, full civil rights. Jews had never before enjoyed such equal status.

Leiden received its ideas from the Renaissance. Humanism and the recognition of the need to limit the powers of religious and political authorities came out of Florence, the capital of the Renaissance, capturing hearts and taking its central place in modern liberal thinking. During the first half of 2010, the great art works of the Renaissance, in particular the sculptures of Michelangelo, inspired me during the composition of the first half of this book. To me, Michelangelo's statues embody the human spirit's ability to shape the world's hardest materials and imbue them with life and emotion. On a Tuscan hill from which one can view Florence in its full beauty stands the European University Institute, standing among vineyards, sculptures, and well-tended gardens. I was a Fernand Braudel fellow in the History and Civilization Department of this young academic institution, founded on the long higher education tradition of humanistic Europe.

I think of the social relations generated by the principles that emerged in Florence and which made their way not only to Holland but also to America. At the end of the nineteenth century they also flowed to the eastern Mediterranean coast, in a surging current that reached Jaffa, Jerusalem, and Hebron. In those cities, these Renaissance ways of relating to others produced new ways of life and identities that spoke the land's unique language. It is this fascinating encounter between the ideas of the Renaissance and the land of Israel/Palestine that stand at the center of the first half of this book. The encounter

EPILOGUE

produced a sense of belonging to a place, to a land that was something more than simply the place one lived, a sense shared by all its inhabitants. Jews and Arabs shared this consciousness, which grew hand in hand with modernization and rapid changes in ways of life. The new consciousness found expression in many areas—spoken language, schools, residential neighborhoods, ways of dressing, the form taken by religious celebrations, kinds of leisure activities and entertainment, the labor market, joint economic, commercial, and political initiatives, and even intermarriages. Local identity was not an abstract idea but a part of daily life. As human life always is, it was not a consistent ideal but rather had many contradictions and rough edges. And, as I have shown, it expressed itself in different ways in each of the three cities I write of here. This local identity joined Jews and Arabs—just as the Palestinian National Movement and Zionism divided them. In their rivalry, each of these two movements sought to appropriate local identity for itself exclusively. The confrontation between Jews and Arabs in Jaffa and Jerusalem escalated after 1945 (in Hebron it had started in 1929), as violent incidents that interrupted normal life turned into a fixed pattern of behavior that became part of life. As this happened, a chasm opened between the two peoples that, in 1948, became a complete disjuncture.

In the book's first part I dispute the accepted scholarly view that sees Jewish relations with Palestine's Arabs at the end of the nineteenth and beginning of the twentieth century only in light of the conflict between two national communities and movements. That pervasive view projects later developments on to this earlier period. It centers on the study of institutions, established organizations, and national ideologies, while failing to appreciate the fact that Zionism and Arab nationalism came into Palestine from the outside and took a long time to take hold in the country and penetrate the hearts of many of its inhabitants. On the contrary, I show that a native identity common to Jews and Arabs developed in Palestine, and that the way to understand and analyze it is through an examination of daily life as it was lived by the inhabitants of cities not yet divided along national lines, who felt themselves and their neighbors to be natives. Furthermore, as opposed to the tendency of historians to seek out a zero point, a historic event prior to 1948 that tore Jews and Arabs asunder, I see the rift as one that developed gradually and became complete only at the time of the 1948 war.

Israel's victories in 1948 and 1967 produced two sharp changes in the relations between Jews and Arabs. First, horizontal relations, which were at times egalitarian, were replaced by hierarchical relations. The victorious Jewish–Israeli side imposed new demographic and geographic realities on the streets of Jerusalem, Jaffa, and Hebron. Second, the governing system of the victorious Jewish–Israeli side rules those same streets. Its agencies and enforcement apparatus shape relations between Jews and Arabs and maintain the hierarchy. This was manifested, for example, in Jaffa after 1948, when the Arabs remaining in the city were subject first to a military government and then to Shin Bet control; by an allocation of resources in Jaffa and East Jerusalem that favored Jews over Arabs; in the imposition of Jewish–Israeli names on streets that run through Arab neighborhoods; in the way in which East Jerusalem was unilaterally annexed to Israel in 1967, while leaving the Palestinians without citizenship; in the expropriation of Palestinian property; and in the establishment of a Jewish settlement in Hebron. It should be noted that, within the Israeli establishment, there were people in whom, and periods in which, the hierarchical approach was restrained. The time Teddy Kollek served as Jerusalem's mayor, from 1966 through 1993, is notable in this regard, alongside the first decade of settlement in Kiryat Arba. The Palestinian side has attempted to restrict the activities of the stronger Israeli side by renovating and preserving buildings in Hebron and Jerusalem as a way of keeping settlers from taking control of them. But the means available to the Palestinian organizations involved in this activity are limited, as thus are their accomplishments.

At the same time, Israelis and Palestinians in Jerusalem, Jaffa, and Hebron established relations more equal than those set by the state. For the most part this happened among neighbors, such as Meron Benvenisti and his neighbors in Abu Tor, and Jews and Arabs who share a neglected neighborhood in Jaffa, and even in Hebron. On top of this were joint business initiatives in East Jerusalem and the Histadrut's work there during the first two decades following 1967. Egalitarian relations in Jerusalem and Hebron were badly hurt by the First Intifada, which began in December 1987, and its aftermath. The intimacy and sense of a brotherhood of the downtrodden that typified Jewish and Arab relations in Jaffa were overridden in the 1990s by two developments that changed the area's social structure and physical landscape. The first was upscale Tel Aviv's penetration of Jaffa, as a result of market forces—an incursion seen only in Jaffa. The second phenomenon, weaker and more limited, was the arrival of religious

EPILOGUE

Jews, who settled in the heart of Arab neighborhoods in fulfillment of their nationalist ideology. This latter phenomenon is not unique—it has happened in all three cities, most intensely in Hebron, less forcefully in several Palestinian neighborhoods in East Jerusalem, and in Jaffa only to a much smaller extent. In all three cities the ethnic divide between Jews and Arabs gaped larger in the 2000s, during the Second Intifada. In the wake of that conflict, relations between Jews and Arabs in all three cities have grown more alienated than at any time since the turn of the last century.

In national conflicts, the stronger side is always eager to establish its superiority by creating an unbridgeable gap between the present and the past—in our case, between the way life was lived prior to the 1948 and 1967 wars and the way it was lived thereafter. Israel accomplished this mostly by changing the demography of the Palestinian state. It seized homes and land that Palestinians had left behind in Jaffa and Jerusalem and settled Jews there. These changes on the ground were accompanied by symbolic changes—for example, the Palestinian past of homes included in the Open House program in Jerusalem and Tel Aviv–Jaffa was disregarded. But the past was not expunged from the consciousness of the defeated. It seems likely that defeat, and Israel's attempt to consign the Palestinian past to oblivion, spurred the Palestinians to tighten their grip on the past and to fashion stronger ties between present and past.

This contrast between past and present is the subject of the second half of the book. It is brought out in its most concentrated form in the chapter in which Palestinian refugees tell of visits they made to the homes they lived in until 1948, and their charged encounters with the current Israeli–Jewish owners. Israeli Jews also went to visit their former homes in Hebron and Jerusalem. Unlike the Palestinians, the Israeli Jews arrived as victors, and were thus better equipped to accept and cope with the disparity between past and present. The Palestinians felt differently. For them, past and present clashed in their minds even before they reached the homes, while they passed through the streets leading to the house that was once theirs. The conflict and alienation between the homes in their minds and the real houses they walk through, the searing memories and their fears, surge as they enter the front yards and erupt with the first words they exchange with the current owners. The Jews who now live in these houses are also fearful when they hear their guests present themselves as the erstwhile owners of the property. From this point onward, however, the encounters take different forms. The ensuing dialogue can be friendly, hostile, suspicious, reserved, arrogant, or considerate. In some cases the current owners allowed their visitors to walk through the houses, while at other times they allowed the Palestinians only into the living room. In other cases they leave the visitors outside and talk to them there. The conversation differs in different cases and with different people. The fact that the interaction between the visitors and the current owners does not take place according to some sort of rigid ideological dictate leaves room for optimism with regard to the future. Wherever human beings are considerate of each other when they meet, there is a possibility of healing even wounds like those incurred by the refugees of 1948 and 1967. Furthermore, quite apart from the refugee issue, there is no way to return to the common native identity that prevailed in Palestine before 1948. Interaction between equal human beings who share the same city—or country—can enable coexistence between nations and enable them to cope with past wounds.

NOTES

ABOUT THIS BOOK

1. Confino 2008: 55.
2. Rabinowitz 1997; Tortrick 2000; Goren: 2006, 2008.
3. Taylor 2008.
4. Ginzburg 2001: 23.
5. Judt 2010: 11.
6. Hobsbawm 2002: 27.

PROLOGUE TO THE PAPERBACK EDITION

1. Nir Hasson, "Jerusalem Through Different Lens", *Haaretz*, 12 June 2016, https://www.haaretz.co.il/news/education/2016-05-28/ty-article-magazine/.premium/0000017f-e8c6-d62c-a1ff-fcff69a20000
2. Yaakov Yehoshua, *Reshimotav Shel Effendi Netul Schar Sofrim [Notes of an Unpaid Scribe Effendi]*, Tel Aviv, 2016, p. 195.
3. Albert Memmi, *Who Is an Arab Jew?*, Jerusalem, 1975, also in http://www.harissa.com/eng/whoisanarabjew.htm
4. Ella Shohat, *Taboo Memories, Diasporic Voices*, Duke University Press, 2006. Eran Kaplan, *Beyond Post-Zionism*, State University of New York Press, 2015.
5. Abraham Hirshberg, *In the Orient Land*, Vilnius, 1910: 393–94 [in Hebrew].
6. Ibid.
7. Laura S. Schor, *The Best School in Jerusalem, Annie Landau's School for Girls 1900–1960*, Waltham MS, 2013, p. 100.
8. Ibid., p. 93.
9. Ibid., p. 87, p. 89, p. 213.
10. Jenifer Glynn, *Tidings from Zion Hellen Bentwich's Letters from Jerusalem 1919–1931*, London, 2000, p. 177.
11. Abigail Jacobson and Moshe Naor, *Oriental Neighbors, Middle Eastern Jews and Arabs in Mandatory Palestine*, Waltham MS. 2016, p. 22.
12. Yuval Evri and Hillel Cohen, "Between Shared Homeland to National Home, the Balfour Declaration from a Native Sephardic Perspective", *The Arab and Jewish Questions, Geographies of Engagements in Palestine and Beyond*. Bashir Bashir and Leila Farsakh (eds), Columbia University Press, 2020, pp. 148–172.
13. Jacobson and Naor, p. 30.

14. Ibid., pp. 101–102.
15. John Tleel, *I am Jerusalem*, Jerusalem, 2000, p. 183.
16. Ibid., p. 184.
17. Alon Confino, 'Between Talbeyeh and Me', in Omer Bartov (ed.), *Israel-Palestine: Lands and People*, New York, 2021, p. 422.

INTRODUCTION: JERUSALEM, JAFFA GATE/BAB AL-KHALIL

1. Chambers 2008: 1.
2. Ayalon 2004: 101; Frumkin 1954: 17.
3. Guri 2010.
4. Kark and Ben Yaakov 2001: 96–136.
5. JCA Street Name Committee 4 Sep. 1967—2655/2/2/1/17.
6. Khalidi 1984: 145.
7. Breen 1906: 25, 118.
8. Khalidi 1997: 47; Graham-Brown 1980: 104.
9. Price 2001: 11–12; Nassar 2006: 317–26; Moors 2010: 93–105; Mendelson 2002: 76.
10. ISA—National Photo Archive: D817–023; D222 031, D129–738; D638–028, D220–104; D543–006, http://147.237.72.31/scripts/topsrch/topapi.dll; Khalidi 1984: 49.
11. Storrs 1937: 291.
12. JCA Street Name Committee: 2655/2/1/17; http://www.jerusalem.muni.il/jer_sys/pro/rehovot/rehovot.asp?STREET_KOD=4060; *Davar*, 5 Dec. 1967; Lurie 1968; Azaryahu 2012: 146–7.
13. Hasson 23 Dec. 2011.
14. Flavius 1968: Book 5, Chapter 4, 1.
15. Sivan 1983; Elad 1994: 132–3.
16. Sasson 1998: 126–33, 284, 317; Brinker 1942: 73; Mishori 2000: 224–5; Yahav 1996; Manor 2005: 46–50, 64.
17. Sivan 1983: 60–6; Levin 2006: 208.
18. Mishori 2000: 226.
19. Goldstein 2007: 176.
20. http://www.towerofdavid.org.il/Hebrew/Category1/About_the_Museum
21. Benvenisti 1996: 10–14.
22. http://www.towerofdavid.org.il/Hebrew/Category3/Permanent_Exhibition
23. Goldstein 2007.
24. Judt 2005: 768.

1. ARAB JEWS

1. Chambers 2008: 27.
2. Khalidi 1997: 58–9.
3. Levi 2008; Snir 2006; Hever and Shenhav 2011; Shenhav 2003: 26.
4. Karmi 2002: 41.
5. Yehoshua 1979a, vol. 2: 213.
6. Sasson 1981: 200.
7. Benvenisti 2012: 71–7, 87–101.
8. Kroyanker 2005: 20.
9. Porath 1976: 11–14.
10. Kroyanker 2005: 24, 35.
11. Kark and Glas 2005: 247–8.
12. Ayalon 2004: 70–3.
13. Khalidi 1984: 62; Auld and Hillenbrand 2000, vol. 1: 260–1; Nassar 2008: 205–23; ISA National Photos Archive: 826–106D; 826–119D; 826–108D; D 220–007D 220–006 in http://147.237.72.31/scripts/topsrch/topapi.dll

14. Storrs 1937: 294.
15. Yellin 1973; Zekharyah 1985: 5–8.
16. Izakson 1994: 53.
17. Holliday 1997: 11.
18. Ayalon 2004: 104–8; Graham-Brown 1980: 125, 132.
19. Khalidi 1997: 35–6, 40, 44, 55.
20. Frumkin 1954: 24, 27, 53 respectively.
21. Press 1964: 40.
22. Photos in http://www.ynet.co.il/articles/0,7340,L-3813552,00.html; Zekharyah 2002: 42, 69–70, 77, 109, 132; Shiryon 1943: 31–3, 100–1; Izakson 1994: 53; Kark and Glas 2005: 145; al-Jubeh 2005; Tamari 2009: 181–2.
23. Yehoshua 1979: 97–8; Kroyanker 2011: 40.
24. Press 1936: 41.
25. Khalidi 1984: 64, 72
26. Zekharyah 2002: 64.
27. MECA Jerusalem Photograph Album, Girls' Day School: GB 165–0505.
28. JCA Oral Documentation: 397.
29. Tamari 2009: 30; Kroyanker 2009: 27–30; 2000: 17–39.
30. Yaffe 2009; al-Jubeh 2005.
31. Mashayof 1978: 25.
32. Tsifroni 1990; Ben-Arieh 2011: 1147–8; Samuel 1970: 91–2; Lazar 2012: 158.
33. Salahiyya 2009: 40; Shiryon 1943: 42; Reiter and Lehrs 2010: 13–19.
34. Cohen 1968: 8, 23–4 respectively; 1995: 1.
35. Yona 1968: 191.
36. http://www.justjlm.org/families
37. Ben Yair Interview: 15 May 2012; 2013: 11–12.
38. Benvenisti 1996: 135–6, 95.
39. Pappe 2002: 140–7; Yehoshua 1979, vol. 2: 215–48.
40. Yahav 2004: 310.
41. Pappe 2002: 171–2.
42. Bareket 2007.
43. Elyashar 1987: 42–3; Yehoshua 1979, vol. 2: 215–48.
44. Pappe 2002: 167.
45. Porath 1976: 19.
46. Arnon 1992; Tamari 2009: 71–3, 82–92.
47. JCA 499, Yehoshua personal records, 25 July 1971.
48. Luncz 1968: 18; JCA 397, Oral Documentation.
49. Yellin 1991: 7; Press 1964: 18; Kark and Glas 2005: 130, 213–14; Elazar 1980: 165; Friedman 1980.
50. JCA Oral Documentation 397.
51. Ibid.; Braver 1966: 450–1.
52. Elazar 1980: 227.
53. JCA Oral Documentation 397; Yellin 1979: 52–3.
54. JCA Oral Documentation 397.
55. Elyashar 1981: 72.
56. Yehoshua 1977: 136; JCA Oral Documentation 397.
57. Elazar 1980: 129.
58. Frumkin 1954: 218.
59. Yehoshua 1988: 191; 1979a: 215–16.
60. Meyuhas 1928: IX–XI.
61. Droian 1980, 1982: 25; Kark and Ben Yaakov 2001.
62. Meyuhas 1919: V, 1937: XI.
63. Meyuhas 1928: VI–VII.
64. Yehoshua 1979a, vol. 2: 240.

65. Press 1936: 4.
66. Press 1964: 18–19.
67. Luncz 1968: 18, 214; JCA Oral Documentation 397; Jacobson 2011: 22–52.
68. Frumkin 1954: 10.
69. Kosover 1966: 98–115, 395.
70. Ben Hananya 1944.
71. Efrati 1975: 178–82.
72. Hamburger 1939: 41; Frumkin 1954: 105; Lev-Tov 2007: 169–85.
73. Rivlin 1967: 50; Yehoshua 1981: 93–127.
74. Frumkin 1954: 22, 23, 281, 33 respectively.
75. Frumkin 1954: 281, 323, 85–6 respectively; Hamburger 1939: 42.
76. Frumkin 1954: 71; Arnon 2012.
77. Tamari 2009: 82–92, 164.
78. Yehoshua 1979a: 93–7.
79. JCA: 501 Yehoshua Personal Records; Tamari and Nassar 2003: 77–9; Tamari 2009: 153–4.
80. Yehoshua 1977: 89–92; Zekharyah 1998: 129–36.
81. Yehoshua 1977: 136.
82. Yehoshua 1979: 93–7; 1982: 137–8; 1979: 230, 235.
83. Yehoshua 1988: 81–81; Karmi 2002: 50.
84. JCA: 499 Yehoshua Personal Records 25 July 1971.
85. Tamari 2009: 82–92.
86. Cohen Hillel 1993; Hannanel 2007: 111; Abu al-Jabeen 2005: 77.
87. Nashashibi 1990: 19; Yehoshua 1979a: 232–4; Lev Ari 2006; Golan-Agnon 2002: 38–40.
88. Shlush 1991: 137–9; Hart 2009: annexes 6, 14; Shohat 2009; Ben-Yehuda 1970: 517.
89. Tamari 2009: 82–92.
90. Sasson 1981: 200–1.
91. Shiryon 1943: 159; JCA Oral Documentation 397; Lev-Tov 2010; Tamari and Nassar 2003: 74.
92. Yellin 1991: 24; Yazbak 2010.
93. Yehoshua 1979a: 66–71.
94. Hamenachem 1988: 49, 51.
95. Mani 1963: 74.
96. Le Bore 2006: 52; Tamari 2009: 138; Khalidi 1997: 69; Pappe 2002: 146.
97. Press 1964: 112.
98. Sakakini Khalil 1990: 11.
99. Laskov: 2010: 66.
100. Sakakini Khalil 1990: 11, 15, 12, 49–50, 52–3; Weigart 2001: 30–42.
101. Laskov 2010: 27.
102. Ben-Arieh 1977: 630–1.
103. Segev 1999: 258–71; Tamari 2009: 5–6; Hamburger 1939: 57, 123; Shiryon 1943: 69.
104. Mani 1963: 103–4.
105. Ibid.: 97.
106. Luncz 1906; Elhanani 1984: 255; Levanon 1936: 8; 2006: 75.
107. Levanon 2006: 48, 75; 1984: 7.
108. Mani 1963: 33.
109. Hever 2007: 61–75.
110. Tamari 2009: 158–9; Ogen 1986.
111. Kannan 1965; Mani 1965.
112. Karlinski 1932.
113. Barkai 1995: 54–5, 60–2, 77.
114. Schneerson 1980: 20–3.

115. Levanon 2006: 75, 72 respectively.
116. Luncz 1906.
117. Tamari 2009: 5–6.
118. Hazan and Monterescu 2011: 57, 98; interviews with Khairi Abu al-Jibein, Malka Ismail, and Khalil Adai in www.jaffaproject.org
119. Moyal 1909.
120. Shlush 1931: Chapter 11.
121. Bezalel 2007: 391; 2011.
122. Laskar 1984.
123. Jacobson 2011a.
124. Jacobson 2003; 2001.
125. Bezalel 2007: 390–401; Albuher 2002: 99–113.
126. Albuher 2002: 99–113; Bezalel 2007: 337–74, 380–2; Lazar 1990: 66.
127. Cohen 2004: 19; Bezalel 2007: 376, 379.

2. MIXED CITIES

1. Klausner 1915: 237.
2. Yazbak 2010.
3. Ben-Arieh 1977: 630–1; Hart 2009: 43.
4. Yahav 2004: 99–100; Scholch 2006: 119–43, 285
5. Le Bore 2006: 12; Hazan and Monterescu 2011: 95.
6. Klausner 1915: 45.
7. Tamari 2009: 9–10, 23; Kimmerling and Migdal 2003: 38–66.
8. Ezrat 1890.
9. Biger 1984.
10. Kark 2003: 263–4, 271–2.
11. Biger 1984; Helman 2007: 11.
12. Porath 1978: 110–11.
13. Razy 2009: 57; Helman 2007: 12; Kimmerling and Migdal 2003: 38–66.
14. Segev 1999: 154.
15. Le Vine 2005: 281–302; Azaryahu 2005: 61–6; Segev 1999: 153–4, 196; Bernstein 2008: 23.
16. Hart 2009: appendix 3.
17. Matalon 2005: 6, 13, 27–9; Rabau 1984: 48–9; Shlush 1991: 79–85.
18. Shlush 1991: 26–30, 46, 80.
19. Le Vine 2005: 134–5, 144, 281–302; Kark and Glas 1993: 155–7.
20. Rabau 1984: 92.
21. Abu al-Jabeen 2005: 77.
22. Lev Tov 2010: 49.
23. Razy 2009: 112–13; Gutman 1999: 45.
24. TAYCA 589/b1/4 neighbor relations
25. Tsur and Rotbard 2010: 167–8, 175, 196–200, 216–19, 226–30.
26. Ibid.: 238–40
27. Le Vine 2005: 41–2, 95–6, 100, 108, 128; Le Bore 2006: 96; Bernstein 2008: 21–2.
28. Le Bore 2006: 53–4, 34; Bernstein 2008: 60–79; Lazar 1990: 185.
29. TAYCA 1320/3642 b r 17, different complaints.
30. TAYCA 1320/4—3642/a r 17, different complaints.
31. TAYCA 589/b 1/4, neighbor relations.
32. Bernstein 2008: 81, 170–1, 187–8, 213–14; Fakhri Jedai and Abu Ilai in www.jaffaproject.org
33. Bernstein 2008: 154–60, 170, 218, 270–1; Razy 2009: 257–68; Gertz 2009: 142–5.
34. TAYCA 1320/3642 r d 17, different complaints.
35. Bernstein 2008: 50–8; Helman 2007: 41, 64, 105, 110, 147, 163, 167–9.

36. Baram 2007.
37. Davis 1999.
38. Laskov 2010: 37; Hannanel 2007: 318; Mass 1974.
39. Golan 2001: 20–1.
40. Karmi 2002: 41–3.
41. Ibid.: 16; Radai 2006; Mass 1974.
42. Levin 2006: 220–3.
43. Lazar 1990: 43–4; Hannanel 2007: 338; Ben-Arieh 2011: 1137; Kroyanker 2000: 17–39.
44. Lazar 1990: 56–8, 63.
45. Davis 1999: 32–53; Benvenisti 1988: 92–5.
46. Ben-Arieh 2011: 831–40, 865; Kroyanker 2011: 22.
47. Kroyanker 2009: 65–7, 74–86, 96–111; Izakson 1994: 45.
48. Karmi 2002: 37.
49. Davis 1999: 32–53; Baramki 2010; Stern 1986: 34; Kroyanker 2005: 52–69.
50. Katinka 1964: 258, 161–2 respectively.
51. Reiter 2011; Hasson 2010; 2010a.
52. Katinka 1964: 169, 260.
53. Ibid.: 161–2.
54. Hasson 2009.
55. Rubinstein 2005; Segev 1999: 228–9.
56. http://www.archive.org/stream/journalofpalesti01paleuoft/journalofpalesti01paleuoft_djvu.txt
57. Tamari 2009: 96–101.
58. Ibid.: 43–5, 178–9.
59. *Hamagid*, 10 Oct. 10, 1867, Year 11, Issue 40, http://www.jpress.org.il/Default/Skins/TAUHe/Client.asp?Skin=TAUHe&enter=true&sPublication=MGD&Publication=MGD&Hs=advanced&AW=1317811776506&AppName=2
60. *Davar*, 20 Aug. 1928, http://www.jpress.org.il/Default/Skins/TAUHe/Client.asp?Skin=TAUHe&enter=true&sPublication=MGD&Publication=MGD&Hs=advanced&AW=1317811776506&AppName=2, and 17 Aug. 1930, http://www.jpress.org.il/Default/Skins/TAUHe/Client.asp?Skin=TAUHe&enter=true&sPublication=MGD&Publication=MGD&Hs=advanced&AW=1317811776506&AppName=2
61. Yazbak 2011.
62. Kapeliouk 1934.
63. Elkayam 1990: 121.
64. Yizhar 1964: 143–4.
65. Tamari 2009: 27–31; Yazbak 2010; Sasson 1995.
66. Shushan 2001.
67. Porath 1978: 74, 81; Cohen 2004: 64, 74–5.
68. Pappe 2002: 97–8; Holliday 1997: 22.
69. Porath 1976: 78.
70. Segev 1999a: 128; Sakakini 1990: 125–6, 137.
71. Sakakini 1990: 137.
72. Segev 1999: 109–10, 117; Pappe 2002: 171–2, 219–26.
73. JCA 330, Shami letter to Avisar Eyar 12, 1921.
74. Segev 1999a: 71.
75. Ibid.: 72.
76. Yehoshua 1992: 151.
77. Storrs 1938: 552–4.
78. Frumkin 1954: 276–9.
79. Pappe 2002: 258–60.
80. Segev 1999: 247.
81. Amit-Cohen 2005.
82. Segev 1999a: 304.

83. Segev 1999: 250; Porath 1976: 214.
84. Yehoshua 1979a: 117.
85. Porath 1976: 211–20.
86. Ibid.: 166–8, 209–22.
87. Segev 1999: 243–4.
88. Ibid.: 251–62; Pappe 2002: 258–71; Alpeleg 1989: 26–7; JCA 397, Oral Documentation.
89. *Haaretz*, 15 Apr. 2011, http://www.haaretz.co.il/news/politics/1.1171293
90. Segev 1999: 258–68.
91. Hazan and Monterescu 2011: 199–200.
92. Segev 1999: 268.
93. Cohen 1986: 16.
94. Levanon 1936: 7.
95. Cohen 1986: 24–8.
96. Avisar 1970: 454–5; Castel 2006: 78, 106.
97. Hayerushalmi 1971.
98. Porath 1976: 16; Hart 2009: 92, 104, 159, 108, 211–12.
99. Hissin 1982: 57–8.
100. Elkayam 1990: 174–5.
101. Krenizi 1950: 24–5; *Hazman*, 1 Apr. 1908, http://www.jpress.org.il/Default/Scripting/ArticleWin_TAU.asp?From=Search&Key=HZN/1908/04/01/1/Ar00100.xml&CollName=HZN_Default&DOCID=36521&PageLabelPrint=1&Skin=%54%41%55%48%65&enter=%74%72%75%65&Publication=%48%5a%4e&AppName=%32&Hs=%61%64%76%61%6e%63%65%64&AW=%31%3%33%39%31%36%32%39%31%32%31%32%30&sPublication=%48%5a%4e&tauLanguage=&sScopeID=%44%52&sSorting=%53%63%6f%72%65%2c%64%65%73%63&sQuery=%u05d9%u05e4%u05d5&rEntityType=%41%52%54%49%43%4c%45&sSearchInAll=%66%61%6c%73%65&sDateFrom=%25%33%30%25%33%34%25%32%66%25%33%30%25%33%31%25%32%66%25%33%31%25%33%39%25%33%30%25%33%38&sDateTo=%25%33%30%25%33%34%25%32%66%25%33%30%25%33%31%25%32%66%25%33%31%25%33%39%25%33%30%25%33%38& ViewMode=HTML; Beeri 1985: 115–17; Le Vine 2005: 44–5.
102. Porath 1976: 24–5, 78, 59–60, 104–8.
103. Litvinski 1920.
104. Shlush 1931: Chapter 26.
105. Porath 1978: 208; Segev 1999: 153–4; Le Bore 2006: 19.
106. Yizhar 2007: 90, 98–100, 128–9.
107. Rabau 1984: 94.
108. Segev 1999: 154–5.

3. LIFE ON THE VERGE OF THE FUTURE

1. Koestler 1949: 196.
2. Segev 1999: 110.
3. Porath 1976: 24–9.
4. Elyashar 1997: 23.
5. Frumkin 1954: 291.
6. Shlush 1931.
7. Arlosoroff 1931: 29 Sep.
8. Laqueur and Rubin 1995: 18; Tessler 2009: 165–6.
9. Crawford 1985: 175–9; Graves 1949: 48.
10. Segev 1999: 56, 64.
11. Storrs 1937: 358.
12. Yehoshua 1992: 151.
13. Storrs 1937: 358.

14. Storrs 1938: 508, 562–4.
15. Lazar 2011: 112.
16. Graves 1949: 52.
17. Porath 1978: 208.
18. Levin 2006: 53; Pappe 2002: 257–8; Frumkin 1954: 287.
19. Levin 2006: 66–8.
20. ISA 327/17 P.
21. Porath 1978: 74, 102–3; Benvenisti 1996: 52, 97–9.
22. JCA 397, Oral Documentation.
23. Porath 1978: 160–2.
24. Ibid.: 25, 63.
25. Ibid.: 60–2, 110–11.
26. Ibid.: 31, 60–2, 82–5, 70–1, 147; Kimmerling and Migdal 2003: 38–66.
27. MECA Green Gerald John, GB165–0404; Jones Frank William, GB165 0389; Robert Hamilton Collection, GB 165 0392.
28. Porath 1978: 173, 195–208.
29. Segev 1999a: 383.
30. Segev 1999: 324–5.
31. Guri 2010a.
32. Segev 1999: 298–9.
33. Laskov 2010: 119; Zekharyah 2002: 71; Kark and Glas 2005: 213–14; Lazar 1990: 45.
34. Radai 2010: 122–3, 129–32.
35. Brinker 1942: 57–8.
36. TAYCA 04–1263.
37. Lapidot 2000; Lazar 1981; Porath 1978: 212–15.
38. Frumkin 1954: 323.
39. ISA National Photo Archive, Zoltan Kluger D23–060 3729, Oct. 1938, http://147.237.72.31/scripts/topsrch/topapi.dll; Khalidi 1984: 210, 228; Sakakini Hala 1990: 56–7; Ricks 2009: 236, 239–44; Lazar 1990: 45.
40. Al-Hout 2007: 24.
41. MECA GB 165–0244; 165–018, John Loxton, *The Survey of Palestine 1937–48*, p. 33.
42. Faierberg 2006; Radai 2010: 130–2.
43. Porath 1987: 106.
44. ISA National Photo Archive, Zoltan Kluger Jaffa, 3 Mar. 1947, D 047–814, D 048; Hans Pinn 17 Mar. 1947, D 836–026; unknown photographer, 1 Mar. 1947, D 005–839; Radai 2006; Mass 1974.
45. Rubinstein 1992.
46. Karmi 2002: 43, 50.
47. Toubbeh 1998: 21.
48. Ibid.: 11.
49. Yehoshua 1979a: 66.
50. Collins and Lapierre 1972: 139, 215.
51. Ibid.: 111–12.
52. Ibid.: 127–8.
53. Toubbeh 1998: 26.
54. Ignatieff 1993: 216.
55. Le Bore 2007/8: 66.
56. Sharabi 2008: 2–19, 51–76.
57. Lazar 2011: 263.
58. Ibid.: 313, 315.
59. Lazar 1990: 40, 46, 51–2, 56, 58, 59, 99.
60. Lazar 1990: 37.
61. Ayalon 2004: 127.
62. Bird 2010: 16–19.

63. Hannanel 2007: 62.
64. Lazar 1990: 116.
65. Lazar 2011: 96.

4. EXPANDING THE BOUNDARIES OF THE POSSIBLE

1. Hobsbawm 2002: 7.
2. Taycher in Bondy, Zmora, and Bashan 1968: 190–2.
3. Laor 2009.
4. Moors 2010.
5. Dromi 2011.
6. Ballas 2009: 100–7.
7. Benziman 1973: 30–7.
8. Oren 2004: 297.
9. ISA 8164 A 10, Cabinet meeting, 19 June 1967.
10. Israel Central Bureau of Statistics 2008, http://www1.cbs.gov.il/shnaton60/st02_27.pdf
11. Wiesel 1968.
12. Klausner 1944: 74–8.
13. Oz 1994.
14. Samuel 1970: 232–3.
15. Izakson 1994: 54.
16. Golani and Manna 2011: 72.
17. ISA 9009–18, a report on Jordanian Jerusalem Municipality, 1 Feb. 1950.
18. Israel Central Bureau of Statistics, Annual Statistical Book 1996: 36–42.
19. Palestine Central Bureau of Statistics 2011, http://www.pcbs.gov.ps/Portals/_pcbs/PressRelease/YOuth2011_E.pdf
20. Katz 2007; Klein 2011; Klein and Yazbak 2011.
21. Golani and Manna 2011: 99.
22. ISA 3729/14, a letter by Uzai, 1 Aug. 1966.
23. ISA 8164/6 A8, Cabinet meeting, 5 June 1967.
24. ISA 8164/6 A–8, Cabinet meeting, 11 June 1967; Ministerial Committee for Jerusalem Status, https://docs.google.com/file/d/0B45gJhLdDCqqNEJ3THAwLXQ4OWM/edit; Benziman 1973: 6–11, 48–50.
25. Benvenisti 1973: 127–35; Benziman 1973: 61–5; IDFA 27/117/1970 Law and Trial, 22 June 1967.
26. Pedazur 1996: 117.
27. ANA Israeli Development and Plans (Old City), Special Folder 1968–1971, arc Identifier 2803130/MLR Number UD–UP 86, container 22, Robert Newman to Josef Sisco.
28. ANA Jerusalem—Israeli Development and Plans (Old City), Special Folder 1968–1971, arc Identifier 2803130/MLR Number UD–UP 86, container 22, consul general on meeting with Kollek.
29. ANA Jerusalem—Israeli Development and Plans (Old City), Special Folder 1968–1971, arc Identifier 2803130/MLR Number UD–UP 86, container 22, consul general reports, 14 Feb., 16 Apr., 3 June 1969.
30. Amir 2007: 95.
31. Bender 2011.
32. ISA 7052/12 A, Sasson report, 22 Jan. 1968.
33. Meital 2000.
34. Sasson 2004: 92–7, 102–20.
35. ISA 7052/12 A.
36. Raz 2012: 33–43.
37. ISA 7052/12 A.
38. ISA 7052/12 A, 22 Dec. 1967.
39. ISA 7052/12 A, Nusseibeh meeting with King Hussein, 24 Feb. 1968.

40. ISA 7052/12 A, Sasson report to minister of foreign affairs and the prime minister, 23 Jan. 1970.
41. Klein 2003: 63–80, 111–26, 199–214; Klein 2007.
42. ISA 7052/12 A, Sasson report on Dayan meetings with mayors; Hadi 1987: 9–12.
43. ISA 7052/12 A, meeting with prime minister, 9 Apr. 1968.
44. Benvenisti Interview, 10 July 2011; 2012: 230–1.
45. ISA Cabinet Committee for Jerusalem Status https://docs.google.com/file/d/0B45gJhLdDCqqNEJ3THAwLXQ4OWM/edit
46. ISA 7052/12 A, meeting with Nusseibeh 19 Apr. 1968.
47. Ibid.
48. ISA 7052/12 A, Even meeting with Nusseibeh, 8 Sep. 1968; Sasson meeting with Shehadeh, 17 June 1968.
49. ISA 7052/12 A, meeting with Abu Zuluf, 21 Oct. 1968.
50. Benvenisti 1988: 123.
51. JCA 499, Yaakov Yehoshua Personal Records.

5. LIKE OWNERS

1. Montefiore 2011.
2. Bauml 2007: 223.
3. Monterescu and Fabian 2003.
4. ISA 2214/2–C.
5. ISA 1874–5 CL.
6. Eldar 2008.
7. Ushpiz 1992.
8. ISA 17078/12–CL Amir to Toledano, 14 July 1968; minister of justice to the prime minister, 14 May 1968.
9. Amir 2007: 78; Nusseibeh 2007: 79; ISCV 282/88.
10. ISCV 282/88.
11. Hoffman 2000: 167–8.
12. ACRI 2010.
13. ISCV 2797/1, http://www.acri.org.il/he/wp-content/uploads/2011/04/hit2797.pdf
14. Klein 2001: 247–93.
15. http://www.btselem.org/hebrew/planning_and_building/east_jerusalem_statistics
16. Amir interview 14 Feb. 2011.
17. Golan 2001: 96–7.
18. Documents 2010: 151.
19. Berger 1988: 55–6.
20. Benvenisti 2012: 106, 172.
21. Rappaport 2007; JCA 1525, Mass private papers; Berger 1988: 56, 61–2.
22. Berger 1988: 55.
23. Amit 2009.
24. Hareven 2002: 78–88.
25. Berger 1988: 61–2.
26. Documents 2010: 154.
27. Hazan and Monterescu 2011: 118, 127.
28. Golan 2001: 118, 127.
29. ISA 2214/2–C.
30. Yahav 2004: 100–1.
31. Weiss 2010: 80.
32. Radai 2006.
33. Ahimeir 2012: 102–3.
34. JCA 1525, Mass private papers; Mass 1974.
35. JCA 5975, Street Names Committee.

36. ISA 17027/17 CL, minister of justice to prime minister, 14 Mar. 1968; Abdelrazek 2011.
37. *Davar*, 12 and 21 July 1967, respectively.
38. ISA 8164/10-A, Cabinet meeting, 19 June 1967; Benziman 1973: 29–30; Halabi 1983: 28; Raz 2012: 115–25.
39. ISA Cabinet Committee for Jerusalem Status June 1967, https://docs.google.com/file/d/0B45gJhLdDCqqNEJ3THAwLXQ4OWM/edit
40. Halabi 1983: 31; Segev 2005: 423; Benziman 1973: 37–45; Hasson 2012a.
41. Benvenisti interview, 5 Jan. 2011.
42. ISA 6423/8-C; Benziman 1973: 44–5; Segev 2005: 511; Misgav 2010.
43. ISCV 114/78.
44. Calvino 1972: 10.
45. Segev 2005: 457–8, 508.
46. Hannanel 2007: 266.
47. JCA 499, Yehoshua personal records.
48. JCA 499, Yehoshua personal records.
49. Ynet 2008, 2009; Villa Salameh http://www.palestine-family.net/index.php?nav=6-24&cid=11&did=733
50. Abowd 2007; Baramki 2010.
51. http://www.mots.org.il/Eng/TheMuseum/TheMuseum.asp
52. Houses from Within 2007, 2008, 2009, http://www.batim-jerusalem.org/
53. http://www.batim-il.org/Tours.aspx?batim
54. Leshem and Ronel 2012.
55. Levne 2009; Rotbard 2005: 195–213; Azaryahu 2012: 82–7.
56. Flavius Josephus 1968: 225.
57. Azaryahu 2012: 109–12; ISCV 4112/99.
58. Azulai 2009.
59. Azulai 2009a.
60. Greenberg Joel 2012.
61. Aderet 2011.
62. Cheshin, Hutman, and Melamed 1999: 146–8.
63. Miller 2011.
64. JCA 502, Yehoshua personal records.
65. Lurie 1968.
66. *Haaretz*, 2 Jan. 2013.
67. Hammudah 2010: 113–14.
68. Bisharat 2004.
69. Sakakini Hala 1990: XV–XI.
70. Sakakini Hala 1997: 28.
71. Ajami 1998: 271.
72. Tamari and Hammami 1998: 67–9; Tamari 2007.
73. Le Bore 2006: 263–8.
74. Al-Qattan 2007: 193–4.
75. Abu Lughd Leila 2007.
76. Cohen Hillel 1995: 50.
77. Husseini-Shahid 2000: 195–200.
78. Aviva Mizrahi in an e-mail to the author by her son Gilad Sher.
79. *Ma'ariv*, 9 June 1970: 37.
80. Ezruni 1967.
81. Ibid.; INLA Yeda Am ARC4 1765/05/10, letter from Menashe Mani, 19 July 1967.
82. Mani 1968.

6. OCCUPATION, ASSIMILATION, OPPOSITION

1. McEwan 2011.

2. ISA 6423 8–C, Eshkol to Bentov, 24 June 1968.
3. ISA 6423 8–C, Bentov to Eshkol, 16 Jan. 1968; *Davar*, 1 Sep. 1967, interview with Kollek.
4. Bar and Rubin 2011.
5. http://www.rova-yehudi.org.il/atar-saruf.asp
6. Bar and Rubin 2011: 780.
7. Ricca 2007.
8. http://www.rova-yehudi.org.il
9. http://www.temple.org.il/show_shgrir.asp?id=46104
10. http://www.temple.org.il/about.asp
11. http://www.ynet.co.il/articles/0,7340,L-3817323,00.html
12. ISA 13908/2.
13. ISA 9009/6, Action Plan to the Eastern Area; Benvenisti 1996: 101.
14. *Kol Hair*, 11 June 1999; 26 May 2000.
15. ISA 17035/2–CL Kollek to Dinitz, 29 Dec. 1971.
16. Benvenisti 1996: 102, 112–29; Benvenisti 1981: 76; Marom 2004: 37; Cheshin, Hutman, and Melamed 1999: 3; ACRI May 2010.
17. Benvenisti 1981: 18.
18. Halabi 1983: 32–5, 50; Segev 2005: 519–20; Ronen 1989: 30.
19. Benvenisti 1973: 187–9; *Davar*, 6 Dec. 1967.
20. Weigert 1975; *Ma'ariv*, 16 Apr. 1968; *Davar*, 23 June, 21 Nov. 1968; 2 June 1969; ISA 6423 8–C.
21. Weigert 1975; ISA 13908/2 Uri More Report, 1972.
22. ISA 17035 2–CL Small Business Association to Alon, 7 Dec. 1969.
23. Caplan 1980: 61–81.
24. JCA 2386 Palmon to Farhi.
25. JCA 1416 Sarig to Tov.
26. ISA 7052/12 a, Sasson talks to Nusseibeh.
27. YYA Gabriel Stern personal records 105469 (5)3–36–95.
28. Cheshin, Hutman, and Melamed 1999: 73–81.
29. JCA 2368.
30. Shlomo Gazit, interview, 22 Apr. 2012.
31. Benziman 1973: 223–9.
32. The Knesset, May 2010: 7–8.
33. Sanders 2011.
34. Iriyat Yerushalayim 1996: 78.
35. Weinstein 1987: 33.
36. Misrad 1993; Nehemya and Perlmuter 1998; Rozenson 1993.
37. ISA 17035 2–CL, Toledano to Hillel, 10 Dec. 1968; Eshkol to Cabinet Secretariat; 13908/2, Toledano to Meir, 5 Mar. 1972.
38. Benvenisti interview, 5 Jan. 2011; Amir interview, 14 Feb. 2011.
39. ISA 7052/12 A, Sasson to foreign minister, 28 Aug. 1969.
40. ISA 7052/12 A, Sasson and Tzafrir meeting with Abu Zuluf, 17 Feb. 1969.
41. Benvenisti 2012: 190–1, 200–7.
42. Cheshin, Hutman, and Melamed 1999: 15–18.
43. Nizan-Shiftan 2006.
44. Kollek 1994: 32, 54–5, 63, 68, 75, 95, 106, 172, 208–13, 273–9; Kollek 1979: 224–5; Benvenisti 1996: 185–94.
45. *Haaretz*, 10 July 1995.
46. Benvenisti 2011: 50.
47. JCA 2386.
48. Rafi Levi interview, 6 Feb. 2011.
49. Amir 2007: 202, 203 respectively, interview 14 Feb. 2011.
50. Amir interview, 14 Feb. 2011.

51. Benvenisti 1981: 85–6; Segev 2005: 518.
52. *Ma'ariv*, 12, 21 Sep., and 3 Oct. 1967; 21 Mar. and 19 June 1968, 21 Mar. 1969.
53. *Davar*, 15 Dec. 1967, 16 June 1968.
54. Rafi Levi interview, 6 Feb. 2011; Benvenisti interview, 14 Feb. 2011.
55. Benvenisti 1996: 154–8.
56. Nusseibeh 2007a: 98.
57. Nusseibeh 2007: 78–105.
58. *Haaretz*, 11 January 1968; *Davar*, 30 Jan. 1968.
59. Amir 2007: 87–8, 117, interview 14 Feb. 2011.
60. Bloch 1967; Benvenisti 1996: 75; *Davar*, 11 July 1969; Pundik 1967, 1967a.
61. JCA 499, Yehoshua personal records, 8 May 1969.
62. JCA 499, Yehoshua personal records.
63. JCA 499, Yehoshua personal records, *al Salam wa-al-Khair* Oct. 1968.
64. Pundik 1967a; Barnea 1969.
65. ISA 6423 8–C; 17035 1–CL.
66. ISA 6423 8–C.
67. Benvenisti 1988: 157–9.
68. Iton Yerushalayim, 2 and 16 Oct. 1998; *Kol Hair*, 11 June 1999, 26 May 2000; *Kol Hazman*, 15 Sep. 2000.
69. Iton Yerushalayim, 26 Feb. 1999.
70. Milne 2010.
71. Hasson 2012.
72. Golan-Agnon 2002: 164–6.
73. Golan-Agnon 2002a: 130.
74. Ibid.: 138–40.
75. Ibid.: 156, 164.
76. Farhat-Naser 2002: 63–8.
77. Ibid.: 149–52.
78. JCA 501, Yehoshua personal records—Our Muslim Neighbors.
79. Benvenisti 2007: 127.
80. Azaryahu 2005: 61–6.
81. Golan 2001: 96–7.
82. Eldar 2013: 106; Azaryahu 2012: 68.
83. Segev 2009.
84. Yahav 2004: 11; Weiss 2009.
85. Paz 1998; Rappaport 2007.
86. http://www.arabyaffa.org/he/index.aspx; Hazan and Monterescu 2011: 24.
87. Hazan and Monterescu 2011:
88. The project marketing as it appeared in *The Marker*, http://cafe.themarker.com/post/470235/ and http://www.humanrights.cet.ac.il/ShowItem.aspx?ItemID=87ef0be8-86eb-402a-be9e-f157205369a1&lang=HEB. After its completion, a similar formulation appeared on the development's website, http://www.andromeda.co.il/submenupage.aspx?menuid=1
89. Levne 2004.
90. Avidan and Heywood 2009; Weiller-Pollak 2010: 7.
91. Luz 2005:
92. Exhibition 2009.
93. Abu Shadeh in Hazan and Monterescu 2011: 103.
94. Abu Ramadan in Hazan and Monterescu 2011: 115.
95. Rabbi Bachar in Hazan and Monterescu 2011: 77, 78 respectively.
96. ISA 2214/2–C Shlush and Malul reports, Oct. 1949, Mar. 1951.
97. Talmi 1979.
98. Ben Shimon in Hazan and Monterescu 2011: 218–23.

99. Amiga in Hazan and Monterescu 2011: 199–204.
100. Andreus sisters in Hazan and Monterescu 2011: 114; Le Bore 2006: 61–75.
101. Siksakk 2004, 2004a, 2004b, 2005, 2005a.
102. www.jaffaproject/org
103. http://www.yafo.org.il/yeshiva/about.html
104. Cook 2010; *Haaretz*, 8 Nov. 2010, http://www.haaretz.co.il/hasite/spages/1149322.html; Ben Simhon 2008.
105. Monterescu and Fabian 2003.
106. http://www.ynet.co.il/articles/1,7340,L-3524625,00.html; http://www.mynet.co.il/articles/0,7340,L-3686408,00.html
107. http://www.mynet.co.il/articles/0,7340,L-3578237,00.html
108. http://www.mynet.co.il/articles/0,7340,L-3582276,00.html
109. *Haaretz*, 31 Oct. 2011, http://www.haaretz.co.il/news/politics/1.1535562
110. Calvino 1972: 124.
111. http://www.mountofolives.co.il/index.aspx?CID=291
112. Soueif 2010; Greenberg 2012.
113. http://www.alt-arch.org/timeline_heb.php
114. *Haaretz*, 24 Oct. 2011, http://www.haaretz.co.il/news/politics/1.1529640
115. ISA 6423 8–C, 17027 15–CL.
116. *Kol Hair*, 29 Nov. 1996; *Haaretz*, 26 and 29 May 1998; Cheshin, Hutman, and Melamed 1999: 215–21.
117. JCA 1417 Committee for Coordinated Operations in the Muslim Quarter, 30 Mar. 1984.
118. Shragai 1995: 202.
119. Cheshin, Hutman, and Melamed 1999: 215–21; http://www.alt-arch.org/settlers_heb.php; Ir Amim 2009; Hasson 2010b.
120. Retranslated from *Haaretz* Hebrew edn, Hasson 2009a.
121. http://www.alt-arch.org/images/yemenite2.jpg; Ir Amim 2010.
122. Reiter and Lehrs 2010: 28–9, 39–41.
123. Rotenberg 2004.
124. YYA 4428 (3) 7.92 Peace Now.
125. ACRI Sep. 2010; Ir Amim 2009; Silwan Information Center, http://silwanic.net/?page_id=49
126. Hammami 2012: 59.
127. Shashar 1997: 18, 86.
128. Dayan 1982: 454, 501–2.
129. IDFA 1688/953/1985.
130. Shlomo Gazit interview, 22 Apr. 2012; Dayan 1976, 1978: 46–7; Karpel 2006.
131. IDFA 88/2846/1997; 3/1460/2002 Matpash 5 June 1975; 10/1460/2002.
132. JCA 1416 Kollek to Peres, 10 and 14 Aug. 1975.
133. http://the-temple.blogspot.co.il/2012/08/blog-post_11.html
134. Vaadat 1994: 135.
135. Admoni 1992: 41, 58–9; Pedazur 1996: 230–2.
136. Divrey Haknesset, 25 Mar. 1970: 1342.
137. Ilani 2009.
138. Frenkel 2003: 201, 437 respectively.
139. Branes and Erlich 1979; Arnon 2008; Dayan 1999; Eldar and Zertal 2004: 336–72; Feige 1995, 2003: 101–25; Neuman 2004.
140. Amru 1985: 9–35.
141. Sharab 2006: 14–27, 66, 155–6.
142. B'Tselem and ACRI 2007: 6, 11.
143. B'Tselem and ACRI 2007a: 47–59.
144. Barel 2008; 2011: 273.
145. Freedland 2011, 2012; Hayes 2010; Barel 2008, 2008a; Rappaport 2005; B'Tselem and

ACRI 2007; Arab Studies Society 2006; TIPH reports http://www.tiph.org; Sellick 1994; Egan 1984.
146. St Margaret's community, http://www.stmgrts.org.uk/archives/2007/12/the_school_on_shuhada_street.html
147. Abu Hashhash 2011.
148. IDFA 953/1985, 1405/83/5 Dayan meeting with Hebron settlers, 5 June 1968.
149. B'Tselem and ACRI 2007a: 27–8, 39–44; Segal 1983: 148–9; Barel 2011: 256.
150. Halabi 1983: 113–14, 117, 122–3, 168–9; B'Tselem and ACRI 2007a: 39–44; Segal 1983: 73–4.
151. Tavger 1999: 155; Barel 2011: 259.
152. Tavger 1999: 129.
153. Ibid.: 129.
154. Ibid.: 120.
155. Tavger 2009: 143–4.
156. Segal 1983: 139.
157. Ibid.: 140, 153–4.
158. Halabi 1983: 112; Rappaport 2005.
159. ISA 6501/24 C, Kiryat Arba Committee to prime minister and minister of defense, July 1975.
160. Barel 2011: 26, 20–2, 30.
161. Shlomo Gazit, interview, 22 Apr. 2012.
162. Segal 1983: 139; Imam Iz al-Din al-Zir, interview, Florence Apr. 2010; Simons 2003: 8–17; Romann 1986.
163. Halabi 1983: 108–9.
164. YLEA, Cable Jabari to prime minister, 7 May 1968; Halabi 1983: 109.
165. IDFA 1985/953 1405.
166. *Ma'ariv*, 17 May 1968.
167. Gish 2001: 35.
168. Stern 2010.
169. http://ocjrp.welfare-association.org/en/article/who-we-are/about-welfare-association.html
170. Ricca 2007: 180–5, 189–93.
171. De Cesari 2010; Vitullo 2003; Ricca 2007: 180–5.

BIBLIOGRAPHY

A = Arabic; H = Hebrew

Archives

ANA American National Archive
Divrey Haknesset [Knesset Protocols] H
IDFA Israel Defense Force Archive
INLA Israel National Library Archive
ISA Israel State Archive
ISCD Israeli Supreme Court Verdicts
JCA Jerusalem City Archive
MECA Middle East Centre Archive, St Antony's College, Oxford
TAYCA Tel Aviv Yafo City Archive
YLEA Yad Levi Eshkol Archive
YYA Yad Ya'ari Archive

Newspapers

Be'sheva [H]
Davar [H]
The Guardian
Haaretz [H]
Hamagid [H]
Hamelitz [H]
Hazman [H]
Iton Yerushalaim [H]
The Jerusalem Post
The Jewish Chronicle
Kol Hazman [H]
Los Angeles Times
Ma'ariv [H]
The Media Line
The Nation
The National
New York Review of Books
The New York Times
The Washington Post

BIBLIOGRAPHY

Yediot Aharonot [H]
Ynet [H]

Books, Reports, and Articles

Abdelrazek, Adnan (2011), "Palestinian Refugees' Property in West Jerusalem—A Fortune Up for Grabs," *Palestine Israel Journal*, 17, 1–2, pp. 88–95.

Abowd, Thomas (2007), "Present and Absent—Historical Invention and the Politics of the Place in Colonial Jerusalem," in Sandy Sufian and Mark LeVine (eds), *Reproaching Borders: New Perspectives on the Study of Israel–Palestine*, New York: Rowan and Littlefield, pp. 243–65.

Abu Hashhash, Musa (2011), "No Religious Conflict in Hebron," *The Jerusalem Post*, 16 Nov. 2011, http://www.jpost.com/Opinion/Op-EdContributors/Article.aspx?id=245852

Abu-Lughod, Lila (2007), "Return to Half-Ruins: Memory, Postmemory and Living History in Palestine," in Ahmad H. Sa'adi and Lila Abu-Lughod (eds), *Nakba—Palestine 1948 and the Claims of Memory*, New York: Columbia University Press, pp. 77–106.

ACRI [Association for Civil Rights in Israel] (May 2010), "Zcuyot Adam Beyerushalayim Mizrahit Uvdot Venetunim" [Human Rights in East Jerusalem Facts and Data], http://www.acri.org.il/he/wp-content/uploads/2011/03/eastjer2010.pdf [H].

――― (Sep. 2010), "Merhav Lo Mugan—Keshel Harashuyot Behagana Al Zechuyot Adam Bezorei Hahitnhalut Shebeyerushalaim Hamizrahit" [Unsafe Space—The Israeli Authorities' Failure to Protect Human Rights amid Settlements in East Jerusalem], Jerusalem, http://www.acri.org.il/pdf/unsafe-space-he.pdf [H].

Aderet, Ofer (2011), "Leavret Et Yerushalayim" [To Hebrewize Jerusalem], *Haaretz*, 7 July, http://www.haaretz.co.il/hasite/spages/1233916.html [H].

Admoni, Yehiel (1992), *Asor Shel Shikul Daat Hahityashvut Meever Lakav Hayarok 1967–1977* [A Thoughtful Decade: The Settlements beyond the Green Line 1967–1977], Tel Aviv, Machon Yisrael Galili [H].

Ahimeir, Ora (2012), *Cala* [Bride], Tel Aviv: Am Oved [H].

Ajami, Fuad (1998), *The Dream Palace of the Arabs: A Generation's Odyssey*, New York: Pantheon Books.

――― (2000), *Armon Hahol Shel Haaravim Odeisah Shel Dor* [The Dream Palace of the Arabs: A Generation's Odyssey], Tel Aviv: Am Oved [H].

Albuher, Shlomo (2002), *Hizdahut Histaglut Vehistaygut Hayehudim Hasfaradim Beeretz Yisrael Vehatnuah Hazionit Beyemei Hashilton Habriti 1918–1948* [Identification, Adaptation, and Reservation—The Sephardi Jews in Eretz Israel and the Zionist Movement During the British Rule 1918–1948], Jerusalem: Hasifriyah Azionit [H].

Alpeleg, Zvi (1989), *Hamufti Hagadol* [The Grand Mufti], Tel Aviv: Misrad Habitahon [H].

Amir, Eli (2007), *Yasmin* [Jasmin], Tel Aviv: Am Oved [H].

Amit, Gish (2009), "Mazevah Meshuna Isuf Hasifryot Hafalastiniyot Mimarav Yerushalayim Bemilhemet 1948 Vegilguleyhen Bebeit Hasfarim Haleumi Vehauniversitai" [A Strange Monument: The Collection of Palestinian Libraries during the 1948 War and their Transformation within the Jewish National and University Library], *Teorya Vebikoret*, 35, pp. 11–36 [H].

Amit-Cohen, Irit (2005), "Bein Maarav Lemizrah Habaron Felix De Menashe Askan Yazam Zioni" [Between Alexandria and Palestine: Baron Felix de Menashe, Entrepreneur and Zionist], *Katedra*, 114, pp. 71–98 [H].

Amru, Yunis (1985), *Khalil al-Rahman al-Arabiyah Madina Laha Taarikh* [Arab Hebron: A City with History], Ramallah: Dar al-Kalm [A].

Arab Studies Society (2006), Land Research Center—the Fieldwork and GIS Unit, *Geopolitical Situations in Hebron Governorate Palestine*, Jerusalem: July, http://www.hic-mena.org/documents/The_Geopolical_situation_in_Hebron_HIC.pdf

Arlosoroff, Haim (1931), "Yoman Yerushalayim" [Jerusalem Diary] (available online: http://benyehuda.org/arlosoroff/jj_sep1931.html) [H].

BIBLIOGRAPHY

Arnon, Adar (1992), "The Quarters of Jerusalem in the Ottoman Period," *Middle Eastern Studies*, 28, 1, pp. 1–65.

Arnon, Noam (2008), *Hevron 4000 Shanah Veod 40—Sipurah Shel Ir Haavot* [Hebron 4000 years plus 40—The Story of the Patriarch's City], Kiryat Arba, http://www.hebron.org.il/hebrew/data/downloads/noamhoverthebron.pdf [H].

—— (2012), "Pothei Hashearim—Elef Shnot Knisat Yehudim Lemearat Hamchpelah" [Gate Openers—Millennium Jewish Entrance to the Cave of Patriarchs], in *Kenes Mehkarei Hevron Divrei Hakenes Harishon* [First Hebron Studies Conference], Kiryat Arba, pp. 21–47 [H].

Auld, Sylvia, and Robert Hillenbrand (eds) (2000), *Ottoman Jerusalem: The Living City 1517–1917*, London: Altajir World of Islam Trust.

Avidan, Lili, and Mathew Heywood (2009), "Zhi Yafo Vegam Zot" [This is Jaffa and This Also], *Marker Week*, 19 Nov., pp. 26–9 [H].

Avisar, Oded (ed.) (1970), *Sefer Hebron Ir Haavot Veyishuva Berei Hadorot* [The Book of Hebron—The City of Patriarchs and its Settlement in Generational Perspective], Jerusalem: Keter [H].

Ayalon, Amy (2004), *Reading Palestine—Printing and Literacy 1900–1948*, Austin: University of Texas Press.

Azaryahu, Maoz (2005), *Tel Aviv Hair Haamitit* [Tel Aviv: The Real City], Sdeh Boker: Machon Ben Gurion [H].

—— (2012), *Al Shem Historia Vepolitika Shel Shemot Rehovot Beyisrael* [Namesakes: History and Politics of Street Naming in Israel], Jerusalem: Carmel [H].

Azulai, Yuval (2009), "Haim Iriyat Tel Aviv Menasah Leyahed Et Yafo" [Is Tel Aviv Municipality Trying to Judaize Jaffa?], *Haaretz*, 16 Nov., http://www.haaretz.co.il/hasite/spages/1128451.html

—— (2009a), "Imam Agadi O Meyasdei Tel Aviv Hakrav Al Hashemot Beyafo Nimshach" [Legendary Imam Or Tel Aviv Founders: The Argument on Jaffa Names Continues], *Haaretz*, 2 Nov., 8 Nov. 2010 [H].

Ballas, Shimon (2009), *Beguf Rishon* [First Person Singular], Tel Aviv: Hakibutz Hameuhad [H].

Bar, Doron, and Rehav Rubin (2011), "The Jewish Quarter after 1967: A Case Study on the Creation of an Ideological-Cultural Landscape in Jerusalem's Old City," *Journal of Urban History*, 37, pp. 775–92.

Barak, Aharon, and Haim Bernzon (1997), *Sefer Bernzon* [Bernzon Book], vol. 1, Jerusalem: Nevo [H].

Baram, Nir (2007), "I Live Again My Forgotten Life," *Haaretz*, 1 Jan., http://www.haaretz.com/hasite/spages/808166.html [H].

Baramki, Gabi (2010), "Education Against All Odds—The Palestinian Struggle for Survival and Excellence," *Mediterranean Journal of Educational Studies*, 15, 2, pp. 11–21.

Bareket, Amiram (2007), "Gam Million Frank Lo Hespiku Lekniyat Hakotel" [Even One Million Francs Were Not Enough to Buy the Wailing Wall], *Haaretz*, 15 May, http://www.haaretz.co.il/hasite/pages/ShArtPE.jhtml?itemNo=859763&contrassID=2&subContrassID=21&sbSubContrassID=0

Barel, Zvi (2008), "Rehov Tarpat Pinat Hashuhada" [Tarpat Street Corner Hashuhada], *Haaretz Weekly Supplement*, 18 Apr. [H].

—— (2008a), "Hevron Online" [Hebron Online], *Haaretz*, 25 Apr. [H]

—— (2011), *Kshemchoniyot Naflu Mehashamayim—Masa Bein Kibushim* [When Cars Fell from Heaven—A Journey Through Occupations], Tel Aviv: Hakibutz Hameuhad [H].

Barkai, Binyamin (1995), *Nahlat Binyamin—Sefer Zicaron* [Benjamin's Estate—Commemoration Volume], Jerusalem [H].

Barnea, Nahum (1969), "Shnatayim Leihud Yerushalayim" [Two Years since Jerusalem United], *Davar*, 16 May [H].

Bauml, Yair (2007), *Tzel Cahol Lavan—Mediniyut Hamimsad Hayisraeli Upeulotav Bekerev Haezrahim Haaravim Beyisrael Hashanim Hameazvot 1958–1968* [A Blue and White

BIBLIOGRAPHY

Shadow—The Israeli Establishment's Policy and Actions among its Arab Citizens: The Formative Years 1958–1968], Haifa: Pardes [H].

Beeri, Eliezer (1985), *Reshit Hasichsuch Yisrael–Arav* [The Beginning of the Israeli–Arab Conflict], Haifa: Universitat Haifa Vesifriyat Hapoalim [H].

Ben-Arieh, Yehoshua, vol. 1 (1977), vol. 2 (1979), *Ir Berei Hatekufah Yerushalayim Bameah Hatesha Esreh* [A City Reflected in its Times—Jerusalem during the Nineteenth Century], Jerusalem: Yad Yitzhak Ben Zvi [H].

—— (2011), *Yerushalayim Hayehudit Hahadashah Betqufat Hamandat—Shchunot Batim Anashim* [The New Jewish City of Jerusalem during the British Mandate Period—Neighborhoods, Houses, People], Jerusalem: Yad Yitzhak Ben Zvi [H].

Ben Hananya, Yehoshua (1944), "Milim Ivriot Vesafradiot Basafa Haaravit Hameduberet" [Hebrew and Ladino Words in Spoken Arabic], *Hed Hamizrah*, 27 Oct., pp. 9–19 [H].

Ben Simhon, Kobi (2008), "Psagot Ajami" [Ajami Heights], *Haaretz Weekly Supplement*, 21 Nov., pp. 16–20 [H].

Ben-Yair, Michael (2013), *Sheih Jarah* [Sheih Jarah], Tel Aviv: Hargol [H].

Ben-Yehudah, Baruch (1970), *Sipurah Shel Hagimnasyah Herzeliyah* [The Herzeliyah High School Story], Tel Aviv: Gimnasysh Herzeliyah [H].

Bender, Aric (2011), "Hehmitz Et Harega Sipur Hatmunah Misheshet Hayamim" [Missed the Moment—The Story of the Six Days War Photo], *Ma'ariv*, 6 June [H].

Benvenisti, Meron (1973), *Mul Hahomah Hasgurah—Yerushalayim Hahazuyah Vehameuhedet* [In Front of the Closed Wall—Jerusalem Divided and United], Jerusalem: Keter [H].

—— (1981), *Yerushalayim Ir Vebeliba Homah* [Jerusalem: City with a Wall at its Center], Tel Aviv: Hakibutz Hameuhad [H].

—— (1988), *Hakela Vehaalah—Shtahim Yehudim Vearavim* [The Sling and the Stick—Territories, Jews, and Arabs], Jerusalem: Keter [H].

—— (1996), *Makom Shel Esh* [City of Stone], Tel Aviv: Dvir [H].

—— (2007), *Son of the Cypresses—Memories, Reflections and Regrets from a Political Life*, trans. Maxine Kaufman–Lacusta, in consultation with Michael Kaufman–Lacusta, Berkeley: University of California Press.

—— (2011), "Ovdan Hapninah" [The Lost Pearl], *Eretz Aheret*, 60, Mar., pp. 46–51 [H].

—— (2012), *Halom Hazabar Halavan* [The Dream of the White Sabra], Jerusalem: Keter [H].

Benziman, Uzi (1973), *Yerushalayim Ir Lelo Homa* [Jerusalem—A City without Wall], Jerusalem: Schocken [H].

Berger, Tamar (1988), *Dionysius Bacenter* [Dionysius in the Center], Tel Aviv: Hakibutz Hameuhad [H].

Bernstein, Deborah (2008), *Nashim Bashulayim—Migdar Uleumiut Betel Aviv Hamandatorit* [Women on the Margins: Gender and Nationalism in Mandate Tel Aviv], Jerusalem: Yad Izhak Ben-Zvi [H].

Bezalel, Izhak (2007), *Noladetem Zionim—Hasfaradim Beeretz Yisrael Bazionut Ubathiyah Haivrit Batkufah Haothmanit* [You Were Born Zionist—The Sephardim in Eretz Israel and the Hebrew Revival During the Ottoman Period], Jerusalem: Yad Yizhak Ben-Zvi [H].

—— (2011), "Halevantinim Harishonim Bayishuv Haothomani Zehutam Hazionit Veyahsam Laarveyut" [The First Levantines in Ottoman Palestine—Their Zionist Identity and Relations with Arab Nationalism], *Peamim*, 125–7, pp. 75–95 [H].

Biger, Gidon (1984), "Hitpathut Hashetah Habanuy Shel Tel Aviv Bashanim 1901–1934" [The Development of Tel Aviv's Built-up Area 1901–1934], in Naor Mordechai (ed.), *Tel Aviv Bereshitah 1909–1934 Mekorot Sikumim Parshiyot Nivharot Vehomer Ezer* [Tel Aviv First Years 1909–1934: Sources, Summaries, Selected Cases, and Assisting Material], Jerusalem: Yad Yizhak Ben Zvi (available online: http://lib.cet.ac.il/Pages/item.asp?item=12795&source=623) [H].

Bird, Kai (2010), *Crossing Mandelbaum Gate—Coming of Age between the Arabs and Israelis 1956–1978*, London: Simon and Schuster.

BIBLIOGRAPHY

Bisharat, George (2004), "The Family Never Lived Here," *Haaretz*, 3 Jan., http://www.freerepublic.com/focus/f-news/1051050/posts

Bloch, Dani (1967), "Yerushalayim Shel Beayot" [Jerusalem of Problems], *Davar*, 13 Oct. [H].

Bondy, Ruth, Ohad Zmorah, and Refael Bashan (eds) (1968), *Lo Al Haherev Levadah—Hasipur Hamufla Al Gvurat Am Yisrael Venitshono Bemilhemet Sheshet Hayamim* [Not Just By Sword—The Miraculous Story of the Israeli Nation's Heroism and its Victory in the Six Days War], Bat Yam: Levin Epstein [H].

Branes, Haim, and Amos Erlich (eds) (1979), *Leket Maamarim Veduyot Utmunot Bimlot 50 Shanah Lemeoraot 1929 Behebron* [A Collection of Articles, Testimonies, and Photos in Commemoration of the 50th Anniversary of 1929 Massacre in Hebron], Kiryat Arba [H].

Braver, Michael, and Avraham Yaakov Braver (1966), *Zichronot Av Uvno* [Father and Son Memoirs], Jerusalem: Mosad Harav Kok [H].

Breen, Andrew Edward (1906), *A Diary of My Life in the Holy Land*, Rochester, NY: J.P. Smith.

Brinker, Dov Natan (1942), *Luah Yerushalayin 1942* [Jerusalem Calendar 1942], Jerusalem: Mosad Harav Kok [H].

B'Tselem and ACRI (2007), *Ir Refaim—Mediniyut Hahafradah Hyisraelit Udhikat Ragleihem Shel Falastinim Memerkaz Hebron* [Ghost Town—Israel's Separation Policy and Forced Eviction of Palestinians from the Center of Hebron], Jerusalem: B'Tselem, May.

B'Tselem (2011), "Statistics on Demolition of Houses Built without Permit in East Jerusalem," http://www.btselem.org/planning_and_building/east_jerusalem_statistics

Calvino, Italo (1972), *Invisible Cities*, Orlando: Harcourt.

—— (1985), *Haarim Hasmuyot Meayin* [Invisible Cities], Tel Aviv: Sifriyat Hapoalim [H].

Canaan, Habib (1980), *Beinei Shoter Falastini* [Through Palestinian Policeman Eye], Ramat Gan: Masada [H].

Caplan, Gerald (1980), *Arab and Jew in Jerusalem: Explorations in Community Mental Health*, Cambridge, MA: Harvard University Press.

Castel, Yosef (2006), *Hashevet Castel Ledorotav* [The History of the Castel Family], Castel Family [H].

Chambers, Ian (2008), *Mediterranean Crossing—The Politics of an Interrupted Modernity*, Durham, NC: Duke University Press.

Cheshin, Amir, Bill Hutman, and Avi Melamed (1999), *Separate and Unequal—The Inside Story of Israeli Rule in East Jerusalem*, Cambridge, MA: Harvard University Press

Cohen, Ben Zion (1986), *Memaamakim* [From the Depth], Jerusalem [H].

Cohen, Hillel (1993), "Etz Vefalastin" [Tree and Palestine], *Kol Hair*, 19 Nov. [H].

—— (1995), "Bayit Hazer Milhama Zicaron" [Home Court Yard Memory], *Col Hair*, 9 June [H].

—— (2004), *Zva Hazlalim* [An Army of Shadows], Jerusalem: Ivrit [H].

—— (2013), *1929 Shnat Haefes Basicsuch Hayehudi Aravi* [1929: Year Zero of the Jewish Arab Conflict], Jerusalem: Keter [H].

Cohen, Yona (1968), *Hacham Gershon Menahlat Shimon* [Rabbi Gershon of Nahlat Shimon], Jerusalem: Mass [H].

—— (1995), *Hapinkas Patuach Vehayad Roshemet* [Hand Writes in the Open Notebook], Tel Aviv: Moreshet [H].

Collins, Larry, and Dominique Lapierre (1972), *O Jerusalem*, New York: Simon and Schuster.

Confino, Alon (2008), "Al Hashihrur Mearizut Haavar Aravim Veyehudim Beyisrael" [On the Liberation from the Tyranny of the Past: Arabs and Jews in Israel], *Alpayim*, 32, pp. 49–59 [H].

Cook, Jonathan (2010), "Jaffa Struggles to be Left in Peace," *The National*, 16 Feb., http://www.thenational.ae/news/worldwide/middle-east/jaffa-struggles-to-be-left-in-peace

Crawford, Allan (1985), *C.R. Ashbee—Architect, Designer, and Romantic Socialist*, New Haven and London: Yale University Press.

Davis, Rochelle (1999), "The Growth of the Western Communities," in Salim Tamari (ed.),

BIBLIOGRAPHY

Jerusalem 1948: The Arab Neighbourhoods and their Fate in the War, Jerusalem: Institute of Jerusalem Studies and Badil, pp. 32–73.

Dayan, Moshe (1976), "Mearat Hmachpela Shemitahat Lamisgad" [The Patriarch Cave below the Mosque], *Kadmoniyot*, 9, 6, pp. 129–31 [H].

—— (1978), *Lehyot In Hatanach* [To Live with the Bible], Jerusalem: Idanim [H].

—— (1982), *Avnei Derech—Autobiographia* [Milestones—Autobiography], Jerusalem: Idanim [H].

Dayan, Yosef (1999), "Mahi Hebron Laumah Haivrit?" [What does Hebron Mean to the Hebrew Nation?], Introduction to Ben Zion Tavgar, *Hebron Sheli* [My Hebron], Jerusalem: Shamir, pp. 9–21 [H].

De Cesari, Chiara (2010), "Hebron, or Heritage as Technology of Life," *The Jerusalem Quarterly*, 41, http://www.jerusalemquarterly.org/ViewArticle.aspx?id=336

Documents (2010), "Mismachim Meginzach Hamedinah—Tikei Misrad Hamiutim" [Documents from Israel State Archive—Minorities Ministry Files], *Mitaam*, 21, pp. 151–6 [H].

Droian, Nitza (1980), "Shchunot Reshonot Leolei Teiman Beyerushalayim 1882–1914" [First Jerusalem Neighborhoods for Yemeni Jews 1882–1914], *Katedra*, 13, pp. 95–129 [H].

—— (1982), *Bein Marvad Ksamim—Olei Teiman Beretz Yisrael 1881–1914* [No Magic Carpet Exists—Yemeni Jews in the Land of Israel 1881–1914], Jerusalem: Ben Zvi Institute. [H].

Dromi, Uri (2011), "Ed Letkufah" [Of Time Witness], *Haaretz*, 24 June [H].

Efrati, Natan (1975), *Mishpahat Elyashar Betochechei Yerushalayim—Prakim Betoldon Hayishuv Hayehudi Beyerushalaim Bameot Hatsha Esreh Vehaesrim* [Elyashar Family inside Jerusalem—Chapters in the History of Jewish Settlement in Jerusalem in the Nineteenth and Twentieth Centuries], Jerusalem: Reuven Mas [H].

Egan, John P. (1984), "Hebron's Mustafa Natshe," *Journal of Palestine Studies*, 13, 3, pp. 49–62.

Elad, Amikam (1994), *Medieval Jerusalem and Islamic Worship: Holy Places, Ceremonies, Pilgrimage*, Leiden: Brill.

Elazar, Ya'akov (1980), *Hatzerot Beyerushalayim Ha'atikah* [Courtyards in Jerusalem's Old City], Jerusalem: Yad Larishonim [H].

Eldar, Akiva (2008), "Hamedinah Moda Larishona Minuyim Shel Anshei Dat Muslemim Mutnim Beishur Hashbak" [Unprecendetedly the State Admits—Security Service Approval is Required for Senior Muslim Appointments], *Haaretz*, 7 Dec.

Eldar, Akiva, and Idit Zertal (2004), *Adonei Haaretz Hamotnahalim Umedinat Yisrael 1967–2004* [Lords of the Land, the Settlers and the State of Israel], Or Yehudah: Kinert [H].

Eldar, Eran (2013), *Bekohoteiha Haazmiyim Hahitpathut Haurbanit Shel Tel Aviv Beshilhei Tekufat Hamandat Ubeasorei Hamedina Harishonim* [By Its Own Effort: The Urban Development of Tel Aviv in the Twilight of the British Mandate and the First Decades of the State of Israel], Tel Aviv: Resling [H].

Elhanani, Avraham Haim (1984), *Beorah Shel Yerushalayim* [In Jerusalem's Light], Jerusalem: Vaad Edat Hasfaradim [H].

Elkayam, Mordechai (1990), *Yafo Neveh Tsedek Reshitah Shel Tel Aviv* [Jaffa Neveh Tsedek—The Beginning of Tel Aviv], Tel Aviv: Misrad Habitahon [H].

Elyashar, Eliyahu (1981), *Lihyot Im Yehudim* [Living with Jews], Jerusalem: Markus [H].

—— (1997), *Lihyot Im Falastinin* [Living with Palestinians], Jerusalem: Misgav [H].

Elyashar, Menashe Hai (1987), *Sherut Leumi* [National Service], Jerusalem [H].

Exhibition (2009), *Asara Mabatim Meyafa/Yafo al Hagigot Hameah Shel Tel Aviv* [Ten Views from Jaffa on Tel Aviv Celebrating One Hundred Years], the author owns the photos and captions [H].

Ezrat, Sofrim (1890), "Michtavim Meretz Hakodesh" [Letters from the Holy Land], *Hamelitz*, 4 July [H].

Ezruni, Nisim (1967), "Im Menashe Mani Bahazara Lehevron" [With Menashe Mani Back to Hebron], *Yedioth Aharonoth*, 25 July [H].

Faierberg, Haim (2006), "Digmei Biluy Betel Aviv Bemilhemet Hazmaut" [Leisure Patterns in

BIBLIOGRAPHY

Tel Aviv during the War of Independence], in Baron Mordechai and Meir Hazan (eds), *Am Bemihamah Kovetz Mehkarim Al Hahevrah Haezrahit Bemilhemet Hazmaut* [Citizens at War: Studies on the Civilian Society during the Israeli War of Independence], Jerusalem: Yad Yizhak Ben Zvi, pp. 375–98 [H].

Farhat-Naser, Sumaya (2002), *Daughter of the Olive Trees*, Basel: Lenos.

Feige, Michael (1995), "Hahitnahalut Hayehudit Behebron Beperspektivah Shel Zicaron Kollectivi bein Merkaz Leperipheriah" [The Jewish Settlement in Hebron in the Perspective of Collective Memory between Center and Periphery], *Yahadut Zmanenu*, 10, pp. 73–111 [H].

—— (2003), *Shtei Mapot Lagada Gush Emunim Shalom Achshav Veizuv Hamerhav Beyisrael* [One Space, Two Places: Gush Emunim, Peace Now and the Construction of Israeli Space], Jerusalem: Magnes [H].

Flavius, Josephus (1968), *Toldot Milhamot Hayehudim Baromain* [The Jewish War], Ramat Gan: Masada [H].

Frenkel, Naomi (2003), *Predah* [Depart], Jerusalem: Gefen [H].

Freedland, Jonathan (2011), "This Is Israel? Not the One I Love," *The Jewish Chronicle*, 7 Nov., http://www.thejc.com/comment-and-debate/columnists/57850/this-israel-not-one-i-love

—— (2012), "An Exclusive Corner of Hebron," *New York Review of Books*, 23 Feb., pp. 21–3.

Friedman, Nahum Dov (1980), *Sefer Hazicaron Hayerushalmi Reshimah Meforetet Mrechushenu Haruhani Vehahomri Beyerushalayim* [The Jerusalemite Memorial Book: A Detailed List of Our Spiritual and Material Properties in Jerusalem], Jerusalem: Ariel [H].

Frumkin, Gad (1954), *Derech Shofet Beyerushalayim* [A Judge Way in Jerusalem], Tel Aviv: Dvir [H].

Gertz, Nurit (2009), *Al Daat Atzmo* [Unrepentant], Tel Aviv: Am Oved [H].

Ginzburg, Carlo (2001), *Wooden Eyes—Nine Reflections on Distance*, New York: Columbia University Press.

Gish, Arthur G. (2001), *Hebron Journal—Stories of Nonviolent Peacemaking*, Scottsdale: Pennsylvania Herald Press.

Golan, Arnon (2001), *Shinui Merhavi—Tozot Milhamah* [Wartime Spatial Changes], Sdeh Boker: Hamerkaz Lemoreshet Ben Gurion [H].

Golan-Agnon, Daphna (2002), *Efo Ani Basipur Hazeh* [Where I Am In This Story], Jerusalem: Keter [H].

—— (2002a), *Next Year in Jerusalem: Everyday Life in a Divided Land*, New York: Free Press.

Golani, Motti, and Adel Manna (2011), *Shnei Tsidei Hamatbea—Azmaut Venakba Shnei Nerativim Shel Milhemet 1948* [Two Sides of the Coin—Independence and Nakba 1948: Two Narratives of the 1948 War and its Outcome], Dordrecht, Republic of Letters and the Institute for Historical Justice and Reconciliation, The Hague [H].

Goldstein, Kaylin (2007), "Citadel into David's Tower—Palestinian Memory and the Multicultural Fantastic," *Radical History Review*, 99, pp. 173–86.

Goren, Tamir (2006), *Haifa Haaravit in 1948* [The Fall of Arab Haifa in 1948], Sdeh Boker: Machon Ben-Gurion [H].

—— (2008), *Shituf Betsel Imut—Aravim Veyehudim Bashilton Hamekomi Behaifa Betkufat Hamandat Habriti* [Cooperation in the Shadow of Confrontation—Arabs and Jews in Local Government in Haifa during the British Mandate], Ramat Gan: Bar Ilan University [H].

Graham-Brown, Sarah (1980), *Palestinians and their Society: A Photographic Essay*, London: Quarter Books.

Graves, Richard M. (1949), *Experiment in Anarchy*, London: Victor Gollancz.

Greenberg, Joel (2012), "An Israeli City: A Tribute to a Palestinian Doctor," *The Washington Post*, 27 Feb., http://www.washingtonpost.com/world/middle_east/in-israeli-city-tribute-to-a-palestinian-doctor/2012/02/27/gIQAJweJeR_story.html

Greenberg, Rafi (2012), *Hasifah Kitzonit—Archeologia Beyerushalayim 1967–2008* [Extreme

BIBLIOGRAPHY

Exposure—Archeology in Jerusalem, 1967–2008], http://www.alt-arch.org/jerusalem_heb.php [H].

Guri, Haim (2010), "Bekafe Hanargilot Bein Natan Alterman Lececil Hourani" [In the Hubble-Bubble Café between Nathan Alterman and Cecil Hourani], *Haaretz*, 22 Jan. [H].

—— (2010a), "Bekafe Hanargilot Im Bialik Vemoshe Dayan" [In the Hubble-Bubble Café with Bialik and Moshe Daya], *Haaretz*, 2 June [H].

Gutman, Nahum (1999), *Ir Ktanah Veanashim Ba Meat* [A Small City with Few People], Tel Aviv: Dvir [H].

Hadi, Mahdi Abdul F. (1987), *Notes on Palestinian–Israeli Meetings in the Occupied Territories, 1967–87*, Jerusalem: PASSIA (available online: http://www.passia.org/publications/information_papers/pub_infopapers_no_01.htm).

Halabi, Rafik (1983), *Yes Gevul Sipur Hagadah Hamaravit* [The Border Exists—West Bank Story], Jerusalem: Keter [H].

Hamburger, Haim (1939), *Sefer Shlosha Olamot* [Three Worlds Book], Jerusalem: Menorah [H].

Hamenachem, Ezra (1988), *Mesipurei Naar Yerushalmi* [Jerusalem's Young Boy Stories], Tel Aviv: Eked [H].

Hammami, Rema (2012), "The Exiling of Sheikh Jarrah," *Jerusalem Quarterly*, 51.

Hammudah, Sahar (2010), *Once Upon a Time in Jerusalem*, Reading: Garment Publications.

Hannanel, Mosheh (2007), *Hayerushalmim—Masa Besefer Hatelephonim Hamandatory 1946* [The Jerusalemites—A Journey Through Mandate Telephone Guide 1946], Tel Aviv: Eretz Vateva [H].

Hareven, Shulamit (2002), *Yamim Rabim—Autobiographya* [Many Days—Autobiography], Tel Aviv: Bavel [H].

Hart, Rachel (2009), "Yahaso Shel Hayishuv Hayehudi El Hayishuv Harvi Beyafo Ubetel Aviv 1881–1930" [The Relation of the Jewish Community to the Arab Community in Jaffa and Tel Aviv 1881–1930], Dissertation, Haifa: Haifa University [H].

Hasson, Nir (2009), "Hazman Havarod Shel Malon Sheferd Beshkhunat Sheikh Jarah Beyerushalayim" [The Pink Time of Shepherd Hotel Sheikh Jarah Jerusalem], *Haaretz*, 3 Sep., http://www.haaretz.co.il/hasite/pages/ShArt.jhtml?itemNo=1112084 [H].

—— (2009a), "Tochnit Hahitpashtut Shel Ateret Cohanim Bemizrah Yerushalayim Kniyat Shisha Batim Bair Haatikah Vbniyah Mehuz Lahomot" [Ateret Cohanim East Jerusalem Expansion Plan Buying Six Houses in the Old City and Building Outside the Walls], *Haaretz*, 27 Sep., http://www.haaretz.co.il/hasite/spages/1117272.html [H].

—— (2010), "Museion Shel Isovlanut" [Intolerance Museum], *Haaretz*, 18 May, http://www.haaretz.co.il/hasite/spages/1169329.html [H].

—— (2010a), "Eduyot Mehaatar Hasodi" [Testimonies from the Secret Site], *Haaretz*, 18 May, http://www.haaretz.co.il/news/education/1.1202691 [H].

—— (2010b), "Kach Mesayat Hamedinah Leamutot Hayamin Lehitnahel Bemizrah Yerushalayim" [How the State Helps Rightist Associations to Settle in East Jerusalem], *Haaretz*, 5 Nov., http://www.haaretz.co.il/news/investigations/1.1228499 [H].

—— (2011), "Kakh Nilhemet Iriyat Yerushalayim Barochlim Memizrah Hair" [The Municipality Campaign against East Jerusalem's Peddlers], *Haaretz*, 23 Dec., http://www.haaretz.co.il/news/education/1.1599110 [H].

—— (2012), "Ir Lekulanu" [City to All of Us], *Haaretz Weekly Supplement*, 28 Dec., pp. 19–25 [H].

—— (2012a), "Edut Nedirah Hasfah Misgad Atik Sheneheras Be-67" [Rare Testimony Reveals a Mosque Destroyed in 67], *Haaretz*, 15 June http://www.haaretz.co.il/news/science/1.1732269 [H].

Hayerushalmi, Lvi Izhak (1971), "Shalosh Dorot Bair Haatikah" [Three Generations in the Old City], *Ma'ariv*, 21 May [H].

Hayes, Christopher (2010), "Postcard from Palestine," *The Nation*, 14 Oct., http://www.thenation.com/article/155400/postcard-palestine

BIBLIOGRAPHY

Hazan, Haim, and Daniel Monterescu (2011), *Ir Bein Arbayim* [A Town of Sundown Aging Nationalism in Jaffa], Jerusalem: Van Leer [H].

Helman, Anat (2007), *Or Veyam Hekifuah Tarbut Tel Aviv Betkufat Hamandat* [Urban Culture in 1920s and 1930s Tel Aviv], Haifa: Haifa University [H].

Hever, Hannan (2007), *Hasipur Vehaleom* [The Narrative and the National], Tel Aviv: Resling [H].

Hever, Hannan, and Yehudah Shenhav (2011), "Hayehudim Haaravim Gilgulo Shel Musag" [Arab Jews: Concept and its Changing Meanings], *Peamim*, 125–7, pp. 57–74 [H].

Hissin, Haim (1982), *Masa Baaretz Hamuvtahat* [A Journey in the Promised Land], Tel Aviv: Universitat Tel Aviv Vehakibutz Hameuhad [H].

Hoffman, Adina (2000), *House of Windows*, New York: Broadway Books.

Hobsbawm, Eric (2002), *Interesting Times: A Twentieth-Century Life*, London: Allen Lane.

Holliday, Eunice (1997), *Letters from Jerusalem during the Palestine Mandate*, London and New York: Radcliffe.

Al-Hout, Shafiq (2007), *Bein al-Watan Waal-Manfa* [Between Homeland and Exile], London: Riad al-Rais [A].

Husseini-Shahid, Serene (1999), *Yerushalmit* [Jerusalemite], Tel Aviv: Andalus [H].

—— (2000), *Jerusalem Memories*, edited by Jean Said Makdisi, Beirut: Naufal.

Ignatieff, Michael (1993), *Blood and Belonging—Journeys into the New Nationalism*, New York: Farrar Straus and Giroux.

Ilani, Ofri (2009), "Kol Hadorot Haavudim Shel Berlin Vehebron" [Berlin and Hebron Lost Generation Voice], *Haaretz*, 23 Nov.

Ir Amim (2009), "Iskah Afela Besilwan" [Shady Dealings in Silwan], Jerusalem: Ir Amim Report, http://www.ir-amim.org.il/_Uploads/dbsAttachedFiles/silwanreport.pdf [H].

—— (2010), "Nifkadim Beal Korham Hafkat Nechsim Beyerushalayim Hamizrahit Tahat Hok Nechsei Nifkadim" [Absentees Against Their Will: Property Expropriation in East Jerusalem Under the Absentee Property Law], Jerusalem: Ir Amim Report, http://www.ir-amim.org.il/_Uploads/dbsAttachedFiles/nifkadim.pdf [H].

Iriyat Yerushalayim Minhal Hahinuch 1996, *Yerushalayim Irenu* [Jerusalem Our City], Tel Aviv: Am Oved [H].

Israel Central Bureau of Statistics (1996) (2008), "Annual Statistics," http://www1.cbs.gov.il/shnaton60/st02_27.pdf

Izakson, Eliyahu (1994), *Mareh Medor Hagesher* [The Bridge's Generation View], Tel Aviv: Or [H].

Al-Jabeen, Abu (2005), *Kitab Hikaya An Jafa* [Narrative on Jaffa], Amman: Dar al-Shuruq [A].

Jacobson, Abigail (2001), "The Sephardi Jewish Community in Pre-World War I Jerusalem," *The Jerusalem Quarterly*, 14, pp. 23–33.

—— (2003), "Sephardim Ashkenazin and the 'Arab Question' in Pre-First World War Palestine: A Reading of Three Zionist Newspapers," *Middle Eastern Studies*, 39, 2, pp. 105–30.

—— (2011), *From Empire to Empire—Jerusalem between Ottoman and British Rule*, Syracuse: Syracuse University Press.

—— (2011a), "Jews Writing in Arabic—Shimon Moyal, Nissim Malul and the Mixed Palestinia/Eretz Israeli Locale," in Yuval Ben Bassat and Eyal Ginio (eds), *Late Ottoman Palestine—The Period of Young Turk Revolt*, London: I.B. Tauris, pp. 165–82.

Al-Jubeh, Nazmi (2005), "Between Damascus Gate and Jaffa Gate—Gates Struggle for Modernization," in Issam Nassar and Salim Tamari (eds), *Pilgrims, Lepers and Stuffed Cabbage—Essays on Jerusalem's Cultural History*, Jerusalem: Institute for Jerusalem Studies, pp. 79–94.

Judt, Tony (2005), *Postwar: A History of Europe since 1945*, London: William Heinemann, 2005.

—— (2009), *Aharei Hamilhamah Toldot Eropa Meaz 1945* [Postwar: A History of Europe since 1945], Jerusalem: Magnes and Dvir [H].

BIBLIOGRAPHY

―――― (2010), *The Memory Chalet*, New York: Penguin.
Kannan, Habib (1965), "Beit Mani Dyukan Shel Mishpahat Maskilim" [Mani Family: A Portrait of Enlightened Family], *Haaretz*, 26 Mar [H].
Kapeliouk, Menachem (1934), "Bikur Lailah Bemahneh Rubin" [Night Visit to Rubin Camp], *Davar*, 26 Nov., http://www.jpress.org.il/Default/Skins/TAUHe/Client.asp?Skin=TAUHe&enter=true&sPublication=DAV&Publication=DAV&Hs=advanced&AW=1329663681589&AppName=2 [H].
Kark, Ruth (2003), *Yafo Zmihatah Shel Ir 1799–1917* [Jaffa: A City in Evolution 1799–1917], Jerusalem: Ariel [H].
Kark, Ruth, and Michal Ben Yaakov (2001), "Yozmot Veyazamut Shel Yehudim Sepharadim Vebnei Edot Hamizrah Bebniyat Shchunot Megurim Bearei Eretz Yisrael Beshilhei Hatekufah Haottomanit Hdugmah Shel Yerushalaim" [Jewish Entrepreneurship in Building Urban Neighborhoods in Palestine at the End of the Ottoman Period: The Case of Jerusalem], in Aaronsohn Ran and Stampfer Shaul (eds), *Yazamut Yehudit Baet Hahadasha Mizrah Eropa Veeretz Yisrael* [Studies in Jewish Economic Entrepreneurship in the Modern Era], Jerusalem: Magnes, pp. 96–136 [H].
Kark, Ruth, and Yosef Glas (1993), *Yazamim Spharadim Beretz Yisrael Mishpahat Amzalak 1816–1948* [Sephardi Entrepreneurs in Eretz Israel: The Amzalak Family 1816–1948], Jerusalem: Magnes [H].
―――― (2005), *Mishpahat Valero Shiva Dorot Beyerushalayim 1800–1948* [Sephardi Entrepreneurs in Jerusalem: the Valero Family 1800–1948], Jerusalem: Gefen [H].
Karlinski, Haim (1932), "Pahad Shav" [Fear of No Reason], *Hayesod*, 17 April p. 3.
Karmi, Ghada (2002), *In Search of Fatima: A Palestinian Story*, London: Verso.
Karpel, Dalia (2006), "Hasambah Bemeart Hamachpela" [The Little Match Girl], *Haaretz*, 31 May, http://www.haaretz.com/the-little-match-girl-1.189081
Katinka, Baruch (1964), *Meaz Vead Henah* [From Then Until Now], Jerusalem: Kiryat Sefer [H].
Katz, Yossi (2007), *Lev Vaeven Sipura Shel Hamazevah Hazvait Beyisrael 1948–2006* [Heart and Stone: The Story of the Military Tombstone in Israel 1948–2006], Tel Aviv: Misrad Habitachon [H].
Khalidi, Rashid (1997), *Palestinian Identity: The Construction of Modern National Consciousness*, New York: Columbia University Press.
Khalidi, Walid (1984), *Before their Diaspora—A Photographic History of the Palestinians 1876–1948*, Washington, DC: The Institute of Palestine Studies.
Kimmerling, Baruch, and Joel S. Migdal (2003), *The Palestinians: A History*, Cambridge, MA: Harvard University Press.
Klausner, Joseph (1915), *Olam Mithaveh* [A World in Making], Odessa: Halperin [H].
―――― (1944), *Am Vearetz Kamim Lethiya* [People and Land Reviving], Tel Aviv: Yavne [H].
Klein, Menachem (2001), *Jerusalem the Contested City*, New York: New York University Press.
―――― (2003), *The Jerusalem Problem—The Struggle for Permanent Status*, Gainesville: University Press of Florida.
―――― (2007), "The Negotiations for the Settlement of the 1948 Refugees," in E. Benvenisti, C. Gans, and S. Hanafi (eds), *Israel and the Palestinian Refugees*, Berlin: Springer.
―――― (2011), "A Choreography of Memories," in Sami Adwan, Efrat Ben Ze'ev, Menachem Klein, Ihab Saloul, Tamir Sorek, and Mahmoud Yazbak (eds), *Zoom In—Palestinian Refugees of 1948 Remembered*, Dordrecht: Republic of Letters and the Institute for Historical Justice and Reconciliation, pp. 153–60.
Klein, Menachem, and Mahmoud Yazbak (2011), "A'ylut and Ma'lul: A Tale of Two Palestinian Villages Before and After the 1948 Nakba and the Birth of Israel," in Sami Adwan, Efrat Ben Ze'ev, Menachem Klein, Ihab Saloul, Tamir Sorek, and Mahmoud Yazbak (eds), *Zoom In—Palestinian Refugees of 1948 Remembered*, Dordrecht: Republic of Letters and the Institute for Historical Justice and Reconciliation, pp. 138–53.

BIBLIOGRAPHY

Kollek, Teddy (1979), *Yerushalayim Ahat Sipur Haim* [One Jerusalem—Biography], Or Yehudah: *Ma'ariv* [H].

—— (1994), *Yerushalayim Shel Teddy* [Teddy's Jerusalem], Even Yehuda: *Ma'ariv* [H].

Koestler, Arthur (1950), *Havtaha Vehagshama* [Promise and Fulfillment], Jerusalem: Ahiasaf [H].

—— (1949), *Promise and Fulfillment—Palestine 1917-1949*, New York: Macmillan.

Kosover, Mordecai (1966), *Arabic Elements in Palestinian Yiddish—The Old Ashkenazi Jewish Community in Palestine: Its History and its Language*, Jerusalem: Rubin Mass.

Krenizi, Avraham (1950), *Bekoah Hamaseh* [With Action Power], Tel Aviv: Masada [H].

Kroyanker, David (2000), *Rehov Haneveim Shchunat Hahabashim Veshchunat Musrrarah Sipuro Shel Makom Dyukna Shel Ir 1850-2000* [Hanevim Street Ethiopian and Musrrarah—Story of a Place and City Portrait], Jerusalem: Keter [H].

—— (2005), *Rehov Yafo Biographia Shel Rehov Sipura Shel Ir* [Jaffa Street: Biography of a Street, Story of a City], Jerusalem: Keter [H].

—— (2009), *Mamilla Geut Shefel Hithadshut* [Jerusalem Mamilla Prosperity, Decay and Renewal], Jerusalem: Keter [H].

—— (2011), *Hameshulash Hayerushalmi Biographia Urbanit* [The Jerusalem Triangle: An Urban Autobiography], Jerusalem: Keter [H].

Laor, Dan (2009), "Hatahat Yerushalayim Tel Aviv" [Tel Aviv in Exchange of Jerusalem?], *Haaretz*, 2 Oct. [H].

Lapidot, Yehuda (2000), *Leidatah Shel Mahteret* [The Birth of an Underground], http://www.daat.ac.il/daat/history/lapidot/2a-2.htm [H].

Laqueur, Walter, and Barry Rubin (1995), *The Arab Israeli Reader: A Documentary History of the Middle East Conflict*, New York: Penguin.

Laskar, Michael (1984), "Avraham Albert Antebi Prakim Bepoalo Beshnot 1897-1914" [Avraham Albert Antebi: Chapters in his Activity 1897-1914], *Peamim*, 21, pp. 50-82 [H].

Laskov, Shulamit (2010), *Lefanim Perkei Zichronot Meeretz Yisrael Shelifnei Milhemet Haolam Hashniyah* [Before: Memories from Palestine before the Second World War], Tel Aviv: Hakibutz Hameuhad [H].

Lazar, Hadara (1990), *Hamandatorim Erez Yisrael 1940-1948* [The Mandate People: Palestine 1940-1948], Jerusalem: Keter.

—— (2011), *Out of Palestine: The Making of Modern Israel*, New York: Atlas.

—— (2012), *Shisha Yehidim Demuyot Harigot Bemahloket Baretz Beshnot Hashloshim* [Six Singular Individuals: Unconventional Figures in Palestine in the '30s], Tel Aviv: Hakibutz Hameuhad [H].

Lazar, Litai Haim (1981), *Kibush Yaffo* [Jaffa Occupation], Tel Aviv: Misrad Habitachon [H].

Le Bore, Adam (2006), *City of Oranges—Arabs and Jews in Jaffa*, London: Bloomsbury.

—— (2007/8), "Zion and the Arabs: Jaffa as a Metaphor," *World Politics Journal*, pp. 61-75.

Le Vine, Mark (2005), *Overlooking Geography—Jaffa Tel Aviv and the Struggle for Palestine 1880-1948*, Berkeley: University of California Press.

Leshem, Noam, and Ayala Ronel (2012), "Salame Kfar Shalem—Likrat Historiah Merhavit Beyisrael" [Salame—Kfar Shalem—Towards Israel's Spatial History], in Haim Yaacobi and Tovi Penster (eds), *Zicaron Hashcaha Vehavnayat Hamerhav* [Remembering, Forgetting and the Construction of Space], Jerusalem: Van Leer, pp. 81-105 [H].

Lev Ari, Shiri (2006), "Zarim Ukrovim" [Stranger Relatives], *Haaretz*, 16 July, http://www.haaretz.co.il/hasite/pages/ShArtPE.jhtml?itemNo=738833&contrassID=2&subContrassID=7&sbubContrassID=0; [H].

Lev-Tov, Boaz (2007), "Biluyim Bemahloket—Dfusei Biluy Vetarbut Polularit Shel Yehudim Beretz Yisrael 1882-1914" [Leisure and Popular Culture Patterns of Eretz Israel Jews in the Years 1882-1914 as a Reflection of Social Change], Dissertation, Tel Aviv University [H].

—— (2010), "Shchenim Nochehim Ksharim Tarbutiyim Bein Yehudim Learvim Beretz Yisrael Beshilhei Hatekufah Haothmanit" [Present Neighbors: Cultural Relations between Jews and Arabs in Eretz Yisrael in the Late Ottoman Period], *Zmanim*, 110, pp. 42-54 [H].

BIBLIOGRAPHY

Levanon, Eliyahu Yehoshua (1936), *Bemisholei Moledet* [In Homeland Pathways], Jerusalem [H].

—— (2006), *Shichehat Hebron* [Forgotten Hebron], Jerusalem: Hayu Beahava [H].

Levi, Lital (2008), "Historicizing the Concept of Arab Jews in the Mashriq," *The Jewish Quarterly Review*, 98, 4, pp. 452–69.

Levin, Menachem (2006), *Shloshah Ohazin Bairiyah Toldot Iriyat Yerushalayim Betkufat Hashilton Habriti 1917–1948* [Three are Holding the Municipality: The History of the Municipality of Jerusalem under British Rule 1917–1948], Jerusalem: Levin-Kinhi [H].

Levne, Neri (2004), "Killelat Andromeda" [Andromeda Curse], *Haaretz Weekly Supplement*, 5 May, http://www.haaretz.co.il/misc/1.964357 [H].

—— (2009), "Bli Shemot" [With No Names], *Haaretz*, 24 May [H].

Litvinski, Moshe (1920), *Nahpesah Dracheinu* [Rethinking Our Ways], Jaffa [H].

Luncz, Avraham Moshe (1906), *Hair Kivrot Avotai* [My Forefathers' Cemetery City], http://www.benyehuda.org/lunz/kivrot.html [H].

Luncz, Bolotin Hannah (1968), *Meir Netivot Yerushalayim* [Illuminating Jerusalem Routes], Jerusalem: Ahiever [H].

Lurie, Benzion (1968), "Shemot Lerehovot Yerushalayim" [Naming Jerusalem Streets], *Davar*, 24 June [H].

Luz, Nimrod (2005), *Kehilat Yafo Haarvit Umisgad Hassan Bec* [The Arab Community of Jaffa and the Hassan Bek Mosque], Jerusalem: Floresheimer Institute.

Mani, Menashe (1963), *Hebron Vegiboreiha* [Hebron and its Heroes], Tel Aviv: Yavneh [H].

—— (1965), "Yosef Mani" [Yosef Mani], *Haaretz*, 1 Mar. [H].

—— (1968), "Eich Nitnahel Behevron" [How We Should Settle in Hebron], *Haaretz*, 20 May [H].

Manor, Dalia (2005), *Art in Zion—The Genesis of Modern National Art in Jewish Palestine*, London: Routledge.

Marom, Nati (2004), *Milkud Tichnuni Mediniyut Tichnun Hesder Karkaot Heteri Bniyah Veharisot Batim Bemizrah Yerushalayim* [The Planning Deadlock: Planning Policies, Land Regulations, Building Permits and House Demolitions in East Jerusalem], Jerusalem: Ir Shalem Vebimkom [H].

Mashayof, Shemuel Meir (1978), *Betochechei Yerushalayim* [Inside Jerusalem], Jerusalem [H].

Mass, Reuven (1974), "Prakim Mehayai" [Autobiography Chapters], in Avraham Ben Shushan, A.H. Elhanani, Aharon Bir, A.M. Haberman, and S. Shalom (eds), *Veim Begvurot* [When You Celebrate 80], Jerusalem: Yedidim, pp. 349–60 [H].

Matalon, Yavnel (2005), *Tel Aviv—Zichronot* [Tel Aviv—Memoirs], Ramat Gan [H].

McEwan, Ian (2011), "Speech at Jerusalem Award Ceremony," http://www.ianmcewan.com/bib/articles/jerusalemprize.html

Meital, Yoram (2000), "The Khartoum Conference and Egyptian Policy after the 1967 War: A Reexamination," *Middle East Journal*, 54, 1, pp. 64–82.

Mendelson, David (2002), *Zel Vehizayon Beyerushalayim Beriyatam Shel Hasofrim Hanosim Ubaomanuyot Shel Hameah Ha-19* [Shadow and Scenery in Jerusalem in the Nineteenth-Century Traveler Writers and Artist], Tel Aviv: Miscal [H].

Meyuhas, Yosef (1919), *Mehayei Haezrahim Beretz Yisrael* [Citizens' Life in Eretz Israel], Jerusalem: Mehadshot Haaretz [H].

—— (1928), *Yaldei Arab* [Arab Children], Tel Aviv: Dvir [H].

—— (1937), "Hafalahim Hayei Hafalahim Behashvah El Hayei Hayehudim Betkufat Hatanach Vehatalmud" [The Fallahs—Fallah Life Compared to the Life of Jews During the Bible and Talmud Periods], Jerusalem [H], http://he.wikipedia.org/wiki/%D7%A1%D7%99%D7%9C%D7%95%D7%90%D7%9F

Miller, David (2011), "Palestinian Road Warriors Give Jerusalem Street New Names," *The Media Line*, 10 Apr., http://www.americantaskforce.org/daily_news_article/2011/04/11/1302494400_2265

Milne, Seumas (2010), "The Palestinians of Israel are Poised to Take Centre Stage," *The*

BIBLIOGRAPHY

Guardian, 10 Nov., http://www.guardian.co.uk/commentisfree/2010/nov/10/palestinians-poised-to-take-centre-stage

Misgav, Uri (2010), "Tahant Mishtarah Zo Hukmah Baavurcha Biedey Amutat Yamin" [This Police Station Built for You By a Right Wing Association], *Yedioth Aharonot*, 22 Jan. [H].

Mishori, Alik (2000), *Shuru Habito Ureu—Ikonot Usmalim Hazutiyim Zionim Batarbut Hayisraelit* [Look, Gaze, Glance—Zionist Icons and Figurative Symbols in Israeli Culture], Tel Aviv: Am Oved [H].

Misrad, Hahinuch Vehatrabut (1993), *Yerushalayim Ladat Lehakir Velehov* [Jerusalem—To Know, To Understand, To Love], Jerusalem: Misrad Hahinuch Vehatarbut [H].

Montefiore, Simon Sebag (2011), "Oh Jerusalem! My Family, My History," *Haaretz*, 16 June.

Monterescu, Daniel, and Roy Fabian (2003), "Kluv Hazahav Gentreficasiah Veglobalizazyah Beproiect Givat Andromeda" [The "Golden Cage"—Gentrification and Globalization in the Andromeda Hill Project Jaffa], *Teoryah Ubikoret*, 23, pp. 141–78 [H].

Moors, Annelies (2010), "Presenting People: The Politics of Picture Postcards of Palestine/Israel," in Jordana Mendelson and David Prochaska (eds), *Postcards: Ephemeral Histories of Modernity*, University Park, PA: Penn State University Press, pp. 93–105.

Moyal, Shimon Yusuf (1909), *al-Talmud Asluhu Watasalsuluhu Waadabuhu* [The Talmud: It Origin, Transmission, and Ethics], Cairo: Matbaat al-Arab [A].

Nashashibi, Nasser Eddin (1990), *Jerusalem's Other Voice—Ragheb Nashashibi and Moderation in Palestinian Politics 1920–1948*, Exeter: Ithaca.

Nassar, Issam (2006), "'Bibilification' in the Service of Colonialism—Jerusalem in Nineteenth Century Photography," *Third Text*, 20, 3–4, pp. 317–26.

—— (2008), "Jerusalem in the Late Ottoman Period—Historical Writing and the Native Voice," in Tamar Mayer and Suleiman A. Mourad (eds), *Jerusalem: Idea and Reality*, London: Routledge, pp. 205–23.

Nehemya, Ronit, and Nediva Perlmuter (1998), *Ani Hoker Et Yerushalayim* [I Study Jerusalem], Even Yehuda: Reches [H].

Neuman, Tamara (2004), "Maternal 'Anti-Politics' in the Formation of Hebron's Jewish Enclave," *Journal of Palestine Studies*, 33, 2, pp. 51–70.

Nizan-Shiftan, Alona (2006), "Lehalim Ulehalim Tfisat Hamakom Beyerushalayim" [To Nationalize and Hide the Concept of Jerusalem Space], *Alpayim*, 30, pp. 134–70 [H].

Nusseibeh, Sari (2007), *Hayo Haytah Eretz* [Once Upon a Country], Jerusalem: Schocken [H].

—— (2007a), *Once Upon a Country: A Palestinian Life*, New York: Picador.

Ogen, Zfira (1986), "Yizhak Shami Haish Veyezirato" [Yizhak Shami: The Man and his Writing], *Bikoret Veparshanut*, 21, pp. 35–52 [H].

Oren, Michael (2004), *Shisha Yamim Shel Milhamah Hamaarach Sheshintah Et Penei Hamizrah Hatichon* [Six Days of War: June 1967 and the Making of the Modern Middle East], Or Yehuda: Devir [H].

Oz, Amos (1994), "Ir Zarah" [Foreign City], in Bareli Avi (ed.), *Yerushalayim Hahazuyah* [Divided Jerusalem], Jerusalem: Yad Yizhak Ben Zvi, pp. 294–7 [H].

Palestine Central Bureau of Statistics (2011), "Annual Statistics," http://www.pcbs.gov.ps/Portals/_pcbs/PressRelease/YOuth2011_E.pdf

Pappe, Ilan (2002), *Atzulat Haaretz Mishpahat Husseini Biographia Politit* [The Rise and Fall of a Palestinian Dynasty 1700–1948], Jerusalem: Mosad Bialik [H].

Paz, Yair (1998), "Shimur Hamoreshet Haadrichalit Bashchunot Hanetushot Leahar Milhemet Haazmaut" [Conservation of the Architectural Heritage of Abandoned Urban Neighborhoods following the War of Independence], *Katedra*, 88, pp. 95–134 [H].

Pedazur, Reuven (1996), *Nizhon Hamevucha Mediniyut Yisrael Bashtahim Leahar Milhemet Sheshet Hayamim* [The Triumph of Embarrassment: Israel and the Territories after the Six Day War], Tel Aviv: Bitan [H].

Porath, Yehoshua (1976), *Zemihat Hatenuah Haleumit Haaravit Falastinin 1918–1929* [The Emergence of the Palestinian Arab National Movement 1918–1929], Tel Aviv: Am Oved [H].

—— (1978), *Memehumot Lemeridah Hatnuah Haleumit Haaravit Falastinit 1929–1939*

BIBLIOGRAPHY

[The Palestinian Arab National Movement 1929–1939: From Riots to Rebellion], Tel Aviv: Am Oved [H].

Porath, Zipporah (1987), *Letters from Jerusalem 1947–1948*, Jerusalem: Association of Americans and Canadians in Israel.

Press, Yeshayahu (1936), *Ele Toldot Beit Hasefer Lehaazil Lebeit Lemel Beyerushalkayim* [History of Lemel School in Jerusalem], Jerusalem [H].

—— (1964), *Meah Shana Beyerushalayim* [One Hundred Years in Jerusalem], Jerusalem: Mass [H].

Price, Elizabeth (2001), "Jerusalem for Sale: Souvenirs, Tourism and the Old City," *The Jerusalem Quarterly*, 11–12, http://www.jerusalemquarterly.org/ViewArticle.aspx?id=198

Pundik, Nahum (1967), "Hahomot Habilti Nirot" [The Unvisible Walls], *Davar*, 14 July [H].

—— (1967a), "Yeh Yeh Bair Haatikah" [Yeh Yeh in the Old City], *Davar*, 15 Dec. [H].

Al-Qattan, Omar (2007), "The Secret Visitations of Memory," in Ahmad H. Sa'adi and Lila Abu-Lughod (eds), *Nakba Palestine 1948 and the Claims of Memory*, New York: Columbia University Press, pp. 191–206.

Rabau, Ziona (1984), *Ani Tel Avivit* [I Am from Tel Aviv], Tel Aviv: Mishrad Habitahon [H].

Rabinowitz, Dan (1997), *Overlooking Nazareth—The Ethnography of Exclusion in Galilee*, Cambridge: Cambridge University Press.

Radai, Itamar (2006), "Krisato Veakirato Shel Maamad Hebeinayim Haburgani Haravi Falastini Be-1948 Shchunat Katamon Mikreh Mivhan" [The Collapse and Exodus of the Palestinian Middle Class: Qatamon as a Case Study], in Baron Mordechai and Meir Hazan (eds), *Am Bemihamah Kovetz Mehkarim Al Hahevrah Haezrahit Bemilhemet Hazmaut* [Citizens at War: Studies on the Civilian Society during the Israeli War of Independence], Jerusalem: Yad Yizhak Ben Zvi, pp. 339–272 [H].

—— (2010), "Bein Hapatish Lasadan Krisatah Shel Hahevrah Haravit Falastinit Beyafo Unefilatah Shel Hair" [Between the Hammer and the Anvil: The Collapse of the Palestinian Society in Jaffa in 1948, and the Fall of the City], in Bar On Mordechai and Hazan Meir (eds), *Ezrahim Bamilhamah Kovetz Mehkarim Al Hahevrah Haezrahit Bemilhemet Hazmaut* [Citizens at War: Studies on the Civilian Society during the Israeli War of Independence], Jerusalem: Yad Yitzhak Ben-Zvi, pp. 120–49 [H].

Rappaport, Meron (2005), "Ir Refaim" [Ghost City], *Haaretz Weekly Supplement*, 17 Nov., http://www.haaretz.co.il/misc/1.1058996 [H].

—— (2007), "Hamivtsa Lepitzus Hamisgadim" [Blow-up the Mosques Operation], *Haaretz*, 4 July, http://www.haaretz.co.il/hasite/spages/878239.html [H].

Raz, Avi (2012), *The Bride and the Dowry Israel Jordan and the Palestinians in the Aftermath of the June 1967 War*, New Haven: Yale University Press.

Razy, Tammi (2009), *Yaldei Hahefker Hahazer Haahorit Shel Tel Aviv Hamandatorit* [Forsaken Children: The Backyard of Mandatory Tel Aviv], Tel Aviv: Am Oved [H].

Reiter, Yitzhak (2011), *Makom Mivtaho Shel Allah Parashat Beit Hakvarot Mamilla Vemuseion Hasovlanut Hamavak Al Hanof Hasimli Vehaphisy* [Allah's Safe Haven? The Controversy Surrounding the Mamilla Cemetery and the Museum of Tolerance], Jerusalem: Machon Yerushalayim Leheker Yisrael [H].

Reiter, Yitzhak, and Lehrs Lior (2010), *Sheikh Jarrah Harachat Mazav* [The Sheikh Jarrah Affair], Jerusalem: Machon Yerushalayim Leheker Yisrael [H].

Ricca, Simon (2007), *Reinventing Jerusalem: Israel's Reconstruction of the Jewish Quarter after 1967*, London and New York: I.B. Tauris.

Ricks, Thomas M. (2009), *Turbulent Times in Palestine—The Diaries of Khalil Totah*, Jerusalem and Ramallah: the Institute of Palestine Studies and PASSIA.

Rivlin, Yosef Yoel (1967), "Memhoz Hayaldut Bair Haatika" [From Childhood Area in the Old City], *Hauma*, 6, pp. 45–51 [H].

Romann, Michael (1986), *Jewish Kiryat Arba versus Arab Hebron*, Jerusalem: the West Bank Data Project.

Ronen, David (1989), *Shnat Hashabk* [The General Security Service Year], Tel Aviv: Misrad Habitahon [H].

BIBLIOGRAPHY

Rotbard, Sharon (2005), *Ir Levana Ir Shora* [White City, Black City], Tel Aviv: Babel [H].
Rotenberg, Hagit (2004), "Kol Yom Shihrur Yerushalayim" [Liberating Jerusalem Every Day], *Besheva*, 13 May, http://www.inn.co.il/Besheva/Article.aspx/2781 [H].
Rozenson, Yisrael (1993), *Zot Yerushalayim* [This is Jerusalem], Jerusalem: Misrad Hahinuch Vehatarbut [H].
Rubinstein, Danny (1968), "Yerushalayim Nichbesha Hlevatim Nisharu" [Jerusalem Occupied Dilemmas Still], *Davar*, 27 Aug. [H].
―――― (1992), *Or Leyerushalayim Sipurah Shel Hevrat Hahashmal Beyerushalayim* [Light to Jerusalem: The Story of the Electricity Company in Jerusalem], Israel Electricity Company [H].
―――― (2005), "Reichman Rakhash Leatsmo Tsatatsua" [Reichman Bought Himself a Toy], *Haaretz*, 18 Nov., http://www.haaretz.co.il/hasite/pages/ShArt.jhtml?itemNo=647169 [H].
Sakakini, Hala (1990), *Jerusalem and I—A Personal Record*, Jordan: The Economic Press.
―――― (1997), *The Years in Ramallah*, Jerusalem: The Commercial Press
Al-Sakakini, Khalil (1990), *Kazeh Ani Rabotai* [Such Am I O World], Jerusalem: Keter, 1990 [H].
Salahiyya, Muhammad Issa (2009), *al-Quda al-Sukan w-al-Ard al-Arab w-al-Yahud* [Jerusalem—Jewish and Arab Residents and Land 1858–1948], Beirut: Markaz al-Zaytun [A].
Samuel, Edwin (1970), *A Lifetime in Jerusalem*, London: Vallentine Mitchell.
Sanders, Edmund (2011), "East Jerusalem School Textbooks are a War of Words," *LA Times*, 24 Oct., http://www.latimes.com/news/nationworld/world/la-fg-palestinian-textbooks-20111025,0,216250,full.story
Sasson, Arieh (1981), *Yerushalayim Iri Hayei Anshei Yerushalayim* [Jerusalem My City, the Jerusalemites Life], Rehovot: Shoshanim [H].
Sasson, Avi (1995), "Haziara Benabi Rubin Beshalhei Hatkufah Haothmanint Vebetkufat Hamandat Habriti" [The Ziarah of Nabi Rubin at the Late Ottoman Period and during the British Mandate], *Hamizrah Hahadash*, 45, pp. 209–18 [H].
Sasson, Avraham (1998), "Sofrim Vehokrim Ivreyim Bameah Hatsha Esreh Vetrumatam Lamehkar Hageography History Shel Erez Yisrael Bameah Hetsha Esreh" [Nineteenth-Century Hebrew Writers and Scholars and their Contribution to the Geographic and Historical Studies of Eretz Yisrael of the Nineteenth Century], Dissertation, Ramat Gan: Bar Ilan Uiniversity [H].
Sasson, Moshe (2004), *Lelo Shulhan Agol* [Talking Peace], Or Yehuda: *Ma'ariv* [H].
Schneerson, Yehuda Leib (1980), *Ho Hebron Hebron* [Ho Hebron Hebron], Tel Aviv: Yair [H].
Scholch, Alexander (2006), *Palestine in Transformation 1856–1882, Studies in Social Economic and Political Development*, Washington, DC: Institute for Palestine Studies.
Segal, Hagai (1983), *Ahim Yekarim Korot Hamahteret Hayehudit* [Dear Brothers, the Jewish Underground Chronicle], Jerusalem: Keter [H].
Segev, Tom (1999), *Yemei Hakalaniyot Eretz Yisrael Betkufat Hamandat* [One Palestine, Complete: Jews and Arabs under the British Mandate], Jerusalem: Keter [H].
―――― (1999a), *One Palestine, Complete: Jews and Arabs under the British Mandate*, New York: Henry Holt.
―――― (2005), *1967 Vehaaretz Shinta Paneiha* [1967: Israel the War and the Year that Transformed the Middle East], Jerusalem: Keter [H].
―――― (2009), "Maaseh Beshtei Arim" [A Tale of Two Cities], *Haaretz Hashavua*, 13 Mar.
Sellick, Patricia (1994), "The Old City of Hebron: Can it be Saved?" *Journal of Palestine Studies*, 23, 4, pp. 69–82.
Sharab, Muhammad Hassan (2006), *al-Khalil Madinah Arabiyah Filastiniyah* [Hebron—An Arab Palestinian City], Amman: al-Ahaliyah [A].
Sharabi, Hisham (2008), *Embers and Ashes—Memoirs of an Arab Intellectual*, Northampton: Olive Branch Press.
Shashar, Michael (1997), *Milhemet Hayom Hashvie* [The Seventh Day War], Tel Aviv: Sifriyat Hapoalim [H].

BIBLIOGRAPHY

Shenhav, Yehuda (2003), *Hayehudim Haaravim Leumiyut Dat Veetniyut* [The Arab Jews: A Postcolonial Reading of Nationalism, Religion, and Ethnicity], Tel Aviv: Am Oved [H].

Shiryon, Yizhak (1943), *Zichronot* [Memories], Jerusalem [H].

Shlush, Aharon (1991), *Megalabiya Lecova Tembel Sipurah Shel Mishpaha* [From Galabiya to Tembel Hat: Story of a Family], Tel Aviv [H].

Shlush, Yosef Eliyahu (1931), *Parashat Hayai* [My Life Story], Tel Aviv, http://benyehuda.org/chelouche/parashat_xayay.html [H].

Shohat, Zipi (2009), "Tosca Daniel Oren Haabir Shel Puccini" [Tosca Daniel Oren Puccini Knight], *Haaretz*, 23 Apr. [H].

Shragai, Nadav (1995), *Har Hameriva Hamavak Al Har Habayit Yehudim Vemuslemim Dat Vepolitika Meaz 1967* [The Contested Mount: The Struggle Over Temple Mount—Jews and Muslims, Religion and Politics since 1967], Jerusalem: Keter [H].

Shushan, Avraham (2001), "Hatahlich Haamami Shel Hitkadshut Kvarim Beyisrael" [The Popular Way of Cemetery Sanctification in Israel], *Kivunim Hadashim*, 4, pp. 153–70 [H].

Siksakk, Aiman (2004), "Hem Meabu Gosh" [They Are From Abu Gosh], *Haaretz Tarbut Vesifrut*, 10 Sep. [H].

—— (2004a), "Tapuhim Bedvash Behinam" [Apple with Honey for Free], *Haaretz Tarbut Vesifrut*, 1 Oct. [H].

—— (2004b), "Hasufganiyah Vehamuazen" [The Donut and the Muezin], *Haaretz Tarbut Vesifrut*, 24 Dec. [H].

—— (2005), "Ma Sheelef Bialikim Lo Yerzu" [What a Thousand Bialiks Would Not Want], *Haaretz Tarbut Vesifrut*, 27 July [H].

—— (2005a), "Ani Hasiba Sheavarta Lagur Beyafo" [I Cause You Moving to Live in Jaffa], *Haaretz Tarbut Vesifrut*, 16 Dec. [H].

Simons, Chaim (2003), *Three Years in a Military Compound—Reminiscences of a Hebron Settler*, Kiryat Arba: C. Simons.

Sivan, Rina (1983), *Migdal David Museion Hair Yerushalayim* [David's Citadel—Jerusalem's Municipal Museum], Jerusalem: Museion Hair Yerushalayim [H].

Snir, Reuven (2006), "Arabs of the Mosaic Faith: Chronicle of a Cultural Extinction Foretold," *Die Welt des Islam*, 46, pp. 43–60.

Soueif, Ahdaf (2010), "The Dig Dividing Jerusalem," *The Guardian*, 26 May http://www.guardian.co.uk/world/2010/may/26/jerusalem-city-of-david-palestinians-archaeology

Stern, Gabriel (1986), *Al Hamirpeset Shel Musa Hagingi* [On Musa the Red Haired Balkoni], Tel Aviv: Al Hamishmar [H].

Stern, Marik (2010), *Besdot Zarim Defusei Interakzia Bein Yisraelim Lefalastinim Bemithamei Mishar Meoravim Beyerushalayim* [In Foreign Fields: Interaction Patterns between Israelis and Palestinians in Mixed Commercial Zones in Jerusalem], Jerusalem: Mehkarei Floersheimer Hauniversita Haivrit, http://www.fips.org.il/Site/p_home/home_he.asp [H].

Storrs, Ronald (1937), *The Memories of Sir Ronald Storrs*, New York: Putnam's Sons.

—— (1938), *Zichronot* [Memoirs], Tel Aviv: Mizpeh [H].

Talmi, Menachem (1979), *Tmunot Yafoeyot* [Jaffa Portraits], Tel Aviv: Ma'ariv [H].

Tamari, Salim (2007), "Bourgeois Nostalgia and the Abandoned City," in Daniel Monterescu and Dan Rbinowitz (eds), *Mixed Towns—Trapped Communities, Historical Narratives, Spatial Dynamics, Gender Relations and Cultural Encounters in Palestinian–Israeli Towns*, Aldershot: Ashgate, pp. 35–49.

—— (2009), *Mountain against the Sea—Essays on Palestinian Society and Culture*, Berkeley: University of California Press.

Tamari, Salim, and Issam Nassar (eds) (2003), *al-Quds al-Othmaniyyah Fi Mudhakirat al-Jawhariyyeh* [Ottoman Jerusalem in al-Jawhariyyeh Memoirs], Jerusalem: Muassat al-Dirasat al-Maqdisiyyeh [A].

Tamari, Salim, and Rema Hammami (1998), "Virtual Returns to Jaffa," *Journal of Palestine Studies*, 27, 4, pp. 65–79.

Tavger, Ben Zion (1999), *Hebron Sheli* [My Hebron], Jerusalem: Shamir [H].

—— (2009), *My Hebron*, Hebron.

BIBLIOGRAPHY

Taylor, Paul (2008), "Saudi Prince Offers Israelis a Vision of Peace," *New York Times*, 1 Feb., http://www.nytimes.com/2008/01/21/world/africa/21iht-saudi.4.9385352.html?scp=1&sq=TURKI%20JANUARY%2021,%202008&st=cse

Tessler, Mark (2009), *A History of the Israeli–Palestinian Conflict*, 2nd edn, Bloomington and Indianapolis: Indiana University Press.

The Knesset Center for Information and Research (May 2010), *Maarechet Hahinuch Bemizrah Yerushalayim—Kitot Limud Vetochniyot Limudim* [East Jerusalem Education System—Classes and Curriculum], Jerusalem, http://www.knesset.gov.il/mmm/data/pdf/m02507.pdf [H].

Tortrick, Rebecca L. (2000), *The Limits of Coexistence—Identity Politics in Israel*, Ann Arbor: University of Michigan Press.

Toubbeh, Jamil I. (1998), *Day of the Long Night—A Palestinian Refugee Remembers the Nakba*, Jefferson, NC: McFarland.

Tsifroni, Gabriel (1990), "Kol Ehad Vehagernika Shelo" [Each One and His Guernica], *Igra*, 3, pp. 277–95 [H].

Tsur, Muki, and Sharon Rotbrad (eds) (2010), *Lo Beyafo Velo Betel Aviv Sipurim Eduyot Veteudot Meshchunat Shapira* [Neither in Jaffa nor in Tel Aviv: Stories, Testimonies and Documents from Shapira Neighborhood], Tel Aviv: Babel [H].

Ushpiz, Ariela (1992), *Ajami—Monologim Shel Toshavim* [Ajami Residents' Monologues], Tel Aviv [H].

Vaadat, Shamgar (1994), "Vaadat Hahakirah Leinyan Hatevach Bemearat Hamachpelah Behebron 1994, Din Veheshbon" [Shamgar Commission Report on the Patriarch Cave in Hebron Massacre], Jerusalem [H].

Vitullo, Anita (2003), "People Tied to Place—Strengthening Cultural Identity in Hebron's Old City," *Journal of Palestine Studies*, 33, 1, pp. 68–83.

Weigert, Gideon (1975), *The Histadruth in East Jerusalem—Seven years of Trial and Error 1967–1974*, Jerusalem: Weigert.

——— (2001), *Hayai Im Hafalastinim* [My Life with the Palestinians], Haifa: Universitat Haifa [H].

Weiller-Pollak, Dana (2010), "Dayar Hamishne Amidar" [Amidar the Second Resident], *Haaretz Weekly*, 20 Nov. [H].

Weinstein, Assi (1987), *Hamisha Yeladim Vekol Yerushalayim* [Five Kids and Whole Jerusalem], Tel Aviv: Modan [H].

Weiss, Aric (2009), "Tel Aviv Hogeget Yafo Mamash Lo" [Tel Aviv Celebrates Jaffa Not At All], *Ma'ariv Sofshavua*, 9 May http://www.nrg.co.il/online/1/ART1/887/176.html [H].

Weiss, Yfaat (2010), *Wadi Salib Haocha Vehanifkad* [Wadi Salib—A Confiscated Memory], Jerusalem: Van Leer Vehkibutz Hameuhad [H].

Wiesel, Eli (1968), "Halomo Shel Kovesh Yerushalaim" [The Dream of Jerusalem Occupier], in Bondy Ruth, Ohad Zmorah, and Refael Bashan (eds), *Lo Al Haherev Levadah* [Not Just on Sword], Bat Yam: Levin-Epshtein, pp. 202–7 [H].

Yaffe, Aharon (2009), "Zoanim Beyerushalayim" [Gypsies in Jerusalem], *Kivunim Hadashim*, 21, pp. 229–37 [H].

Yahav, Dan (1996), "Migdal David [Hamezudah] Baomanut" [David's Tower [the Citadel] in Art], http://www.acpr.org.il/nativ/articles/1996_5_yahav.pdf [H].

——— (2004), *Yafo Kalat Hayam Meir Roshah Leshchunot Oni* [Jaffa the Sea Bride—From Major City to Slama], Tel Aviv: Tamuz [H].

Yazbak, Mahmoud (2010), "Holy Shrines (Maqamat) in Modern Palestine/Israel and the Politics of Memory," in Marshal Breger, Yitzhak Reiter, and Leonard Hammer (eds), *Holy Places in the Israeli–Palestinian Conflict—Confrontation and Co-Existence*, London: Routledge, pp. 231–48.

——— (2010), "The Islamic Waqf in Yaffa and the Urban Space from Ottoman State to the State of Israel," *Makan*, 2, pp. 23–46.

——— (2011), "The Muslim Festival of Nabi Rubin in Palestine—From Religious Festival to Summer Resort," *Holy Land Studies*, 10, 2, pp. 169–98.

BIBLIOGRAPHY

Yehoshua, A.B. (1990), *Mar Mani* [Mr Mani], Tel Aviv: Hakibitz Hameuhad [H].
—— (1992), *Mr. Mani*, London: P. Halban.
Yehoshua, Yaakov (1977), *Yerushalayim Tmol Shilshom* [Jerusalem of Yesterday and the Day before Yesterday], Jerusalem: Mass.
—— (1979), *Habayit Veharehov Beyerushalayimm Hayeshanah* [Home and Street in Old Jerusalem], Jerusalem: Mass [H].
—— (1979a), *Yaldut Beyerushalayim Hayeshanah* [Childhood in Old Jerusalem], Jerusalem: Mass [H].
—— (1982), *Yerushalayim Tmol Shilshom* [Jerusalem of Yesterday and the Day before Yesterday], vol. 3, Jerusalem: 1981 [H].
—— (1988), *Yerushalayim Hayeshanah Baayin Ubalev* [Old Jerusalem Seen and Appreciated], Jerusalem: Keter [H].
Yellin, David (1973), *Yrushalayim Shel Tmol* [Jerusalem of Yesterday], http://benyehuda.org/yellin/temol.html [H].
Yellin, Ita (1979), *Lezezaai—Zichronotay* [To My Children—My Memoirs], Jerusalem: Mass [H].
Yellin, Yehoshua (1991), *Zichronot Leben Yerushalayim* [Memoirs of a Jerusalemite], Jerusalem: Ariel [H].
Yizhar, S. (1964), *Sepurei Mishor* [Stories of a Plain], Tel Aviv: Hakibutz Hameuhad [H].
—— (1992), *Mikdamot* [Preliminaries], Tel Aviv: Zmorah Bitan [H].
—— (2007), *Preliminaries*, New Milford: Toby Press.
Ynet (2008), "Villa of Contention," 21 Dec., http://www.ynetnews.com/articles/0,7340,L-3641731,00.html
—— (2009), "Belgium to Pay Rent in Jerusalem," 16 Dec., http://www.ynet.co.il/english/articles/0,7340,L-3820280,00.html
Zekharyah, Shabtai (1985), *Batim Umosadot Yehudim Barova Hamuslemi Beyerushalayim Hatikah—Rova Rehov Hebron Harova Hayehudi Hayashan* [Jewish Homes and Institutions in the Muslim Quarter of the Old City Jerusalem, Hebron Street—The Old Jewish Quarter], Jerusalem: Haagudah Al Mishmar Yerushalayim.
—— (1998), *Yerushalayim Habilti Nodaat—Prakim Betoldot Hayishuv Hayehudi Bair Haatikah Badorot Hahronim* [The Unknown Jerusalem—Chapters in the History of the Jewish Settlement in the Old City During Latter Generations], Beit El [H].
—— (2002), *Soharim Ubaalei Melacha Yehudim Beyerushalayim Haatikah Baavar—Ishim Dmuyot Veatarim* [Past Jewish Merchants and Craftsmen in Old Jerusalem—Personalities Characters and Places], Jerusalem: Tsur Ot [H].

Links to Map Sites

Jerusalem Historical maps and photos up to 1967 in Martin Gilbert, Jerusalem Illustrated History Atlas, Oxford 1987: http://www.scribd.com/doc/19551586/JERUSALEM-Illustrated-History
Present Jerusalem: http://www.goisrael.com/Tourism_Eng/Tourist%20Information/Planning%20your%20trip/Online%20tools/Documents/JerusalemNew.pdf
Collection of Jerusalem maps: https://www.google.co.il/search?tbm=isch&source=univ&sa=X&ei=bqe6UvC0OYLB7AaUzICgCg&ved=0CHsQsAQ&biw=1092&bih=513&q=Jerusalem%20map%201948%20zochrot#q=Jerusalem%20map%20before%201948&tbm=isch
Hebron 1912 map: http://www.lib.utexas.edu/maps/historical/hebron_1912.jpg
Present Hebron map: http://www.btselem.org/sites/default/files2/map/200705_hebron_center_map_eng.pdf
Also: http://www.ochaopt.org/documents/ocha_opt_hebron_h2_area_closure_map_october_2010_a0_web.pdf
Collection of Hebron maps and photos: https://www.google.co.il/search?tbm=isch&source=univ&sa=X&ei=bqe6UvC0OYLB7AaUzICgCg&ved=0CHsQsAQ&biw=1092&bih=513&

BIBLIOGRAPHY

q=Jerusalem%20map%201948%20zochrot#q=Hebron%20West%20Bank%20map&tbm=isch

Jaffa 1912 map: http://www.lib.utexas.edu/maps/historical/jaffa_1912.jpg

Jaffa and Tel Aviv on the eve of the 1948 war: http://zochrot.org/en/content/about-map-tel-aviv-and-its-palestinian-villages

Collection of Jaffa maps and photos: https://www.google.co.il/search?q=jaffa+map+1948&tbm=isch&tbo=u&source=univ&sa=X&ei=H6a6UqTiA7PQ7AbGloDQDg&ved=0CCoQsAQ&biw=1092&bih=513

INDEX

'Abdallah of Transjordan 115
'Abd al-Gahni Street 195
'Abd al-Ghani Kamleh 181
'Abd al-Hadi 'Awni 80
'Abd al-Mu'atazim al-'Alami
'Abd al-Nasser Gamal 158 161–163 170
'Abd al-Raziq 'Adnan 264
'Abduh Mohammad Street 79
Abkarius Mikhail 47
Abu Ajwa Ahmed 173
Abu Ghosh Salim 48
Abu Jabein Khairi 59
Abu Kabir 172
Abu Laban Ahmed 177
Abu Nasser Nimri 207
Abu Shehadeh Isma'il 59, 253
Abu Tor 5, 6, 152, 178, 183 196–197 241–242
Abu Zayad Basam 196
Abu Zuluf Mahmoud 166, 230
Acre VIII
al-Adasi Malikah 59
al-Afghani Jamal al-Din Street 79
Aflalo David 36
Ahdut Ha'Avodah 107
Amiga Musa 101
al-Alami Musa 80
Agnon-Golan Dafna 47 243–246
Agnon Shmuel Yosef 47

Ahimeir Ora 181–182
Ajami 68, 194 196 249–252
Al-Akhbar 63
'Alami Musa 134
al-'Alami Sa'ad al-Din 240
Alaska Café 82
Albina Josef 82
Alhambra Cinema 236
Allenby Edmond 11, 86, 96
Allenby Square and Street 6, 81 122 127, 152
Alliance Israelite Universelle 24, 51, 81
Allon Yigal 143, 153 216, 221, 225–227 270 275
Alterman Natan 5, 124
American Colony 29–30, 31, 167, 192
Amdursky Yehiel 26, 45
American Tourists 9–10, 23
Amir Eli XI 174 175 234–234
'Amro Yunes 272
Amzaleg Ben-Zion 71
Amzaleg Yosef 60
Andreus Amin 180 255
Andromeda Hill 250
Anglo-Palestine Bank 56, 81, 105
Antebi Albert 61
Antonius George 85
Antonius Katy 85 134 235

INDEX

Assaf Mohammad 104
Arab Chamber of Commerce 221–222
Arab Club 68 104
Arab Jamusin 70
Arab Nationalism 111–112
Arafat Yasir 163
Arens Moshe 276
Aran Zalman 153
al-'Arif 'Arif 80, 94
Arab Othman Bank 82
Arlosoroff Haim 114
Aroches 26
Artists Quarter 254
Ashkenazi Jews 21, 27, 32, 36, 40–42, 46, 54, 58, 60, 61, 63
Association to Maintain Historical Sites in the Land of Israel 34
Atara Café 82 131 134
Atara LeYoshna 261–262
Ateret Cohanim 261–263
'Awad Anton 178–179
Augusta Victoria 156 186
Austrian Hospice Hotel 192
Avi Yona Michael 185
Avicenna Street 6
Avisar David 95
Avneri Uri 169–170
Azuri Najib 36

Bab al-Hutah 36
Bagdad IX
Baghdadi Café 70
Bagio Haim 54
Balfour 63, 94, 96, 97, 104, 112–113, 117
al-Bakri Yasin 167–168, 239
Ballas Shimon 142
Baiover Berl 26
Banet David Zvi 80
Bachar Avraham 253
Bechar Nissim 34
Barclay's Bank 25, 81
Barkai Binyamin 57–58
Barker Evelyn Hugh 134

Barghuthi 'Omar Salah 82, 87
Beit Dajan
Beit Hadassah 275 279
Beit Hanina 167 197–198
Beit Orot 156
Beit Safafa 197
Baq'a 29, 47, 52, 78–80, 125, 129 178 196
Barakat Fa'iq 164
Baramki 191–192
Barel Zvi 280
al-Bashurah Café 45
Bat Shalom 243–246
Batei Mahseh 41
Bathhouses 46
Batito Yosef 75
Batrak Street 25, 42
Bauhaus 70 194
Bayt Jubrin 120
Be'erot Yitzhak Street 80
Begin Menachem 153–154
Beit HaKerem 78
Beit Ya'akov 24
Ben Atar Haim 62
Ben Gurion David 124, 153 168 180 247–248
Ben Maimon Street 47
Ben Maimon Ya'akov 89
Ben Naim 26
Ben Shimon Amram 254–255
Ben Yair Michael XI, 32
Ben Yehuda 82, 87, 128
Ben Zvi Yitzhak 55
Beni Tzion 33
Bentov Mordechai 154 165
Benvenisti Meron XI, 16, 17 164–165 167–168, 177, 217–218 226, 230–234 236 241–242, 246
Berenson Zvi 200–201
Bergman Hugo 30
Berman Bakery 27
Bethlehem 157, 161
Bezalel Art Academy 14, 15, 28
Bikur Holim Hospital 81
al-Bina Josef 83

INDEX

Biram Arthur 87
Bisharat George 199–201
Blau Amram 100
B'nai Brith Library 28
Boehm Aryeh 30
Bokovsky Michael 207
Borton William 11
Braudel Fernand 3
Brenner Yosef Hayyim 55
Bristol Gardens Café 25
Brit Shalom 79
Bruner Ilan 157
Bukharin Neighborhood 100
Burg Avrum XI
Burg Yosef 47
Burqan Mohammad Sa'id 187–188
Butrus Street 68, 75

Cairo IX
Calvino Italo 188 258
Can'an Habib 56, 123
Can'an Hamdi 163
Can'an Tawfiq 80, 87, 125 134
Capelnian's 82
Capucci Hilarion 162
HaCarmel Street 124
Cave of the Patriarchs 14, 44, 50 55, 57, 91, 143, 267–270
Central Bus Station Jerusalem 7
Central Post Office 81
Chancellor Street 81
Charteris Martin 117 133–134
Chizik Yitzhak 177
Churchill Winston 115
Citizenship and residency for Jerusalemites 174–175, 223–225 242–243
Clock Square 68 128
Cohen Ben Zion 101
Cohen Haim 187–188
Cohen Yonah 31
College des Freres 59
Confino Alon VII
Cordoba School 275

Custodian of Abandoned Properties 181 190

Dabash Ben-Zion 45
Dai'is Nadi 131
Damascus Gate 7, 8, 25, 27, 29, 31
Danon Nissim 50, 93
David's Citadel 11–17
Dayan Moshe 47 157 163 184–185, 226, 234 267–269 275 280–282
al-Dajani 'Arif 118
al-Dajani al-Daudi 'Abdallah 47
al-Dajani Fuad Isma'il 194 196
al-Dajani Hassan Sadki 30
Dajani Hospital 194 196
Dajani Issa 48
al-Dajani Jamal
Diab Nafa' 172
Dizengoff Meir 69, 104
Dunieh Tovia 83
al-Dusturiyah School 27

Eban Abba 165–166
Eden cinema 72, 82
Eder David 113
Edison cinema 82, 125–126
Ekron 68
'Ein Karem 79, 120 153, 185 193
Elad 40, 259–260 263–264
Elazar Ya'kov 36, 37, 38, 43
Elbaz David, 45
Elkayam Mordechai 103
Elkayam Yehoshua 60
Elmaliah Avraham 60
Eliyahu Yosef 60
Elyashar Eliahu 38, 62
Elyashar Menashe Hai 34, 52–53, 58, 81, 113
Elyashar Ya'akov Shaul 42
Emek Shaveh 260
Emir Abdallah Street 80
Eshel Avraham 31
Eshko Levi 143 157–170 174 181 185 186 229 239

INDEX

East Jerusalem Development Company 152
Etz Haim 42
Europa Café 82 134
Evelina de Rothschild School 39
Even Yisrael 24
Ezra Ya'akov 101–102
Ezrat Yisrael 24

al-Faisal Turki X
Faisal–Weizmann Agreement 115
Falastin Newspaper 20, 26, 66, 102
Farhat-Naser Sumaya 243–246
Farhi David 155 230
Fast Hotel 81, 117 201
al-Farabi Street 79
Festival of the Tamarisk 54
Fink's 130–131
Flavius Josephus 13 195
Florence 286
Florentin 69, 70, 73
Frankel Naomi 271–272
Franz Joseph Emperor 23
Freij Elias 159
French Hill 165 242
Frumkin Gad 26, 38, 42, 43–44, 52, 97, 113, 127
Frumkin Israel Dov 43
Frutiger Johannes 6

Gaberdian's 82
Gazit Shlomo XI
Gemilut Hesed Alley 43
German Colony 79–80 125 128 178 196 201
al-Ghussei Nuzha 81
Ginzburg Carlo XI
Goitein Shlomo Dov 79
Gorenberg Gershom XI
Gozlan Mohammad 210
Gradstein Rivka 48
Grand New Hotel 26
Graves Richard 116–117
Greek Colony 79, 178, 193
Gretz Tzvi Street 80

Gur Mordechai 143–144
Guri Haim 12, 76, 124–125
Gutman Nahum 76
Gypsies 29

Hadad Elias 87
Hadassah Hospital 47
Hadawi Sami 79
al-Hadi Shaira 240
Hadoar Café 25
Haetzni Elyakim 276
Haganah 107 129
Hai Mas'ud 59
Haifa VIII
Hahavatzelet Newspaper 26
Haherut Newspaper 61
Halevy Assaf 51
Hamagen 60
Hamagid Street 80
Hamami Ahmed 73
Hamami Rima 203–205 266
Hamburger Haim 53
Hamelitz Street 80
Hamburger Meir 42
Hamburger Yair 88
Hamelitz Street 80
Hammudah Sahar 199
Haim Baruch Hotel 104
Han al-Zayt Street 44
Hananya Ya'akov 70
HaPoel HaTz'ir 55, 104
Hareven Shulamit 178–179
Haroun al-Rashid 181 199–201
Hasan Bek 252–253
Hashalshelet Street 43
Hashkafa Newspaper 26
Hasson Haim 62
Hatikvah 69, 70, 126–127
Hatzefirah Street 80
Havilio Sweets 26
Hayarkon Street 5
Hayl Mishmar Street 79
Hayl Nashim Street 79–80
Hazan Eliyahu 59
Hazvi Newspaper 26

INDEX

Haykal Yusif 180
Hebrew University 57 219
Hebron Road 5, 6, 242
Hebron Rehabilitation Committee 283–384
Hebron Yeshiva 56–58
Hefetz Meir 38
Hesse Max 130–131
Herod the Great 13, 91
Herzliya Hebrew Gymnasium 48, 56
Herzog Chaim 184
Hill of Evil Counsel 5
Hildesheimer Wolfgang 135
Hilmi Pasha 85
Hiriyya 172
de-Hirsch Maurice 61
Hirschberg Haim Ze'ev 177
Hisin Haim 103–104
Histadrut 219–220
Hobsbawm Eric XII 139
Hoffman Marvin Arthur and Adina 175
Hoisman Shimon 53
Holy Sepulcher 25 50 214
Hourani Albert 134–135
Hurva Synagogue 215–216
al-Hussayni 'Abd al-Qadir 198
al-Hussayni Amin 44–45, 83, 94, 99, 100, 121, 168, 198 236
al-Hussayni Amina 240
al-Hussayni Ibrahim Sa'id 33
al-Hussayni Ishaq Musa 189, 197–198
al-Hussayni Jamil 35
al-Hussayni Jawad 81
al-Hussayni Mohammad Salah 30
al-Hussayni Mussa Kazem 41, 94, 95, 113, 118, 198
al-Hussayni Mustafa 34
al-Hussayni 'Omar 93
al-Hussayni Rabah 33
al-Hussaynin Sa'id 51
al-Hussayni Salim 33, 35, 41
al-Hussayni Tewfiq 34
al-Hussayni Taher 33

Ibn Batuat Street 6, 30
Ibn Khaldun Street 6 79
Ibn al-Khatab 'Omar 12, 13
Ibn Yunus 'Abdallah 93
Ibrahim Pasha Street 79
IDF 172, 180 181 267
Ignatief Michael 132
Igum 260
Intifada 85 257–258, 288–289
'Isa al-'Isa 62
Israel Defense Forces 6
Israel Land Authority 186 251 257 260
Ivri Binyamin 51
IZL 123–124, 126 128 130

Jabaliyya 68 173 180, 194
Jabal Mukabar 197
al-Ja'abari Mohammad 'Ali 159, 280–282
Jabotinsky Ze'ev 80, 95
Jacobson Abigail XI
Jadai Fakhri 59
Jaffa's Boy Scout 89
Jaffa Trade and economy 65–66
Jaffa Road 3, 5, 6, 23, 24, 25, 28, 82, 140
Jam'ah al-Islamiyyah 76
Jarisah 70
Jawhariyyeh Café 82
Jawhariyyeh Tawfik 79
Jawhariyyeh Wasif 45, 48
Jebusite Music Festival 87
Jerusalem Brigade Street 6
Jerusalem Communities 1905 32–33
Jerusalem Municipality Culture and Names Committee 12
Jerusalem Municipal Museum 16–18
Jerusalem population 76–77, 175–176

INDEX

Jerusalem Small Business Association 220–222
Jerusalem Women's Center 243–246
Jerusalem Workers Council 219–220
Jewish Agency 180 181
Jewish Citrus Growers Association 73
Jewish Colonization Association 61, 104
Jewish Demography 143, 151
Jewish Quarter rebuilt 187–188, 214–217
Jewish Quarter Development Company 215–216
al-Jihad al-Muqaddas 122
Jordan 69, 92, 154, 155, 159–170
Judt Tony XII
Julian Street 81–82

Kahanov Nehemiah 42
Kakal Street 126
Kalvarisky Haim Margaliot 87
Kantrowitz Avraham 120–121
Kapeliuk Menachem 89
Kapulski Café 82
Kalisher Street 74
Karlinski Haim 57
al-Karmel Newspaper 102
Karmi Ghada 21, 78 129
Katinka Baruch 83–85
Katoul Gibril 131
Kendall Henri 185
Keith-Roach Edward 99
Kerem Temanim 68
Keren Kayemet 14, 16, 78
al-Khalidi Amina 81
al-Khalidi Dawish 47
al-Khalidi Fuad 47
al-Khalidi Husayn Fakhri 119
al-Khalidi Lina 240
al-Khalidi Othman 51
Khalidi Rashid 26
al-Khalidi Taher 47

Khalidi Walid 134
Khartoum Summit 159, 162–163
al-Khatib Anwar 158 161
al-Khatib Rukhi 143, 155, 184
King David Hotel 17, 83, 86, 128 134–135 166–168
King George Street 140
King Hussein 143, 153, 156 158 161 163
Kinor Tzion 72
Kiryat Arba XII 267–282
Kisch Frederick 97
Klausner Yosef 65, 67, 144–146
Klein Shmuel Street 80
Klein Rivka XI
Kleiger Israel 30
Klonski Eliezer 53
Klugman committee 262–263
Knesset Information and Research Center 227
Kochav Yerushalayim 220
Kollek Teddy 12, 143, 155–157 167 184–185, 188 218 223 230–234 260 269–270 288
Konstrum Shalom 6
Kosover Mordechai 41
Kostler Arthur 111
Krenitzi Avraham 104
Krikorian Photo 27
Kulliyyat al-Nahad 52
Kupat Am Eretzyisraeli Bank 82

Lag BeOmer 48
Lagerlof Selma 8
Ladino 45, 67
Lahat Shlomo 184–185 249
Landau Hannah Yehudit 80, 87
Laskov Shulamit 51, 52, 78
Legacy Hotel 192
LEHI underground 58, 126 128
Leiden 285–286
Lemel School 27, 51
Levanon Eliyahu Yehoshua 58, 101
Levi Rafi XI 161 186 234–236
Levi Yitzhak 53

INDEX

Levin Alter 51–52, 87
Levinger Moshe 269, 279–280
Lifta 153, 185
al-Liftawi Salah 47
Lilienblum Street 72
Lincoln Street 167
Lisan 63
Literary Club 68, 104
Litvinsky Moshe 105–106
Lod/ Lydda 172 180
Looting and expropriation 177–211
Loretz Café 27
Lunz Avraham Moshe 54
Lunz-Boltin Hannah 37
Lusidu's 81
Luria Ben Zion 12

Ma'aleh Adumim 157 187
Ma'aqhelah Alley 44
Ma'aref Café 82
Madafat Ibrahim 91
Malul Avraham 172
Magnes Judah Leib 30, 52
Mahaneh Yehuda 24, 82, 102
Mahaneh Yisrael 36
Makor Barukh 129
Maliha 79 120 153 185, 227
Malul Nisim 60–63, 66, 172
Mamilla 3–4, 7–8, 11, 24, 28, 36, 52, 81, 83, 100, 122, 127, 130 -131, 190 201
Mani Eliyahu 56
Mani Menashe 50, 54, 56, 81 210
Mani Mikhaiel 56
Mani Yosef 56
Mapai 172
Manshiyya 70, 71, 74, 75 107 124 127 249–250, 252–253
Mantura Layla 127
al-Maqased al-Khiriyya al-Islamiyya 252
Mar Elias Monastery 8
Mas Reuven 78, 182
Mashaiof Shmuek Meir 29 -30
Matalon Moshe 60, 70

Matson Eric 11
McEwan Ian 213
Meah She'arim 36, 100
Medini Hezkizhu 55
Meir Golda 162, 181 183 218 229
Melissanda Street 82
Menachem Ezra 50
de-Menasce Felix 97
Mendel Aharon 59
Meyer Ludwig 81
Meyuhas Yosef 30, 39–40, 43, 59 210
Migdal Joel XI
Mikveh Israel 51, 126
Ministerial Committee on Jerusalem Affairs 154
Ministry of Commerce and Industry 86
Ministry of Education 225–227, 240
Ministry of Interior 223
Ministry of Health 218
Ministry of Interior 173, 176
Ministry of Labor and Welfare 218 220
Ministry of Minorities 172 174 181
Ministry of Religion 214–215 240
Mix marriage 47–48
Mizrahi Elazar 39
Mizrahi Eliahu 209
Moial David 60
Moial Esther 60
Moial Shimon 59–62
Montefiore [neighborhood] 70
Montefiore 42, 171
Morgenthau Henry Jr. 34
Mughrabi Quarter 96, 97, 175 184–185
al-Mukhtar 25, 224–225
al-Muna Café 45
Museum on the Seam 191
Muslim-Christian Association 67, 104
Muslim Ensemble Orchestra 89

INDEX

Musrara 29, 78, 80, 126–127, 178 193 196
Mustafa Muhammad 72

Nadim 'Abdallah 60
Nahalat Shimon 31–32
Nahalat Shiv'ah 23 -24, 42, 126
Namir Mordechai
Napoleon 11
Narkis Uzi 141, 155 157 184–185 275
Nashashibi Fakhri 81 134
Nashashibi Jajati 34
Nashashibi Nasser al-Din 134
Nashashibi Raghib 6, 47, 81, 83, 95, 114, 118
Nashashibi Rene 47
Nathseh 'Abd al-Nabi 276
National Emergency Committee 180
Nature and Park Authority 185
Nea Church 214
Neveh Shalom 104
Neve Tzedek 71, 72
Navon Joseph 6
Nazareth VIII
Nebi Musa 49, 50, 85, 92, 93, 94, 95, 107, 118
Nebi Rubin 87–90
Nebi Samuel 49
Negba Street 80
Negotiating with Palestinian Leaders 157–170
Newman Robert 156
Neve Tzedek 33, 68, 74
Nisan Beq 31, 100
Nordiya 124
Notre Dame 177
Nusseibeh Anwar 81, 158–159, 161–162 164–166, 175 224
Nusseibeh Sari 237
Nuzha 68 178

Ohel Shlomo 24
Olmert Ehud 228

Olshan Yitzhak 82
Open House 192–194
Oren Daniel 48
Ottomans VII, IX, 11, 12, 13, 19, 20, 22–23, 24, 28, 33, 34, 38, 49, 51, 53, 56, 60–61, 65, 72, 75, 98, 104, 111–112, 117–118
Oz Amos 146–147

Palace Hotel 83–85
Palestinian Authority 227
Palestinian Central Bureau of Statistics 151, 227
Palestinian Executive Committee 122
Palestinian Nationalism VIII
Palestine Oriental Society 86
Palestine Symphony Orchestra 82
Palmon Yehoshua 223
Palumba of Rhodes 47
Pape Ilan 97
Paratrooper Road 6
Park Lane Hotel 177
Peres 180 182 269–270
Peri Yoram XI
Piamenta Yehuda 52
Piccadilly Café 52, 82, 201
Pilgrims 8–9
Pinto Diana XI
Pisgat Ze'ev 188
PLO 149 163 227
Po'alei Tzion 104
Porat Tzipora 128
Pres Yeshayahu 40–41
Princess Mary Street 81–82, 128
Pro-Jerusalem Society 15
Prophets Street 28
Prostitutes 75, 240
Public Work Department 82
Purim 48, 58

Qabani Ibrahim 78
Qabatiyyeh Canaanite Festival 87
Qaloniyah 33

INDEX

Qaryat al-'Anab 120
Qatamon 29, 31 78–80 127–129 131–132 147, 178, 181, 196 201 227 233
Qatan 'Abd al-Muhsan and Omar 205–206
Qatan Henry 82 134
al-Qawasma 'Ali 283
al-Quds Newspaper 20, 26

Rabau Tziona 72, 109
al-Rabita Liri'ayat Shuon 'Arab Yafa 249–253
Rachel Yanait 55
Rafaelowitz Yeshayahu 44
Ramadan Nights 45–46
Ramallah 157
Ramat Eshkol 165
Ras al-'Amud 29, 186
Red Crescent Society 45
Rechtman Chava 48
Refugees 174, 176–211 264–265, 289–290
Reichman Family 86
Reiner Elchanan XI
Rehavia 30, 78, 128 130
Reich Ronny 259–260
Revolt 1936–39 21, 39, 52, 71, 74, 85, 101, 119 121–122, 124–127, 131
Rex Cinema 82 130
Riad Khalil 51
Riad Mahmoud 162
Rifa'I 'Abd al-Mun'im 162
Riots 1929 54, 88, 100–101, 271–272
Riots 1920–21 1 71, 88, 94–96, 100, 105, 107–109, 118, 125
Rishon LeTzion 72
Rivlin Alter 53
Rivlin Yosef 42–43, 120–121
Rocach Street 74
Rogers William 162
Rokach Shimon 33, 104
Rokach Yitzhak 33, 72, 195 248

Romema 129
Rosenblit Felix 82
Rosenthal Yosef 42
Rotary Club 128
Rothschild Bank 27
Rothschild Edmond 33, 34
de-Rothschild Evelina School 80
Rubin Reuven 15
Rupin Arthur 63, 102
Russian Compound 23–24, 45
Ruzat al-Ma'araf 36

Sa'd WaSa'id 31
Sa'adeh Antun 133
Safini's 81
Sakakini Hala 201–202
Sakakini Khalil 51–52, 79, 94, 125, 178 201
al-Salah 'Omar 51
Salah al-Din 8, 65, 83, 92, 156 228
Salah George 82
al-Salam 63, 66
Salameh 69, 70, 172 190–191
Salman Ya'akov 155 185
Sansur Mikhail 79, 82 188–189
Salant Shmuel 42
Samuel Edwin 30–31
Samuel Herbert 30, 86
Sarig Aharon 223
Sasson Aryeh 21
Sasson Eliyahu 161
Sasson Moshe 157–170, 224, 230
Sardis Iris XI
Saudi Arabia X
Sha'aya Huri 251
Sharabi Hisham 202
Shilo Efrayim 261
Shin Bet 172 173
Schneersohn Yehudah 58
Selassie Haile 47
Separation fence 49
Silwan 37, 39, 263–265
Simon Wiesenthal Center 84
Simon the Just 31, 48
Sha'ar Tzion 33

335

INDEX

Sha'arei Tzedek Hospital 82
Shabazi Street 70
de-Shalit Meir 183
Shama Eliyahu 81
Shamgar Meir 187–188
Shami Yitzhak 55–56, 95
Shar'iah Court 36
Sharon Ariel 265
Sharon Aryeh 185
al-Shark cinema 82
Schwartz Miko 70
Schwartz Reuma 80
Schwartz Ruth 80
Schwartz Yehosef 14
Shehadeh 'Aziz 163
Shertok–Sharet 71
Sho'afat 183
Sephardi Jews 22, 36
Sepharadi Orphanage 24
Sevidas Photo 27
Sha'arei Yerushalayim 24
Shahid Hussayni Serene 207–209
Shapira 69, 70, 73
Shapira Haim Moshe 153, 247–248
Shapira Ya'akov Shimshon 81, 154 174, 185
Shlomo HaMelekh Street 126
Shlush Aharon 71
Shlush Avraham 59, 181 253
Shlush Ya'akov 60
Shlush Yosef Eliyahu 107, 113–114
Shehadeh Fuad 134
Sheikh Jarrah 29, 31–32, 48, 78, 167 227 232–233 265–266
Sheikh Muwanis 70
Sher Aviva 209
Sher Gilad XI
Sheikh Jarrah 6, 85
Shepherd Hotel 85 236
Shirion Yitzhak 26
Siksik Ayman 256
al-Siksik Mohammad 48
Sisco Joseph 156
Shitrit Bechor 48
Slouschz Nahum 87

Smuts Jan Street 80
Social and religious norms 238–240
Spector Hotel 104
St. Artemius Street 79
St. George School 27, 51, 189
St. Nikoforos Street 79
Stephan Hana 87
Storrs Ronald 11–12, 15, 24, 25, 95–97, 116–117
Straus Nathan 97
Streets re-named 6, 12, 79–80, 194–198
S. Yizhar 76, 90, 107–108, 125, 151
Sykes-Picot 112, 115
Suk 4, 7–10, 12–13, 37, 238 282
Sultan Bibars Street 79
Supreme Court 183, 187–188 195
Supreme Muslim Council 44, 83, 91, 239
Szold Henrietta 30

Tahon Yaakov 30
Talbiyeh 29, 78–80 127–130, 178, 181 196 207 233
Talpiot 5, 52, 78, 125
Tamir Yehuda 186
Tamra 172
Tamari Salim X, 87 202–203
Tannenbaum Leah 47
Al-Tarhi Yusuf 207 228
Tavgar Ben Zion 276–278
Tel al-Rish 172
Tel Aviv 3, 21, 56, 59, 62, 67–76, 106–107, 113, 122–123, 126–127, 247–249, 254 -256 288
Tel Or Cinema 82
Talmi Menachem 254
Temple Institute 216–217
Temple Mount / Haram al-Sharif 5, 8, 14, 15, 16, 25, 48, 50, 91, 92, 93, 95–100, 163–164, 185, 216–217 238–239
Temporary International Presence in Hebron 275
Tenuva 37

INDEX

Terra Sancta 130
Text books 225–229
Toledano Shmuel 174 217 229
Tomb of Absalom 14
Tomb of Rachel 6, 14
Torat Chaim 98
Totah Khalil 87
Toubbeh Jamil 129–130
Touqan Fadwa 79
Tourjeman Hassan / Tourjeman House 191–192
Tuchner's 81
Tusiyah Cohen Shlomo 81
al-Tur 186
Tzafrir Eliezer 230
Tzifroni XI, 134–135, 142

Um Jabara 47
Umayah Café 82
United Committee of the Hebrew Neighborhoods 73
UNRWA 183
UN Security Council 156
USA 156–157 162
Ussishkin Menachem 87, 97, 113–114

Violence in Hebron 273–275
Valero Gabriel and Victoria 134
Valero Haim Aharon 23, 36
Valero Bank 26
van Vriesland Siegfried 30
Vally of Hinnom 5, 152
Vienna Café 82 134

Wadi Joz 29 232
al-Wad Street 36
Wahaba Jamil 47
Waldorf Astoria Hotel 86
Wallach Yair XI
War 1948 IX, X, XII, 18, 79 122 124–135, 139–153
War 1967 IX, 5, 6, 9, 12, 16, 17, 43, 49, 102, 139–143, 146, 150–157

Warhaftig Zerach 153
Weigert Gidon 52
Weiner Esther 47
Weingarten Avraham and Esther 102
Weizmann Chaim 83, 95–97, 112–116
Weizmann Vera 96
Weizmann Ezer 80
Welfare Association 283–284
West Bank 171 173 230
Western Wall 14, 15, 25, 34, 95–100, 140, 142–145, 162–163 216 231
Wiesel Elie 143
World War I 51, 65, 95, 112
World War II IX, 4, 52, 75, 86, 126–127, 147
Watzman Haim XI

Ya'akobi Paul 196
Yad Mordechai Street 80
Yadin Yigael 143, 153
Yafa Café 256
Yafo Yefat Yamim 249
Yazur 172
Yaffe 43 172 186
Yahud 172
Yazur 126
Yehoshua A. B. 21, 116
Yehoshua Ya'akov 21, 38, 39, 40, 43, 45, 46, 47, 49, 52–53, 58, 97, 98, 167–168, 189–190, 197 230 239
Yehuda Halevi Street 75
Yehuda HaYamit 195
Yeivin Shmuel 249
Yellin Avinoam 52
Yelin David 25, 30, 34, 87
Yellin Yehoshua 36
YMCA 79, 82, 83 134, 201
Yemin Moshe 100 128
Yeshiva 257
Yoav 59

Zahalon Geriatric Center 194 196

INDEX

Zanziri's 81
Zarsifi Café 27
Zeitlin Y. H. 177
Zemora Moshe 82
Zion Cinema and Square 27, 82, 125 131, 189, 234
Zionism VIII, IX, 14, 16, 17, 22, 23, 33–35, 45, 50–51, 55–58, 61, 63, 66–67, 73–74, 76, 80–81, 84, 91, 93, 95–97, 100, 102, 104–109, 112–118, 121, 125, 147 -148, 151–152, 235 258–259 266 271–272 287
Zuckerman